SOUTHEAST ASIA
AMONG THE WORLD POWERS

Southeast Asia
AMONG THE WORLD POWERS

AMRY VANDENBOSCH
and RICHARD BUTWELL

UNIVERSITY OF KENTUCKY PRESS - LEXINGTON

Reissued, with supplement, 1958
© 1957 BY THE UNIVERSITY OF KENTUCKY PRESS
PRINTED AT THE UNIVERSITY OF KENTUCKY
Library of Congress Catalog Card No. 57-9768

The publication of this book is possible partly because of a grant from the Margaret Voorhies Haggin Trust established in memory of her husband James Ben Ali Haggin

PREFACE

FIFTY YEARS AGO several areas of the globe were little touched by the main currents of world affairs. Others escaped involvement altogether in the rivalries of international politics. This era is no more. Today, the former colonial territories of Asia, Africa, and the Middle East comprise key arenas in which crucial struggles are taking place: struggles which could determine whether men will look back on the twentieth century as an age in which freedom flourished or was dealt a formidable setback.

One of these former colonial areas is Southeast Asia, the subject of this book. The eyes of an entire world seemed focused on Southeast Asia in the spring of 1954 when the French fortress of Dien Bien Phu fell to the Communist Viet Minh in once-remote Indochina. Most of these eyes were turned toward Southeast Asia for the first time—but probably not the last.

This book seeks to provide the reader with a brief yet comprehensive picture of this increasingly important region in the hope that he may understand more fully future developments in the lands which are China's southern neighbors. There are six chapters dealing individually with the countries comprising the area. Three other chapters offer a general introduction to the area, analyze the international relations of Southeast Asia, and describe the approach of American foreign policy toward the countries of this part of the world. A select and late bibliography is provided for the reader who will wish to examine further the past and the prospects of Southeast Asia.

An effort has been made to focus attention on major problems of the area and on recent important happenings. Because the events taking place in Southeast Asia at the present time are both swift and basic, the authors have sought to include significant developments right up to the eve of publication. The immense changes which were registered in Southeast Asia between 1939 and 1945 are continuing, and no work which fails to take cognizance of this fact can hope to offer a true picture of today's Southeast Asia.

The authors have drawn upon the writings of the increasing number of scholars who specialize in the governments and politics of the region; to them they owe a debt of gratitude. They have also drawn on their own published writings. Much of the subject matter of this work, however, is presented for the first time in book form here. It is based on the research and observations of the authors, both of whom have traveled recently in Southeast Asia. A considerable debt is owed to those who assisted them in meeting leaders and representative figures of the area.

The senior author wishes to acknowledge his indebtedness to the Social Science Research Council for a research fellowship and a travel grant which enabled him to visit the countries of the region in 1929-1930 and again in 1950 for the purpose of studying their governments and politics.

Mr. Butwell wishes to express his thanks to the United States Fulbright Program for providing him with the opportunity of two years of study of Southeast Asian international relations at St. Antony's College, Oxford University, and the Institute of Pacific Relations for a grant for travel in Southeast Asia in 1953.

AMRY VANDENBOSCH
RICHARD BUTWELL

The publishers wish to acknowledge with thanks the cooperation of the Institute of Pacific Relations in the distribution of this book.

CONTENTS

Preface	page v
1. Southeast Asia: Contemporary Power Vacuum	1
2. Indonesia: Restless Insular Empire	26
3. The Philippines: Showcase of Western Democracy	69
4. Indochina: Gateway to Southeast Asia	110
5. Thailand: Diplomatic and Political Phenomenon	156
6. Malaya: A Problem in Nation Building	186
7. Burma: Land of Contradictions	212
8. The International Relations of Southeast Asia	246
9. American Policy in Southeast Asia	284
Recent Developments	327
Bibliographical Note	351
Index	357

CHAPTER I

SOUTHEAST ASIA CONTEMPORARY POWER VACUUM

NOT SO LONG AGO the people of the Western world knew only vaguely of the existence of the countries of Southeast Asia. India, on the fringe of the region, had for several decades attracted a great deal of attention because of its heroic struggle for national independence under a very unusual leader. The Philippines were known to Americans, though in a superficial manner, because the United States had the responsibility for governing the islands. Their country's respective Southeast Asian colonial holdings were likewise known in a general fashion to Englishmen, Frenchmen, and Dutchmen. As a whole, however, the people of the West knew little of the lands east of India and south of China.

Today the Western world is conscious of Southeast Asia and of its importance in world politics. The change in attitude began with the Japanese invasion of Southeast Asia during the Second World War, which dramatically emphasized the strategic importance of the region. Interest sharpened when the loss of China left to the free world only the fringes of the continent and the off-lying islands and insular countries. The fall of Dien Bien Phu, lending itself to colorful news coverage, caught virtually everyone's attention; as a result of its successes in Vietnam, the Communist bloc now also had a foot squarely in a country known as the "gateway" to Southeast Asia.

If the Communists gain control of Southeast Asia, the West is now fully aware, India will be threatened and the strength of Australia will be partially neutralized. The free world cannot afford to lose any more territory or prestige in Asia.

A LITTLE-KNOWN REGION ENTERS WORLD POLITICS

Southeast Asia consists of Indonesia, Vietnam, the Philippines, Thailand, Burma, Cambodia, Laos, Malaya, and the British Borneo possessions. The total land area of the region exceeds 1,600,000 square miles, and because much of it is insular, it covers a large expanse of ocean. Southeast Asia's significance in world politics is particularly due to its strategic location at the southeastern extremity of the great Asian land mass. A tropical extension of the continent, the region consists of a two-pronged peninsula on the mainland and a vast string of islands stretching along both sides of the equator for a greater distance than that between New York and San Francisco. The main sea route between the Pacific and Indian oceans passes through the area, which also serves as a link between Asia and Australia. With the important exception of northeastern Indochina, an extension of the south China littoral, Southeast Asia's boundaries effectively separate it from the nearest land masses on all its sides. In the north, high mountains divide the region from China and India—except for the northeast coastal region of Vietnam in Indochina. Southeast Asia is bordered by water to the east, south, and west.

As a consequence of the events of the post-Second-World-War years—and the headlines which chronicled them—the term Southeast Asia is now common in discussions about international political, social, and economic developments. Before the war, however, these tropical-equatorial lands were thought of almost exclusively as overseas extensions of the Western metropolitan powers which controlled their destinies. They had little political identity or significance apart from their colonial connections. Nor was there any reason why this should have been otherwise. As late as the nineteen-twenties and early thirties Southeast Asia's was not a role of vital importance on the stage of international politics, although the area produced most of the world's rubber and tin and more than two-thirds of the rice entering world trade.

Today all the major foreign offices have, or seek to have, a "Southeast Asian policy." The British and the Australians, as examples, have resident commissioners in Southeast Asia to coordinate policy in this area of more than 170,000,000 inhabitants. Political developments in individual countries—Vietnam or Malaya, for instance—are no longer important only locally or to an imperial ruler. Ho Chi Minh's is a name known to at least some men in all lands; Philippine President Magsaysay and Indonesian President Sukarno also have international reputations.

All of this indicates a major change in the attitude of the world, the West in particular, towards this region, which, it should be noted, is itself as big as all Europe. The occasion for this change has been the emergence of a new and dynamic Southeast Asia—a politically independent Southeast Asia demanding a greater voice in the settlements of international politics. The change also relates to recent developments in other parts of Asia—the rise of Moscow-fathered communism in China and the achievement of independence by India, which have had tremendous consequences for Southeast Asia—and to events in the world at large, especially as these have been reflected in the "cold war" of the years since the Second World War.

From the point of view of the United States, one of the most important characteristics of contemporary Southeast Asia is the fact that it constitutes a power vacuum of rather sizable proportions and with significant consequences. For more than forty years preceding the outbreak of the Second World War, Southeast Asia had comprised a series of mutually accepted Western colonial regimes. During these years Southeast Asia, together with British India and Ceylon, formed a single defense unit, based on the naval power of the British and part of a larger defense arc which reached westward as far as Suez. Stability at the price of national freedom was a keynote of the area. The postwar years, however, witnessed an eclipse of this stability with the attainment of independence, if not always complete, by all the lands of the area except Malaya and northern Borneo. The old chain of defense which once extended from Suez to the eastern reaches of Southeast Asia was broken, as India, Pakistan, and Ceylon also achieved national independence, although within the British Commonwealth. Stability was replaced by turmoil. A power vacuum followed the demise of Western colonialism.

This vacuum derives importance from the existence, to the north of Southeast Asia, of the huge Chinese state, which has traditionally regarded the lands to its south as a proper outlet for its expansive tendencies. Its present membership in the international Communist coalition makes Peiping's dominating geographical and political position more ominous for its southern neighbors today than ever before. China is not the only power, however, which might seek to fill this important vacuum. To the west of Southeast Asia lies India, which has contributed several million immigrants to the countries of South Asia and East Africa in the present century and which also is enjoying a period of resurgence, regarding itself as the key power in the Indian Ocean area. And to the northeast a crowded and once-covetous Japan watches Southeast Asia with an obviously interested eye, the same Japan which in 1941-1942 succeeded in bringing all of the region under a single ruler for the first time in history.

Like other of history's power vacuums, Southeast Asia may not remain a vacuum long, particularly in light of the fact that geographically it is composed principally of islands and peninsulas with a high ratio of coastal area to total land surface, a physical condition highly favorable to external penetration.

TRADITIONAL "LOW-PRESSURE AREA"

It is no new thing for Southeast Asia to be subjected to pressures from all sides. This, indeed, has been its historical lot, causing one prominent observer of the region to term it a "low-pressure area."[1] The description is apt.

---

[1] Cora DuBois, in *Social Forces in Southeast Asia* (Minneapolis, 1949).

Southeast Asia

One of the most important of these pressures has been population. Southeast Asia has been peopled for the most part by successive migratory waves forced to move south by ever-increasing pressure upon them, stemming in the last analysis from the Chinese, who pushed down from their early home in north China.

The first of the migrations of importance to contemporary Southeast Asia was that of the Indonesians or Malays, who, beginning about 2500 B.C., pressed south into the mainland portion of Southeast Asia and moved on to the archipelago beyond. The direct impetus to their migration was not the Chinese themselves, but other Mongoloid peoples who had in turn been pushed south by the Chinese. These were later to be pushed out of south and west China by Chinese population pressure, various groups of them becoming the Vietnamese, Thai, Burmese, and Cambodian peoples of modern Southeast Asia.

Traditionally, in comparison with China to the north, Southeast Asia has been a region of low population density. It was this comparatively sparse settlement of the area that permitted the peoples now inhabiting the region to move into it. This situation has not basically changed. The gap, in fact, has greatly widened in modern times. China, with its population of approximately 600,000,000, continues to exert pressure upon the lands to its south, which have less than one-third its inhabitants. Southeast Asia, though possessing patches of overpopulation, has vast areas of sparsely settled land. If anything, an increase rather than a lessening of Chinese population pressure is to be expected. It is highly significant that large numbers of Chinese have migrated to Southeast Asia during the past one hundred years, almost all of them coming by sea. There are today more than ten million of them in the area.

Southeast Asia is faced with population pressure from another direction. Indeed, it is situated between two of the heaviest concentrations of population to be found in the world —the Indian and the Chinese. The pressure of population upon available resources caused large numbers of Indians to seek their fortunes in British-held Burma and Malaya. That they did not do so in greater numbers elsewhere in the area is probably due to policies designed by the colonial rulers of these territories to exclude them. It certainly is not due to the absence of a desire to move into Southeast Asia.

Expansion of adjacent populations has been only one of several pressures converging upon the region. Culturally, Southeast Asia also has always been a low-pressure area. The advanced level of civilization achieved by the Indonesian kingdoms of Java and Sumatra in the eighth and fifteenth centuries largely resulted from the penetration of the area by Hinduism and associated social elements. Much that owes its origin to Indian cultural influence is evident today in most of Southeast Asia. The same might be said of Chinese-derived cultural factors, although to a lesser degree. The Arabs also have made a substantial cultural contribution to Southeast Asia, although Indians were the direct bearers of Islam. And though they gave little of substance to Southeast Asian life in the early years of contact, the Europeans have to an ever-increasing extent left a pronounced imprint on virtually all aspects of life in this part of the world. Although much is made of the truth that Southeast Asians adapted many of these borrowings to their own particular needs and environment, the fact remains that they did borrow them. Cultural influences converged upon the area from India, Europe, China, the Middle East, and America, and they were accepted. Traffic, however, was one way. No such influences made their way out from the area to these or other parts of the world.

This was also true in the realm of economics. It cannot be shown that the Indian or Chinese or European economic structures were modified in any way as a result of any efforts by native Southeast Asians. The markets of this region were opened by traders from other countries; they were not the development of indigenous commercial enterprise. Before the advent of European traders, Indians, Chinese, and Arabs had been prominent in fostering the commerce of Southeast Asia. With the establishment of European power, the economic structure of the area underwent a revolutionary transformation. What had previously been a self-sufficient food-producing economy became a raw-material supplier to the industrialized countries of the West and a leader in world trade in rice. Few events in economic history have been comparable to the impact of the Western commercial invasion upon Southeast Asia and similar underdeveloped regions. Historically, Southeast Asia has certainly been an economic low-pressure area.

It has been an area of convergent political interests, too. China on several occasions has moved south to increase its power and territory. Vietnam was long under the Chinese yoke, and Khubilai Khan attacked Burma, Cambodia, and Champa (part of present-day Vietnam) and sent a punitive expedition to Java, which had given Champa some assistance in its war with China. An aggressive Chinese foreign policy was most evident, however, under the Ming emperor Yung Lo (1403-1424), who occupied much of Vietnam, acquired control over Upper Burma, and sent several tribute-seeking naval expeditions to the lands of the south to induce local rulers to acquiesce, either peaceably or under duress, in Chinese overlordship. In contrast with China, the relations of India with the area on the whole have been most peaceful. The expansionist policy of the Chola emperors of Tanjore in the eleventh century, however, is an example of what India could do, although in fact it has made the attempt only once. Japan, though it also struck at the region but once, would have been successful in that effort, had it encountered only Southeast Asia's resistance and not that of the allied West. The West in its own penetration of the area successfully and for a limited time took over full political control of the region. And today the forces of the powerful contestants in the worldwide cold war converge on this politically, economically, and militarily weak area. Simultaneous with this convergence is the impact of China, India, Japan, Australia, the United States, the Soviet Union, and the United Kingdom functioning as traditional influence-seeking national states, possessing objectives which exist apart from the present encounter between democracy and communism—objectives, however, frequently not perceived due to the shadows cast by the bigger and more novel cold-war interests. As much in terms of international relations as of population, culture, and economics, Southeast Asia can best be understood in terms of a low-pressure area.

Two factors especially explain why alien powers have been so successful in their numerous attempts at penetration of various parts of the region. The first is the continuing division of the area into a multiplicity of small political units, partially a consequence of its marked geographical fragmentation. When the West began its penetration of Southeast Asia in the sixteenth century, it found a "patchwork quilt of kingdoms, principalities and tribal chieftainships, independent cities, and local or regional confederations."[2] This division is an outstanding factor in explaining the ease of European conquest of the area. Divided, it could be, and was, taken over territory by territory. After a series of squabbles in which the contestants varied, the area was finally stabilized into several mutually accepted Western colonial holdings. But if it had become stabilized, it was still divided. There was British Malaya, the Dutch East Indies, French Indochina, British Burma, and the American-held Philippines, as well as nominally sovereign Thailand.

The existing divisions, in the sense of there being a multiplicity of ultimately responsible rulers, and the metropolitan power-imposed stability were wiped out by the Japanese invasion which struck at the region in late 1941 and early 1942. For the first time in all its history Southeast Asia knew a common ruler, although in fact, for all practical purposes, divisions continued much as before under Japan's temporary overlordship. But there can be no doubt that the old stability disappeared. The very change of rulers, whatever their respective merits, encouraged this. The use of local puppets by the Japanese was fuel to the flame of incipient nationalism. And as the Japanese began to be forced out of the region, it became their deliberate policy to give active encouragement to this rapidly growing nationalism. Although this may have arisen from a reckless determination to create turmoil and confusion for their own sake, there can be no question that it gave considerable impetus to the nationalist movements in Southeast

[2] H. J. van Mook, *The Stakes of Democracy in Southeast Asia* (London, 1950), 36-37.

Asia. It also created conditions favorable to the spread of communism, which has benefited from the region's widespread poverty as well as its postwar political instability.

RISE OF NATIONALISM

Nationalism, as contrasted with more primitive hostility to the foreigner, dates its active existence in the region from the period following the First World War. An importation from the West, it existed in embryonic form before then, but only in the Philippines had it assumed substantial strength before the 1914-1918 war. In the nineteen-twenties and thirties, although granted a few concessions, it continued to feed on the ever-increasing frustrations of an ever-expanding body of sympathizers, modeling itself in many respects after Indian Congress and Chinese Kuomintang nationalism. On the eve of the Japanese invasion it was still a force of limited strength, but it emerged from the devastations of the Second World War a militant movement. Taking advantage of the almost complete destruction of existing and accepted institutions and values by the Japanese occupation, the nationalists raised the standard of revolt. Although they met with armed resistance from the French and the Dutch, national independence was for the most part obtained. The Philippines, Indonesia, and Burma have joined the family of nations, and French colonialism is dead in Indochina, although it is not yet clear what will take its place. It may very well be succeeded by Communist Chinese colonialism. Malaya, which until the Second World War seemed utterly without political consciousness, is about to take its place as a self-governing dominion in the British Commonwealth.

But although the colonial powers have departed, the divisions solidified by their arbitrary partition of the region remain. The new national states for the most part follow the boundaries of the old colonial domains. Division continues, but the old stability is gone. The door perhaps is again open to external penetration. The situation bears a close analogy to the condition of Southeast Asia at the time of the coming of the West. Forces exist today ready once more to converge upon the area.

The old pattern of division may facilitate the progress of these forces.

In addition to political divisions, however, there was another conspicuous characteristic about Southeast Asia that facilitated Western penetration of the region. This was its backwardness in economic development. It was in part because of this material weakness that the several lands of the area fell under the sway of the powerful European imperial powers seeking to expand their trade. This is most important in understanding the region's present character and its possible future development, for predominantly agricultural Southeast Asia today is still backward in economic achievement. In terms of industrialization, the main criterion in ascertaining economic might in the modern world, it is exceptionally weak. And it is very likely that this lack of industrial strength will continue for some time to come. Thus, once again a situation is observed comparable to the past—more specifically, to the time of the coming of the Westerner. As political division encouraged or tempted external penetration, so also did economic backwardness. And as political division continues today, so, too, does this comparative backwardness.

NO LONGER AN OUTPOST OF WORLD POLITICS

If there are many similarities between Southeast Asia's past and its present, there are also some extremely significant differences. The world has become considerably smaller since that distant day in the sixteenth century when the Spanish ships of the daring Magellan reached the Philippines from across the wide Pacific, and this has had important consequences for all nations. To state that Southeast Asia was an outpost of world politics until recent times is to assume that there were no international relations outside of Europe till Europe expanded to the far corners of the globe. Such is not true, of course. As there was considerable intercourse among the nations of Europe before Europe and Asia came into continuous direct contact, so, too, was there such intercourse among the lands of Asia, although it may have differed in kind from its European counterpart. But in modern times—that is, since Europe effectively gained its ascendency over most of the rest of the world (however transitory that ascendency may turn out to have been) — it is true to say that Southeast Asia has been far from the main arenas of conflict in world politics. For the last one hundred and fifty years, if not longer, world politics has been in fact European politics. Southeast Asia, though an aspect of the rivalry between the Western states, was not a key area in the international struggle for power. This changed with Japan's rise to power in Asia in the nineteen-thirties, which was but one indication of the expansion of European politics into truly world politics and of that island nation's bid for hegemony in the Far East. The geography of decreasing distances among the nations of the world and the not unrelated expansion of European politics into world politics thus combined to bring Southeast Asia closer to the threshold of conflict in modern international relations. It did not, however, bring it quite over that threshold.

The factor which has accomplished this more than any other has been the rivalry between the United States and the Soviet Union in the years since the end of the Second World War. This rivalry has taken the form, among several others, of a competition for control of all areas of the world which have not committed themselves in this titanic struggle of the mid-twentieth century. Wherever a power vacuum has existed in the postwar years, these two nations have sought to fill it. Such was the case in Central Europe, as it was in Korea. It explains the ever-increasing attention which is focused today on the Middle East. Greece was a player in the drama in the early postwar years, and Africa would appear slated for a larger role in the years which lie ahead.

The nationalist revolutions of the postwar years which catapulted European colonialism out of Southeast Asia left a vacuum in the wake of the Western withdrawal. As the cold war between the United States and the U.S.S.R. increased in intensity in the years after 1945, the importance of Southeast Asia in world politics loomed larger. It would appear greater today than at any other time in modern history. It is in light of its role as a "battlefield" in the Western-Communist conflict that its continuing divisions and its economic backwardness are to be appraised. China's nearness and historic pattern of domination of Southeast Asia, coupled with Peiping's present partnership with Moscow, only serve to intensify the complexity of the problems faced by the new nations of this part of the world. Whether it likes it or not, and the so-called "neutralist" foreign policies of some of its states would seem to indicate it does not, Southeast Asia is today very much a part of the world about it.

The world has come to Southeast Asia in yet another sense. Not only is this region of the world of increased importance in modern international politics, it has itself become "modern" in the sense that it is trying desperately to catch up with the world politically, economically, and socially. It is still a backward area, but the desire to transform itself has become strong. Democracy may not reign in Southeast Asia, but modern Western political forms and ideas are at work in the region. The sultans and other old hereditary rulers are passing from the scene; they are being succeeded by the organizational structure of the European political units—prime ministers, parliaments, foreign offices, bureaus of the budget, labor arbitration boards, and all. Industrialization is invading the area, although on a modest scale, while state planning has captured the imagination of the region's several national leaders, even though they do not always understand the nature of their captor. Socially, class lines are shifting as a result of the new mobility, physical and otherwise, introduced by the West. Southeast Asia is today undergoing a vast and varied revolution in behalf of modernization, of which the nationalist political revolt is the most conspicuous but by no means the exclusive symptom. This revolution cannot help but distinguish the Southeast Asia of the present from the Southeast Asia of the past.

One thing is clear above all others in contemporary Southeast Asia: important changes are taking place. At the same time, much of the old pattern persists, so that today the region represents a combination of the traditional and the new. What kind of adjustment will result from the final union of the two will not depend only on Southeast Asia itself. Too many external influences are today converging on the area. One of the costs of involvement in world politics is the impact international relations inevitably have on domestic affairs. This fact Southeast Asia is today learning—in some respects rather reluctantly.

If external developments have effects on domestic politics in contemporary Southeast Asia, so also domestic Southeast Asian developments are producing reactions, some of them significant, on the international scene. The internal struggle for power in Vietnam, for instance, is carefully watched by Americans, Russians, and Chinese, as well as others.

Surely, in the light of such circumstances, there can be little doubt that Southeast Asia today is very much a part of the world about it—and of the conflicts and tensions which distinguish that world.

CULTURAL DIVERSITY

Culturally the countries of Southeast Asia have many things in common. A majority of the inhabitants of all the lands of the region possess a primitive belief in animism and spiritism. Everywhere are to be found cultural practices and devices derived from the extensively felt Indian and Western social impacts. The entire region, moreover, is today marked by the disintegration of village life and the eclipse of the traditional social system associated with it. Wet rice agriculture is a major economic factor in every country of Southeast Asia. Similar types of food, housing, and dress, as well as almost identical forms of art, entertainment, and games, distinguish the several lands of this part of the world.

Southeast Asia, however, also is marked by considerable cultural diversity. Linguistically the area is possessed of nearly four hundred different languages and dialects. Ethnically its wide variety of human species range from pygmy negritos, to tall, graceful brown peoples of mixed Caucasoid-Mongoloid stock, to virtually pure Mongoloids. Although an all-pervading belief in animism and spiritism seemingly lends Southeast Asia a large degree of unity, the region is at the same time marked by four major organized religions which divide it in a far more decisive fashion than its common pagan practices unite it. While most of Southeast Asia bears the imprint of Indian cultural penetration, the nature of this legacy varies from place to place. Chinese cultural influence, for example, clearly predominates in Vietnam. Most of the area also has experienced the impact of Western social forces. As there is a difference between the British and French cultures, so, too, is there a difference between the imprints these cultures have left upon other lands. Differences among Southeast Asians of language, race, and religion, as well as those deriving from distinct responses to Indian, Western, and Chinese cultural forces, are further sharpened by the several nationalisms of the area, which tend to exalt the uniqueness of native culture and history.

Southeast Asia has been described as an ethnographic museum, and probably no more fitting analogy could be offered to describe the complex pattern of peoples who reside in this region of the world. There is a relative ethnic unity among the inhabitants of insular Southeast Asia—Indonesia, the Philippines, and British Borneo—who are mainly of Malay or Indonesian stock. For this reason, enduring racial antagonisms are least likely to develop in this part of the area. The native population of Malaya is part of this same ethnic grouping, but the presence of more Chinese than Malays on Malayan soil, including Singapore with Malaya, is sufficient reason for not placing these territories in the same category with Indonesia and the Philippines.

The Malays and the closely related Indonesians are sharply differentiated from the peoples who populate the greater part of mainland Southeast Asia. More Mongoloid in their physical traits, the inhabitants of the mainland represent a later migratory invasion of the region by a series of distinct groups who have retained their separate ethnic identity through the years with the help of the mountain ranges which divide them from one another. After their arrival in Southeast Asia many centuries ago, these peoples formed and maintained separate pockets of settlement along the various river valleys of the Southeast Asian peninsula. Although there are various mixtures of these main migratory groups in Southeast Asia today, the groups themselves remain as distinct ethnic concentrations, comprising the Thai, Vietnamese, Burmese, and Cambodian peoples.

That ethnic differentiation is a divisive factor socially in present-day Southeast Asia is evident from the nationalism-inspired pride of race which marks this part of the world. While racial antagonisms between the several countries of the area are not yet apparent, serious ethnic friction has broken out within almost all of the Southeast Asian lands. Burma, Indonesia, and the Philippines, for example, are today faced with serious sociopolitical problems deriving specifically from internal ethnic rivalries. It is difficult to envisage the pride of race presently marking the peoples of Southeast Asia encouraging closer relations among them in the near future.

If Southeast Asia is a veritable museum as regards its ethnic diversity, it presents an even more complex pattern linguistically. Of the two, its linguistic diversity is the more important. Although it is of little consequence if men differ ethnically—unless their ethnic groups possess diverse cultural characteristics or men themselves think them of consequence—it is important if they do not speak the same language. In Southeast Asia they do not.

The least complex lands of the area, from a linguistic as well as an ethnic point of view, are clearly the island countries, demonstrating again the unifying effect of insularity. Nonetheless, more than 87 different languages and dialects are spoken in the Philippines, while some 30 languages and 250 dialects are identifiable in Indonesia. Vietnamese, Thai, Burmese, and Cambodian are the main languages to be found in mainland Southeast Asia, but several minor tongues also exist. The major languages are quite separate tongues, although they have interacted considerably upon one another in the past. The important fact, however, is that the peoples speaking these various languages do not understand one another. Nor does proficiency in Vietnamese, for example, lead to easy mastery of Burmese—as French does to Italian, or Dutch to German.

Religion also divides Southeast Asia. Burma, Thailand,

Cambodia, and Laos adhere to Buddhism of the Hinayana (or Little Vehicle) School. Most of Indonesia, Malaya, and peninsular Thailand are Moslem, as are some islands in the Philippines. The ranking faith of the Philippines, however, is Christianity, which also is the religion of significant groups of peoples in Indonesia. The religion of Vietnam represents the curious Chinese scrambling of Confucianism, Mahayana (or Greater Vehicle) Buddhism, and Taoism, the result of which appears to be a species of ancestor worship more than anything else. The Chinese themselves practice their own version of this blended faith, while Hinduism survives in an attractive form on the Indonesian island of Bali.

While overtly offering primary allegiance to Christ, Mohammed, Buddha, or Confucius, the mass of Southeast Asians are animists and ancestor worshipers basically. Christianity, Islam, and Buddhism are in a sense only new names for old ways of looking at life. What the Southeast Asian has done in the case of these imported religions is to adopt the form of the new faith and use it as a sort of window dressing for his age-old views about the world of seen and unseen things.

Yet the form of the Southeast Asian's faith is extremely important. While Indonesians and Malays regularize a large portion of their lives according to pagan concepts of spiritism, ancestor worship, and magic, they also regard themselves as devout Moslems. Thailand's Buddhists, as well as those of Burma, Cambodia, and Laos, may be thoroughgoing animists, but they think they are good Buddhists. The Philippines' Catholics, though they are basically animistic, consider themselves as highly orthodox followers of the faith of Rome. The claim that Islam, Buddhism, and Catholicism are of only secondary importance religiously in this part of the world today is one of the most misleading of the many myths about spiritual Southeast Asia. Most of Southeast Asia's people serve two masters. While the doctrinaire doubtlessly would not regard them as real Moslems, Christians, or Buddhists because of their simultaneous attachment to rival pagan practices, they nevertheless see themselves as devoted followers of their organized faiths. And what men think they are can be just as divisive as what they really are. Moreover, since nationalism puts such great pride in a country's spiritual heritage and so much of Southeast Asia's spiritual heritage concerns its organized religions, these have gained in stature in the recent years of rabid nationalism in the area.

INDIAN AND WESTERN SOCIAL IMPACTS

The common experience of the Indian cultural impact was one of the most important events in Southeast Asia. As a result of more than a thousand years of Indian cultural dominance, the cultures of these several lands resemble one another in a multiplicity of ways. This resemblance, on the other hand, is far from a complete one. Most of Vietnam never fell within the cultural sphere of India, being influenced instead by China, while Thailand and the Philippines were Hinduized mainly by non-Indian peoples, who had themselves, however, felt the direct impact of cultural contact with India. Moreover, although Indian cultural influences gave the region a considerable degree of social unity, they served at the same time to differentiate key areas of it. Although Buddhism and Islam were both carried to Southeast Asia by Indians, they are, nonetheless, quite different creeds and so a divisive influence in the region.

More important today than India's influence is the impact of the West. Each of the lands of Southeast Asia came under varying degrees of Western cultural as well as political and economic influence. However, Western influence was not everywhere the same. Despite the broad designation of "the West," Europe and North America themselves represent much in the way of cultural divergencies, language being only one example of their several differences. Since the Western countries are differentiated and since they impinged upon the even more strongly differentiated countries of Southeast Asia in different ways, at different times, and to different degrees, it was only natural that they should have further divided the peoples of Southeast Asia culturally.

The languages in which the European colonial powers transmitted their cultural influences were different, and the institutional and administrative forms which they introduced varied from country to country. The political boundaries they established cut across oldtime contacts, and the orientation of the peoples of the colonial lands became focused primarily upon different metropolitan powers: Burmese and Malays upon Britain, Indochinese upon France, Indonesians upon the Netherlands, and Filipinos first upon Spain and then upon the United States. The ideological motivation of their colonial undertakings also varied among the imperial powers. France and Spain thought of colonies as devices for cultural expansionism as well as in terms of trade and political power. The Dutch, on the other hand, were traders first and foremost; their cultural impact on Indonesia, not surprisingly, was less imposing than that of Spain on the Philippines or France on Indochina. Finally, for those people affected by European influences, the very contact itself with the West made them more aware of the outside world and, as a result, more conscious of their own identity and the distinctness of their culture —a tendency further encouraged by nationalism.

On the whole, although most of Southeast Asia has felt the impact of Western cultural influences, the result thus far of this experience would appear to be more divisive than unifying. The peoples of Southeast Asia have derived common material devices from this experience, village life has almost everywhere been disrupted, and similar ideas have made their way into all the lands of the area. Yet the most important ideological force contributed by Europe, that of nationalism, is probably the most singularly disunifying factor operative in Southeast Asia today.

Southeast Asia today is a culturally divided region. Although social differentiation has marked its several parts throughout recorded times, this differentiation seems greater in many ways today than ever before, partially as a consequence of such events as the Hindu and Western cultural intrusions. This is important because of the roots political behavior has in cultural considerations. These are by no means all determining, but they are influential. Before the new nation states of this part of the world draw closer together politically— before introversion is eliminated from their political and economic policies— cultural horizons will have to be broadened. They are being broadened in many respects at the present time, but they are simultaneously being narrowed in other respects. Except as a consequence of major crisis or through external action, any political drawing together of the Southeast Asian peoples would seem to have to be preceded, or at least accompanied, by greater social or cultural cohesiveness among them. Unfortunately, no such cultural rapprochement seems likely in the near future. Cultural divisions—and, partially because of them, political divisions—continue to characterize the several lands of Southeast Asia. Such divisions may well prove to be twentieth-century Southeast Asia's undoing. Comparable conditions have caused the region's downfall in the past.

ECONOMIC INADEQUACY

Southeast Asia has been variously described as a rich region— and a poor one. It all depends on the type of yardstick used. If one looks at the area's natural resources, which are considerable, Southeast Asia can be termed an area of much wealth. However, if attention is focused on the standard of living of the masses of humanity who inhabit the region, it is obvious that Southeast Asia is marked by widespread poverty. It is not that there are pockets of poverty to be found in every part of the area, but that the overwhelming proportion of Southeast Asia's peoples—not just a minority—live at a low level of subsistence. The annual average family income for the region was only $55 in 1950. This low level of subsistence, however, still is relatively high in comparison with the rest of Asia. Compared with their neighbors the peoples of this part of the world eat and live quite well.

The seeming economic paradox of Southeast Asia's considerable natural resources and the low living standard of its peoples has produced much talk of "poverty amidst plenty." This would be an accurate enough analysis, if material resources were the only criterion in measuring an area's economic wealth.

They are not. Other factors also contribute to an area's economic wealth, and many of these—for example, capital and technical ability—are sadly lacking in present-day Southeast Asia. The region's economic wealth at the present time is largely limited to its natural resources.

These resources include most of the world's natural rubber, tin, and hemp. Rice dominates agricultural production throughout the area and is a major export commodity. Copra, sugar, petroleum, tea, quinine, tungsten, manganese, teakwood, kapok, coffee, and pepper are among Southeast Asia's other major products. Prior to the Second World War the area, then still under colonial rule, was of considerable economic importance to the several European metropolitan powers, as indicated by the scope of its exports. Burma, Thailand, and Indochina annually exported 6,000,000 tons of milled rice. In 1940, Southeast Asia grew 20 percent of all the rice grown in Asia and contributed more than two-thirds of all the rice entering world trade. Malaya and Indonesia sent about 800,000 tons of rubber a year into international commercial channels. From Burma and Indonesia 8,500,000 tons of crude petroleum were exported annually; from Malaya, Indonesia, and Thailand, 90,000 metric tons of tin concentrates; and from Indonesia, the Philippines, and Malaya, 1,600,000 tons of copra.[3]

The products of Southeast Asia in the years both before and after World War II have been primarily agricultural or mineral. The area is not yet able to meet its own needs for various manufactured goods, being still in an early stage of industrial growth. This is partly due to the direction of its economic development as formulated during the period of Western colonial rule. It also is due, among other factors, to the area's limited coal and iron-ore resources. These two minerals were a backbone of European and North American industrial growth, and their limited occurrence in Southeast Asia is one of the reasons why the West did not make more of an effort to industrialize the area, as well as a good reason why Southeast

---

[3] See Frank N. Trager, "Problems of Economic Development in Southeast Asia," *Journal of International Affairs*, X (1956), 60.

Southeast Asia

Asia's own efforts at industrialization must be limited in the immediate future.

The coming of the European wrought great economic changes in Southeast Asia. Prior to the advent of the West, Southeast Asia had been marked by an economic system combining subsistence agriculture with cottage industries and limited barter. This system was disrupted by the impact of Western economic imperialism. Rubber, tin, and other Southeast Asian products became the raw materials for the industries of the West. Sugar, coffee, tea, and other items left the region to meet the expanding needs of growing overseas populations. New products from the West invaded the area, changing the cultural as well as the economic life of the Southeast Asians who came into contact with them. A money economy was introduced by the Europeans. Because of the emphasis placed by the colonial powers on the development of agricultural and mineral products, Southeast Asia became highly dependent upon the fluctuating economic needs of distant overseas nations. These nations lent considerable instability to Southeast Asian life, for Southeast Asia had no control over the overseas demands for its products.

The economic personality of Southeast Asia has not changed in essentials with the replacement of European colonial rule by the new national governments. Native governments increasingly direct the economic affairs of the several Southeast Asian lands, but although this has generally meant economic development by state planning rather than by foreign commercial concerns, it has not changed the character of Southeast Asia's primary reliance on the export of its agricultural and mineral products. The dangerous dependence of the Southeast Asian lands upon foreign demands for its products was amply illustrated by the boom in raw material prices occasioned by the Korean War—and the subsequent rapid decline in the prices offered for these products. Rubber, for example, dropped from about 80 cents a pound in late 1950 to about 30 cents in mid-1952, quite a fall in price in less than two years. Copra, as another illustration, dropped from $261.50 per ton in March, 1951, to $112 a ton in the middle of 1952, a period of little more than a year.[4] This has made it difficult for governments and individuals alike to plan on the economic resources available to them. This has been especially so in Southeast Asia, so highly dependent on its exports of raw materials and the import of various capital and consumer goods. If world prices drop and no loans or grants are made to a country so reliant on international price levels, obvious contractions in foreign purchases must follow— even though such contractions mean reducing the already low living standards of the masses.

The living standards of today's Southeast Asians, however, are not the only ones to be affected by such foreign-purchase contractions. The lives of tomorrow's Southeast Asians also are affected. Most of the leaders of contemporary Southeast Asia are cognizant of the dangers inherent in their nation's heavy reliance on world prices for primary products. They are seeking the rapid industrialization of their lands in order to remedy this situation as quickly as possible. Although their efforts have been halting to date, their plans remain ambitious. But they need capital goods, or heavy equipment, to achieve their economic objectives. These must come from abroad, and all sorts of obstacles have greeted the efforts of Southeast Asian leaders to obtain such necessary capital equipment. The post-Korean-War fall in international commodity prices has made it difficult for Southeast Asian governments to pay for such capital goods themselves. At times when they have had the money, as during the Korean War boom, these goods were not always available, and so the money was spent in other ways, not always wisely. Plans nevertheless are going forward for the diversification of Southeast Asian economic life, and definite progress has been registered. The road ahead, however, is still a long one.

Foreign economic assistance, both private and governmental, has been, and probably will continue to be, of considerable help to the Southeast Asian countries in hastening their economic advancement. There are signs that the leaders of this area are today better disposed towards accepting foreign aid

---

[4] Frederick T. Koyle, in Philip W. Thayer (ed.), *Southeast Asia in the Coming World* (Baltimore, 1953), 119.

than in earlier periods of their newly won national independence. As a consequence of the long era of Western imperial rule, the leaders of the new Southeast Asian states have been fearful of economic assistance as a means of reasserting old controls over their countries. Both Burma and Indonesia have recently displayed new interest in United States economic assistance, however—an indication, perhaps, of emergent political self-assurance. At the same time, the Soviet Union has moved into the picture as a major broker of foreign economic aid, a development which could prove most unfortunate to Southeast Asia's plans for the future in light of Moscow's known general policy objectives.

The economic backwardness of Southeast Asia was one of the conditions which made Western domination of the area possible. The Southeast Asia of today has come a long way from the Southeast Asia of the days of the first European arrivals. But so, too, have Europe, North America—and Russia. Southeast Asia's continued dangerous reliance on foreign purchases of its products and its crying need for capital to effect a change in this situation both afford excellent opportunities for the extension of foreign control over these countries. It may well be that Southeast Asia does not possess sufficient economic strength for independent political survival—except at the sufferance of the big powers or because of rivalries among these powers. It may also be that new developments in the fields of energy and matter will enable Southeast Asia to achieve this economic strength—for the first time in its history.

CHAPTER 2

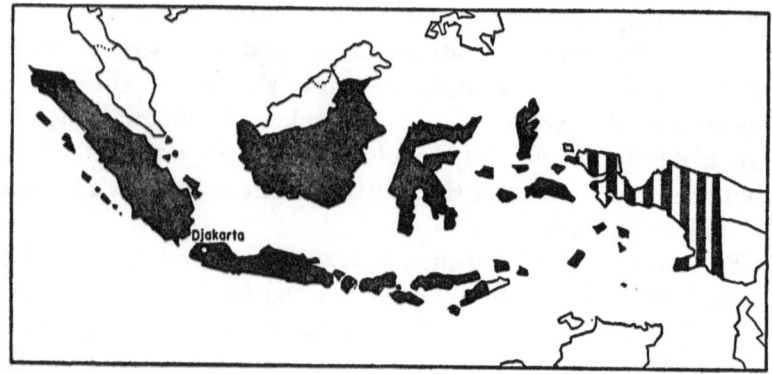

INDONESIA
Restless Insular Empire

THE INDONESIAN NATION is the product of the more than three centuries of Dutch rule which was terminated by the transfer of sovereighty to the new state on December 27, 1949. Nationalism was, of course, bound to come to the peoples of the region, but under other circumstances it might have been Javanese, Sumatranese, or other island or island-group nationalism. Such feeling of unity as now exists among the varied peoples of the insular state has in large part come about as the result of the long period of common Dutch administration.

For their population and resources the Dutch had an enormous colonial task which at times appeared beyond their strength. At the time of Pearl Harbor the Netherlands had an area of 12,850 square miles and a population of over 9,000,000; it governed an overseas territory in Southeast Asia of 733,000 square miles with a population approaching 70,000,000. There were Netherlanders in the last years of the nineteenth century who advocated giving up some of the islands

Indonesia 27

of the East Indies on the ground that to administer them was too costly.

The Dutch first went to the East Indies in 1595 as traders sent out by a large number of companies. The disadvantages of this unrestricted competition were so great that the States General in 1602 incorporated the East Indies traders in the United East India Company and conferred upon it divers rights of monopoly and sovereignty. The company's charter gave it a monopoly against all Netherlanders, but it had to compete with other European traders. This problem led the company involuntarily to shift from a commercial to a territorial basis, because it discovered that it could not trade unless it also governed. It took the forts and factories of its rivals, the Portuguese and Spanish, but found in time that this was not enough. Because of the chronic warfare among the native peoples, the company was led to a steadily deepening penetration. The East India Company was taken over by the Netherlands government in 1798, but even then the authority of the Dutch had not yet been thoroughly established everywhere in the archipelago. Indeed, it was to be another century and more before the whole region was brought under Dutch control.

The Dutch government had deliberately abstained from penetrating with its administration all of the territory it claimed, but because of the imperialist pressure at the end of the nineteenth century, an extension of effective administration to the whole territory of the dependency could no longer be delayed. In certain areas the Dutch effort to intensify their administration encountered bitter hostility. The pacification of some of these peoples required many years and was costly in men and money. This was especially true in the case of the Achinese, an ethnic group inhabiting the northern part of the island of Sumatra. Their geographic position at the northern entrance to the Malacca Straits made their piratical activities exceptionally dangerous and might easily have caused international complications. Fanatically Moslem in faith, these people resented the penetration of Western influences. In 1953 these same people rebelled against the Indonesian government.

The effects of this tardy extension of governmental administration to the remote parts of the archipelago can be seen today. It has given the Indonesian government considerable trouble in the form of local unrest and armed insurrection. The many different peoples of the archipelago had not reached the same stage of development when the Dutch came upon the scene, and the character of Dutch rule was not such as to reduce the differences much. The Dutch avoided the introduction of direct rule as much as possible, leaving the inhabitants under their sultans or the semihereditary regents and allowing them to continue under their local customary law. This policy of protecting the native customs and institutions tended to retard the cultural unification of the scores of ethnic groups which composed the population of the dependency. According to the 1930 census, there were nearly fifty ethnic groups, most of them with their own separate language. The Javanese, with nearly half of the total population, constituted the largest group. The Sundanese were next, with about 14 percent, followed by the Madurese with 7 percent.

The Dutch were also slow in developing educational facilities for the Indonesians. Closely related to their general policy of respecting native customs and institutions was that of differentiation in accordance with need in the field of education. This led to a great variety of schools to meet the supposedly peculiar needs of the various population groups—folk and standard schools, Dutch-Indonesian and Dutch-Chinese and Link or connecting schools—while all higher education was Western, with Dutch as the medium of instruction. The Dutch were determined that all Western education should maintain the same standards as similar education in the Netherlands; as a result, many non-Dutch students quickly dropped out. Moreover, this variety of schools did not help to merge the different ethnic groups into a nation; rather it tended to keep them apart. The Indonesian educational system was thus complicated and the facilities were limited. In all of Indonesia there were fewer than 2,000 college and university students on the eve of Pearl Harbor. The Philippines with about one-fourth of the population of Indonesia had more than four times as many young people pursuing higher education, though the standards were considerably lower. Thus the young Indonesian Republic began its independent existence with a dearth of educated persons for positions of leadership.

The situation with respect to government was similar. Standards of public administration were exceptionally high, but few Indonesians were found in the higher positions of government. Representative bodies had not yet been granted wide powers, and Europeans held membership in them far out of proportion to their numbers in the population. The Indies Civil Service was composed of a body of highly selected and well-trained persons, who until the last two decades could carry on their work free from political interference and the pressure of public opinion. Within the limits of the system they acquitted themselves well. But the system did not develop a democratic society or government. At the time of the fall of the country to Japan no Indonesian had yet been appointed to the governorship of a province and only one to a headship of a department of the central government.

The first representative body for the whole of the Indies, called the Volksraad, was established in 1917. During the first decade of its existence it had only advisory powers. After 1927 it enjoyed colegislative powers; that is, its approval was necessary for all legislation with the exception of emergency measures. Though the number of Netherlanders in the Indies constituted less than one percent of the population, nearly one-half of the seats of the Volksraad were reserved for them. In the provincial councils the membership was distributed in about the same way, but in the regency councils the Indonesians predominated. The urban councils were dominated by Europeans. The provincial and regency councils had functioned for only about a decade before the Japanese invasion. Thus when the Indonesians upon the capitulation of Japan in 1945 determined to take over the reins of government, they had had little experience in administration.

It is generally assumed that Indonesia received a bitter and meager heritage from the long years of Dutch rule. While the inheritance was poor on the educational, administrative, and political side, it was good in at least three respects. In many other dependencies foreigners acquired ownership of much of the land, which is about the only form of wealth in underdeveloped countries, but Indonesia began its independence with no such handicap. Under the provisions of the Netherlands Indies' Government Act only indigenous persons could own land; thus the natives could not sell their land to foreigners. Not even Indo-Europeans or Indo-Chinese, though their families had been residents of the country for many generations, could acquire ownership of agricultural land. The Indonesian Republic took over its national estate without a heavy mortgage on it by foreigners.

Secondly, the Indies government owned and operated most of the public utilities and in addition engaged in a wide range of economic activities. It owned and operated pawnshops, railroads, telephone and telegraph services, tramcars, bus lines, gold, silver, and coal mines, teak forests, and large cinchona, rubber, tea, and guttapercha plantations. In some years as much as 30 percent of the total revenue of the government came from this source. The government itself exploited the tin mines of Banka purely for profit-making purposes. The government was also part owner of corporations which exploited some of the richest oil fields in the country. The new state of Indonesia fell heir to all of these assets.

Thirdly, the Dutch followed a policy of the open door with respect to the external trade of the Indies. Dutch goods received no tariff preference over goods coming into the Indies from other countries. While the Indies' economy was "colonial" in that it produced chiefly primary commodities, it was not heavily dependent upon the market of a single foreign country, as was the case of its neighbor the Philippines, where an abrupt imposition of the full American tariff would have produced serious economic trouble. Indonesia had no such readjustment problem.

THE STRUGGLE FOR INDEPENDENCE

When the Dutch sought to return to the Indies after the capitulation of Japan in 1945, they were astonished and dismayed at the fierceness of the Indonesian nationalism they encountered. On the eve of World War II the Indonesian nationalist movement was relatively mild and immature and seemingly under control. The forces and events which wrought the transformation are not yet completely known.

The Netherlands was overrun by the Germans in May, 1940, and Queen Wilhelmina and her ministers fled to London, where they set up a government in exile. Thus abruptly cut off from the Netherlands, society in the Indies, Dutch as well as Indonesian, underwent a change. Nearly every aspect of life became more autonomous. Both Dutch and Indonesians felt their stature increased and became more assertive. The war had created a strong demand for the products (oil, rubber, tin, bauxite) of Indonesia, and as a result the economic position of the country was strong. The Dutch in Indonesia desired greater autonomy from the mother country, and the Indonesians demanded political reforms which would make Indonesia a parliamentary democracy with "dominion" status. These requests were made by moderate nationalists, and had the Dutch government dealt with them more constructively in the short time remaining before the Japanese invasion, the postwar story might have been somewhat different. But the Dutch government in exile replied to all demands for political reforms that it could do nothing without consulting the Dutch nation, and that was now impossible because of the German occupation. Its only promise was that an imperial conference would be called after the war to consider constitutional reforms. This negative attitude disillusioned and embittered the moderate nationalists and tended to drive them into the camp of the irreconcilables.

The three and one-half years of Japanese occupation most profoundly changed the Indonesian attitude and aroused the national consciousness to the fighting pitch. In the rapid conquest of the region by the Japanese the West suffered such a loss of prestige that Western rule could never again be restored on anything like the old basis. The Dutch in Indonesia were treated by the Japanese in such a manner as to humiliate them before the Indonesians. "Asia for the Asians" propaganda fell in fertile soil, and the general idea could never be uprooted.

The top Dutch officials were replaced by Japanese, but the latter, being wholly ignorant of the local situation and conditions, had to allow the Indonesian subordinates in effect to run the government offices. When in 1944 the Japanese leaders became alarmed at the American advance in the Pacific, they decided that their position in Southeast Asia had to be strengthened, and to secure the cooperation of the Indonesians, they promised them national independence. From that time on, more Indonesians were admitted to positions in the government, including those in the top ranks. Many of these new officials were young men who had been especially trained in various Japanese youth and military organizations and were fanatic nationalists. After the capitulation some Japanese officers allowed the nationalists to seize stores of arms.

The Netherlands had been completely liberated only a few months before the capitulation of Japan; hence the Dutch government was hardly prepared to meet the problems in its huge dependency on the other side of the world. The Indonesian nationalists, encouraged by the Japanese, used their opportunities and time well. A week before the surrender, Sukarno and Hatta were summoned by the commander in chief of the Japanese armies in Southeast Asia to fly to Saigon to confer about an immediate proclamation of Indonesian independence. Within a few days the Indonesian leaders returned to Batavia (Djakarta), and on August 17, 1945, independence was proclaimed. The Indonesian nationalists still had six weeks of unhampered freedom in which to consolidate their position. Not until September 29 did the British arrive with a small force to disarm and repatriate the Japanese troops.

The Dutch government was prepared to grant Indonesia a large amount of autonomy within an imperial union, but the representatives of the newly proclaimed republic demanded recognition as a sovereign state, after which, they declared, they would be willing to accept close political relations with the Netherlands with cooperation in many fields. After three years of intermittent negotiations, with two "police actions" by Dutch armed forces, followed each time by United Nations' intervention, an agreement was finally reached at a Round Table Con-

Indonesia 33

ference at The Hague in November, 1949. On December 27, 1949, sovereignty was transferred to the United States of Indonesia. The two sovereign states agreed to enter a Netherlands-Indonesian Union for "organized cooperation" in the fields of foreign relations, defense, and financial, economic, and cultural relations. The chief organ of the union was to be a conference of ministers, three designated by each member, meeting at least twice a year. The Union Statute also contained a vague provision for discussion between representatives of the parliaments in order "to effectuate good contact and regular cooperation" between the national representative bodies of the "partners." A court of arbitration composed of six members, three appointed by each government, was to have jurisdiction over legal disputes which might arise between them. Queen Juliana, and in case of death her successors, was named head of the union.

SHORT-LIVED FEDERAL GOVERNMENT

The heart of the nationalist revolution was located in Java and in certain areas of Sumatra. These territories constituted the core of the 1945 Republic, which the Dutch could not crack even though they penetrated them deeply in their "police actions." Outside of Java and Sumatra the Dutch had little difficulty in reestablishing their authority, and there they proceeded to organize states with plans to unite them in a federal structure. The Republicans felt that the "Federalists" were pro-Dutch, not true patriots, and there was considerable hostility between them. But when the Rum-Van Royen agreement, signed on May 7, 1949, made it clear that the Netherlands was about ready to grant Indonesian independence, representatives of the nationalist republic and of the Federal Consultative Assembly met in an inter-Indonesian conference during July and August to determine the main outlines of the provisional constitution for Indonesia. The draft of the constitution was completed at The Hague during the Round Table Conference (August 23 to November 2, 1949). The Dutch were merely informed that the Federalists and Republicans had agreed on a constitution and were given a copy of the text.

The title assumed by the former Dutch dependency was "Republic of the United States of Indonesia," and the first article declared it to be "a democratic state of federal structure." The position of the nationalist Republic of Indonesia in the federation was somewhat like that of Prussia in the German Empire. The republic had over 40 percent of the population of the country, and Sukarno and Hatta, respectively its president and vice president, were chosen to fill the same offices in the federal republic. The parliament was composed of a senate and a house of representatives. The former had a membership of 32, two from each of the 16 states and "units." The house had a membership of 150, with one-third of the number reserved for the nationalist Republic of Indonesia. Nine, six and three members were guaranteed the Chinese, European, and Arab minority groups respectively, either by election or appointment. The members of the first and only federal parliament were not popularly elected; they were delegated by their state governments. The government set up by the provisional constitution was a parliamentary system, but one in which the head of the state, the president, had far more power than is generally found in this type of political organization.

It is impossible to know whether the Republicans ever intended to give the federal government a real trial, for the movement to dismantle it began immediately after the transfer of sovereignty. The opposition to the federal system was powerfully aided by the attack on Bandung on January 22 by a rebel force under the leadership of a Dutch adventurer by the name of Captain Raymond ("Turk") Westerling. According to the Indonesian government's report, the force contained or was assisted by a number of soldiers and officers of the Netherlands and Netherlands Indies army. Members of this force later infiltrated into Djakarta, the capital, apparently with the object of overthrowing the government. Shortly thereafter, Sultan Hamid II of West Borneo, a leader among the Federalists and a member of the cabinet, was arrested as the mastermind behind the plot. Westerling escaped to Singapore on a Dutch military plane. This affair fanned anti-Dutch sentiment and helped to discredit the federal system, which was largely regarded as originally an invention of the Dutch "to divide and rule" and, even after independence, was looked upon as tainted with colonialism. The old federal states collapsed under hostile attacks, chiefly in the form of organized popular demonstrations. The federal system was not given a decent legal or constitutional burial; it was just abandoned.

A number of reasons were advanced to justify this action. It was asserted that the federal system was too costly, that it required a far larger experienced and trained personnel than Indonesia possessed, that the territories of the "states" and "units" were poorly drawn, and that the populations of the "units" were grossly unequal. It is certainly true that the federal structure as set up in the constitution had many weaknesses and defects, but it is difficult to escape the conclusion that the chief motivating force for its destruction was psychological.

The Republican leaders felt that they had been deprived of a complete victory by being compelled by force of circumstances to go to The Hague and negotiate a settlement. The federal constitution was a symbol of that failure of complete triumph, and it had to go. Later the Netherlands-Indonesian Union had to go for much the same reason. All this is understandable but nevertheless unfortunate. For months the government was paralyzed when much needed to be done quickly. Moreover, it was a poor beginning in establishing a democratic government; the federal system was destroyed by undemocratic means in violation of the constitution. Events were soon to demonstrate that another important factor was the matter of positions. Most of the offices in the governments of the federal states were held by persons regarded by the Republicans as cooperators with the Dutch. A quick means of getting the "cos," as the cooperators were called, out of all government positions and filling them with faithful Republicans was to replace the federal with a unitary government. For a country with the geographic and ethnic structure of Indonesia, however, the creation of a highly centralized government was ill considered. Dissatisfaction with the centralization of the new regime quickly developed.

Indonesia as a federal state had only one cabinet. Hatta, who was vice president of the state, was also the prime minister. Hatta probably represents the best political leadership Indonesia possesses, and he had in his cabinet a number of very able men, but his government had to work under extremely unfavorable conditions. Besides the Hamid-Westerling attempted coup d'etat, it had to deal with disorders and an army insurrection which broke out in South Celebes and with a rebellion on the island of Ambon, where the people proclaimed a Republic of South Moluccas. The latter affair was especially unfortunate because it further strained Dutch-Indonesian relations. The Ambonese were a Dutchified people who for generations had furnished large numbers of soldiers to the Netherlands Indies army; hence the plight of the Ambonese was bound to arouse a certain amount of sympathy among Netherlanders even if they did not approve of the Ambonese action. Many Indonesians were certain the Dutch had instigated the rebellion, or at least encouraged the Ambonese in their defiance of the Indonesian state.

It was probably foolish for the Dutch to hope that they would still be able to play a large and effective role in Indonesia after independence, though the hope was understandable. Netherlanders had large sums of money invested in the country, they had a profound scientific knowledge of every aspect of Indonesian life, and in some respects they had brought the islands to a remarkable development. Moreover, the delegates of Indonesia at The Hague had agreed to take over the Dutch civil servants of the former Indies government. To the Indonesians, however, all of these things were evil vestiges of colonialism, which had to be eradicated as soon as possible. The federal system, regarded as a Dutch imposition, was the first to go. The Netherlands-Indonesian Union followed a few years later.

In the discussions leading up to the conversion of the federal into the unitary state a big question was whether the old nationalist republic was swallowing up the federal government or a new republic was being formed. Though the change represented a tremendous psychological triumph for the Republicans, the new government did not, at least legally, mean the annexation of the whole of the country by the 1945 republic, for the new provisional constitution was a revision of the provisional constitution of the Republic of the United States of Indonesia. The outlines of the new constitution, except for the federal features, were practically the same as the old. The senate was abolished, but its membership was incorporated in the new house of representatives. The constitution contained a marked social and economic emphasis, but probably no greater than other basic political documents drafted since World War II.

POLITICAL DEVELOPMENTS UNDER THE UNITARY SYSTEM

The provisional constitution of the unitary state went into effect on August 17, 1950, the fifth anniversary of the proclamation of the original republic, but not until September 6 was a new cabinet ready to take over the government. Mohammad Natsir, the leader of the Masjumi (Moslem) party, the largest in the parliament, became the new prime minister. His cabinet represented a coalition of the Masjumi and a number of small parties, of which Sjahrir's Socialist party was one of the most important. Not a member of the coalition was the Nationalist party, which, after the Masjumi, had the largest number of seats in parliament. The general position of the Natsir cabinet was one of moderate liberalism. Though it was on the whole a strong cabinet, its life was short. It resigned March 20, 1951.

The Natsir cabinet had to struggle with a number of difficult problems, nearly all of which continued to plague succeeding governments. There was first of all Indonesia's relations with the Netherlands, including the dispute over West New Guinea. The Dutch and Indonesian representatives at The Hague had been unable to agree on the disposition of this vast jungle area of over 150,000 square miles but with a population estimated at less than a million. Indonesians insisted that it be included in their domain, since it was a part of the former Netherlands Indies, but the Dutch maintained that this relationship had been only incidental and that the territory was not an integral part of Indonesia geographically, ethnically, or otherwise. In order to conclude the main business of the conference, it was agreed that "the status quo" of the territory would be maintained "with the stipulation that within a year from the date of transfer of sovereignty . . . the question of the political status of New Guinea be determined through negotiations" between the parties. This was in effect an agreement to continue the disagreement, but with the immediate advantage with the Dutch, since the "status quo" was that the Netherlands was administering the territory. The unwillingness of the Netherlands to surrender the territory to Indonesia has embittered Indonesian-Dutch relations, and led to popular demands for nullification of all the agreements with the Netherlands and even for reprisals against the Dutch.

Other issues which caused the Natsir cabinet political difficulties were the high cost of living, a ban on strikes and lockouts, budget deficits, and the manner of choosing the members of local councils until the permanent constitution should be adopted. A rash of strikes broke out, threatening to paralyze the economic life of the country, and in February, 1951, the government prohibited strikes and lockouts in essential industries. This was an issue which the leftists could exploit effectively.

Thirty-seven days after Natsir's resignation, Sukiman of the Masjumi and Sidik of the Nationalist party succeeded in forming a coalition government, which took office on April 28. Since the cabinet represented a coalition of the two largest parties plus a few small parties, it was expected to have strong support in parliament. The Sukiman cabinet was regarded as conservative. In August it rounded up thousands of persons alleged to be subversive, including sixteen members of parliament, some for questioning, others for detention and arrest. It signed the treaty with Japan at San Francisco, instituted some monetary reforms, and devaluated the rupiah.

The Sukiman cabinet came to grief over a matter of foreign policy. The foreign affairs minister signed an agreement with the United States for Mutual Security Agency assistance involving only eight million dollars, largely in the form of badly needed equipment for Indonesia's internal security forces. When the agreement became public, however, a political furor instantaneously developed, for the Mutual Security Act required all governments receiving aid under it to agree to contribute "to the defensive strength of the free world." Practically every Indonesian political leader regarded the acceptance of even such a mild, vague commitment as a departure from Indonesia's independent, or neutralist, foreign policy. When the two major parties of the coalition refused to support the agreement, the foreign minister resigned, but his departure failed to still the political storm. The entire cabinet submitted its resignation a short while later, on February 23, 1952, after having held office for nearly ten months.

On April 1 a new cabinet was announced. It represented a coalition of the Masjumi, the Nationalist, and five small parties. The prime minister and formateur of the new government was Wilopo, a Nationalist and secretary of economic affairs in the previous cabinet. While the new government represented primarily a Nationalist-Masjumi coalition, the most important positions in it were held by Nationalists. The program of the Wilopo government included general elections for the constitutional assembly within one year, increased welfare through an increase in national production, strengthening the national security, improved labor legislation, modernization of the educational system, an active and independent foreign policy, and termination of the Netherlands-Indonesian Union.

The Wilopo cabinet lived a precarious existence for fourteen months. Its beginning was inauspicious. A vote of confidence was obtained from parliament only after forty days of debate, though the vote when finally taken was substantially in its favor. The cabinet wobbled through one crisis after another until it finally fell on the issue of the handling of the land-distribution problem on the east coast of Sumatra. But this was not the cause of the downfall of the cabinet, only the occasion. The two major parties supporting the government became deeply divided on a number of issues, so that cooperation between the two became difficult. Wilopo had much trouble with the leftwing members of his own party, who frequently voted with the opposition, thus putting the cabinet in a weak position.

On October 17, 1952, there occurred an extraordinary affair, one which deeply involved the political stability of the country. From this event until its resignation on June 3, 1953, the Wilopo government existed in a "political oxygen tent." The background of the affair was complicated. The minister of defense, Sultan Buwono of Djokjakarta, aided by a military mission from the Netherlands, was carrying out plans for modernization of the army. The group of former guerrilla officers in the army disliked this policy, chiefly because of their inadequate training, and the large number of former guerrilla fighters within the army likewise feared the plan would mean their removal from the service when the strength of the army would be reduced from 200,000 to 100,000 men.

The issue was politically explosive. A foreign military mission—worse still, a Dutch mission—was advising and aiding the sultan in carrying out the plan. Opponents of the plan charged that the army was losing its revolutionary character and was again acquiring a "colonial" status. Apparently also involved was rivalry between President Sukarno and Sultan Buwono. The former seemed to fear the role and ambitions of the latter. It was also charged that the top members of the Defense Ministry were sympathetic with the Socialist party and that political considerations influenced promotions.

The issue came up in parliament. There were debates. Voices were raised demanding changes in the defense ministry, whereupon a number of army officers petitioned President Sukarno to dissolve parliament, since it had no mandate from the people and therefore no moral authority to pass judgment on other departments of the government.[1] On October 16 parliament passed a resolution, introduced by a member of

[1] Members of parliament were not popularly elected, but were appointed by the political parties according to a system of proportional representation established by a presidential committee.

Indonesia

the Nationalist party, calling for early withdrawal of the Netherlands military mission and the appointment of a committee "to bring forward concrete proposals for changes in the top echelons of the Defense Ministry and in the Armed Forces." On the next day the capital witnessed a wild popular demonstration against parliament and in support of the defense minister, with the army much in evidence. The crowds entered the parliament building, destroying furniture and finishings, and then marched to the presidential palace, demanding the dissolution of parliament and early elections for a new national assembly. With his customary skill in handling crowds President Sukarno succeeded in calming the demonstrators without promising anything more than the first general elections would be held as soon as possible. The parliament did not assemble again for a number of weeks.

These remarkable events were followed by others no less strange. A few days after the October 17 affair three territorial commanders (in East Java, East Indonesia, and South Sumatra) were removed by subordinate officers, apparently in protest against what they believed to be the actions of the military clique in Djakarta. The usurping officers declared allegiance to President Sukarno while engaged in their acts of insubordination. The government in a public statement strongly rebuked the officers who had participated in the October 17 demonstration and promised "to restore integrity and unity" in the armed forces. However, instead of disciplining the rebellious officers, the new chief of staff formally appointed them to the positions they had usurped, over the protests of Defense Minister Buwono. When the cabinet backed the appointments, the sultan resigned.

The resignation of the Wilopo cabinet was followed by a 58-day political crisis. After several leaders had failed in forming a cabinet, the president called upon Wongsonegoro, the chairman of the United Greater Indonesian party (P.I.R.), with a membership of only fifteen in the temporary parliament. He succeeded in forming a coalition cabinet composed of the Nationalist and a number of small nationalist and Marxist parties, with Ali Sastroamidjojo, at the time ambassador to the United States, as prime minister and himself as vice prime minister. The new cabinet had only a slight majority in parliament, and it was apparent that its political life would frequently be dependent on the Communist members of parliament. The new cabinet was markedly leftist. Among the new ministers was Iwa Kusuma Sumantri, who had spent some time in Moscow and was imprisoned in 1946 for participation in the attempted Communist coup of that year. He was given the sensitive post of minister of defense.

Another important factor which helps to explain the character and history of the Ali-Wongsonegoro cabinet was its peculiar relation to President Sukarno. It seems clear that without his influence and active support it could not have been formed or remained so long in power. The prime minister and the minister for foreign affairs were old and close friends of the president. An informed American observer concluded that the cabinet was "presidential" in everything but name. "In terms of effective policy control, the Ali-Wongsonegoro Cabinet offers the president all the advantages of a presidential cabinet without the responsibility of accepting blame for any failures."[2]

The Ali cabinet remained in office two years, which was considerably longer than any of its predecessors. Wongsonegoro, who formed the cabinet and served as vice premier, resigned toward the end of 1954 when his party withdrew its support. The cabinet weathered the loss of some support in parliament, a cabinet reshuffle, widespread corruption in administration, deteriorating economic conditions, continued internal insecurity, and a revolt in North Sumatra. It won considerable prestige in promoting the Bandung Conference and serving as host to this important diplomatic meeting. It looked as if its life was secure, at least until the general election, which was scheduled for the end of September, 1955. Suddenly it ran into political trouble and fell.

The manner of the fall of the Ali cabinet points up the political instability of the country. The prime minister, flush

[2] Robert C. Bone, Jr., "The Future of Indonesian Political Parties," *Far Eastern Survey*, XXIII (1954), 23.

with the diplomatic festivities and honors enjoyed on an official visit to Communist China from which he had just returned, suddenly found himself and his cabinet in serious trouble arising when the minister of defense filled the vacancy caused by the resignation of the army chief of staff. When the appointment was announced, the deputy, serving as acting chief of staff, and seven colonels, all territorial commanders, refused to accept the newly appointed chief. The colonels successfully defied the prestige, power, authority, and combined efforts of President Sukarno and Prime Minister Ali. Not only did they refuse to accept the appointee, but they acted as if he did not exist, and the deputy continued to function as chief of staff. They rejected all offers of compromise. On July 26, 1955, the cabinet handed in its resignation.

Just what motivated the army leaders in their defiance of the government is not clear. They had demanded the right to be consulted in the appointment of a chief of staff, but had been ignored. They may have felt that the appointment was political. They stated that their aims were nonpolitical, that they had in view only the efficiency of the army. It has been suggested that the army leaders were weary of trying to keep the army at a high level of efficiency under the government of Ali and used the chief-of-staff appointment as a means of forcing the cabinet out of office.

The affair which brought the Ali cabinet and the government to its sad plight is not incomprehensible. The government claimed to be democratic, yet after more than five years after the transfer of sovereignty it was still operating under a provisional constitution and a nonelected parliament. The government no longer had moral authority. The army leaders apparently felt no strong obligation to respect the decisions of the Ali government. Whatever the explanation, the affair revealed a critical situation. Natsir, the leader of the Masjumi party, succinctly summarized the gravity of it when he stated that Indonesia was confronted not only with a cabinet crisis but with "a crisis of authority."

A new ministry under the leadership of Burhanuddin Harahap, the chairman of the Masjumi party in the parliament, took office on August 13. It was formed under peculiar circumstances. President Sukarno had nothing to do with the formation of the Harahap cabinet. Part of the time of the political crisis he was out of the country on a pilgrimage to Mecca, and on his return he did not assume the usual functions of his office but instead went "on vacation." Moreover, Vice President Hatta, who was functioning as the head of the state, was himself considered for the role of prime minister. The plan to form a strong national cabinet under his able leadership fell through because agreement could not be reached on his status while premier. The Harahap ministry, representing a coalition of 12 of the 20 parties represented in the provisional parliament, was conservative in character. The chief points in its program were restoration of the moral authority of the government and the confidence of the armed forces and people in the government, checking of inflation, combating of corruption, and continuance of the struggle to "reincorporate" West New Guinea into the territory of Indonesia. The main parties in opposition were the Nationalists and Communists.

FIRST PARLIAMENTARY ELECTIONS

At long last the first general elections were held, on September 29, 1955 (in some outlying districts on subsequent dates). The voting took place fairly peacefully, with about 90 percent of the eligible voters going to the polls. Thirty-four political groups and individuals conducted a nationwide campaign for seats, and forty-four others tried their fortunes in restricted or local areas. Twenty-eight parties and individuals won seats— twelve winning only one seat. The results of the election were rather surprising. It was thought that the religion of the masses would work to handicap the Nationalist party and would favor the Masjumi, the leading Moslem party. However, in the country as a whole the Nationalists' vote slightly surpassed that cast for the Masjumi, and on Java the vote ran three to two in favor of the former. On the other hand, a splinter Moslem party, the Nahdatul Ulama (Moslem Schoolmen's League or Moslem

Indonesia

Teachers' party), received nearly as many votes as the Masjumi. One of the most startling aspects of the election returns was the large vote of the Communist party—more than 16 percent of the total vote.[3] Sutan Sjahrir's Socialist party made a very poor showing, and a number of small parties received too few votes to win a single seat in the new national parliament, even under the system of proportional representation by which the seats are distributed.

The success of the Nationalist party may in part be explained by the support which it received from President Sukarno, while the large vote for the Moslem Teachers' party reflects the conservative character of many Indonesian Moslems. The Moslem Teachers' party is orthodox; the Masjumi is reformist and pro-Western. Though more conservative religiously, the former was less outspokenly anti-Communist. However, the Masjumi is the most national of all the parties; its votes were more evenly distributed over the whole country than those of any other party, and its representation in parliament is accordingly more nationwide. The Moslem Teachers' party found itself in an awkward position. It had unexpectedly come into a position of real power, but it was without experienced or strong leadership.

On December 15, 1955, Indonesia held a second national election, this time to elect the members of the constituent assembly which was to draft a permanent constitution. In this election, in which fewer votes were cast than in the earlier one, the Nationalists received a larger and the Masjumi an even smaller percentage of the total vote.[4] The two national elections seem

[3] The number of votes cast in the election was 37,785,299. Six parties received more than a million votes each. The number and percentage of their votes and the resulting distribution of seats in parliament is as follows:

	Votes		No. Seats	
	No.	%	Parl.	Prov. Parl.
Nationalist	8,434,653	22.3	57	42
Masjumi	7,903,886	20.9	57	44
Moslem Teachers'	6,955,141	18.4	45	8
Communist	6,176,914	16.4	39	17
Moslem Association	1,091,160	2.9	8	4
Christian	1,003,325	2.6	8	5

[4] The popular vote received and the seats in the assembly won by the four largest parties is as follows: Nationalists—9,070,218 votes, 119 seats; Masjumi—7,789,619 votes, 112 seats; Moslem Teachers' party—6,989,333 votes, 91 seats; Communists—6,232,512 votes, 75 seats. There are 520 members in the constituent assembly.

to indicate a strong trend toward extreme nationalism, radical economic policies, and militant, orthodox Islamism.

The elections called for a new cabinet based on the new parliament. On March 16, 1956, Ali Sastroamidjojo informed President Sukarno that he had succeeded in forming a ministry. After some days of hesitation the president approved the ministry, which was based upon the three largest parties in parliament—the Nationalist, the Masjumi, and the Moslem Teachers—and a number of smaller parties, including the Parkindo (Protestant) and Catholic parties. The new ministry's program embraced twelve points, all general in character.

The new Ali cabinet started with a strong numerical backing in a parliament only recently elected by the people; it nevertheless soon found itself in difficulty. In August the army, under authority of martial law, attempted to arrest Foreign Minister Ruslan Abdulgani on charges of corruption, just as he was about to leave for a conference in London. A cabinet commission cleared him of the charges. Also under authority of martial law, the army jailed a leading newspaper editor for criticizing the government. In November an army officers' group in Djakarta apparently sought to overthrow the Ali government, and in December there were a series of military revolts in Sumatra. The Sumatrans are discontented because of the failure of the government to build up the country, and they demand greater local autonomy. Because of its wealth, Sumatra produces a large part of the revenues of the central government, and its exports produce over two-thirds of the country's foreign exchange earnings. The revolutionary councils set up in South Sumatra demanded the right to keep more of the revenues collected in the area for local use. The central government seems to have yielded to these demands. In January the Masjumi and several small parties withdrew from the ministry, leaving the Ali cabinet in a precarious position.

The response of President Sukarno to these developments is worth noting, as he is still the idol of the Indonesian masses. He has twice publicly appealed for the "burial" of Indonesia's political parties and the replacement of the present political

Indonesia

system by a "guided" democracy. He regards the formation of parties in 1945 as a grave mistake which has caused discord among the people. In opening the constituent assembly, he declared that "For the time being our democracy must be a guided democracy—thus not a democracy that is based on conceptions of liberalism." This desire for unity was probably stimulated by his visits in 1956 to the Communist countries. He apparently is convinced that this unity is necessary for Indonesia, if it is to have security and prosperity. He suggested that once the parties were dissolved, political leaders should decide "whether a one party system should be formed, a mass movement, or some well-founded parties."[5] There were reports that he was planning to play a more direct role in the government by setting up a council whose approval would be necessary for all major decisions taken by parliament.[6] He strongly asserts, however, that he does not want to become a dictator.

After many weeks of expectation the president on February 2, 1957, called on his countrymen to abandon the "imported" Western system of democracy and substitute for it a new one which he termed a "conception." He specifically proposed the creation of a cabinet which would comprise all the major parties, including the Communists, which had seats in parliament as a result of the 1955 elections. This cabinet would represent parliament, and a second body, a national council, composed of a cross section of the people, would represent Indonesian society. The latter body, presided over by the president himself, would "advise" the cabinet. If his "conception" were adopted, Sukarno said, there would be an end to the opposition which had paralyzed Indonesian governments; instead, there would be only brotherly discussion.

The Communists greeted the proposal with joy and immediately began a campaign to whip up enthusiasm for it. Buildings were painted with pro-Sukarno and antiforeign slogans. Political leaders opposing Sukarno's proposal received letters threatening them with kidnapping unless they changed

[5] See New York *Times*, November 18, 1956.
[6] New York *Times*, January 16, 1957.

their minds. The Moslem and Christian parties and a number of Djakarta newspapers criticized the plan and announced opposition to it.

On March 2 a dissident group proclaimed a military regime in East Indonesia. They announced dissatisfactions similar to those of the Sumatrans. The leader of the revolt in the east presented President Sukarno an ultimatum demanding the dismissal of Prime Minister Ali Sastroamidjojo and his cabinet, and warning the president that they would not tolerate any Communists in the government. There were reports that both the Communists and anti-Communist factions in Sumatra had received arms from Malaya.

After South Sumatra and Borneo had joined the procession of revolts, the Ali cabinet resigned (March 14). President Sukarno promptly proclaimed a state of war and seige, legally giving him virtually dictatorial authority, but how much power in fact remained to be seen in view of the involvement of the army in the defiance of "Javanese centralism."

The situation has become very serious for the central government. Cut off from the rich tax-producing and large foreign-trade-earning outer islands, the government, situated in overpopulated Java, would soon experience financial strangulation.

The ideas advocated more recently by President Sukarno are consistent with basic ideas frequently expressed by him. In his view the national revolution is never completed but is continuing. He once pleaded for a "Peoples Congress" in which all the national forces would be represented to carry on the national revolution. As a result of his advocacy, such a congress was held. The democratic parties shunned it, enabling the Communists and fellow travelers to dominate it. In his speech to the constitutent assembly, Sukarno stated that the constitution must prevent the growth of a "capitalistic system in Indonesia."

A rift between President Sukarno and Vice President Hatta had been developing for some time. The latter became outspokenly critical of ideas advocated by the president. On December 1, 1956, he resigned, presumably to have freedom to follow an independent political course. Hatta is known as an able economist, respected for his integrity, and widely regarded as a strong man of judicious temperament. Some political groups, especially the Masjumi, strongly advocate the appointment of Hatta as prime minister.

INTERNAL SECURITY

If orderly and democratic government is to survive in Indonesia, a number of difficult problems must be solved; and improvement must come soon, for the situation is grave indeed.

There is unrest, banditry, lawlessness, and large-scale resistance against the government in many areas of Indonesia. This is a problem which every government since 1950 has promised to deal with drastically, but conditions improve slowly, if at all. There is stealing, murder, the burning of villages. This extraordinary phenomenon is the product of the Japanese invasion and occupation, guerrilla activities against the Dutch, extreme poverty, political discontent, and religious fanaticism.

The revolt in the South Moluccas is not difficult to understand. The Ambonese, who constituted the heart of the movement, are a Dutchified people who supplied large numbers of men to the Netherlands Indies army. Many of them found it difficult to transfer their loyalty to the independent Indonesia; several thousand Ambonese soldiers chose to go to the Netherlands rather than be discharged in Indonesia. Moreover, some of their leaders may honestly have felt tricked when the provisional federal constitution was abolished for another provisional but unitary constitution by means that could hardly be called democratic. The political leaders of the territories outside the nationalist republic had joined in a common front against the Dutch at The Hague Round Table Conference on the basis of the federal constitution. They feared government from Djakarta by Javanese and the consequent loss of local autonomy. The revolt seemed to have been crushed by the Indonesian army by November, 1950, but smoldering embers remained.

The military disorders, guerrilla activities, and terrorization in South Celebes seem to be a mixture of political and social discontent and religious fanaticism. Some of the leaders of disorder in this region seem to be in contact with the Darul

Islam on Java and sympathetic with it. In Java the heart of the disorder and resistance to the government is Darul Islam, a group which seeks to overthrow the present government and set up a "pure Moslem state." Before independence the Darul Islamists fought alongside other groups against the Dutch, but steadily refused incorporation with the nationalist Republic of Indonesia. For them the winning of independence was merely a necessary step in the creation of a theocratic Islamic state. Violence is their method, and they have used it as vigorously against the Indonesian government as they did against the foreign ruler. They have kept a considerable area of Java in a state of terror. In 1953 a revolt closely allied to Darul Islam broke out among the Achinese in North Sumatra.

Internal insecurity has been the central problem of Indonesia during the first seven years of independence. In his independence day speech on August 17, 1952, President Sukarno declared that "the state is still shaky because it is being disturbed in various areas by marauding bands." That condition seemed chronic. In 1953 there were 4,295 persons killed in Java alone, and 11,494 houses burned down. The government reported that 137,379 persons had been evacuated from Central Java during the first three months of 1955 as a result of bandit activities. During the same period 76 villagers were killed and five persons kidnapped by bandits in this area alone.

GENERAL WELFARE AND ECONOMIC PROSPECTS

If Indonesia is to become politically stable and not fall under Communist control, living levels will have to rise. The nationalist revolution in Indonesia was in part a "revolution of rising expectations." Per capita and national incomes were low. About the only affluent people in the country were foreigners: Westerners, Chinese, Arabs, and Indians. It is wholly understandable that people living under these conditions would ascribe their poverty to foreign exploitation aided by foreign rule. For them Marxism seemed to explain nearly everything. Many of the nationalist leaders became strongly Marxist in their thinking, and moreover, they found the Marxist theories useful in arous-

Indonesia

ing resentment against foreign rule. The masses were led to believe that with independence, living conditions would immediately improve, because there would be an end to foreign exploitation. The fruits of Indonesian resources and labor would remain in Indonesia and go to Indonesians.

Unfortunately, the lively and pleasant expectations of improved living conditions have not been realized. Instead, living levels have declined. Needless to say, this creates a dangerous situation. The head of the Bank of Indonesia in his report for the year 1952-1953 stated that real per capita income was only about 60 percent of what it was in 1938, and production was only 65 to 70 percent of the prewar levels. There has been little if any improvement since 1953. In the meanwhile the population has increased considerably. The 1954 production of rubber, petroleum, and rice, however, exceeded that of 1938. In 1952, 760,000 tons of rice had to be imported; by 1955 self-sufficiency had been nearly achieved. With regard to nearly every other commodity the story is not so favorable. Production of tea, coffee, cinchona bark, sugar, palm oil, palm nuts, and hard fiber in 1954 was considerably below that of 1938.

Indonesia's balance-of-trade picture is not encouraging. During 1950, the first year of its independence, the Korean hostilities broke out and the prices of rubber and tin, two of the country's chief exports, shot up, producing a large balance of trade in Indonesia's favor in 1950 and 1951. Unfortunately, the foreign exchange thus earned was largely squandered on the importation of luxury goods. In 1952 the balance was unfavorable. The price of tin and rubber slumped badly, and the price of the manufactured goods which Indonesia imported went up rather than down. To keep the foreign trade in balance, a number of measures restricting imports were resorted to, but this led to all sorts of difficulties. Plantations and factories were unable to import necessary supplies and equipment, and some factories actually had to cease operations. The rise in the price of rubber and tin in 1955 considerably eased Indonesia's foreign-exchange position.

If it were not for the Western-operated industries, the trade balance would be strongly adverse. Rubber and petroleum account for over half of the total exports in value, and nearly all of the petroleum and much of the rubber is produced by Western capital and management. Exclusive of petroleum alone, the Indonesian trade balance is heavily adverse. If capital goods for economic development are to be imported, the great export industries will have to earn the foreign exchange, but the conditions under which they have to operate is discouraging. Labor troubles, hostility toward foreign capital, large-scale thievery and brigandage, illegal occupation of concession lands by peasant squatters, heavy taxes, and exchange restrictions make it difficult for Western enterprises to carry on profitably. There is a 15 percent ad valorem sales tax, a 52 percent tax on profits, and a 66.6 percent tax on dollar remittances out of the country. Some of the large Dutch companies are transferring their operations to other countries, notably Ethiopia. This is a serious matter for Indonesia, for the Western enterprises are the earners of foreign exchange and a rich source of public revenue. Until Indonesian capital and enterprise can fill this role, the economic outlook will remain gloomy and the government's fiscal situation precarious.

Government finances naturally reflect the unsatisfactory economic conditions of the country. Expenditures far exceed income; revenue falls short of outgo by about 20 to 30 percent. Expenditures in 1956 were about 19,000,000,000 rupiahs and receipts 17,000,000,000. The deficit in 1955 was about 3,000,-000,000 rupiahs. The national public debt practically doubled during the first four years of independence, having increased from 6,894,000,000 rupiahs in 1949 to 13,385,000,000 by the end of 1953. The country is caught in an inflationary spiral. By June, 1955, salaries had fallen so far behind the rapidly rising price level that they were woefully inadequate, with inefficiency and corruption as a result.

POPULATION PRESSURE AND SOCIAL STABILITY

Judged by Asian and tropical standards, Indonesia as a whole is not densely populated. It is nevertheless troubled with a serious demographic problem. It is essentially a problem of

Indonesia

underdevelopment and the concentration of the population on one island. Java (with the dependent island of Madura) with only one-eleventh of the area of Indonesia has two-thirds of the estimated 85,000,000 inhabitants of the country. An idea of the intense population pressure on Java can be obtained by comparing its area and population with those of the state of New York. The two have practically the same area, but Java has about 55,000,000 people to 16,000,000 for New York. Thus the former, which is still overwhelmingly agrarian, has nearly four times the population of the latter, which is highly commercial and industrial. Such a population mass weighs heavily on the production and the available resources, and depresses the levels of living.

There is no easy solution to this problem. Significant extension of agriculture is no longer possible. Intensification, including heavier application of fertilizers and the use of higher producing seeds, is still possible and is being achieved. Rapid industrialization would relieve population pressure on the land, but when the comparison with New York is recalled, this solution does not seem bright. It would take a tremendous industrial development to draw half of the population of the island from the countryside into the cities within a period of two decades, and by that time the total population would have increased by at least a third, since Java has a natural increase of over 700,000 per year.

There remains transmigration to the less populated islands, a scheme begun by the Dutch decades ago. As early as 1905 the Netherlands Indies government encouraged Javanese to move to the Outer Islands, as they were called. The colonists were given free transportation and financial support during the first years of settlement. The scheme was too costly, and the number of migrants remained small. Some of the more difficult problems connected with the scheme were solved, and in the last years before the war the number of colonists increased rapidly, from 13,152 in 1936 to 55,000 in 1940. The Indonesian government has resumed the policy of resettlement. The number of transmigrants was 27 families with a total of 45 persons in 1950, 769 families (2,923 persons) in 1951, 3,829 families

(17,430 persons) in 1952, 9,854 families (39,284 persons) in 1953, and 7,846 families (27,643 persons) in 1954. Plans for the next four years are rather ambitious. The government planned to resettle 40,000 families in 1955, 80,000 in 1956, and in the years 1957 to 1960 a total of 280,000 families, or a grand total of more than 2,000,000 persons for the six-year period. It is estimated that the cost to the government will run over 4,000,000,000 rupiahs. The resettlement areas are in Sumatra, Borneo, and Celebes.

Transmigration in such large numbers might be expected to relieve the population pressure on Java somewhat, but large as the numbers are, the total will not equal the natural increase of Java's millions. Moreover, the scheme does little or nothing to raise the level of production. The small-farm peasantry system is merely being spread to the Outer Islands; the conditions of Java are extended over an area which should be jealously conserved for maximal production by the use of more capital, relative to labor, on larger tracts. Only by this means can per capita income be increased.

A Dutch sociologist, Dr. J. H. Boeke, after long study of the problem of raising the general welfare concluded that "a real solution can be found only by instilling into the masses of the people a Western spirit which will bring forth a rationalistic view of sex relations and a dynamic view of production. This is the only conclusion that can be reached by those who desire to make actual a general mass-welfare policy."[7] There is little evidence to indicate that a basic change is taking place in the attitude of the masses with respect to these matters.

It is frequently asserted that Indonesia is a very rich country. It does possess considerable natural resources, but riches must always be related to the number of people who have to share them, and Indonesia cannot be "rich" for an unlimited number of people. It is generally assumed that tropical soils are very fertile, but this is far from the truth. In fact, tropical soils are generally poor, for the reason that the heavy rains leach the soil of its mineral elements. It is only where there has been recent volcanic action, as in Java, that the soils are fertile.

[7] *The Structure of Netherlands Indian Economy* (New York, 1942), 163.

Indonesia

A danger to which Indonesian soil is especially exposed is erosion. The land is hilly, frequently mountainous, and the average annual rainfall in some places runs as high as 250 inches. To prevent destructive erosion, it is necessary to keep the hillsides covered with vegetation. The Dutch had early learned their lesson in this matter. Squatters who denuded the hillsides which had been set aside as reserves were severely dealt with, and as a result the Netherlands Indies forestry service was hated by the peasants. During the Japanese occupation and the revolution these conservation measures were neglected, with erosion, floods, the filling of streams, and the covering of lowlands with silt as a consequence. The weak, cruelly beset Indonesian governments have not dealt with this problem as resolutely as they should, if the national heritage is not to be seriously impaired.

It is not only Java that is suffering from the pressure of population on land. The Indonesian government is considering the resettlement of Balinese on the island of Sumbawa, and there is evidence to indicate that north central Sumatra is beginning to experience difficulties.

On the east coast of Sumatra a peculiarly difficult problem has arisen. In the last decades of Dutch rule this area attracted large Western agricultural enterprises, which acquired access to the soil by means of concessions of public lands for periods not exceeding 75 years. This Western plantation area became an important source of government revenue and foreign exchange, for practically the total production of the area was exported.

Signs of approaching trouble appeared even before the war. There were complaints that the best land had been leased to European planters or added to the public forests, so that the native population was left with poor and insufficient land. The government, sorely in need of increased revenue, could ill afford to see the land transferred to native agriculture, which is much less productive than plantation agriculture.

During the years of Japanese occupation and the revolution, thousands of illegal squatters settled on these lands. The Indonesian government found itself caught between the foreign planters' demands for restoration of the land and its own desperate need for revenue and foreign exchange on the one hand, and on the other, the squatters' unwillingness to move. The foreign operators, realizing the difficulties of the government and the explosive character of the situation, relinquished about a third of their concession areas with the understanding that the government would guarantee them full use of the remainder.

The government now faced the unpleasant task of removing the squatters from the land that was to be returned to the planters. The government scheme called for the transfer of squatters to other areas where they received small tracts of land and 300 rupiahs as indemnification. This was a delicate operation in an area where there were many Communists (among the large Chinese population) and where many native laborers and peasants had been drawn into leftist organizations. Forcible removal of tillers of the soil in favor of "foreign imperialists" was a situation which lent itself to exploitation. About half of the 30,000 families which were to be moved had been resettled when an outbreak occurred. The police fired on the demonstrators, and a number of people were killed and wounded. Naturally the matter was discussed in parliament. The Communist and other leftist members of parliament united in support of a resolution calling for a revision of the land-distribution policy. This was the immediate cause of the downfall of the Wilopo cabinet, which resigned on June 3, 1953.

POLITICAL INSTABILITY

Politically the early years of the republic have been marked by uncertainty, tension, and conflict. By June, 1955, the situation had become grave and the political life of the country seemed to be at a dead end. Only an early and honest general election offered any hope of restoring respect for, and confidence in, the government. The condition of the country was graphically and frankly described in an open letter to President Sukarno in June, 1955, by his old friend and fellow revolutionist, Dr. Halim, former premier of the early nationalist republic of Indonesia and at the time head of a large government hospital in Djakarta. Prices had so far outrun salaries, declared Dr.

Halim, that a month's salary could meet family needs for only two weeks, or at most twenty days. As a result, capacity for work had seriously declined, and absence from work two days a week in order to earn some money on the side had become a common practice among government employees. If reprimanded, these people asked why petty corruptionists should be arrested when big thieves were permitted to go free and remain "honored persons." Laborers wishing to strike were threatened by the government, and the general fear prevailed among government employees that they might be discharged at any time without explanation or statement of cause. While the government declared that the security situation was improving daily, the opposite was the fact. More and more persons feared to sleep in their own homes at night, and in some districts the number of fugitives was increasing daily. Differences in political views were less and less tolerated, even by the government radio. Dr. Halim ended his description of conditions by stating that he tried to see the good as well as the bad, but that he was convinced that at the moment far more was being torn down than was being built up. Many, he concluded, sought the cause of this in the presence of the evil influences of the Netherlanders and of the Western imperialists, though as far as he was concerned there was no difference between Eastern and Western imperialism. He was of the opinion that the fault must be sought primarily among Indonesians themselves. Because of envy, jealousy, and suspicion, Indonesians had not placed high-minded, able, conscientious persons in responsible positions.

This political crisis should cause little surprise. Indonesians had had little training in representative government or public administration under the Dutch, and they took over the government for the entire country after nearly a decade of war, foreign occupation, and revolution. The new state retained a large number of former Netherlands Indies officials to advise and help administer the public services, but the trained and experienced Dutch civil servants quickly dwindled away, leaving some of the government services in a bad way.

Indonesians like to compare the situation of their country today with that of the United States in the critical period of

1783-1789, but this comparison is not wholly sound. The new American government was simple, its functions limited, and the problems it faced not extremely difficult. In every respect the position of the Indonesian government is quite different. It has a relatively large, complicated machinery to regulate a wide variety of interests, it owns and operates large economic enterprises, and it is responsible for the welfare of 80,000,000 people (as compared with the 3,500,000 inhabitants of the United States in 1789). The young American republic could work out its problems in relative isolation, but there is no isolation anywhere today, least of all for a country with the location of Indonesia.

Aside from such matters as corruption, administrative inefficiency, and internal insecurity, Indonesia faces a number of political problems. Probably the chief of these is national unity. The country has become deeply divided on the basic issue of what the nature of the state should be. There are the Darul Islamists who wish to establish a theocratic or "pure Islamic" state. The fanatic adherents of this view are in open rebellion against the existing government. At the other end of the spectrum are the Communists, who are atheist in their outlook but who make considerable effort to conceal this. The Nationalist and related parties hold that the state must be secular. The Masjumi and other Moslem parties do not demand a theocratic state, but do desire to see Islamic principles applied in politics as far as possible. A Catholic and a Protestant Christian party wish to see laws and governmental policies imbued with Christian principles. By 1955 the rivalry between the two big parties, the Nationalist and the Masjumi, had become so bitter and the Masjumi distrust (shared by several other parties) of the leftist and Communist-supported Nationalist cabinet had become so great that democratic government was no longer possible. The Masjumi leaders smarted especially under what they felt were grossly unfair tactics of the Nationalists in trying to identify the Masjumi with the Darul Islamist insurrectionists. Had the general elections been held under the authority of the Ali government, serious trouble would almost certainly have developed.

Indonesia

During the two years of the Ali cabinet the Communist party prospered. Communists were freer to carry on public activities and even engage in demonstrations. Party membership increased. In 1953 there were reports that the government had yielded to Communist pressure to allow armed, Communist-led volunteer bands to enter the field against the Darul Islam rebels. Former Prime Minister Natsir, leader of the Masjumi, declared in parliament that such action might result in civil war. "Those who demand weapons," he declared, "must themselves be destroyed."

National political unity is frequently sought by emphasizing the Pantja Sila, the five principles of political philosophy on which, according to the preamble of the provisional constitution, the Indonesian state is based. They were first enunciated by Sukarno in a speech on June 1, 1945. These five basic principles—"recognition of the Divine Omnipotence, Humanity, National Consciousness, Democracy and Social Justice"—are sufficiently general to leave ample room for widely varying interpretations. However, they do serve as something of a unifying influence. In 1955 a Pantja Sila political party was organized as a rallying point for all those weary of the welter of the many conflicting parties. However, it became merely another political group.

The substitution of the unitary for the federal system in 1950 has not settled the issue of the geographic distribution of governmental power in Indonesia. There has been much dissatisfaction with the centralization of power in Djakarta. There have been demands for greater provincial autonomy. The federal idea is not dead; in 1955 a federalist party was organized. Federalism is one of the most important issues before the constituent assembly.

The position of the president in the governmental system needs clarification. President Sukarno's role has been much greater than that customarily enjoyed by the titular head of a parliamentary government. His great popularity and own inclination to be a real political leader, as well as constitutional ambiguities, account for his peculiar position in the government. Sukarno makes innumerable speeches, not all of which can have been previously approved by the cabinet. Occasionally he makes strange statements for the titular head of a state. For example, in a speech at Palembang on November 9, 1954, he declared, "There are Indonesian leaders who actively take part in the effort of foreigners to set Indonesians against each other in the interest of these foreigners. These people have for millions of rupiahs betrayed their country and people by their efforts to bring this cabinet to a fall." Eighteen months later the opposition in parliament was still trying to get an explanation of this statement, but to no avail. The only answer they received was that the matter was still under investigation by the ministry of justice. Similar statements were made by Sukarno subsequently. The charges were vague, though they were declared to be based upon documents in his or the government's possession; but they carried the implication that the Dutch were plotting to regain control of the country. Members of the government seemed to know nothing of the documents. Relations between the Harahap ministry and the president became strained.

The ambiguous position of the presidency in the present constitutional system is in no small part responsible for the political crisis which has developed. In the constituent assembly, which in November, 1956, began drafting the permanent constitution, there may well be demands for a clearer delimitation of the powers and responsibilities of the presidential office. But whether President Sukarno can be made to fit into a more restricted framework is another matter. He is very popular with the masses and insists upon a role of political leadership. His obvious backing of the Ali cabinet and his equally obvious hostility to the Harahap ministry placed him in the role of a partisan and caused him to lose some popularity. In January, 1956, Sukarno publicly endorsed the inclusion of Communists in future ministries. His taking a second wife was met with much criticism and even protest. Nevertheless, Sukarno is still the predominant single political force in Indonesia.

Ever since the October 17, 1952, affair the army has been an uncertain quantity, plagued with intrigue and disunity. In giving the weak Ali cabinet the push which caused it to fall, the army demonstrated what it can do in a political situation of confusion and weakness. After the fall of this cabinet the army arrested a number of high government officials on charges of corruption, yet without indicating any intention of taking over control. Unfortunately, the army itself is not free from corruption. In 1955 the commander of the Celebes area frankly admitted that he engaged in large-scale smuggling, justifying his act by saying that he had to do it in order to get funds to maintain his military unit; and the territorial commander in North Sumatra publicly announced that his unit was engaged in smuggling out rubber to obtain funds to construct necessary barracks. Whether the army is sufficiently unified to maintain order if called upon by the civil authorities in a grave political and social crisis, or whether its leaders plan to assume control over the government in case such a crisis should arise, can only be a matter of speculation. The army might decide to support a strong personality seeking to establish himself as dictator. In any case the relation of the army to the civil government is at the moment unsound and can be improved only by the establishment of vigorous democratic government.

EDUCATION

After the long recital of disintegrating tendencies, it is pleasant to be able to take note of real achievement in the field of education. The republic has tackled this problem in earnest and put behind it all the enthusiasm and idealism of a vigorous nationalism. The number of elementary schools has been enormously increased; the number of children in school is now more than three times as great as it was in the last year of Dutch administration, and the number of students in the secondary schools is over six times as large. In higher education the achievements are even greater. Here a complete transformation has been wrought. In addition to the University of Indonesia a number of regional institutions have been erected, and the number of students is more than twenty times as great as before. The educational problem has not yet been solved by any means. There are not yet facilities for anywhere near all the children of school age, and the problem of financing even the school system that has been erected remains formidable. Nevertheless, Indonesians have every reason to be proud of their remarkable achievement in this field, which in the long run may be the determining factor in the country's future.

In addition to expanding the school facilities and training the teachers, the Indonesians had to cope with a difficult language problem. There was no national language, unless "market" Malay could be called such. The Nationalists were determined to develop a national language. This was done (it is still in process) by using Malay as a base. Furthermore, English instead of Dutch was made the second language, in order that educated Indonesians might have command of a world language. When it is remembered that formerly all higher education was in Dutch, the enormous difficulties that have to be overcome in this transition period are apparent. In the field of education and language the Indonesians have shown themselves truly capable of constructive work in nation building.

FOREIGN POLICY

Though Indonesia is independent and geographically widely separated from the Netherlands, the chief problem of its foreign policy continues to be its relations with that nation. This is due to a number of factors. The Dutch were psychologically ill prepared to accept the fact of the "loss" of the Indies. They had been in the archipelago for about three and a half centuries, and many roots had become deeply embedded in Indonesian soil and many institutions in the Netherlands were dependent upon the economic, cultural, and political relationship with Indonesia. Once the connection was severed, these institutions would wither. Large numbers of Netherlanders had made Indonesia their home, either on a permanent or semipermanent basis, and Dutch investments in Indonesia were large, especially for a country of the size and population of the Netherlands. The Dutch therefore were insistent that some tie between the two countries be preserved. Prominent statesmen like H. Colijn believed that the Netherlands had an enduring function as

Indonesia

the supreme authority over the different islands and peoples. Before the war there had been much discussion of the desirability of an imperial union between the Netherlands, Indonesia, and the Dutch territories in South America and the Caribbean, and a conference with this end in view was to have been called shortly after the war.

The Indonesians indicated little enthusiasm for the union at the Round Table Conference, and that little was thoroughly dissipated within a year of the transfer of sovereignty. Though the language of the Union Statute clearly safeguards the independence and sovereignty of the two members, the Indonesians feared that their country would be regarded as the junior partner. They looked upon the union as in some sense a vestige if not a continuation of the colonial relationship, or as Sukarno once put it, "the Union kept too much alive the memory of the unhappy past." A series of events occurred during 1950 which caused a serious deterioration in the relations between the two countries, namely, the participation of Captain Westerling and some other Netherlanders in the attempted overthrow of the government by Sultan Hamid of Borneo, the support of a few Netherlanders of the Darul Islam guerrilla activities, the revolt of Dutchified Ambonese in the South Moluccas, and the refusal of the Netherlands to cede West New Guinea to Indonesia.

Negotiations to settle the political status of West New Guinea were conducted in 1950, but led to no result. The Netherlands government proposed putting the territory under the administration of the Netherlands-Indonesian Union, but the Indonesian government demanded transfer of sovereignty over the territory to Indonesia. The Indonesians were under the impression that the Dutch delegation at the Round Table Conference had insisted upon tabling the West New Guinea issue merely as a face-saving device which would enable the Dutch government to get the Round Table Agreements approved by parliament, and that once this was obtained, Dutch public opinion on the issue would change and permit the government to yield to the Indonesian demand for West Irian (the name given the territory by Indonesians). Instead, Dutch public opinion hardened rather than softened on the issue, and the government seems determined to hold on to the territory. On the Indonesian side, President Sukarno never makes a speech, regardless of the occasion, without including a rousing demand for the "restoration" of West Irian to Indonesia. A West Irian bureau has been established in the government to direct the drive for the "return" of the territory. The Dutch authorities in New Guinea assert that they have seized Indonesian soldiers attempting to infiltrate into the territory, but the Indonesian government denies that any such attempt was made.

The Indonesian government bases its claim to the territory almost solely on the ground that it was a part of the Netherlands Indies, to which the Republic of Indonesia has become the successor. President Sukarno declares that the Indonesian national revolution will not be completed until West Irian again becomes a part of Indonesia. The Netherlands government claims that the territory has a geological, biological, and geographical character of its own which cannot be classified as Indonesian, and that from the point of view of culture, religion, language, and ethnology the Papuans, as the inhabitants of New Guinea are called, are quite different from Indonesians. In these respects they are more closely related to the peoples east of them.

Australia has also become involved in the issue. Australians have not forgotten the Japanese conquest of New Guinea, both the Dutch and Australian administered parts, in World War II and the serious threat to the Australian mainland from this direction. Australians feel that the defenses of the region are stronger with West New Guinea under Dutch administration than they would be with the territory under Indonesian rule. Moreover, if the Indonesian contention that the inhabitants of West Irian belong to the Indonesian nation were to prevail, it is difficult to see why the argument could not easily be extended to include the inhabitants of the eastern part of the island, which is under Australian administration.

The Indonesian government tries to win international support for its claim to the territory by asserting that the chief issue involved is "colonialism." On this issue it can always obtain a great deal of support especially in the United Nations,

Indonesia

whose membership is so largely made up of states with a colonial background. Indonesia nearly succeeded in getting the 1954 session of the General Assembly to adopt a resolution requesting the Netherlands government to resume negotiations on the matter. It succeeded in getting the African-Asian Conference at Bandung in 1955 to adopt a resolution vaguely supporting its position. The matter was again before the General Assembly at its 1955 session, but when the Indonesian and Dutch governments issued a joint statement announcing early negotiations to settle differences between them, that body merely expressed the hope that the problem would soon be peacefully resolved. A resolution sponsored by African-Asian and some other countries to set up a good-offices committee to assist in negotiations between the two countries failed to receive the necessary two-thirds approval in the General Assembly when it came up for a vote on February 28, 1957.

Though Netherlanders have left Indonesia in droves, a considerable number still live there, and these people bear the brunt of the Indonesian ill will toward the Netherlands. The arrest and long-delayed trial of a score of Dutch citizens accused of complicity in plots against the government, and the alleged unfair methods of conducting the trial, has aroused the whole Dutch nation. The substantial Dutch investments are, of course, also exposed to Indonesian pressure.

A Dutch military mission which was in Indonesia at the request of the government to help train its army was withdrawn in 1953. Its presence in the country had become a source of embarrassment to both governments because of continued attacks made on it. In 1954 the two governments signed an agreement to terminate the union, which after the first few months of its existence had ceased to have any life in it anyway, but ratification of the agreement was defeated five times in the Indonesian parliament in a very odd manner. Every member of the parliament wished to see the union formally buried, but most of them wanted the burial accompanied by a modification of the economic and financial agreements signed at the Round Table Conference. A large number of members felt so strongly about this that they absented themselves from the meeting of parliament whenever this item was on the agenda. In this manner they were able five times to prevent a quorum.

A ministerial conference between the two governments for the purpose of reaching an agreement on a formal dissolution of the union accompanied by new economic and financial agreements was begun in December, 1955, in Geneva. The conferences, suspended several times, became deadlocked in February, whereupon the Indonesian government unilaterally denounced the union, including the economic and financial agreements signed at The Hague Round Table Conference. In August, 1956, the Indonesian government announced the repudiation of the debt to the Netherlands which it had assumed in the Round Table Conference agreements.[8]

The bad relations existing between Indonesia and the Netherlands is a tragedy for both countries. Indonesia desperately needs Dutch capital, technology, administrative ability, and experience. No other people know so much about Indonesian conditions and problems as the Dutch, and it is a pity that Netherlanders are not used more extensively. Their help can probably be obtained at considerably lower cost than aid from any other country in a position to render assistance. Likewise, the Dutch, crowded in their small territory on the North Sea, would find the outlet for their energy and talents very welcome. Moreover, Indonesians allow their anticolonialism and the West Irian issue to blind them to unpleasant facts at home which they ought squarely to face. On the former Dutch rule and the continued presence of Dutch interests in the country is laid the blame for all of their troubles. It would be better for the Indonesians if this convenient escape were not at hand and they were compelled to examine themselves and their problems honestly.

NEUTRALISM

Indonesian foreign policy is modeled after that of India. In attempting to define this policy, Indonesian spokesmen use very much the same language employed by the Dutch in prewar days

---

[8] According to the announcement from Djakarta, the sum involved is $963,000,000, but according to Dutch figures, only $170,000,000.

Indonesia

to explain the foreign policy of their country. Vice President Hatta, a person of moderate views, has described the Indonesian attitude toward foreign policy as follows:

"Western nations tend to hold that there is no middle position for the weaker countries, and that they must choose between the one bloc or the other. . . . The policy of the Republic of Indonesia is not one of neutrality, because it is not constructed in reference to belligerent states but for the purpose of strengthening and upholding peace. Indonesia plays no favorites between the two opposed blocs and follows its own path through the various international problems. It terms this policy 'independent', and further characterizes it by describing it as independent and 'active'. By active is meant the effort to work energetically for the preservation of peace and the relaxation of tension generated by the two blocs, through endeavors supported if possible by the majority of the members of the United Nations."[9]

Prime Minister Ali in a statement to the press in July, 1956, declared that Indonesia's "independent and active" foreign policy was the result of the following factors: (1) the historical developments which lead to national independence, and the current problems connected with advances in the social and economic field; (2) the fact that the economy of Indonesia is dominated by foreigners; (3) the desire of Indonesia to form its own personality in the world; (4) the fact that in the atomic age the possibilities for peace are much greater if military pacts are changed into active cooperation in economic and technical assistance.[10]

Indonesia has rejected membership in Seato; it signed but did not ratify the San Francisco treaty with Japan; it has refused to accept any American economic or military aid which involves any sort of commitment to support or strengthen the "free world." It has taken an active part in the Colombo Powers conferences and took the initiative in convening the Asian-African Conference of 1955 and served as host to that conference. The Ali government was rather cool to the West

[9] "Indonesia's Foreign Policy," *Foreign Affairs*, XXXI (1953), 444.
[10] Djakarta *Nieuwsgier*, July 13, 1956.

and went a long way to establish cordial relations with Communist China, and its domestic policy was characterized by friendliness towards the Communist party. The Masjumi party, while basically in accord with the independent foreign policy, is inclined to be cooler toward the Communist bloc and more cordial toward the West, as well as hostile to communism at home. Indeed, the Harahap cabinet, which succeeded the Ali ministry and from which the Nationalists were excluded, displayed a distinctly more friendly attitude toward the United States and the West, but the relatively poor showing made by the Masjumi in the general elections makes it unlikely that this was more than an interim manifestation.

Indonesians reacted violently to the French-British military action against Egypt. Egypt is a Moslem country and was the first to recognize the Republic of Indonesia. On November 7, 1956, mobs heavily damaged the building of the British Information Office, carried out the books and journals, and burned them. A demonstration was also made before the French embassy. The British and French flags were hauled down and the Indonesian flag hoisted in their stead. The government strongly condemned the British-French action, and after some delay, also censured the Russian action in Hungary.

In May, 1956, President Sukarno made an official visit to the United States, where he was cordially received. In September and October he visited Russia and Communist China. Foreign Minister Ruslan Abdulgani in Moscow signed a joint communique with Andrei Gromyko, Soviet deputy foreign minister, in which colonialism was condemned and world disarmament and the banning of nuclear weapon tests were called for. About the same time an agreement was also signed for a $100,000,000 Russian loan to Indonesia for economic and technical aid, with specific projects to be agreed upon later. The joint communique was sharply criticized in the Indonesian parliament, and even in the cabinet, as a departure from the country's foreign policy. The United States has granted Indonesia a total of $41,000,000 technical assistance, the amount for 1956 being $11,100,000. In 1955 Indonesia obtained a $96,000,000 loan for the purchase of surplus American commodities.

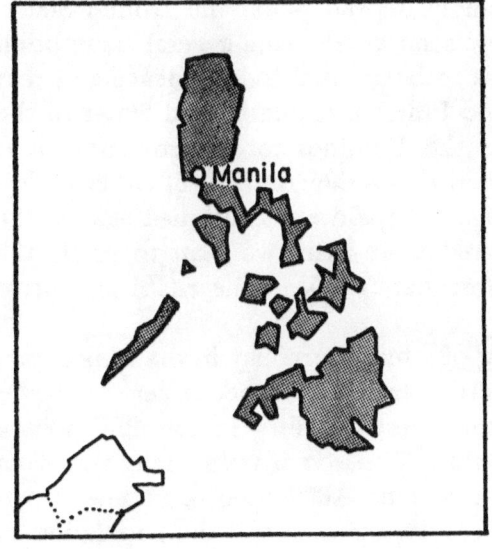

CHAPTER 3

THE PHILIPPINES
Showcase of Western Democracy

THE ESTABLISHMENT of United States sovereignty over a territory many miles from the American mainland and inhabited by an alien people who were already engaged in a bitter struggle for national independence presented a new departure in American policy, the meaning of which was not at once apparent to the American nation. Assuming responsibility for the destiny of the Philippines was not expansion into sparsely peopled areas awaiting American settlement, but imperialism, and for this the American people were not prepared. As a result there was little consistency in Philippine policy. In many respects the distant tropical territory was treated as if it was to become a part of the Union. English was made the official language of the islands, even though another Western language, Spanish, already enjoyed a wide use. Much of the American legal system was extended to the overseas territory, and as soon as the treaty with Spain permitted it, tariff barriers between the two countries were removed and the economic life of the Philippines thus was made increasingly dependent on the United States. On the other hand, there soon developed a general assumption that the Philippines was to be granted independence and that the only justification and function of the United States in the islands was to prepare the Filipinos for self-government as rapidly as possible. The Filipinos thought little of either policy, and the revolt begun against Spain was continued against the United States. It required more than two years to pacify the islands, causing an unfortunate delay in the establishment of civil government.

For an understanding of American policy in the Philippines it is necessary to keep certain factors in mind. Americans never became conscious of their responsibility in the Philippines. There were reasons for this. The islands were a long way from continental United States—some 8,000 miles—and few Americans visited them. Moreover, the area and the population of the United States was large in comparison with that of the Philippines, and there was little pressure on Americans to seek outlets for people or capital in the dependencies overseas. In the Congress the interests of the Philippines rarely played an important role. But the cause of the Philippines had one marked advantage, which Filipino nationalist representatives in this country fully exploited, and that was the generally strong anticolonial sentiment of the American people.

The United States had been an immigrant-receiving country on an enormous scale, and in order to assimilate these vast numbers, the American people had unconsciously come to emphasize cultural assimilation or uniformity. The situation was not one to develop sympathy for foreign cultures. In contrast with the Dutch, who did not try to Dutchify the Indonesian peoples, Americans quite naturally followed a policy of cultural assimilation in the Philippines.

EARLY HISTORY

The Philippine Islands constitute a compact archipelago of over 7,000 islands with a total area of nearly 116,000 square miles. The two largest islands, Luzon with 40,814 and Mindanao with

The Philippines

36,906 square miles, account for 67 percent of the total area of the archipelago, and the eleven largest islands account for 95 percent of the total land area. Over 6,500 of the islands have areas of less than one square mile each; some are little more than rocks jutting above the sea. The islands are strategically situated about 200 miles south of Formosa and 700 miles east of Indochina. Lying between the fifth and twentieth parallels, they have a tropical climate. The population at the time of the 1948 census was 19,234,182 and is now (1957) about 22,000,000.

Something of the history of the country is revealed in its name. In 1521 Ferdinand Magellan, a Portuguese navigator in the service of Spain, came upon the islands while on the expedition to circumnavigate the globe. The islands were claimed for Spain and named in honor of Prince Philip, later Philip II. Not until about half a century after Magellan's discovery of the archipelago did the Spanish make permanent settlements. As the result of an expedition sent out from Mexico under the command of Miguel Lopez de Legaspi, settlements were established on Cebu in 1569 and at Manila in 1571. Gradually Spanish administration was extended over the archipelago, and Spanish culture spread widely among the people. In 1611 there was founded the Royal and Pontifical University of Santo Tomas in Manila.

As a result of the Spanish rule, the Filipinos became Christianized and the most Westernized of the Asian peoples. Islamism had come to Mindanao and the Sulu islands about two centuries before the Spanish arrived, and the natives of these islands have remained Moslems, numbering about 800,000. About 90 percent of the population is Christian, with 80 percent belonging to the Roman Catholic church. Protestantism, which dates from the American occupation, has made considerable progress. Pagans, constituting some 5 percent of the population, are found in the mountain fastnesses of northern Luzon and Mindanao. According to the 1939 census, nearly 3 percent of the population could speak Spanish and about 30 percent could speak English.

While the Spanish did practically nothing to advance or train the Filipinos in self-government, they indirectly created the conditions which were bound to produce a nationalist movement. Spain brought the peoples of the many islands under one administration and gave the upper classes a common language and the masses a common religion, thus gradually welding the different ethnic groups into a nation. A revolt against Spanish rule broke out in 1896, put down only to break out again a few years later. It had made considerable progress when the United States acquired the islands from Spain in February, 1899. The United States government now found itself in the awkward position of having to put down a movement for national independence which had already adopted a constitution and organized a government. Not until April, 1901, did General Emilio Aguinaldo, the leader of the revolt, surrender.

AMERICAN ADMINISTRATION, 1899-1933

A year before Aguinaldo's surrender, President McKinley appointed a commission to set up a civil government in the Philippines. On July 4, 1901, William H. Taft, the chairman of this commission, became the first American civil governor. With this event, two years of military administration and the first phase of American rule came to an end, although the islands were not yet completely pacified.

The commission, composed of Governor Taft, four other Americans, and three Filipinos, served as the chief governing body of the Philippines for six years. Collectively the commissioners served as a legislative body and individually as heads of governmental departments. Thus Filipinos were given responsible positions in government from the first days of American civil administration. Though Governor Taft adopted the slogan "The Philippines for the Filipinos," he took a rather conservative view as to the time that would be required to prepare the people of the archipelago for independence. By the Organic Act of 1902, the Philippines were authorized to send two resident commissioners to Washington with seats in the House of Representatives, but without the right to vote. In 1904 Taft was succeeded by General Luke E. Wright, a member of the commission, who characterized his policy as one of "making the Philippines worth something to the Filipinos." During the administration of James F. Smith as governor general (1906-1909) an elective assembly was established. This body, which met for the first time on October 16, 1907, constituted, with the Philippine commission as the appointive upper house, the Philippine legislature. Upon Smith's resignation Vice Governor W. Cameron Forbes was appointed to the office, serving until succeeded in 1913 by President Wilson's appointee.

The twelve years from 1901 to 1913 may be called the period of the Taft policy. Successively chairman of the Second Philippine Commission, first civil governor, secretary of war, and President of the United States, Taft throughout these years was in a position to formulate and direct American policy in the Philippines. During this period the organs of self-government were set up and a civil service system based upon the merit principle was established. The latter, first created by act of the commission in 1900 and extended by the act of 1907, was in its provisions much in advance of similar legislation in the United States. Absence of extreme partisanship also characterized the appointments to the highest positions. Of the five governors general of these years, only two, Taft and Henry C. Ide—who served less than six months in 1906—were Republicans.

Independence became an issue in the first popular general election. In the 1907 campaign for the newly created assembly the Nationalist party stood for "immediate independence of the Philippine Islands to constitute it into a free and sovereign nation under a democratic government," and the Progressive party called for increasing autonomy and eventual independence. The former, under the leadership of Manuel Quezon and Sergio Osmeña, won an overwhelming victory. The Nationalist party so increased its strength in succeeding elections that by 1916 the Philippines had a one-party political system. In 1909 Quezon, the tireless and resourceful young advocate of immediate independence, was chosen by the assembly as one of the two resident commissioners to the United States. For the next twenty-five years he skillfully kept the cause of Philippine independence steadily before the American people.

In the campaign of 1900 the Democratic party had advocated independence for the Philippines. That continued to be its position in all of its platforms until the islands acquired commonwealth status in 1936. Wilson was strongly committed to this policy. His appointee as governor general, Burton Harrison, eagerly carried out the President's directive to do everything possible to prepare the territory for ultimate independence and "to move toward that end as rapidly as the safety and the permanent interests of the islands will permit." As an immediate first step the commission was reconstituted to give the Filipinos a majority of that body.

In 1916 Congress provided the Philippines with a new organic act, which in the preamble declared that it always had been "the purpose of the people of the United States to withdraw their sovereignty over the Philippine Islands and to recognize their independence as soon as a stable government can be provided therein." An elective senate replaced the appointive commission as the upper house of the legislature. Directly or indirectly, however, all bills, including appropriations, could be vetoed by the President of the United States. Governor General Harrison interpreted the Jones act, as the new organic act was called, very liberally in favor of Filipino self-government. Except in matters affecting public order and protection of American interests, he followed the advice of the council of state, composed of the speaker of the house, the president of the senate, and heads of the executive departments. The council of state became in effect a cabinet in a parliamentary government. The governor general rarely exercised his veto power. Moreover, Filipinos replaced Americans in administration. By 1920 the government of the Philippines in all of its branches had been almost completely Filipinized. In his report for that year Harrison declared that the people of the Philippines were ready for independence. President Wilson in his last annual message to Congress endorsed this view and recommended that independence be granted.

The Philippines

The Republicans, who came to power in 1921, were not convinced that the dependency was ready for independence. President Harding sent a mission to the islands to make a survey of conditions and to ascertain the real wishes of the people. The mission, headed by General Leonard Wood and former Governor General W. Cameron Forbes, reported that the government was wasteful and inefficient, and that it had entered into a number of unsound business ventures. The mission found a very general desire for independence, except among the non-Christian peoples and the Americans, but accompanied with the assumption that American protection would be continued. It recommended that no change be made in the status of the islands "until the people have had time to absorb and master the powers already in their hands," that the powers of the governor general be reestablished or recovered, and that the United States should not permit a situation to develop which would leave it in a "position of responsibility without power."

The appointment of General Wood as governor general implied the approval by President Harding of the mission's recommendations, but unfortunately Wood's efforts to recover the relinquished authority of the office led to increasing friction with the Filipino political leaders. The crisis which had developed under Wood ended with his death in 1927 and the appointment in 1928 of Henry L. Stimson as his successor. In his short term of office Stimson succeeded in restoring good relations with the political leaders and in reestablishing much of the authority of the office. His Republican successors, Dwight Davis (1929-1931) and Theodore Roosevelt, Jr. (1931-1933), continued the Stimson policies.

During these years the Filipino leaders exerted continuous pressure for independence. Mission after mission was sent to Washington requesting it. In reply to comments in the United States that the people of the Philippines did not want independence, the insular legislature in 1927 passed a bill over Governor General Wood's veto providing for a plebiscite which would enable the people of the islands to demonstrate their desire for national freedom. The measure was disapproved by President Coolidge.

The independence issue entered a new phase with the depression. Heretofore the Filipinos ardently pressed the issue upon a reluctant Washington, but after 1930 the American Congress was determined to sever the colonial relationship with the Philippines, but on terms which the Filipinos were loath to accept. Filipino leaders, having become somewhat aware of the cost, were not so certain that they wanted complete independence. Panic stricken by the deepening depression, several important sections of the American public wished to deprive Philippine products of the advantages they enjoyed on the American market because of the 100 percent tariff preferences between the two countries. Sugar-cane and sugar-beet growers and dairy farmers felt especially aggrieved, because of the large imports of sugar and coconut oil from the Philippines, though the latter commodity came into competition with butter only indirectly as an ingredient in oleomargarine. American investors in Cuban sugar production were likewise interested in restricting the entrance of tariff-free Philippine sugar to the American market. Labor also supported the movement to grant the Philippines independence, since Filipino laborers were coming to the United States in increasing numbers. It was generally assumed that free entry would have to be granted Filipinos and Philippine goods so long as the islands remained under the sovereignty of the United States.

With American interest groups joining the idealists in demanding independence for the Oriental dependency, the national freedom of the Philippines was assured. Congress, on January 17, 1933, passed the Hare-Hawes-Cutting Act over President Hoover's veto. The law was not to become effective until accepted by the Philippine legislature, but this body, under the influence of Senator Quezon, rejected it. Quezon himself headed a new independence mission (the tenth) to Washington to plead for more liberal terms, but Congress was in no mood for major concessions. Quezon won just enough to help him in his battle for political power in Manila. The Philippine Commonwealth and Independence Law, generally

The Philippines

known as the Tydings-McDuffie Act, was signed by President Roosevelt on March 24, 1934, and was accepted by the legislature of the Philippines on May 1.

THE COMMONWEALTH ESTABLISHED

The Tydings-McDuffie act provided for an intermediate stage to independence. In accordance with the provisions of the act, a constitution for the Philippine commonwealth was drafted by a popularly elected convention and ratified in a popular referendum. During the commonwealth period of ten years, foreign relations remained under the control of the United States government. Instead of the governor general there was established the office of high commissioner. Free trade between the two countries was continued for the first five years, but beginning with the sixth year the Philippine government was to levy an export tax of 5 percent "of the rates of duty which are required by the laws of the United States to be levied, collected, and paid on like articles imported from foreign countries." The rate was to be increased by an additional 5 percent each year, and with the termination of American sovereignty the United States would levy the same import duties that it levied on goods coming from other foreign countries. For the purpose of the regulation of immigration the Philippines would immediately be regarded as a foreign country and was granted a quota of 50 immigrants a year. During the commonwealth period the President of the United States had a limited authority to suspend laws, contracts, and acts of the commonwealth government.

The constitution which the Philippines adopted was basically the United States Constitution with such changes as some political scientists and progressive reformers have from time to time suggested be made in it. Its legislative body, called the national assembly, consisted of only one house. The president's term of office was six years, but he was not eligible for immediate reelection. He had the power to veto items of appropriation bills. He also had the power to make treaties, with the concurrence of a majority of all the members of the national assembly. The supreme court was specifically given the power to declare laws and treaties unconstitutional, but only with the concurrence of two-thirds of all the members of the court. The Philippine constitution had a rather marked economic and social emphasis. With some changes, this is the constitution under which the Philippines is governed today.

The constitution went into effect on November 15, 1935, and the commonwealth was inaugurated. Manuel Quezon became the first president and Frank Murphy, who became governor general in 1933 by appointment of President Roosevelt, became the first American high commissioner.

THE CHARACTER OF AMERICAN RULE

With the establishment of the commonwealth the primary responsibility for the government of the islands had passed from the American to the Filipino people. During the commonwealth decade the United States government through the high commissioner was to have only a supervisory and restraining power. Since the direct United States administration ended in 1935, the American achievement in the Philippines has to be assessed as of that year.

First of all, the United States was generous with the Philippines. It bore the total cost of defense, a burden which in most other colonies was borne by the colony itself. This enabled the Philippines to spend a larger percentage of governmental income for welfare and education than was the case in other dependencies.

Secondly, the United States rapidly reduced the number of Americans in the Philippine service and replaced them with Filipinos, even in the highest government positions. This was in sharp contrast with the policy of the French in Indochina, of the Dutch in Indonesia, and even of the British in Malaya. The number of Americans in the classified service of the Philippines reached its peak in 1905, when the total was 3,307. By 1914 the number had declined to 2,148. Under the administration of Governor General Harrison the number shrank rapidly. In 1921 there were only 614 Americans in the service

The Philippines

of the Philippine government, and about half of these were teachers. In 1913 all but two or three of the bureaus were headed by Americans; in 1921 nearly all of the bureau chiefs were Filipinos.

On the political side the story was the same. From a minority in an appointive commission in 1901, the Filipinos were granted in a series of acts ever greater self-government, until on July 4, 1946, the Philippine Islands received their independence, in spite of the fact that the ten-year commonwealth period had been interrupted by war, much destruction, and over three years of hostile occupation.

Good as the American record was on the political side, the United States shared with other colonial powers in the region the failure to develop the economic and social conditions which are necessary if real democratic self-government is to flourish. That American policy failed to lay the basis for a sound democratic society is evident from the data on social conditions revealed by the 1939 census reports and official reports since the war. Over half of the wage earners in 1939 received less than 35 cents a day, and 38 percent had no work animals. Aliens conducted 87 percent of the business of the country and controlled over 85 percent of the invested capital. Farm tenancy increased during the period of American rule. In spite of the great effort made in the field of education, only 41.4 percent of the children between the age of 7 and 10 were in school. Moreover, the holding power of the schools was low. Half of the children entering the first grade dropped out of school before they completed the third grade, and only about a tenth of them remained to complete the seventh grade.

The annual national income was low, and it was very unequally distributed. About half of the Filipino people received an annual income, largely in kind, of about $62.50 per family, and although only one percent of the people received an annual family income of over $500, their combined incomes amounted to about one-third of the total national income.[1]

---

[1] Shirley Jenkins, *American Economic Policy Toward the Philippines* (Stanford, Calif., 1954), 41. Her statement is based on the *Report and Recommendations of the Joint Philippine American Finance Commission*, H. R. Doc. 390 (Washington, July 8, 1947), 11. The estimated figures are for 1938.

The United States did little in a positive, direct way to improve economic conditions. By measures to improve health and by releasing funds for education the American government indirectly did much to improve social conditions, but this was in considerable part nullified by the policy of preferential tariffs between the United States and the Philippines. Americans liked to call it the free-trade policy, but it was free only for Americans and Filipinos. For others it was a door very nearly completely closed: about 80 percent of the Philippine exports in value was artificially channeled to the United States, and about 60 percent of the islands' imports came from this country. By encouraging Filipino producers to concentrate on a few specialized export crops, this policy tended to keep the economy of the islands predominantly dependent and agricultural. Sugar alone accounted for over 40 percent of the exports in value, while the four chief export commodities—sugar, abaca (Manila hemp), copra, and coconut oil—accounted for three-fourths of the total exports in value. About 12 percent of the population was dependent upon the sugar industry for its livelihood. The country had so specialized on a few export commodities that it failed to produce enough food to feed its own people, even though it was predominantly agricultural. The "free trade" relationship with the United States also tended to discourage home industries.

When the United States transferred direct responsibility for administration to the commonwealth government in 1935, it could not boast of what it had achieved in improving the life of the masses. In his annual message to the national assembly in October, 1937, President Quezon, speaking of the results of the American rule for the working man said: "His hopes have been raised, his vision has been broadened, and his outlook has been painted in bright colors. But 35 years of American regime has brought him only disappointment and sometimes despair. . . . The poor has still to drink the same polluted water that his ancestors had drunk for ages. Malaria, dysentery, and tuberculosis still threatened him and his family at every turn. His children cannot all go to school, or if they do, they cannot even finish the whole primary instruction for one

The Philippines

reason or another. Roads from his barrio or his little farm to the town there are none. Only trails are within his reach—trails that have been formed by the daily pressure of his bare feet and not because they have been constructed. As he works from sunrise to sundown, his employer gets richer while he remains poor. He is the easy prey to the heartless usurer because usury is still rampant everywhere despite legislative enactments intended to suppress it."[2]

Under the conditions, agrarian unrest was to be expected; it was not a postwar development.[3] In 1935, the last year of American rule, an armed uprising occurred in the provinces around Manila by the Sakdalistas, a minor political party. The leaders of the movement charged the party in power with indifference and insincerity toward the demands of the poor and advocated a drastic reduction in the taxes paid by the poor, a more equal distribution of property, and a division of the large landed estates.

With the economic and social conditions such as they were, it is not surprising that political life did not develop along truly democratic lines. The Filipinos had developed a one-party government, with President Quezon as very nearly the absolute boss of that party. The government became highly centralized; the larger cities had practically lost the right of self-government. The national assembly had not the prestige nor the power, and

---

[2] *The Second Annual Report of the United States High Commissioner to the Philippine Islands. Covering the calendar year 1937. Manila, September 1, 1938* (Washington, 1939).

[3] "During the period covered by the present report there was an increase in both labor and agrarian unrest. . . . The spread of agrarian unrest has been more serious than urban labor disputes. All efforts on the part of the Commonwealth government to obtain settlements of tenancy troubles in Bulacan and Pampanga Provinces have been of little avail. . . . Basic faults in the technique of agriculture, extreme parcelling of the land, resulting in tenant holdings too small for family subsistence, absentee-land-lordism, and a perhaps socially premature abandonment of the paternalistic features of the hasama system, are the accountable roots of this very serious problem. . . . While the present administration of the central government has proclaimed widely the extension of a 'social justice program' to include tenant and small-scale farmers, and has passed some meritorious laws, it has been unable, through lack of money, personnel, and the inertia of a traditional system, to arrive at a program for definite solution. Meanwhile, agrarian leaders, those of sincerity as well as many acting from motives of personal profit, have organized numerous country societies, some of which are so radical as to appear subversive of government itself."

Third Annual Report of the United States High Commissioner to the Philippine Islands. Covering the Calendar year 1938 and the first six months of 1939. Manila, Oct. 1, 1940 (Washington, 1943), 36-37.

generally lacked the will, to check the president. When Quezon wanted the national assembly made bicameral and the president's term reduced from six to four years, with the right of reelection subject to the provision that no person could serve more than eight years in the office consecutively, his wishes were granted with practically no debate. "By 1940," wrote Ralston Hayden in his great work on the Philippines, "President Quezon had taken the position that parties are not necessary to democratic government. Further party organization, he declared, should be postponed in the Philippines."[4]

Americans liked to refer to the Philippines as the showcase of democracy in Asia. While there is much in the record of the United States in its administration of the islands which is praiseworthy, it is not as good as most Americans like to think. For a number of years after the war the exhibit in the showcase looked very bad indeed.

WAR AND JAPANESE OCCUPATION

Some people in the United States were in favor of granting the Philippines independence out of isolationist sentiments. Japanese aggression in Manchuria in 1931-1932 had caused Americans grave concern over the possibility of a war in the Far East. Some believed that the danger of involvement in future hostilities in the Western Pacific would be greatly reduced by the United States' withdrawal from the Philippines. As Japan continued its aggression and moved southward, finally occupying Indochina in 1940, Americans and Filipinos became alarmed. General Douglas MacArthur was induced by President Quezon to come to the Philippines to build its defenses. However, the Philippine and United States governments disagreed over the responsibility for the complicated, expensive undertaking. President Quezon argued that so long as sovereignty over the islands remained with the United States, and with it exclusive American control over Philippine foreign policy, accountability for any war in which the Philippines might become involved would rest with the United States. Pearl

---

[4] *The Philippines: A Study in National Development* (New York, 1942), 450.

The Philippines

Harbor found the Philippines inadequately prepared, but the fighting spirit of the American and Filipino defenders, aided by the favorable setting of Bataan and Corregidor, denied victory to the enemy until May 6, 1942. President Quezon and Vice President Osmeña had departed before the surrender and had set up headquarters in Washington.

Because of the advanced stage of the Philippines on the road to independence, Japanese policy there differed from its policy in the other dependencies of the region. Japan "granted" the Philippines "independence" and permitted the establishment of a puppet government with José P. Laurel as president. Many of the Filipino leaders collaborated with the Japanese, whatever their motives may have been. As elsewhere, collaborationists sought to justify their acts or excuse themselves with the protestation that their object was the protection of the Filipinos from worse Japanese treatment. The puppet government, no doubt under Japanese pressure, declared a state of war on the United States and Great Britain. In contrast with the collaboration of the leaders was the heroic conduct and resistance of the rank and file.

Some of the Filipino leaders apparently succumbed to Japanese propaganda of "Asia for the Asiatics" and the "Greater East Asia Co-Prosperity Sphere." Some of the collaborators proclaimed their conversion to the "true Oriental spirit" in perfervid eloquence, according to statements received by shortwave radio in the United States. Jorgé B. Vargas, former secretary to President Quezon and later ambassador of the puppet government to Japan, for example, declared: "We were in hopeless bondage . . . and Japan liberated us. We were deluded victims and Japan redeemed us. We were divided by political dissensions, weakened by imitation and frivolity, deluded by a sense of inferiority and Japan uplifted us." General Aguinaldo, the old revolutionary leader, who in all the years after his surrender had been friendly toward the United States, saw "all troublesome doubts dispelled by the light of Japan's rising sun, by whose rays we have found the central fact of our national existence, the eternal truth which eluded us, but to which our national soul was anchored from the beginning, namely, that we are Orientals and that it is our God-given duty to do our part as members of that proud race."[5]

POSTWAR POLITICAL DEVELOPMENTS

President Quezon did not return to his country; he died in August, 1944, while in exile in the United States. He was succeeded by the vice president, Sergio Osmeña. The latter had enjoyed a long, distinguished political career, but he lacked the remarkable resourcefulness and force of Quezon. Osmeña returned to a country which had suffered severe war damages and was plagued with financial, economic, social, and political problems. Chief among the latter was the issue of collaboration with the Japanese. President Roosevelt had declared that the collaborators must be punished, and President Truman criticized the Osmeña government for its failure to take action against the leaders of the Japanese puppet government. The matter was never vigorously pushed for a number of reasons. Except among dissident groups, there seemed to be little popular demand for it. Too many of the old-time political leaders were involved, and when Manuel Roxas was cleared by General MacArthur and in 1946 was elected president, the movement was robbed of logic and force. Although for the next two years treason trials were held, no one had been finally judged. All of the convictions were appealed to the supreme court, which had not confirmed any; on the contrary, it had granted a full pardon to Sergio Osmeña, Jr., son of the former president, who had been convicted of selling war materials to the Japanese and had been sentenced to a long term in prison. In January, 1948, President Roxas proclaimed amnesty to all Filipino citizens accused of political or commercial collaboration with the enemy. With this the issue was as good as buried.

In the general election held in April, 1946, Manuel Roxas ran for the presidency as the candidate of the Liberal party. The chief issue in the campaign was collaboration, but in spite of this, Roxas received the support of the veterans, the press,

[5] *Radio Reports on the Far East* (Broadcast Intelligence Service, Federal Communications Commission, Washington, 1943).

The Philippines

the landlords, and influential Americans. He seemed to have convinced a majority of the voters that he could get more aid from the United States than Osmeña. When Roxas died suddenly in April, 1948, the vice president, Elpidio Quirino, succeeded him. In the presidential election of 1949 the Nationalists chose José Laurel as their candidate. Only four years after the end of the war the chief collaborator with the enemy, the man who had been president of the puppet government, was chosen by one of the great political parties as its leader. Laurel, who vigorously disclaimed being a collaborationist, wanted his war record vindicated by popular endorsement. Quirino's government had become unpopular because of alleged corruption and incompetence. However, by using all of the great powers of the presidential office and by exerting extreme pressure on officials and voters, President Quirino managed to win the election, at least officially. The Laurel forces charged that the election had been stolen.

Under Quirino the government of the Philippines reached near collapse. Economic and financial conditions had become so bad that President Quirino appealed to President Truman for American aid. Before making any recommendations to Congress, Truman sent Daniel W. Bell to the islands to make a survey of conditions. In its report,[6] made in October, 1950, the Bell mission laid bare the unpalatable facts. It declared that the basic economic problem in the Philippines was inefficient production and low incomes. Although population in the last decade had increased by 25 percent, agricultural and industrial output in 1950 was still below the prewar level and the standard of living of most people was lower than before the war. The mission declared that wages were wholly inadequate for many agriculture workers. The situation, it indicated, had become critical. Among the conclusions of the Bell mission were:

"The inequalities in income in the Philippines, always large, have become even greater during the past few years."

[6] *Report to the President of the United States by the Economic Survey Mission to the Philippines. Oct. 9, 1950* (Department of State, Publication 4010, Far Eastern Series 38).

"Because of the deteriorating economic situation there is a widespread feeling of disillusionment. Most agricultural and industrial workers have no faith that their economic position can or will be improved. Business men fear a collapse of the peso."

"The Philippine farmer is between two grindstones. On top is the landlord, who often exacts an unjust share of the crop in spite of ineffective legal restrictions to the contrary. Beneath is the deplorably low productivity of the land he works. The farmer cannot see any avenue of escape."

"Inefficiency and even corruption in the government service are widespread."

"The public lacks confidence in the capacity of the Government to act firmly to protect the interests of all the people. The situation is being exploited by the Communist-led Hukbalahap movement to incite lawlessness and disorder."

"The finances of the Government have become steadily worse and are now critical. The Treasury has a large mounting deficit, with taxes covering little more than 60 per cent of the expenditures."

The Bell report examined at some length many aspects of the economic problems of the Philippines. It strongly recommended that the budget be balanced by reforming the tax system and increasing revenues. It further recommended direct financial aid by the United States of some $250,000,000, chiefly on a project basis and subject to supervision in order to guarantee effective use of the funds. An agreement for the implementation of the Bell program was signed on November 14, 1950, but before it could go into effect, President Quirino had to induce the legislature to pass the reform measures which the program called for. There was much opposition to the proposed legislation, especially to the tax measures and the minimum-wage law for agricultural workers. After several months of debate the measures were passed, though in somewhat diluted form.

It is not surprising that there was some resentment against the United States among Filipinos because of the pressure exerted upon them to enact the reform measures. The basic

The Philippines

ills which the Bell report laid bare were of long standing. In the decades when the United States had the responsibility for governing the islands it did little to change the pattern of the economic life of the country; now, when it no longer had the responsibility, it was using pressure to induce the Philippine government to make the reforms which it itself had not even attempted.

THE HUKBALAHAP MOVEMENT

Smoldering discontent periodically breaking out into violence is an important trend in Philippine history from the earliest days of Spanish rule until today. There were peasant uprisings under American rule: in northwestern Mindanao in 1923-1924 by a secret society known as the Colorums, in northern Luzon in 1931 by another secret organization called the Tangulans, and in 1935 in the provinces surrounding Manila by a party calling itself the Sakdalistas. The last-named group had elected three of its members to the house of representatives in the elections of the previous year. All of these uprisings reflected deep, bitter discontent among the peasants.

Rural society in the Philippines is composed of two main classes, the landlords and the tenants, with the former getting many of the good things of life and the latter practically none. Moneylenders and overseers quite naturally were lined up with the landowners, and most of the politicians either were landlords themselves or dependent upon them. The government and its agents, the constabulary and the army, were generally on the side of the landlords. Tenants and agricultural workers deeply distrusted and even feared the constabulary.

Ralston Hayden, foremost student of the political development of the Philippines and the last American vice governor of the islands, described the social and political problem of the tenants, which he called "the unrepresented minority," as follows: "As represented by the Sakdals and Communists, they came from the other side of a deep political, social and economic chasm, and had already shown that they were ready to resort to violence in order to overcome the handicaps placed upon them by the existing political system. By far the largest portion of them are rural laborers—the common *Taos* who as tenant farmers, renters or virtually landless workers eke out a miserable living from the rich Philippine soil. These people constitute a depressed minority which has been largely left behind in the march of Philippine progress. Astonishingly ignorant, for the most part unable to use effectively any language save their local dialect, it is they who are the most complete victims of the local *cacique,* the remorseless usurer and the exploiting political or religious charlatan."[7]

President Quezon became concerned about the agrarian unrest and in 1936 announced his program of "social justice." However, little of this program reached the statute books.

Various liberal and radical groups came together shortly after the invasion to form a united front against the Japanese. They became popularly known as the Huks, an abbreviated form of Hukbalahap (*Hukbong Bayan Laban Sa Hapon,* which is Tagalog for People's Anti-Japanese Army). Peasants constituted the base of the group, but among the leaders were a number of intellectuals. At the head of it was Luis Taruc, labor organizer and editor of labor publications. Huk guerrillas were effective in operations against the Japanese, but throughout the war they apparently carried on hostilities against landowners and those associated with them with even greater vigor. The ideology of the movement steadily became more openly communist.

After the war the Huks demanded that they be taken into the national armed forces as a unit with the retention of their identity. When this was denied them, they went underground again. They continued to kidnap and execute collaborators and traitors, and to take levies on harvests. In short, they set up a government within their area of control and carried on war against the national government at Manila.

The Huks in the 1946 election supported Osmeña against Manuel Roxas for president. They regarded Roxas as a collaborator and friend of the landowners, but curiously, in 1949 they backed José Laurel, who had headed the puppet government under the Japanese. Roxas tried to cope with the move-

---

[7] *The Philippines,* 378.

ment by inaugurating some agrarian reforms and by vigorous military action against the Huks. Quirino began a resettlement program and made a peace overture with amnesty to Huks. For a while it looked as if this move might be successful. As an act of good faith the Huks were expected to register their arms, but few did so. Taruc, who had come to Manila to take the seat in congress to which he had been elected in 1946, suddenly disappeared, and the hostilities broke out again.

The situation had become desperate by 1950. The Huks seemed to be everywhere; their strength was estimated at 40,000 fully armed members, with about 2,500,000 reserves. They made attacks on towns on the outskirts of Manila, and the capital itself seemed in danger. At this critical juncture (September, 1950) President Quirino appointed a young congressman, Ramon Magsaysay, as secretary of defense. He reorganized the army and got it to pursue the Huks deep into the jungle. He rooted out inefficiency and corruption. He was convinced that misery, bad government, and exploitation by the landlords was at the bottom of the discontent, and so he followed a policy of all-out friendship for all who were prepared to surrender, and all-out force against the Communist core of diehards. Among those who capitulated was the leader, Luis Taruc. Surrendered Huks were resettled on small farms in attractive communities. Within a year the whole situation had changed and the Huk menace had been greatly reduced. In 1951 the army was called upon to police the elections. The fact that the Nationalists, the opposition party, won a sweeping victory in the midterm elections is good evidence that the elections that year were conducted honestly, in contrast to what happened in 1949.

THE MAGSAYSAY POLITICAL REVOLUTION

Ramon Magsaysay, the young secretary of defense who had in a short period broken the back of the Huk movement and electrified Filipinos by the vigor and honesty with which he administered his department, had become a national hero. There were suggestions that he be chosen as his party's candidate for the presidency. Whether for this or other reasons, there developed a coolness between President Quirino and Secretary Magsaysay. The Nationalists now became interested in making the defense secretary their candidate. On March 1, 1953, Magsaysay resigned his post, justifying his action with the statement that "It would be useless for me to continue as Secretary of National Defense with the specific duty of killing Huks as long as the administration continues to foster and tolerate conditions which offer a fertile soil for Communism."[8]

Magsaysay left the Liberals and became the candidate of the Nationalist party for president. A short time before the Liberal party held its convention in May, General Carlos P. Romulo resigned as the ambassador to the United States and permanent representative at the United Nations, and announced his candidacy for nomination for president by the Liberal party. The convention was firmly in President Quirino's control, however, and he secured his own renomination. General Romulo and his supporters bolted the convention and organized a new Democratic party, which nominated him as its candidate for president. In August, Romulo withdrew his candidacy and formed a coalition with the Nationalists.

The election campaign was hard fought. Magsaysay carried the campaign into the *barrios* (villages), which was something new in Philippine politics. He charged the Quirino administration with incompetence, corruption, graft, and failure to carry out basic agrarian reforms and to provide education and welfare services. President Quirino stood on his record, stressed his opponent's lack of experience, and charged the Nationalists with seeking American intervention in the Philippine elections. He belittled the "new knight" of the Nationalists, he accused the elder statesmen Senators José Laurel and Claro Recto of tax frauds, and characterized the Magsaysay movement as one of "ultranationalism, foreign interventionism, pro-Communism and sheer opportunism."[9]

Magsaysay and the Nationalists won an overwhelming victory, receiving over two-thirds of the vote cast. They carried

[8] New York *Times*, March 2, 1953.
[9] New York *Times*, April 17, 1953.

The Philippines

24 of the 28 cities and 48 of the 52 provinces. Magsaysay's election was hailed as a triumph of the masses and a victory for honest government, inaugurating a new day in Philippine politics. After conceding the election, President Quirino in a radio address declared the election had proved that "a working democracy" had been built in the Philippines.[10] Magsaysay had a clear mandate from the voters to carry out the reforms he had advocated, but he soon ran into trouble with the old guard of the party, who were reluctant to acknowledge his leadership. This was especially true of Senators Laurel and Recto. The president emerged from a party caucus in June, 1954, as the apparent victor, with all in attendance signing a set of party principles, but Recto continued critical and uncooperative. Congress delayed and sometimes diluted administration bills.

As secretary of defense and as president, Magsaysay said repeatedly that merely killing dissidents would not solve the Communist problem, but that "its solution lies in the correction of social evils and injustices and in giving the people decent government free from dishonesty and graft." Corruption was deeply imbedded in the government, and while a profound change has been made in the general atmosphere, it has not yet been rooted out. Magsaysay invited everybody in the land, whatever his economic or social status, to bring his complaints to Malacanang Palace, the official residence of the president. The president himself frequently goes out into the villages to adjust the complaints. This has made him very popular with the masses, but trying to settle everybody's little problems has tended to leave him little time or energy to work at the large national problems. Magsaysay began haltingly, but he has gained confidence and momentum with experience.

President Magsaysay was able to get a new law, called the Agricultural Tenancy act, which codifies and regulates the relationship of the landowner and sharecropper or leaseholder, giving more security to the tenant and farm worker. The law limits the rate of interest on loans to tenants at 8 percent. Later an agrarian court was created, which operates very much

[10] New York *Times*, November 17, 1953.

like the court of industrial relations. A land-tenure law was enacted to permit expropriation of large estates and their redistribution where "justified agrarian unrest exists."

The Magsaysay administration in the 1955 election campaign claimed a number of other accomplishments, such as building many miles of roads connecting the hinterland with trading centers, stimulating an increase in food production, constructing 3,000 public buildings and schools, completing irrigation projects providing 157,000 hectares with water, providing more credit facilities for farmers, and revising the Bell Trade Act agreement to give the Philippines certain economic advantages and benefits.

While these are all creditable achievements, the question still remains whether they are enough. The basic problem of underproduction has hardly been touched; unemployment is high and is decreasing little, if at all. The number of unemployed in 1956 was estimated at about 2,000,000 in a population of 22,000,000. Budgets and foreign trade remain unbalanced. The international dollar reserves continued to drop in 1955 and stood at only $213,000,000 at the end of the year, in spite of considerable United States government spending. Congress is reluctant to pass adequate tax measures, and tax collection efficiency is poor. There will be a strong temptation to use the Japanese reparations payments to make up government budget deficits rather than use them on development projects as planned.

FOREIGN POLICY

The Philippine Islands became a sovereign state on July 4, 1946, but already before that date its government had actively entered world politics. As president of the commonwealth, Quezon signed the United Nations Declaration (June 10, 1942). Throughout the war the Philippines, represented by Quezon and after his death by Osmeña, was a member of the Pacific War Council. The commonwealth government in exile signed the UNRRA agreement on November 9, 1943, and the Bretton Woods agreement in December, 1945. The Philippines also participated in the San Francisco conference which drafted the Charter of the United Nations and became one of the original members of this organization. The chief of its delegation, General Carlos P. Romulo, took an active part in the movement of the small states to restrict the great power veto and to make the provisions of the articles on non-self-governing territories as broad as possible. Romulo's attitude at San Francisco established the pattern of Philippine foreign policy. While in some matters the island republic follows American policy rather closely, it is quite independent in others.

The foreign policy of the Philippines, according to Carlos P. Garcia, vice president and concurrently secretary of foreign affairs under President Magsaysay, rests on three cornerstone principles, namely, (1) to maintain, deepen, and broaden the Philippine—United States relations, (2) to maintain and continually improve her good-neighbor relations with the sister countries in Asia, and (3) to maintain and continually improve the Philippine historic relation with Spain and other Latin countries. To these three principles should be added active participation in the United Nations and adherence to the principles of the Charter. The third principle stated by Secretary Garcia is more a matter of sentiment than of practical importance. It reflects a certain pride of Filipinos in the culture they acquired in three centuries of Spanish rule and which has survived five decades of American administration and influence. Upon the invitation of Generalissimo Francisco Franco, President Quirino made a state visit to Spain in 1951. The Philippines joined a group of Latin American countries in 1950 in getting the General Assembly of the United Nations to rescind the resolution passed by it in 1946 recommending that the members withdraw their ambassadors and ministers from Madrid and barring Spain from membership in the specialized agencies of the United Nations.

Many Filipinos are convinced that their country has a special role to play in world politics, which is to serve as "the intermediate means through which the West can earn the friendship and faith of the Asians." A Filipino newspaper editor has stated the argument as follows: "Geographically, in a military sense, politically, culturally, and even economically, the Philippines is in a most enviable location in Asia. We are of Asia and yet not a part of the Asian mainland, unlike Thailand, Vietnam, Malaya and South Korea; kept apart and at a reasonably safe distance by the China sea, unlike Hong Kong and Formosa, which are dangerously close to a land mass that bodes ill for lesser territories adjoining it. We are equally well situated to serve as a base against a continental enemy or as a base from which to bolster the ideals of democracy and to win friends throughout Asia."[11]

President Quirino cherished the idea of the formation of a regional association or union of "the little democracies" of Southeast Asia and the Pacific for collective defense. He pressed the project vigorously for nearly four years, with meager results. The Philippine government called a conference which met at Baguio in May, 1950, to which Australia, Ceylon, India, Indonesia, Pakistan, and Thailand sent representatives. The conference revealed the sharp differences in foreign-policy attitudes of the countries of the region. In July, 1949, Quirino had been visited by Chiang Kai-shek, who, speaking also for Syngman Rhee of South Korea, had urged the formation of a Far East anti-Communist pact. The neutralist countries, however, were so opposed to taking a collective anti-Communist stand that neither Chiang's nor Rhee's government was invited to the conference. Philippine Foreign Secretary Carlos Romulo reassuringly stated that the conference would not be "Anti-Communist or anti-anybody." Resolutions on cultural, economic, and social relations and cooperation were adopted. The suggestion of the Philippines for a permanent organization was not acted upon. Romulo called the conference an "epoch-making" event, "the first formal articulation of Asian consciousness along a broad political basis," but its impact on world politics was somewhat less than that. In fact, the conference made no provision for meeting again and was overshadowed by

[11] Modesta Farolan, New York *Times*, July 8, 1956. President Roxas in a speech in the United States in 1946 declared, "We are not of the Orient except by geography. We are part of the Western world by reason of culture, religion, ideology, economics. . . . We expect to remain part of the West, possibly as the ideological bridge between the Occident and the Orient." See George A. Malcolm, *First Malay Republic* (Boston, 1951), 161.

The Philippines

the Asian-African Conference held at Bandung, Indonesia, in April, 1955, where the Philippines delegation, headed by Romulo, took an active part in diluting the strongly neutralist trend of the proceedings.

After the election of Ramon Magsaysay as president, some Filipinos and Americans urged him to step forward as the leader of the Pacific countries. Senator William F. Knowland, at the time Republican majority leader of the upper house of Congress, called upon him to take the leadership in organizing seven Far Eastern countries "to challenge the Communist scheme for the conquest of the Orient."[12] With rare good sense President Magsaysay modestly brushed aside the suggestions that he play the role of leader of the Asian peoples by saying that he had homework to do.

The Philippines, through its very able representative General Romulo, has played an active part in the United Nations. Romulo's election as president of the General Assembly in 1949 was a tribute to his country and to him. The Philippines has served as a member of the Trusteeship Council (1948-1950), and in 1955 after a protracted contest and many ballots it won a split term (with Yugoslavia) on the Security Council. In the United Nations as at Bandung, the Philippines has sought to serve as a bridge between the Asian-African countries and the West.

Filipinos are trying to develop closer relations with their neighbors, but with only moderate success. The Philippines has been host to a number of regional meetings of various kinds. The University of the Philippines has a program known as Scholarship and Exchange of Professors for Southeast Asia, and it has also established a Center of Asian Studies, to which it is attempting to draw students from all the countries of Southeast Asia. There have been a number of exchanges of high official visits, but the results of all of these efforts are still rather meager. The truth is that the Filipinos are not generally popular with Asians. The latter feel that the Filipinos regard themselves as different, and indeed, as superior to their neighbors. The Asians

[12] New York *Times,* November 21, 1953.

regard the Filipinos as Westernized, as alienated from their native culture. Sometimes they are caustically characterized as the strange product of three centuries of life in a Spanish convent followed by forty years in Hollywood. President Sukarno of Indonesia in his address to the congress on the occasion of his official visit to the Philippines in 1952 chided the Filipinos for their radical desertion of their indigenous culture. The countries of Southeast Asia which follow a neutralist foreign policy naturally view the Philippines with some distrust. They regard it as a client, or somewhat of a satellite, of the United States.

An effort to develop closer relations with Cambodia took a queer turn. Upon invitation, Prince Norodom Sihanouk Varman of Cambodia made an official visit to the Philippines. In a speech upon his arrival at the airport in Manila on January 3, 1956, he stated that "although we obtained our independence by peaceful means from France, who remains our friend, we had to defend it sword in hand for eight years against foreign Communist invasion, brutal and unprovoked." Before a joint session of the Philippine congress he declared: "if Cambodia is neutral she does not conceal that she intends to closely cooperate with countries who have the same democratic and social ideals, the same aspiration for justice, liberty and well being of the masses," and at a reception given him by the secretary of defense and the army chief of staff he remarked that he wished the Philippine armed forces success in defending the security of Southeast Asia. Upon his departure he said that he was "convinced" that he had obtained good results in strengthening the "century-old" ties existing between Cambodia and the Philippines, and that he would tell his people and government that the solidarity of the Cambodians and the Filipinos "is once again alive, tangible." These remarks quite naturally led the Filipinos to think that if the prince was a neutralist, he was a neutralist with strong anti-Communist sympathies. Upon his return home, to the amazement of Manila, he charged that the Philippine hospitality was part of an American plot to draw Cambodia into Seato. Sometime later he accused the Philippine

The Philippines

government of having exerted strong pressure on him to join Seato. He later visited Communist China, signed a coexistence treaty with Peiping, and denounced Seato in the strongest terms. Shortly afterward, he made a visit to Moscow.

The attempt to develop closer relations with Indonesia ran into a difficulty which caused some tension. An issue arose between the two countries, which though it was not serious, was not easily solved. Over the years a number of Indonesians had illegally entered the Philippines and made their home there. The proximity of little islands between the Sulu Archipelago and the groups of islets north of Indonesia, the fact that the natives on both sides of the boundary are Moslems, and the absence of an adequate patrol system encouraged illegal immigration. The number of Indonesian immigrants was estimated at 6,000. There were unofficial reports from Djakarta that as many as 20,000 Filipinos were entering Indonesian Borneo annually, but apparently very few Filipinos have migrated to Indonesia, either legally or illegally. The official estimate of illegal Filipino immigrants was 3,000. A reason for Filipino concern about the relatively small number of illegal immigrants involved was probably revealed by an editorial in the Manila *Times* of August 24, 1954. "It should be realized," declared the newspaper, "that 6,000 Indonesians with a mission to perform, such as the dissemination of Communist propaganda, could do a lot of damage in areas where social conflicts are unresolved."

After two years of intermittent negotiations an agreement was reached. Immigration regulations for the inhabitants of the frontier areas for temporary visits were simplified. With respect to the illegal immigrants it was agreed that those who had crossed the frontier before October 29, 1954, would be repatriated unless they satisfied certain legal requirements. About 1,600 Indonesians and 80 Filipinos would be repatriated under the agreement. All those who crossed the national frontier after October 29, 1954, would be returned to their original homes.

The Philippine government is solidly behind the United

States policy with respect to China. Sometimes it fears that the American government is not thoroughly and definitely committed to this policy, and may ultimately deviate from it. Formosa is only a few hundred miles distant from Luzon, and most Filipinos quite naturally fear any new Communist territorial gains in their area. The Philippines strongly supported the American position on Korea and was one of the small number of countries to support the United Nations action with military contingents.

The determination to support Nationalist China against Communist China does not mean the relations between Manila and Taipei always run smoothly. The Chinese constitute a problem in all of the countries of Southeast Asia, and though their number in the Philippines is relatively small, the Filipinos are much concerned about some of their activities. Chinese control a large share of the retail trade. According to the bureau of census and statistics, aliens (mostly Chinese) controlled more than half of the retail business in 1953. A law designed to put all retail trade ultimately in the hands of Filipinos was enacted in 1954. Foreigners doing business in the Philippines fear that the provisions of this law will gradually be extended to cover the wholesale, import, and export trade and other businesses. This law has been a severe blow to the Chinese community in the Philippines.

Another problem which has caused some difficulties between the two countries is the supervision of Chinese schools in the Philippines. These schools were suspected of being centers of Communist infiltration. Charges were also made that the Chinese schools followed the curricula prescribed by the Nationalist government in Taipei and not those prescribed by the Philippine government. A committee appointed by the board of national education to investigate these schools reported the total absence of the Filipinization process. The children of Chinese immigrants were becoming Philippine citizens without acquiring any knowledge of the country's system of government, history, or the customs and traditions of the people. Taipei was as much concerned about Communist infiltration in these

The Philippines

schools as was Manila, and it offered to do all in its power to prevent it, but the Nationalist government did insist upon the right, under the terms of the Treaty of Amity with the Philippines, of the Chinese communities to operate them. After considerable diplomatic discussion China did concede the sole and exclusive jurisdiction of the Philippine government over all schools in its territory, but the latter agreed to permit the 137 Chinese schools to operate subject to a "joint supervision" over them. According to the agreement, signed January 23, 1956, Manila will prescribe the basic curricula but the schools may offer additional subjects.

Another troublesome issue between Manila and Taipei has arisen over Chinese who have entered the Philippines as temporary visitors and have overstayed the period allowed them by law. The Philippine government wants to expel them all and has insisted that Formosa receive them. The Nationalist government is reluctant to yield to this demand, since most of the Chinese involved came from the mainland in the years 1947-1951, and some of them presumably are Communists.

Filipinos are much worried about the presence of Chinese in their country, regardless of whether the latter are Communists or not. The non-Communist Chinese are disliked because of their aggressiveness in business, and the Communists are distrusted because of their revolutionary activities. On March 27, 1955, the army announced that it had crushed a nationwide conspiracy organized in China to overthrow the Philippine government. A number of ringleaders were arrested.

The political connection with the United States, and especially the preferential tariff arrangement, prevented the development of close cultural and economic relations between the Philippines and Japan. What would have been the outcome if the Philippines had obtained its independence several decades earlier can only be a matter of conjecture. At long last, with the ratification in 1956 of the reparations agreement between the two countries, the road has been cleared of major obstacles to the development of closer relations, but as a result of the war and the Japanese occupation there still remain psychological barriers in the way of such relations.

The Philippine government signed the Japanese peace treaty at San Francisco on September 8, 1951, but it was not happy about it. There was strong popular opposition to some of the terms of the treaty. In Manila, feeling against signing the treaty ran high, taking the form of public demonstrations. Filipinos were opposed to the reparations clauses of the treaty, which drastically restricted Japan's obligations to pay. Filipino bitterness was undoubtedly heightened by the economic, social, and political conditions, which at the time were bad and seemed to be getting worse. It was natural for Filipinos to ascribe all of their troubles to the Japanese invasion. This attitude was poignantly expressed by an indignant Filipino in a letter to the editor of the New York *Times*.[13] He wrote, "Whatever is the state of affairs in the Philippines at present, is the result of enemy atrocities in the new nation. Not only that there was physical and human devastation, but a moral breakdown was a natural negative result of four long years of enemy domination, when there was not enough food and no opportunity for work."

Under the terms of the peace treaty Japan accepted the obligation to pay reparations, but no amounts were specified. This was left for determination by bilateral negotiations between the occupied countries and Japan, subject to the restriction, however, that reparations were to be limited to goods and services. This provision made it unlikely that the Philippines would get anything like the eight billion dollars in cash it was demanding. The Philippines originally had insisted also upon the branding of Japan as an aggressor in the war and upon a stringent limitation of Japan's capacity for resurgence as an economic and military power. The sad experience with the reparations problem after World War I had made the United States and Great Britain wary of creating a situation like that again. Moreover, as a result of the developments in world politics, especially the triumph of communism on the

---

[13] Vincente D. Gabriel in the issue of August 13, 1956.

mainland of China, the United States could not afford to see economic and social conditions in Japan deteriorate further. Japan's economy had to be made viable, or the Japanese government might have to cope with a rising Communist movement in the country and feel compelled to make trade and possibly other arrangements with Soviet Russia and Communist China as a solution to its economic problems. Japanese economy at the time was still at a dangerously low level. During the period of occupation, Japan had failed to meet its food and raw-material requirements by about two billion dollars. This huge deficit was made good by the United States.

When the Philippine senate gave notice that it would refuse to approve the peace treaty until after a reparations agreement had been reached, negotiations on this matter began. The Philippine government first demanded $8,000,000,000, and Japan's initial offer was only $250,000,000. By an interim agreement signed April, 1953, Japan acknowledged the moral validity of the Philippines' claim and undertook the task of salvaging the sunken ships in Philippine waters as a first step in meeting its obligations. After several years of negotiations the Philippines had scaled its demand down to $1,000,000,000 and Japan had increased its offer to $400,000,000. At one point in the negotiations, Vice President Garcia, the representative of the Philippines, signed a memorandum providing for payment of the amount offered by Japan, but this was repudiated by President Magsaysay.

Agreement on a reparations settlement was finally reached in August, 1955, but it took almost a year more to obtain the consent of the Japanese parliament to its terms. According to the provisions of the agreement, which was signed May 9, 1956, Japan will pay $500,000,000 in capital goods, $20,000,000 in cash, and $30,000,000 in services over a period not to exceed ten years, and $250,000,000 in long-term development loans. Although the Filipinos insisted on the reparations, they are not altogether happy now that agreement has been reached. They fear the influx of Japanese capital, goods, and services may reopen their country to Japanese economic penetration.

Ratification of the reparations agreement finally cleared the way for ending the state of war between Japan and the Philippines. On July 16, 1956, the senate of the Philippines gave its consent to the Japanese peace treaty of 1951.

POSTWAR RELATIONS WITH THE UNITED STATES

As has already been noted, the system of preferential tariff between the Philippines and the United States during the colonial and commonwealth periods had reduced the former to almost complete economic dependence on the American market. Thus when the Philippines became politically independent on July 4, 1946, the republic had still to gain its economic independence. Trade between the two countries had been completely severed during the three years of Japanese occupation, and much of the economy of the country had been badly damaged. In view of this it might have been better not to have reinstituted the trade preferences. The United States could have helped the Philippine economy make the adjustment to the full tariff schedules of both countries by means of subsidies. However, the trade preferences were reinstituted and the colonial character of the Philippine economy perpetuated for a number of years.

Economic relations between the Republic of the Philippines and the United States were regulated by the Philippine Trade act of 1946, passed by the United States Congress just shortly before the commonwealth became the republic. The act provided for reciprocal free trade until July 3, 1954, followed by increasing duties (5 percent each year) until July 3, 1973, when the full rates would become effective. However, seven of the most important exports of the Philippines were made subject to absolute quotas. The act also contained the so-called "parity clause" which guaranteed to nationals of the United States the right to exploit the natural resources of the islands and to operate utilities on equal terms with Filipinos. A third restrictive provision tied the peso to the dollar. Without the agreement of the President of the United States, the government of the Philippines could not change the value of its currency in relation to the dollar, nor suspend the convertibility of pesos into dollars, nor impose restrictions on the transfer of funds from the Philippines to the United States.

Filipinos had protested the institution of trade preferences in 1909, but pleaded for their continuation in 1945 and 1946. They believed that this was the surest and quickest way of securing the rehabilitation of their country. American capital would be induced to restore the old economy and create new industries. The "parity clause" was a high price to pay for the hope of American investments and caused special difficulties, for it was in conflict with a provision of the Philippine constitution which restricted the exploitation of natural resources to citizens of the Philippines or to corporations of which at least 60 percent of the capital was owned by Filipinos. There was much sharp criticism of the Trade act as being "non-reciprocal and one-sided." The Nationalist party denounced it, declaring that it would "condemn the Filipino people to slavery." In spite of a growing opposition, President Roxas was able to get it approved by his congress. By a vigorous campaign he also won the popular referendum on the constitutional amendment which would give American capital equal rights with Filipino capital in developing the country's resources and acquiring franchises for public utilities. An important factor in the referendum was the popular impression that further American aid for rehabilitation and reconstruction was dependent on acceptance of parity.[14] There was a provision in the Philippine Rehabilitation act passed by the United States Congress in 1946 which limited payment on any war-damage claim to $500 until the Trade Agreement act should go into effect, and the latter was made dependent on acceptance by the Philippines of the "parity" provision.

Demands for revision of the Trade act of 1946 became more insistent as the time approached for the graduated imposition of duties on trade with the United States. Filipinos believed that the act was in a large measure responsible for the retarded condition of their economy, and that it prevented the development of industries in the Philippines by keeping the country

---

[14] See Jenkins, *American Economic Policy Toward the Philippines*, ch. 7.

dependent on a few export crops. Young industries in the islands could not hope to compete in the home market against duty-free goods from the United States, the most highly advanced industrialized country in the world.

The Philippine government first asked that the 100 percent preferences on trade between the two countries be extended for 18 months, to January 3, 1956. This request was granted by the United States government as preliminary to negotiations to revise the Trade act. A Philippine panel headed by Senator José P. Laurel and an American panel headed by James M. Langley carried on negotiations in Washington during the closing months of 1954. A new agreement was concluded in December, 1954.

Filipino leaders were determined to obtain a revision of the agreement of 1946, threatening trade with Communist China in case the United States Congress should fail to approve the Laurel-Langley agreement. When in May and June, 1955, it looked as if the agreement might be defeated in Congress, Senator Gil Puyat, who had been deputy chairman of the Philippine panel, urged the abrogation of the 1946 agreement and trade with China as an alternative to the existing agreement. He declared that "It appears that we must now turn to Red China for economic survival because our democratic friends choose to abandon us."[15] He was not alone in these views. Senator Claro M. Recto, in supporting Puyat's suggestion, stated that he had always favored economic ties with Communist China because it would be beneficial to the Philippine economic stability, and Senator Edmundo B. Cea, chairman of the senate committee on commerce and industry, declared that too much dependence on the American market was "unwise and dangerous." The agreement was signed September 6, 1955, and went into effect January 1, 1956.

The new trade agreement is more reciprocal than the old, and its provisions generally are more favorable to the Philippines. It eliminated United States control over the exchange rate of the peso in terms of dollars, while the so-called "parity"

[15] *News From the Philippines* (Division of International Information, Department of Foreign Affairs, Manila, June 6, 1955).

The Philippines

provision, which allowed Americans to exploit natural resources and to operate public utilities in the Philippines on the same basis as Filipinos, was made reciprocal. The Philippines were granted the right to accelerate the imposition of import duties on American manufacturers, and the United States agreed to impose duties on Philippine goods at a slower pace than under the 1946 agreement. Full tariff rates will be applied by both countries in 1974, as in the agreement of 1946. It is hoped that the new trade regulations will stimulate industrial expansion in the Philippines.

A large amount of American money has gone into the Philippines since the end of the war, some of it in direct aid and the rest in government expenditures. The total dollar receipts in the decade 1946-1955 have been estimated at nearly 2,500,000,-000 as follows: military expenditures, 1,039,000,000; Veterans Administration, 562,000,000; economic aid, 85,000,000; and war damages, 768, 000,000.[16] Under the military expenditures come such items as back pay for Philippine armed forces, civilian claims against the military, civil relief, and redemption of guerrilla currency. The Veterans Administration paid compensation to Filipino veterans.

Filipinos are not satisfied with the amount of war damages they have received. They argue that since the United States was sovereign over the islands at the time of the war, it should reimburse Filipinos 100 percent for all losses sustained. They also have the feeling that the fact of American sovereignty at the time was the cause of their misfortunes. It is interesting to speculate on what would have happened if the Philippines had been independent at the outbreak of the war. The republic could not have remained neutral in the struggle. It would have had to choose between collaboration with Japan or resistance to Japanese aggression. If it chose the first course, it probably would have been battered by the United States and its allies; if it chose the second, its fate would have been the same as in 1941-1945. In either case it would have had no legal claims against the United States for war damages.

The republic also has become dependent on the United

[16] *The Philippines: A Report on Business and Trade* (New York, 1956).

States for defense. In 1947 it signed an agreement granting the latter a number of naval and military bases for ninety-nine years. In accordance with a Military Assistance agreement signed in the same year, the United States undertook to aid in the development and training of the Philippine armed forces, and in 1951 the two countries entered into a mutual-defense treaty. They agreed "separately and jointly by self-help and mutual aid" to "maintain and develop their individual and collective capacity to resist armed attack." Unlike Nato, the obligation to provide military aid in case of attack is not automatic. According to Article IV, "Each party recognizes that an armed attack in the Pacific area on either of the parties would be dangerous to its own peace and safety and declares that it would act to meet the common dangers in accordance with its constitutional processes."

Filipinos have not been happy about the clause which presumably requires action by the American Congress before the treaty becomes effective in case of armed attack. Both the President of the United States and the secretary of state have sought to reassure the Philippines that it would regard an attack upon the Philippines as an attack upon the United States, but Filipinos would like to have this incorporated in the treaty itself.

There is also dissatisfaction with the agreement on military and naval bases. The opinion issued in 1954 by Attorney General Herbert Brownell that the United States held title to the base lands became the center of sharp controversy. Many Filipinos regarded the opinion as in conflict with Philippine sovereignty. The United States government yielded on the title issue even before negotiations on a revision of the bases agreement began in Manila in August, 1956. President Magsaysay was being pressed by extreme nationalists to demand more than the United States could possibly yield, even to help meet the political necessities of a stanch friend. The Philippine house in July, 1956, passed a resolution urging the president to demand, among others, the following changes in the agreements: that mineral, forest, and water rights within the bases remain with the Philippines; that the laws of the Philippines

The Philippines

be enforced on the bases and that the jurisdiction of Philippine courts be extended to all offenses against Philippine law whether committed on or off the bases; that the period of the leases be reduced from ninety-nine to twenty-five years; and that for use of the bases during wartime Philippine congressional action be necessary. The delimitation of present base areas and the acquisition by the United States of limited new areas for radar warning centers and airstrips for the dispersal of jet planes were problems, but the jurisdictional question seemed to be the key issue. On this issue the two governments were far apart. While the negotiations were going on, a Philippine congressional committee was investigating the whole scope of Philippine–United States relations, including the American economic aid program and military advisory group. However, when negotiations were suspended in December, 1956, other important issues seemed to have been interjected. The Philippine panel insisted upon the right to control the use of the bases in the event of war, and on including the bases agreements as part of a "package deal" which would make the United States' rights to the bases contingent on an annual plan of military aid.[17]

Filipinos were not altogether happy with the special relations with the United States, and least of all with the special privileges which the Philippines had been called upon to grant. Two measures especially were resented, namely, the demand for "parity," already described, and the so-called 1946 Property act passed by the United States Congress before the Philippines became independent. The latter gave agencies of the United States government the right to acquire title to property in the islands. The American explanation that the act was designed to help the United States to discharge its commitments to the Philippines and its people, and that it merely reserved to the United States title to certain physical properties to which it already had title, did little to placate the feeling it aroused. The act evoked bitter anti-American editorials and comments in Philippine newspapers.

The special relationship with the United States quite natu-

[17] New York *Times,* December 6, 1956.

rally has become an issue in Philippine politics. There is always the temptation for a presidential candidate to claim the favor of the United States government and thus to be able, if elected, to obtain more United States aid than his opponent. This was a background issue in the election of 1946, and probably won the presidency for Roxas. Many Filipinos undoubtedly voted for Quirino in 1949 because they feared that the United States would not welcome the election of Laurel, a collaborationist, as president. In the election of 1953 this consideration clearly favored Magsaysay, as he was generally regarded as strongly favored by Americans and their government. Magsaysay and his followers contended that United States aid would not cease if the Quirino administration was turned out. To counteract this, President Quirino accused American officials and military men of meddling in Philippine politics and the Nationalist party of seeking American intervention in the election. Quirino's effort to arouse and draw Filipino nationalism to his support failed, but there is always the temptation in Philippine politics for someone to seize upon this issue. Senator Claro Recto has caused President Magsaysay much trouble by charging him with subservience to the United States and with following an American rather than a Filipino foreign policy. Others have chided him for not getting more aid from the United States.[18]

At the end of the first decade of Philippine independence, relations between the United States and its former dependency had deteriorated somewhat. A number of factors explain this situation. The presence of foreign troops, even of close allies, has caused trouble all the way from Iceland to Okinawa, and the situation in the Philippines is no exception.[19] Filipinos also feel that their country has not been treated as generously in economic aid as European or even other Asian states, and

[18] See summary of editorial in the *Philippines Herald*, March 12, 1955, as given in *Editorial Trends*, March 15, 1955. The latter is issued by the Division of International Information, Department of Foreign Affairs, Manila.
[19] Ernesto O. Granada, who conducts the column "Behind Page One" in the Manila *Chronicle*, wrote "The observation is well worth repeating that it is the American soldier in these parts who is stirring anti-American feeling. For the average American soldier seems unaware that the country has been independent since 1946. He is as pompous, as abusive and as demanding as when he was here last to scare off the Japanese." May 28, 1956.

that in wooing neutralist countries the United States has forgotten its stanchest friends. Domestic politics also enters the picture. Enemies of President Magsaysay's land and other reforms dare not attack him on these issues, but seek to discredit him by attacks on the United States and by branding him as too pro-American. The sugar lobby in Manila also has its ax to grind. It is angry and fearful because of the suggestion in the United States that the import quota for sugar from the Philippines be cut in retaliation for the restrictions on the import of American tobacco by the Philippines. Filipinos are also critical of the small annual quota (fifty) which the American immigration laws grant them, and they chide the United States for giving more economic aid "to Japan, a former enemy, than she has granted to the Philippines, a traditional ally."[20] While the strain in the relations between the two countries has become serious, it is by no means critical.

[20] Remarks by Pedro Padilla at Rizal Day banquet in San Francisco. New York *Times*, December 31, 1956.

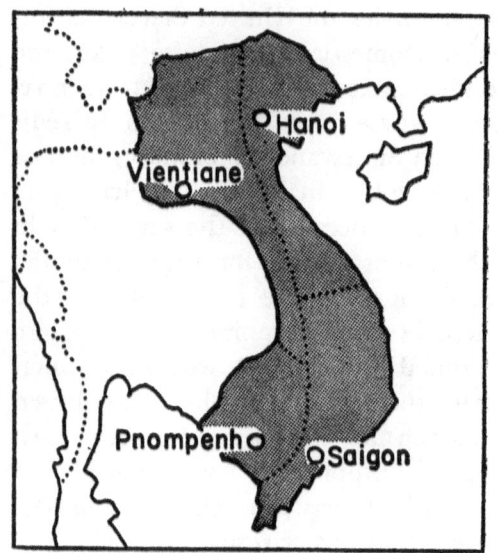

CHAPTER 4

INDOCHINA
Gateway to Southeast Asia

THE FALL OF Dien Bien Phu to the forces of Viet Minh on May 8, 1954, dramatized to the whole world the growing military and political weakness of the French in Indochina. The negotiations at Geneva in the summer of 1954 which resulted in the partition of Vietnam confirmed Western pessimism about the future of this section of Southeast Asia. During the next year the gloomy outlook of the West was justified in large part by the fact that the north Vietnamese regime of the Communist Ho Chi Minh had got off to a much faster start than its southern rival, the anti-Communist government of Premier Ngo Dinh Diem. This pessimism was further deepened by the realization that the loss of Indochina would mean more than the enslavement of yet another distant country by the international Communist camp. As President Eisenhower had put it in the spring before Geneva, Indochina was "the cork in the bottle," and if that cork were removed, Communist aggression would be able to spread out through all of Southeast Asia.

Indochina

Although conditions in south Vietnam in early 1957 were not such as to occasion unbridled optimism, the situation had improved markedly over that prevailing fifteen months earlier. Significant areas of the troublesome internal divisions had been eradicated. The Binh Xuyen, the notorious gangster clique which once controlled Saigon's police, had been defeated, and Premier Diem was in control of his own police force, which he had not been at the start of 1955. Moreover, not only had his army demonstrated its competence in defeating the Binh Xuyen as well as in engagements with the rebellious religious sects, but it also had proved its loyalty to Diem and his government. This, too, was a distinct improvement over conditions of a year earlier, when south Vietnam's strength-sapping personal rivalries had raised grave doubts concerning the army's reliability as a prop of the Diem regime. The threat to the government deriving from the activities of the feudalistic religious sects also had been eliminated. The leadership of one of these sects, the Cao Dai, had thrown in its lot with the government, and its private forces had been integrated into the national army. The other major rebellious religious group, the Hoa Hao, proved less than a match for the military arm of the Diem regime. Bao Dai, the anachronistic playboy emperor, had been ousted as chief of state, and Diem had been voted president (as well as premier) of the newly proclaimed south Vietnamese republic. On March 4, 1956, elections were held for south Vietnam's first national assembly. Communist elements were unable to disrupt either balloting. Communist infiltration of the government (including the armed forces) seemed to have been checked, while the rural areas—formerly dominated by Communist cadres—were coming gradually under the authority of Saigon.

To the leadership of Ngo Dinh Diem should go primary credit for the marked improvement in conditions in south Vietnam. Diem's outstanding leadership notwithstanding, however, it is certain that south Vietnam's record would have been less impressive without American diplomatic and financial support. In the fiscal year 1954-1955 the United States allocated $320,300,000 worth of aid to non-Communist Vietnam and

$196,500,000 the next year. American aid accounted for an estimated 65 percent of south Vietnam's total expenditures, including most of the military budget. Without Diem's leadership, the United States' economic and military assistance might have been aid down the drain. Without this assistance, on the other hand, Diem would have had an even more difficult time keeping his portion of divided Vietnam from succumbing to chaos and subsequently to Communism. He might not have been able to do so. Progress clearly was being registered by the Diem regime, but would it result in an ultimate triumph over the Communists? This was the big question.

FRANCE AND COLONIALISM

French action against the Communist Viet Minh movement in the post-war years was primarily in behalf of the continuation of French colonial rule in Indochina. Political intervention by France in Indochina (about the size of France itself) had begun in 1786, when a Catholic bishop led a group of soldiers into Cochin China, the southernmost part of present-day Vietnam. France did not actually acquire territory in Indochina at that time, however; the three eastern provinces of Cochin China came under its rule only in 1862. When the century ended, France was in control of all of Indochina. Cochin China was a colony in both name and fact, but Tongking (northern Vietnam, including the important cities of Hanoi and Haiphong), Annam, Cambodia, and Laos were called protectorates. The difference between colony and protectorate was more in theory than practice, for a powerful governor general, appointed by Paris, ruled over a highly centralized administration which included all five territories.

Opposition to French imperial control clearly was present from the start of French domination. During the First World War this resistance began to assume the form of Western-type nationalism, imported to distant Indochina through the writings of its greatest French spokesmen. Nationalism as a movement gained further strength as a consequence of France's use of more than 100,000 Indochinese troops in Europe, where they

Indochina

came into direct contact with Western democratic concepts and ideas. The next two decades witnessed ever-increasing agitation for the ending of French imperial rule in Indochina.

Vietnamese nationalism constituted the core of French problems in Indochina. As it gained momentum in the years leading up to the Second World War, France fought primarily to retain its colonial domination. The native elite developing in Vietnam was denied political and economic responsibility, and so equal social status as well. The situation could hardly have been more explosive.

The explosion came shortly after the conclusion of the Second World War. The French administration in Indochina had acquiesced in the Japanese occupation of the land, although more for reasons of expediency than affinity with Japan's aims. It continued nominally to govern Indochina until almost the war's end, but Japan was the real ruler of the country. After the war, Indochina was occupied by British and Chinese troops. The French also wanted American help in returning to Indochina—indeed, General Charles de Gaulle flew to Washington to ask this of President Truman—but the United States refused.

Vietnam having been the hotbed of nationalism in Indochina during the twenties and thirties, it was not unnatural that the French should come to a settlement more easily with Cambodia and Laos, less aroused and less strong. The agreement with Cambodia was signed January 7, 1946, and with Laos on August 27 of the same year. Both states were granted a degree of "autonomy," checked by the peculiar position of the French governor in the two territories, his function being simultaneously to "advise" the king and to represent the French Union and the Indochinese Federation, bodies the French envisaged all three Indochinese states joining. The role of past French governors in Indochina gave grounds for fearing that the promised autonomy might be without substance.

On March 6, 1946, the French and Ho Chi Minh's Viet Minh concluded an agreement which was supposed to establish a new relationship between Vietnam and the old imperial power. In the wake of the Japanese withdrawal in August, 1945, the Viet Minh, which had possessed a monopoly of the resistance to

Japan during the war years, had established the "Democratic Republic of Vietnam." When the French returned to Vietnam in September, 1945, they found most of the country in Viet Minh hands. The French were able to drive the rebels from the cities and to establish their rule once again in the urban areas, but the countryside, for all practical purposes, remained Viet Minh–governed territory. By the March 6 agreement the French recognized the Democratic Republic of Vietnam as "a free state with its own government, parliament, army, and finances, forming part of the Indochinese Federation and the French Union." The two sides disagreed over whether Cochin China should be included as part of Vietnam, which otherwise consisted of Tongking and Annam, both protectorates under the prewar arrangements. The French, however, pledged themselves to hold a referendum on the question. Ho Chi Minh's side, for its part, agreed not to oppose the French when they arrived in Tongking and northern Annam to relieve the Chinese occupation troops who were still located there.

French actions after the accords with the Ho government leave no doubt whatsoever that there were men in key positions who had not the slightest intention of honoring the promises of their government.

In April, 1946, the month after the agreement had been signed with the Viet Minh, representatives of the two sides met at Dalat, Cochin China, to discuss, among other matters, diplomatic relations between Vietnam and other states, French economic and cultural interests in Vietnam, and the future status of Indochina as a whole. No real agreement was reached on any of these topics, although the Vietnamese did agree that there should be some kind of a federal assembly for all the Indochinese states and that there might also be a customs and monetary union among them. The French reiterated their promise to conduct a referendum in Cochin China.

On June 1, in apparent direct violation of the French pledge, Admiral Thierry d'Argenlieu, high commissioner for Indochina, announced French recognition of the "free republic" of Cochin China—without the holding of a referendum. Termed "provisional" by the French, the move was not in the slightest way necessary for France's administration of the area pending agreement upon its fate. Representatives of the Vietnamese republic and France met in July at Fontainebleau in France to discuss two of the thorniest problems facing them, the status of Cochin China and the position of Vietnam within the Indochinese Federation, a federal political grouping which the French envisioned as including Vietnam, Cambodia, Laos, and possibly Cochin China. While the Fontainebleau talks were in session, Admiral d'Argenlieu convened a second conference at Dalat in Indochina of representatives from Laos, Cambodia, south Annam, and Cochin China, but not the Viet Minh, which had not been asked to attend. So struck were the Vietnamese delegates at Fontainebleau by this highhanded conduct of d'Argenlieu's that they walked out of the conference in protest.

All but one of the members of the Vietnamese delegation returned home. Ho Chi Minh remained behind in Paris and on September 14 finally signed with Marius Moutet, minister of France overseas, a modus vivendi providing for the cessation of hostilities and the settling of certain cultural and economic questions. To Moutet, Ho is reported to have said, "Don't leave me this way. Give me some weapons against the extremists. You will not regret it." Although the sly Ho probably was not sincere in his protestations of opposition to the "extremists," his prediction of future French regret for omissions of this period appears to have been vindicated by the events of the years which followed.

The September 14, 1946, modus vivendi was the last agreement to be signed by France and the Viet Minh until July 21, 1954, when signatures were affixed to the Geneva documents. Skirmishes between the French and the Vietnamese had been continuing since France's return to Indochina, but they were a far cry from the type of warfare which was to engulf the unfortunate peninsula in the years which lay ahead. War broke out in full force after November 23, when the French bombed Haiphong, killing or wounding thousands of persons and indicating that France's aim was not settlement with the Viet Minh but its annihilation. In December the Viet Minh retaliated with a surprise attack on French forces in north Vietnam. From then through the summer of 1954, war raged in Indochina.

Regardless of the political orientation of the rebels, there can be little doubt that the main objective of the French in prosecuting their long war against the Viet Minh was to retain their colonial hold over Indochina. That Ho Chi Minh and his close associates were Communists was only incidental to this primary French purpose.

BAO DAI AND "ASSOCIATED STATEHOOD"

Further indication of French intentions is to be found in France's action in bringing Bao Dai back to Vietnam in 1949. Rather than attempting to seek a settlement with Ho Chi Minh, the French decided to establish the abdicated emperor of Annam as "head of state" of Vietnam, hoping that the Vietnamese would rally around the emperor, a personage of traditional veneration, and so cut down popular support for the Viet Minh. This hope was but slightly vindicated. Ho Chi Minh's prestige was of such stature that it would have taken a real patriot and politician to rival him in the affections of the Vietnamese people. This Bao Dai was never able to do, having little association with his people, lacking in political ability or inclinations, leading a life of luxury, and spending considerable periods of time away from Vietnam in the sunny resorts of southern France. Tainted in Vietnamese eyes as pro-French, if not a puppet of Paris, the former emperor of Annam also was remembered as having abdicated in favor of Ho's republic in 1945 and even having served as "supreme councilor" to that government. The negligence and incompetence of the playboy emperor were not to be compared with the austerity and apparent national devotion of the astute Ho.

At the same time that France enticed Bao Dai from his Hong Kong nightclub life to be the "head of state" in a pro-French Vietnam, it attempted another political sleight of hand, the so-called "associated statehood." Abandoning earlier proposals for an Indochinese federation, the French billed associated statehood as something akin to independence—only better because of its continued bond with Paris. Vietnam, Cambodia, and Laos were to comprise the Associated States of Indochina, in which they would possess "internal sovereignty," as the French called it. Each was to be theoretically sovereign in internal matters, except for affairs best handled on an Indochina-wide basis. Externally, control over foreign affairs and the armies of the three associated states was to be in the hands of Paris. The Elysee Agreements, ratified by the French national assembly in late January, 1950, made Vietnam an associated state, and other agreements gave a similar status to Cambodia and Laos.

That associated statehood was not real independence was nowhere more evident than in the statements of French spokesmen themselves. In a solemn declaration on July 3, 1953, for example, France expressed its formal desire to "perfect the independence and sovereignty of these States." Quite obviously if they were to be perfected, they were not already perfect, which more than a few French officials had declared on a variety of occasions since 1950. On April 28, 1954, indeed, after the start of the Geneva Conference on Indochina, the French and Bao Dai issued a "joint declaration" on the basis of which, it was claimed, Vietnam's "total independence" was finally secured. Only a few details, it was announced, remained to be smoothed out.

Despite the fact that on March 6, 1946, France had recognized Ho Chi Minh's Democratic Republic of Vietnam as "a free state with its own government, parliament, army and finances," in April, 1954, it still was not completely willing to accept the fact of the nationalist revolution. As it was announced, a few details remained to be smoothed out.

Much had happened since March 6, 1946. There is little in the record, however, to indicate that anywhere in the long years of tragedy and chaos had the French given up their primary objective of retaining at least a degree of colonial hold on Indochina. Never were they willing to grant the reality of independence, even to pro-French elements, which might have taken much of the fire from the Communists' opposition.

Always there was a French foot placed in the doorway—just in case it might be possible to effect a resurgence of imperial domination in the future. Much of the blame for what happened in Indochina must be placed on the shoulders of those Frenchmen who set colonialism above all else in their evaluation of the Indochinese problem.

THE COMMUNIST BACKGROUND

But even though the French were not fighting Communism as their primary objective, they were battling against it in pursuance of their main aim, for the Ho Chi Minh–directed Viet Minh was a Communist as well as an anti-French nationalist movement. There is no doubt that Ho Chi Minh, redoubtable leader of the Viet Minh in its war with France, has been a Communist throughout the long years of his struggle against French imperialism in Vietnam. As early as 1917 Ho organized the first Vietnamese Marxist group in Paris. In 1920 he joined the Communist International (Comintern), and the next year he organized the Intercolonial Union, which was sponsored by the French Communist party. Two years later the Vietnamese revolutionary attended the Congress of International Peasantry (Krestintern) in Moscow. In 1925 Ho—then known as Nguyen Ai Quoc—appeared in Canton in south China, where he not only worked as translator-assistant to Michael Borodin, Russian adviser to the Chinese Nationalists, but also formed the Revolutionary Youth Fraternity of Vietnam. The uneasy alliance between the Chinese Nationalists and Communists came to an abrupt end, however, when Chiang Kai-shek turned on the Communists, who were out to infiltrate his movement as a means of taking over the Chinese revolution. Ho fled to the Soviet Union with many of the Russian and Chinese Communists.

In 1928 Ho Chi Minh returned to his native Vietnam, where he commenced active agitation in behalf of Vietnamese independence. Two years later he organized the Vietnamese Communist party at a conference of previously rival revolutionary groups in Hong Kong. The Ho Chi Minh–directed Vietnamese

Indochina

Communist party was to occupy a position of prime importance in the country's nationalist movement until its dissolution in 1945, a move designed to win the support of non-Communists for the Vietnamese revolution.

Nor were Ho Chi Minh's efforts in the thirties confined to revolutionary activity in his native Vietnam. Although his actual position in the Southeast Asian Communist liaison is difficult to define because of its clandestine nature, it can be documented that he was on several occasions charged with coordination of various aspects of Communist activity elsewhere in this part of the world, especially in Thailand. The degree of Ho's devotion to Communism is indicated by the fact that he labored in behalf of the movement in other Southeast Asian lands than his own.

The Viet Nam Doc Lap Dong Minh Hoi (Vietnam Independence League), or Viet Minh, was founded in May, 1941. It represented a coalition of sixteen revolutionary groups which had as their common objective the abolition of French and Japanese rule in Vietnam. The evidence in existence does not support the thesis that the Viet Minh at the time of its inception was a Communist-dominated movement. Communists were included in it, as were a variety of other organized groups, but they constituted only a minority of the movement's members and had no more than a corresponding voice in its policies and activities. As the war years progressed, Ho Chi Minh emerged as the coalition's leader, but he led the movement as a nationalist—not as a Communist. Similarly, the very able General Vo Nguyen Giap, victor at the tragic battle of Dien Bien Phu, commanded the liberation army formed under Viet Minh auspices, but he owed his position to his nationalist rather than his Communist orientation.

When avowed Communists like Ho Chi Minh and Vo Nguyen Giap emerge as the leaders of a political grouping, it is not unnatural to assume that the movement they head is Communist as well. Perhaps in an area of the world like Southeast Asia where individual leadership has showed itself to be so decisive in recent years, it is misleading to distinguish between the leaders of a movement and the movement itself, including those who support it. Yet in Vietnam this differentiation does appear to have considerable pertinence. The crux of the problem for the West in Vietnam has been—and continues to be—the difficulty in determining where nationalism ends and Communism begins. In the last five years, Communists have come to completely dominate the Viet Minh movement. Yet, even so, they receive the support of a large proportion of the Vietnamese people, because they are conceived of as unselfish and devoted supporters of Vietnamese nationalism. Ideologically, Ho Chi Minh is clearly a Communist; politically, the movement he heads is undeniably nationalist in terms of its mass support. There are those, indeed, who believe Ho himself to be both a nationalist and Communist. This is what makes Vietnam the problem it is today.

The problem of Vietnam is not a unique one, however. It is in a sense the problem of China in miniature. The popular backing which the Chinese Communists received in their ascent to power in rivalry with the Kuomintang, or Nationalists, was not pro-Communist but ardently nationalist. The people of China supported Mao Tse-tung when he took over the Chinese government from Chiang Kai-shek because of the adept way in which he and his colleagues identified themselves with, and generally utilized, Chinese nationalism. The same is true of Vietnam. Ho's popular appeal stems not from his position as a Communist but from his role of leadership through the years of the Vietnamese nationalist revolution.

A major result of French efforts against the Viet Minh movement was to drive the non-Communist moderates from positions of influence within the movement and replace them with Communist extremists. What had once been a predominately nationalist coalition with important Communists in some key positions became in the years between 1945 and 1954 an overwhelmingly Communist organization which played upon the nationalist sympathies of the Vietnamese people. There is no doubt whatsoever that the Viet Minh today is a thoroughly Communist body.

Had the French not opposed so vehemently the tide of Vietnamese nationalism, it is possible that the Bao Dai experiment—

Indochina 121

but with a more adroit figure than Bao Dai—might have undermined Ho's leadership. But France was never quite ready to make the requisite concessions. The whole objective of the Bao Dai experiment, if the French view is accepted, was to build up non-Communist-directed nationalism as an alternative to Communist-led nationalism in Vietnam. But when non-Communist nationalism began to assert itself in Vietnam, as it did in the fall of 1953 in the form of two congresses, the French flouted it. The first congress, organized unofficially by the brother of Ngo Dinh Diem, demanded independence, and so a second was called, its membership carefully selected by Bao Dai. This second congress, however, declared that Vietnam, when independent, should leave the French Union. French Premier Joseph Laniel retorted that if Vietnam had such an intention, there would no longer be any reason for France to keep on fighting against the Viet Minh—an unmistakable indication that colonialism, not anti-Communism motivated the French in Indochina.

THE POST-GENEVA ERA IN SOUTH VIETNAM

Principals in south Vietnam's demoralizing rivalry for power in the first stages of the post-Geneva era were American-supported Premier Ngo Dinh Diem, a sincere but administratively inexperienced nationalist of long standing, and a pair of prominent military figures. These latter were General Nguyen Van Hinh, former army chief of staff and son of former Premier Nguyen Van Tam, who started out with Bao Dai's support in his clash with Diem, and General Le Van Vien, an old friend of Bao Dai and head of the Binh Xuyen, a gangsterlike outfit which controlled both Saigon's police and gambling houses. General Hinh, by no means as reactionary as some Western observers painted him, was backed by considerable military support, and General Vien was reported as having about 2,000 troops under his command, a figure which turned out to be somewhat exaggerated. Premier Diem, on the other hand, counted among his allies at this time two unique and powerful religious sects, the syncretist Cao Daists and the allegedly reformed Buddhist Hoa Hao, both possessing private armies. As if this rivalry for power among the non-Communists were not enough to sap the limited stability of the country, there also were the continuing Viet Minh efforts to organize local governments and committees to support the Communist cause in south Vietnam. The Geneva agreement had stipulated that the Viet Minh withdrawal from this part of the partitioned state be complete, but the Communists left large numbers of political cadres behind them. Their activities only accented the political instability stemming from the disunity among rival non-Communist south Vietnamese forces.

The threats which faced the inexperienced Diem at the start of the post-Geneva period were partially resolved—only to be succeeded by new threats, stemming in part from the very successes which seemed at times to strengthen the premier's hand. In his rivalry with General Nguyen Van Hinh, for example, Diem emerged apparently victorious, although not wholly as a consequence of his own actions. Backed at first by Bao Dai, highly incensed at Diem's attempts to unseat him as head of state, General Hinh was subsequently abandoned by the playboy titular ruler of Vietnam. Pressured apparently by the United States, Bao Dai dismissed the former leader of the Vietnamese national army on November 29, 1954, from his residence in southern France. General Hinh, whose rivalry with Premier Diem had resulted in several bloody clashes between factions supporting the two men, had—according to Bao Dai—"made regrettable statements."

At first it appeared that Bao Dai's action had considerably improved the position of the premier. Not only was General Hinh removed as a rival to Diem, but Bao Dai also acquiesced, however reluctantly, in a move which strengthened the premier. Premier Diem's hour of triumph, however, was very short lived. General Le Van Ty, whom Diem appointed as the new chief of staff of the Vietnamese national army, and General Nguyen Van Vy, who became inspector general of the army, accepted their posts only after the premier "had agreed to grant 'virtual autonomy for the Army as a semi-independent corps' and to pardon all officers and men who had rebelled against the government."[1] Such developments undoubtedly played a prominent role in the decision by Diem to reduce the 270,000-man Vietnamese national army to a 90,000-man "security force." The settlement of the Hinh affair, permitting a virtual formalization of the army's almost independent status in south Vietnam, can hardly be said to have increased unity in the disunited territory governed by Premier Diem.

The Binh Xuyen of General Le Van Vien, an early opponent of Diem's after the signing of the Geneva accords, were river pirates who dominated both the police and gambling establishments of Saigon, capital of the free Vietnamese territory. Seeking power for the rewards it thought would come its way materially if it toppled the Diem regime, or if a situation could be brought about whereby Diem remained as premier partly at its sufferance, it was more akin to oldtime oriental warlordism than to a movement of truly political proportions like the Viet Minh. Premier Diem, displaying the sort of strength that justified the high hopes many Americans had in him, moved with vigor against these unscrupulous river pirates, as he closed down the Saigon gambling dens they ran, removing a major source of their financial support. He also battled the Binh Xuyen for control of Saigon's police, in which struggle he emerged triumphant. His army, moreover, showed favorably in victorious clashes in April and May, 1955, with the once powerful gangster clique. The consequence was that Binh Xuyen strength diminished drastically—although it never had been quite as imposing as some observers have suggested. In late 1955 a government spokesman announced that only 600 irregular forces of the original Binh Xuyen rebels remained in action against the army. The Diem regime was subsequently successful in wiping out the Binh Xuyen insurgents.

If Diem was successful in his efforts to reduce the troublemaking power of one of the groups which divided unfortunate south Vietnam, he was faced with increasing difficulties from two other groups which originally supported his government. These were the colorful religious sects known as the Cao Dai,

[1] Bernard B. Fall, "Indochina since Geneva," *Pacific Affairs,* XXVIII (March, 1955), 7.

a syncretist movement which includes Victor Hugo and Jeanne d'Arc as well as Christ, Confucius, and Buddha among its "saints," and the reformed Buddhist Hoa Hao. Without parallels in the political groupings of the West, even in earlier days, these sects combined at least a superficial devotion to religious principles with the opportunism and cunning of Chinese-style warlordism. The Cao Dai, influenced in many ways by Roman Catholicism though by no means even a distant relative of that church, has its own "pope," whose seat is at Tay Ninh, south Vietnam, religious headquarters for an alleged two million believers. The Buddhism-professing Hoa Hao was in reality a federation of several wardlord-led bands. Both sects, significantly, possessed private armies, which showed themselves at times to be very effective. Resentful of the efforts of Premier Diem—whom they first supported, if unenthusiastically and for their own material ends—to limit their influence in south Vietnam, these religious groups and their private armies engaged in determined warfare with the premier's troops, who eventually eliminated the sects as a serious threat to his regime.

At the same time that Premier Diem was plagued by his troubles with the Binh Xuyen, Cao Dai, and Hoa Hao, he also was bothered by the instability lent his regime by the continuing Viet Minh control of much of the countryside in south Vietnam. Americans in Indochina in the spring of 1955 claimed that from 40 to 70 percent of the villages outside the areas controlled by the religious sects were under de facto Viet Minh jurisdiction; some French estimates placed the figure as high as 90 percent.[2] Indeed, the attempts at land reform made by the Diem government sometimes met almost open resistance from villagers, who followed instructions of Viet Minh agents because they believed it would not be long before the Viet Minh operated the government in south Vietnam and they had no desire to face later reprisals for cooperation with its enemies. The Diem government moved to counter such feelings on the part of the peasantry, but its efforts to convince the villagers of its stability met only limited success when confronted by

---

[2] See Joseph Alsop, in New York *Herald Tribune*, March 1, 1955.

the presence of courts operated by the Viet Minh in various areas of south Vietnam more than two years after the signing of the Geneva agreements.

In late 1955 organized units of the Viet Minh army began to penetrate repeatedly into southern territory. According to one such report in early 1956, for example, four battalions of Communist soldiers in the guise of anti-Communist refugees crossed into the south to set up military strongholds.[3] In late 1955, indeed, one southern official reported that an entire Viet Minh regiment had appeared on the road joining the important cities of Saigon and Dalat, more than 350 miles south of the partition line. At the same time the Communist radio at Hanoi hurled forth at the world variegated charges of south Vietnamese violations of the July, 1954, armistice accords in which, for some important non-Communist areas, it clouded effectively the Communists' own and more numerous infractions of these same agreements.

Concurrently with its military infiltration, the Viet Minh increased its overt efforts to win friends among the population of south Vietnam. A new "front" organization, the "Fatherland Front of Vietnam," was formed by the north Vietnamese Communists ostensibly to promote the unification of the divided country's two parts. The Communist national assembly of north Vietnam, in an obvious effort to strike at the morale of the south Vietnamese government and people, adopted a resolution calling on all south Vietnamese to join with their northern comrades in a struggle for a united homeland under the Fatherland Front. Although some non-Communists were included in the organization, the key officers of the front gave away its sinister intention. The venerable Ho Chi Minh was honorary chairman of the organization, and its president and vice president were both veteran Communists.

As it had done so skillfully in the past, the Viet Minh sought to cloak its real purpose in the garb of nationalism. It was for this reason that the leadership of the Fatherland Front included several prominent non-Communists—Duong Duc Hien,

---

[3] See *Christian Science Monitor*, January 23, 1956.

head of the Vietnamese Democratic party; Cao Trieu Phat, leader of a group of Cao Dai dissidents; and the Reverend Vu Xuan Ky, a Roman Catholic priest, among others.

Nationalism also was being employed for a similar purpose within north Vietnam, where several non-Communists received minor posts in the government shuffle of mid-1955. The Communists quite obviously wished to continue to appear as Vietnamese nationalists first and foremost.

Not all of Premier Diem's woes stemmed from Viet Minh, Cao Dai, Hoa Hao, or Binh Xuyen activities. Some of them resulted from the personality and actions of Diem himself. An ardent Roman Catholic, he had an obvious handicap in a country where Christianity was an import from the suspect West and where most of the population professed belief in a Chinese-derived syncretist faith combining elements of Buddhism, Confucianism, Taoism, and traditional animism. His popularity did not increase when he made some rather pointed political appeals to his fellow Catholics on religious grounds. Moreover, despite his acknowledged longtime devotion to the cause of Vietnamese nationalism, Diem began his premiership comparatively inexperienced in political and administrative matters. More French than Vietnamese in many of his traits, including his dress, he was a colorless figure, lacking—at least during the first year and a half of his regime—in contact with the masses of Vietnam. Diem was further handicapped in his first year in power because, as an appointee of the thoroughly discredited Bao Dai, he had difficulty saying that he spoke for the people of Vietnam. Although he had promised elections in south Vietnam—as on April 23, 1955, for example, when he delivered a forthright defense against attacks on his right to speak for the people of free Vietnam—the months passed and elections were not held. Major obstacles, particularly the warfare against the sects, stood in the way of polling, but although these may explain why elections were not possible, they did not supply the premier with evidence that when he spoke, he did in fact speak for free Vietnam.

Diem's seemingly genuine moral fervor in opposition to Communism was inspiring; the ruthlessness with which he went about building his anti-Communist state was frightening. If totalitarian government was what Diem opposed, it also was the kind of government he was constructing in the territory he ruled himself. Diem, on the basis of his performance as premier during the first two years of the regime, was an autocrat in the best oriental traditions of craftiness and unscrupulousness. Of freedom of the press, speech, or political opposition there was little in late 1956 in south Vietnam. Of the eleven political parties opposing Diem, only two, the weak Socialists and Republicans, operated in the open. The others, including the Communist party (called the Viet-cong), opposed the government in a variety of illegal and extralegal ways. Political prisoners, held without charges or trial, were not an unknown commodity.

"The most serious mistake of Premier Diem," a generally respected Vietnamese opposition leader told a visiting American editor early in 1956, "is to crack down so hard on those nationalist groups which are not Communist and which are frustrated by his dictatorship. His strategy is pushing them over into the other camp. If we continue with a tight dictatorship like this, the word will get around the country that things under Diem are not much better than things under the French, and then Ho Chi Minh and his fifth column will have another real wave of popular discontent to exploit."[4]

If Diem did not seem to be setting up a democratic government in south Vietnam, he was establishing an increasingly efficient one. Little by little he was conquering those who opposed him. The achievements of the Diem regime in consolidating itself resulted from totalitarian tactics not much different from those used by the Viet Minh in the north. Diem's very successes seemed to underscore his primary weakness—his was an authoritarian, not a popular government.

The first step toward eliminating this handicap was taken by Diem on October 23, 1955. On that day, for the first time since the Geneva accords, a referendum was held throughout south Vietnam to choose between Diem and the absent Bao Dai as head of state. When the ballots were counted, Diem

[4] Saville R. Davis, in *Christian Science Monitor*, January 10, 1956.

was declared the victor—with more than 98 percent of the vote. The election left much to be desired from a strictly democratic point of view. Critics claimed that neither Diem nor Bao Dai was nominated by the people to stand for office, that the electorate resultingly had only the choice of voting for the premier or the almost universally disliked Bao Dai, that Bao Dai in effect forfeited any chance of victory by his nonparticipation in the prereferendum campaigning, and that the government's several-sided efforts to insure a maximum turnout at the polls made even absention from the balloting difficult. Although there is considerable truth to some of these charges, the incontestable fact remains that Diem had taken the first step toward popular approval of his government. Considering Vietnam's recent history, the widespread disruption caused by the warfare against the sects, and the country's lack of a democratic tradition, this was a bigger step than many realized.

As a consequence of the outcome of the October 23 referendum, Diem became president as well as premier of south Vietnam, which itself became a republic—proclaimed by Diem shortly afterward. He was not to be content with the results of the October referendum, however. On March 4, 1956, elections were held throughout the southern portion of Vietnam to select a 123-member national assembly. The new president clearly was moving quickly in his efforts to secure popular endorsement of his government.

The electoral ordinances establishing the national assembly, south Vietnam's first, provided for each member of the legislature to represent 60,000 voters, with each province of the Diem-ruled territory having at least one deputy. In addition, there were provisions for the election of nine representatives by the various ethnic minority groups and twelve by the 800,000 refugees from Communist north Vietnam. All citizens of south Vietnam of eighteen years of age or older were legally permitted to vote, with all south Vietnamese of twenty-five or over eligible to be candidates, provided they had been residents of south Vietnam for the six months preceding the election.

The opposition to the elections comprised two groups. The first of these, not unexpectedly, was the Communists, who were opposed to the voting primarily because of the increased popular quality it would give the Diem regime. They urged the population to abstain from voting, and in various areas they engaged in acts of physical sabotage, such as the burning of school buildings in which polling was to take place. On the whole, however, the voting was not seriously affected by Communist interference. Also opposed to the assembly elections were the non-Communist south Vietnamese foes of the Diem government. These elements, poorly organized and suffering from Diem's control of communication media as well as from a large number of legal restrictions, maintained that the elections were unfair and were merely designed to give Diem a puppet legislature which he could dominate.

The supporters of President-Premier Diem scored a solid victory in the March 4 balloting. As in the case of the October, 1955, referendum, charges were advanced by opposition elements that the national assembly elections were not conducted in the true spirit of democratic government. Nonetheless, the elections marked a step forward toward stable and responsible government in south Vietnam.

The March 4 south Vietnamese balloting was not the only election to attract public attention—and stimulate controversy—in the second year of Vietnam's partition. According to the July, 1954, Geneva agreements, preparations for elections for a unified Vietnam were supposed to commence by July 20, 1955. When then Vice Premier and Foreign Minister Phan Van Dong of Communist north Vietnam proposed talks to begin these preparations in the summer of 1955, Premier Diem came out unequivocably against such conversations. Indeed, the south Vietnamese leader stated in October that he interpreted his referendum victory over Bao Dai as a popular mandate not to proceed with unification elections in divided Vietnam until "true liberty" was established in the Communist-ruled north.[5] Replying to the Communist charge that his stand was in violation of the Geneva accords, the determined Diem retorted that free Vietnam was not a signatory to the agreements of July, 1954, and so was not bound to honor them.

[5] New York *Times*, October 26, 1955.

The premier's opposition may well have been based on the not unreasonable fear that, even given free polling, the Communist Viet Minh would emerge victorious in any electoral contest in which a majority of the Vietnamese people participated. As a consequence of Diem's opposition, which had both American and British diplomatic backing, nationwide elections were not held, as originally intended at Geneva, in July, 1956.

The Diem policy of condemning the 1954 conference on Indochina and the agreements resulting from it may be a temporarily necessary one, but it is not without definite dangers. Already the northern Communist government has seized the initiative and is posing as the champion of Vietnamese unification against what it terms "the American imperialist regime of south Vietnam." The July, 1956, elections were not held as envisaged at Geneva in 1954, the Communists say, because of Diem's opposition. Ho Chi Minh, they claim, strongly desired such elections.

President Diem may be digging his own political grave with his policy of opposition to nationwide elections. The urge toward reunification may be expected to increase in south Vietnam in the future, especially now that the security problem has been greatly eased. If Diem does not adopt a more positive policy than his present "not now" approach, he may find himself playing right into the hands of his astute Communist opponents in the north.

While fear was expressed in some quarters that the Communists might resort to force to unite Vietnam in lieu of the Geneva-envisioned elections, there were no indications that the Viet Minh intended to pursue such a course. Fear of Western intervention, particularly by the United States, and the Communist worldwide air of cordiality—as evidenced at the meeting of the Big Four heads of state in July, 1955, the Khrushchev-Bulganin tour of South Asia in the fall of the same year, and the twentieth congress of the Soviet Communist party in early 1956—probably were factors influencing the Viet Minh decision.

The Communists, always seeking for choice ingredients for their propaganda fare, were not going to let Diem escape participation in all-Vietnamese elections without maximum dimin-

Indochina 131

ution of the international prestige of his regime. Efforts were made by the Communists in the first half of 1956 to convene a second Geneva conference on Indochina to insure that the Vietnamese elections envisaged by the first parley were held on schedule. Chou En-lai, premier and foreign minister of Communist China, called on January 30 for the reconvocation of the 1954 conference on Indochina to "insure implementation of the agreeement" on Vietnam.[6] Not to be outdone by their Chinese Communist "big brothers," the north Vietnamese Communists two weeks later sent a letter to London and Moscow also proposing that the 1954 parley be reconvened. In early March, British Foreign Secretary Selwyn Lloyd sent an invitation to Foreign Minister Molotov to hold talks on the Vietnamese situation—talks which went badly for the Soviets. That Moscow remained very much interested in the struggle for Vietnam, however, was only too evident in the March 3 issue of *Izvestia*, official newspaper of the Soviet government. *Izvestia* declared that the preservation of peace required the convocation of a new international conference on Indochina. On July 14, 1956, the British foreign office announced that north and south Vietnam had agreed to continue to respect the 1954 armistice agreement despite the breakdown in its political provisions.

On October 26, 1956—one year to the day from the election which made south Vietnam a republic and Ngo Dinh Diem its first president—a constitution was promulgated for the southern half of divided Vietnam. This constitution gave broad powers to President Diem and specifically outlawed Communism.

South Vietnam's constitution follows the American model in providing for a division of authority among three separate branches of the national government: executive, legislative, and judicial. The executive, however, is clearly endowed with a preponderance of the power given the national government. The constitution seeks to protect individual citizens from abuses of this power by a number of democratic safeguards—such as the right of free speech and assembly and procedures for protection from administrative arrest. These safeguards, however,

[6] New York *Times*, January 31, 1956.

will not come into full effect for some time, for the constitution specifically provides that during the term of the first national legislature the president may suspend the exercise of freedom of press, speech, association, and circulation and the right to strike. The first legislature's term extends until late 1959.

The president and national assembly of south Vietnam are elected by universal secret ballot. The president's term is five years, and he is eligible for three terms. The chief executive has veto power over all legislation of the parliament (which is a one-chamber body), and his veto can be reversed only by a three-fourths majority. The president, moreover, can rule by executive decree during the five months of the year when the assembly is not in session.

The south Vietnamese constitution is a step in the direction of democratic government, despite the sweeping powers it gives President Diem. Diem probably will work for greater democracy in south Vietnam, if security conditions permit. It may be, however, that he will decide that security conditions do not permit greater democracy in the near future. If Diem comes to such a conclusion, it probably will not be for reasons of personal power, but because he thinks it best for Vietnam.

POST-GENEVA DEVELOPMENTS IN THE NORTH

Although by no means free from troubles of its own, the government of north Vietnam appeared two years after partition to be in a stronger political position than its southern rival. With real power located in the Communist or Lao Dong party, revived after its dissolution in 1945, President Ho Chi Minh's regime tolerated no opposition to its rule. The government reshuffle of mid 1955 was not evidence of instability. It would seem that Foreign Minister Phan Van Dong became premier and Army Commander Vo Nguyen Giap deputy premier to ease the burden of leadership carried by the aging Ho Chi Minh. At the same time, several non-Communists received minor posts in the government, as the Viet Minh sought to broaden its regime to give it the appearance, if not the reality, of nationalist rule. In late 1956 Ho Chi Minh's rule over

Indochina

northern Vietnam appeared to be firmly established. His subjects, used to traditional autocracy and arbitrary colonial rule, were adapting themselves rapidly to the hard facts of life under Communism.[7]

Another reason for Viet Minh stability was the fact that it had operated a de facto government over much of Vietnam long before it assumed legal rule. In those parts of the north under effective French control prior to Geneva, the Viet Minh had only to bring out into the open a governmental apparatus which previously functioned clandestinely, and as the symbol of nationalist resistance to French domination, it commanded considerable popular support.

Reinforcing its stability were the increasingly close relations the Ho government enjoyed following Geneva with the Soviet Union and Mao Tse-tung's Peiping regime. Ho Chi Minh's visits to Moscow and Communist China in the summer of 1955 provided the most conspicuous indication of this growing solidarity. Not only did Ho thus bolster his prestige at home, but he also was successful in negotiating more than $300,000,000 of long-range industrial credits. In addition, north Vietnam's tottering economy was buttressed by an emergency loan to buy from the U.S.S.R. 150,000 tons of rice which Moscow had purchased from Burma in a barter agreement.

The importance of the Soviet Union's rice loan to north Vietnam should not be underestimated. First of all, it strengthened the northern Communist regime at one of its most vulnerable points, its chronic food situation. At the same time a demonstration was given the people of both parts of Vietnam that the Soviet Union had the capacity to assist its friends and that Ho Chi Minh was such a friend.

The loan was not a long-range solution to the threat of famine, however. The partition had cut off the importation of more than 100,000 tons of rice annually from the south, and north Vietnam lacked sufficient foreign exchange to buy rice on the world market. A large portion of the irrigation system upon which north Vietnam's own wet-rice agriculture depended, moreover, was ruined as a consequence of eight years' warfare

[7] See *Christian Science Monitor,* August 9, 1956.

against France. A further complication was the drought which afflicted food-producing sections of the Communist-ruled territory in 1955 and 1956. The Viet Minh's own efforts to solve this food problem resulted in a 10 to 15 percent increase in rice production between 1954 and 1956, but not anywhere near enough for self-sufficiency.

Food shortage was but one aspect of the disturbed economic state of the Viet Minh territory. The greater part of the fighting in the war with France had taken place in north Vietnam, and almost all phases of its economy—from mines to factories—showed marks of this experience. Compounded with this was a critical shortage of trained personnel to run the factories and mines inherited from the French. This condition has been somewhat alleviated by technicians and managerial personnel from the Soviet Union and Communist China, but these have not been sufficient in either number or experience to replace the departed Frenchmen.

The Viet Minh's efforts to continue collectivization of agriculture in the territory under its jurisdiction—to note another of the Communists' economic difficulties—proved increasingly unpopular as the post-Geneva era progressed. Even more unpopular was the use of forced labor to effect much of the reconstruction deemed necessary by Ho and his associates.

A major barrier to the economic rehabilitation of north Vietnam was the badly disrupted transportation system. The greater part of the north's railroad system had been destroyed during the eight-year war. For those lines which had been restored, moreover, there was a serious shortage of railway locomotives and cars. Trucks and automobiles also were scarce, and roads for such vehicles to travel on still were in bad shape in late 1956. Draft animals and human carriers, as a consequence, were the chief means for transportation of many of the goods entering the country from north Vietnam's richer Communist cousins, although in August, 1956, the Communist radio announced that Ho Chi Minh's government had completed the reconstruction of the rail line linking its capital city of Hanoi with Communist China's Yunnan Province, giving the important southern Chinese city of Kunming an outlet to the sea.

Indochina

The north Vietnamese Communists attacked their economic troubles with a two-year version of the Moscow-Peiping type five-year plan. As the primary objective they envisioned rice production increasing by 22 percent in 1956 over the previous year—an increase, however, still not sufficient to permit the Viet Minh to meet its food consumption needs without large rice imports from outside the country.

Second on the list of Communist economic objectives in the national plan was the progressive industrialization of the north Vietnamese economy, calling for the output of coal to be increased by 128 percent in the two-year period of the plan's operation, that of tin by 229 percent, and that of phosphates by 329 percent. The Communists also envisaged a 152 percent gain in electric-power production.

A third objective was an increase in trade with "friendly democracies," aiming specifically at doubling the 1955 volume of such trade in 1956.

Although the first two years following the July, 1954, Geneva agreements were marked by more overt antiregime activity in south Vietnam than in Ho Chi Minh's half of the partitioned former French colony, there was opposition to the Communist government of north Vietnam. This opposition grew as time passed. The north Vietnamese Communist government itself announced that serious "disturbances" broke out on November 13, 1956, in Nghe An province, south of Hanoi. The Communist radio described the revolt (which was put down) as "prepared long in advance" by "reactionary hooligans . . . taking advantage of our mistakes in the application of land reform."

Conducted by longtime Lao Dong (Communist) party stalwart Truong Chinh, the Viet Minh land reform program had resulted in the loss of their land by many small holders as well as by the once powerful large landlords. These small landholders objected to their property being taken from them, and thousands were jailed or executed. The result was unrest and barren rice fields.

This was a situation which the Communists could not long endure, especially in light of north Vietnam's traditional rice deficit. President Ho Chi Minh, therefore, dismissed Truong

Chinh as general secretary of the Lao Dong party, took over the post himself, and promised a drastic liberalization of his regime in general and the land-reform program in particular. Ho's moves had quite the opposite results from those anticipated, however, for it was little more than two weeks after the announced changes that the disturbances in Nghe An province took place.

It was not immediately clear how isolated an event the November 13, 1956, uprising was or whether Ho's changes would have their desired results over a longer period of time. One thing was certain, however: the Nghe An revolt worried the Chinese Communists, for Chou En-lai suddenly appeared in Hanoi. With only two days' notice of his intentions, Chou stopped in Hanoi on his way to Cambodia, which he had been scheduled to visit for some time and concerning which there had been considerable fanfare. The Hanoi visit clearly was decided upon at the last minute and undoubtedly was related to the Nghe An uprising, which may have been a bigger outburst than indicated by the Communist radio and press.

CAMBODIA AND NATIONALISM

The problems of the other two Indochinese states, Cambodia and Laos, were overshadowed by more spectacular activities in neighboring Vietnam. Despite the scanty attention accorded them, however, Cambodia and Laos are of considerable strategic importance as a buffer between pro-American Thailand and Communist-dominated north Vietnam.

Unlike the situation in south Vietnam, the present governments of Cambodia and Laos are considered representative by important fellow Asians, particularly heartening evidence of which was provided in December, 1954, with neutralist India's recognition of the legally constituted administrations. On the other hand, as the Communist-sponsored Vietnam-Khmer-Pathet Lao alliance of March, 1951, clearly showed, the Viet Minh has its eyes on all of Indochina.

Cambodia came under French rule in 1864, when it became a protectorate two years after France's first acquisition of Indo-

Indochina

chinese territory in Cochin China in south Vietnam. For all practical purposes, there was no nationalist movement of any consequence in Cambodia until after the Second World War, and even then, Cambodian nationalism lacked the depth of the movements in such other Southeast Asian lands as Burma, Indonesia, or adjacent Vietnam. The French had asserted their colonial control over the country with the acquiescence of its king, who feared both Thai and Vietnamese encroachments on his territory, with the result that Cambodia's ruling and educated elite were slow to attack imperial rule. However, nationalism received considerable impetus from the period of Japanese control in Indochina, during which the volatile Son Ngoc Thanh served as premier, and after the Japanese withdrawal, the Cambodians voted to end the French protectorate. The French shortly afterward returned to the country, deported the premier, and installed a new administration under King Norodom Sihanouk. On January 7, 1946, an agreement was signed between Cambodia and France reestablishing French control over the country.

The king was not to turn out to be a French puppet—nor, unlike many of the leaders of Vietnamese nationalism, was he to turn to Communism as an alternative to rule by France. Assuming the leadership of Cambodia's growing nationalist movement, he agitated for greater freedom from French rule, and on May 9, 1953, signed a series of protocols with France which, while they did not give his country complete independence, provided for full Cambodian sovereignty in military, judicial, and economic affairs. The agreements permitted Frenchmen, both military and civilians, to remain in Cambodia as advisers, but French troops were required to leave Cambodian soil.

If Sihanouk was devoted to the cause of Cambodian nationalism, he was—partly because of the ways in which he chose to dramatize his devotion—a most controversial political figure. Regarded as immature and erratic by many foreign observers, by some of the very moves which earned him this description he edged Cambodia closer to full independence. When Sihanouk sought exile abroad in an effort to publicize his country's efforts to rid itself of French colonialism, he was criticized by some as irresponsible and naive. But he did successfully dramatize his country's plight—as well as his own devotion to Cambodian nationalism—at home as well as abroad. When in 1955 he stepped down as king of his country in favor of his father, the question of his political competence again was raised. But when he later emerged as Cambodia's premier with a 100-percent majority in the national legislature, it was quite obvious that he was possessed of considerably more shrewdness than generally believed. To be sure, as king he had made—and unmade—premiers as he wished. But in an age when democratically elected prime ministers were far more fashionable than kings, Sihanouk's action could not be considered politically unwise.

Unlike Vietnam, Cambodia was not plagued in the postwar years by a serious Communist problem—through no fault of the Communists. That the Communist Viet Minh in neighboring Vietnam was clearly interested in succeeding to the French position in Cambodia, however, was evident from the links it maintained with the country's indigenous Communists as well as by the guerrilla bands it dispatched to harass the Cambodian government. If it had not been for the fact that its full efforts were required in the war against the French in Vietnam, the Viet Minh probably would have given the Cambodian Communists even greater assistance. As it was, the "Khmer Issaraks" —a revolutionary outfit led by Son Ngoc Thanh—received a significant amount of military help from the Viet Minh, with whom they were linked by the Vietnam-Khmer-Pathet Lao alliance. The Geneva agreements of July, 1954—from which Cambodia probably benefited more than either Vietnam or Laos—reduced the Communist threat to the government considerably. By the terms of the accords, foreign troops, including the Viet Minh guerrilla bands, were required to leave the country within ninety days, while the Khmer Issaraks were to give themselves up within thirty days and be incorporated into either the Cambodian army or police. Although the Geneva agreements were by no means flawlessly adhered to by the Communists in Cambodia, they were for the most part honored,

Indochina

with a resulting significant decrease in overt Communist activity in the country.

Communist hopes for gaining control of Cambodia by peaceful means received a sharp jolt in early September, 1955, when the Popular Socialist Community party of former King Norodom Sihanouk, founded after his abdication in March, 1955, captured all ninety-one seats in elections for the national assembly. Opposition-inspired charges that Sihanouk, an exceptionally independent young man, had "sold" Cambodia to the United States for financial assistance apparently failed to convince the country's electorate, voting in the first post-Geneva election in Indochina and the third in Cambodian history. Far less strong at the polls than expected were the National Democrats, led by Son Ngoc Thanh. The Communist-oriented People's party, making an open bid for power in the former French protectorate, also showed poorly in the balloting. Shortly after the elections, Son Ngoc Thanh took to the bush again, but in early 1956 the Cambodian army inflicted a heavy defeat on his rebel forces, although Thanh himself escaped.

Communism would therefore not appear to constitute a major internal threat in the near future. Were a Communist military attack from north Vietnam to be mounted against Cambodia, however, the former French protectorate's 35,000-man army probably would not be capable of more than the most limited sort of holding action.

That Sihanouk would dominate the new government to be formed by his party soon became obvious. Although he had declared earlier that he would not become premier under any circumstances, he relented sufficiently to take over not only the post of prime minister but also that of foreign minister. Sihanouk remained Cambodia's premier until early 1956, when he resigned to travel abroad as a private citizen—his travels taking him, among other places, to Communist China. He returned to Cambodia in time to resume the premiership on the last day of February, but resigned again a month later. Sihanouk told his people in a radio address that he was resigning because the American press had distorted and attacked his neutralist foreign policy, but a government communique indicated he was stepping down because of "difficulties" between Cambodia and neighboring nations. These "difficulties" presumably were border disputes with Thailand and south Vietnam, who charged lawless acts against their territory by Cambodian nationals. Sihanouk's successor was Khim Tit, a supporter of the former king, who in turn resigned in August, 1956, amid rumors of a return of Sihanouk as prime minister. Sihanouk himself, however, for some time steadfastly refused to become premier again to end the cabinet crisis caused by Khim Tit's resignation, although his father, King Sura Marit, reportedly had ordered him to do so. Finally he did relent, and a new government under his leadership was formed in mid-September. The "on again, off again" premierships of Sihanouk did little to diminish his reputation as an erratic political figure.

If Sihanouk kept changing his mind over whether to be, or not to be, Cambodia's prime minister, he apparently experienced no change of mind concerning one of the key planks in his party's campaign platform: to do everything possible to stimulate the development of democracy in Cambodia. Hardly a month after the elections which swept his party to power, Sihanouk as premier was taking his cabinet "on tour" of the country's provinces in an effort to bring government as close as he could to the Cambodian people. At public meetings attended by the prince and his entire cabinet, members of the government explained its policies as well as answered complaints. In implementation of his "democratization" drive, the former king unfortunately displayed his usual singularly erratic qualities. In February, 1956, for example, he announced a lengthy list of "undemocratic" things members of his government must not do: use official cars for private purposes, benefit from special housing, wear a uniform except at official ceremonies, permit themselves to be addressed as "excellency"—and frequent places of entertainment!

It is not likely that the immediate future will bring closer relations between Cambodia and the United States. Cambodian foreign policy now follows along the lines of the Asian neutralist views espoused by Indian Premier Jawaharlal Nehru, although it is more realistic in its appraisal of the Ho Chi Minh government of north Vietnam. The threat posed by Peiping leadership is largely unperceived, however. Simultaneous with the growth of closer relations with Communist China has been an increase in the number of anti-American statements and actions by Cambodian leaders, particularly Sihanouk's rejection of Seato and his untruthful remarks in France that his country had refused American aid.

During his visit to Communist China in February, 1956, Sihanouk signed a friendship pact which embodied nonaggression, mutual respect for national integrity and sovereignty, noninterference in the internal affairs of other countries, peaceful coexistence, and equality and mutual benefit. Cambodia and China also agreed to strengthen relations in economics and culture and to work for the "removal of doubts" in international relations. In March, Cambodia sent a delegation to negotiate commercial agreements with the government of Mao Tse-tung. Under the terms of an agreement signed in Peiping on June 21, China was to invest $22,400,000 in the construction of textile, cement, paper, and plywood factories in Cambodia, with work on the several projects to begin before the end of 1957.

Sihanouk next made an "unofficial" visit to the Soviet Union, where an agreement for economic and industrial aid to Cambodia also was concluded. The Soviets agreed to supply industrial equipment and technician-instructors to Cambodia, and to build, equip, and staff a hospital in the Cambodian capital of Pnompenh. Sihanouk manifested his appreciation of the Soviet promises by declaring that the hope of his people "rests in the Soviet Union for the realization of our desires for peace and prosperity."

Meanwhile, prominent Cambodian spokesmen were criticizing United States assistance as designed to "buy the country." On a trip to the Philippines in early 1956, as an example of the Cambodian attitude, the easily aroused Sihanouk openly declared that the hospitality the Filipinos had heaped upon him was part of a United States plot to woo his country into the Southeast Asian Treaty Organization. Upon his return to

Cambodia, the prince declared that in the Philippines he had seen many tractors and wonderful hospitals built with United States aid. To Cambodia, however, the prince told his people, the United States gave only refrigerators and automobiles. He ignored the fact that the United States had equipped and was then paying three-quarters of the salary of the Cambodian army; that the United States had started irrigation, school, health, and road projects in his country; that when the Cambodian rice crop had failed, the United States had rushed 20,000 tons of rice to the onetime French protectorate, and that in the fiscal year of 1956, American assistance totaled $50,000,000, slightly more than half of which was in the form of military aid to build up the newly organized army. The prince later retracted his statement that United States assistance consisted mainly of luxury items, but he already had put himself on record for the Communist propagandists to quote.

The explanation of Sihanouk's behavior would seem to lie in his erratic political personality. Lacking in experience in international affairs, Sihanouk was playing one side against the other, in his own inimitable crude way, in an effort to reap the maximum economic benefits for Cambodia. In domestic politics, however, he stanchly rejected the efforts of Cambodian Communists to form a "united front" with his Popular Socialist Community party. Indeed, at an April, 1956, national congress of his party, Sihanouk declared that Cambodia aspired to a decentralized democracy modeled after the United States. There is considerable evidence that Sihanouk meant what he said—but he also knew it would please American ears. He also was quoted as saying that Cambodia "wishes to continue receiving from America economic and military aid that are indispensable to prevent Cambodia from falling under Communist influence." In the spring of 1956 Sihanouk announced that Cambodia's two-year economic development plan was ready to get under way, thanks to "promised aid" from the United States, France, India, certain British Commonwealth countries, "and from new friends such as continental China, Poland, and Russia." The main aim of the plan was an increase in agricultural output and timber, the products of these two sectors of the national economy being the main items of Cambodia's export trade. This two-year plan was to serve as a prelude to a later and more ambitious four- or five-year plan. That Sihanouk appreciated the benefits of a neutralist policy was evident in September, 1956, when he told the national assembly that the country's neutrality should be proclaimed "officially in law."[8]

LAOS: NATIONALISM AND NEUTRALISM

Laos, most of whose 1,300,000 inhabitants are ethnically related to the neighboring Thai, was established as a French protectorate in 1893, the last of the Indochinese territories to come under the rule of France. Like Cambodia, it was mostly untouched by nationalism until after the Second World War, and even now it cannot be said that nationalism has inflamed the sparsely settled Laotian countryside. Members of the ruling and educated elite have felt the impact of nationalism, but their initial contact with this imported political concept came at a much later date than in adjacent Vietnam. As was the case with Cambodia, the pre-French Laotian government welcomed the establishment of a French protectorate in the nineteenth century, because it feared being swamped by the then expanding Vietnamese and Thai populations.

Anti-French feeling grew during the period of the Japanese occupation of Indochina in the Second World War. Shortly after the Japanese broadcast a declaration that "the colonial status of Indochina has ended" on March 10, 1945, the king of Luang Prabang (which forms part of present-day Laos) issued a declaration of independence. King Sisavong Vong, however, was not a leader of the Laotian nationalist movement. Indeed, during the early postwar Chinese Nationalist occupation of the protectorate prior to the French return, a free Laotian movement forced the abdication of the king. Sisavong Vong later returned to his throne at the leave of the revolutionaries, who brought him back as a constitutional monarch. On August 27, 1946, the French concluded an agreement with the king of Luang Prabang, who thus legally became king of

[8] *Christian Science Monitor*, September 17, 1956.

Laos in French eyes, reestablishing the domination of France over the country. Contrary to their actions in other Southeast Asian lands, the Japanese did give virtually full self-government to Laos and Cambodia during their Second World War occupation, and the Laotian nationalists, having felt the exhilaration of this self-rule, were not to be denied by France. Some of the nationalist elements took to the bush under Communist leadership in hopes of duplicating the Viet Minh feats in neighboring Vietnam. Other nationalists agitated for freedom from imperial rule under non-Communist leaders, fully aware that "independence" under Communism was no more independence than continued French colonial rule. As a consequence of the efforts of the latter group primarily, Laos moved slowly forward on the road to self-government. On October 22, 1953, it signed with France a treaty giving it "full independence" within the French Union. Laos was still not a completely sovereign state, but it appeared headed in that direction.

The main barrier to full realization of Laotian national aspirations would seem to come, not from the retreating French, but from the Communists. That the Viet Minh harbors designs on Laos was most evident in its unprovoked thrusts into Laotian territory in 1953 and 1954 as well as in the March, 1951, alliance between the Viet Minh and its satellite movement in Laos, the Pathet Lao Issaraks. In addition, the insurgent Pathet Lao of Prince Souvanna Vong, a relation of the Laotian royal family, received much material aid from their Communist colleagues in Vietnam, without which they would never have been able to make as strong a showing as they did.

As a result of accords reached at the July, 1954, Geneva conference on Indochina, the Pathet Lao on November 6, 1954, allegedly submitted to the political control of the royal Laotian government, although retaining possession of the northern provinces of Phong Saly and Sam Neua. The hollowness of this move was revealed by later armed attacks against royal army units by Pathet Lao bands, operating from the two excluded provinces. In mid 1956, two years after the signing of the Geneva agreements, limited military activity continued, though sporadically, between Communist and government forces.

The result of Pathet Lao control over the disputed northern provinces was a de facto partition in Laos. On November 9, 1955, a royal Laotian government delegation which had been negotiating with the Pathet Lao in Vientiane, capital of Laos, informed the international commission charged with observing the carrying out of the Geneva accords in Laos that it had been unable to reach a political settlement with the rebels and would hold national elections without their participation. These elections were held on December 25, 1955, with more than 300,000 out of approximately 360,000 Laotian electors going to the polls, according to the royal government, in spite of Communist propaganda urging voters not to participate in the balloting. In only one area, the village of Muong Peun in Sam Neua province, did the Communists actually prevent Laotian voters from participating in the election. There about 1,000 Pathet Lao troops used mortar and machine-gun fire to keep government soldiers from casting their votes. A government spokesman charged that these Pathet Lao troops included north Vietnamese soldiers.

As a consequence of the elections, the ten participating provinces came under the national government, and the other two—the disputed northern provinces of Phong Saly and Sam Neua—were held by the Communists. Such partition clearly was not the intent of the Geneva agreements. The submission of the Pathet Lao to government political control was supposed to have set the stage for the resumption of government jurisdiction over the northern provinces, but subsequently military activity by the Communists made this impossible. In November, 1955, the Pathet Lao leaders once again had publicly voiced their willingness to recognize the right of the government to extend its control over the disputed provinces, if this were done "progressively." The Pathet Lao also indicated a willingness to permit elections in the two provinces—on its own terms.

The fact that elections were held in Laos in December, 1955, with such a large turnout under strained conditions in such a primitive country, was a tribute to the resourcefulness of the non-Communist elements, particularly veteran nationalist Kathay Sasorith. But not until mid-March, 1956, were non-

Communist politicians able to agree on a government to succeed Premier Kathay and his cabinet. On March 21, however, a new Laotian government headed by Prince Souvanna Phouma was voted into office, ending the longest cabinet crisis Laos had known.

Meanwhile, Pathet Lao attacks in northern Laos continued. On November 11, 1955, the Laotian foreign minister declared that the Viet Minh had attached both political commissars and military cadres to the Pathet Lao forces, which were, he said, receiving military and food supplies from the Vietnamese Communists. In addition, he charged that Ho Chi Minh's north Vietnamese government had broken the promise it gave at the Bandung Conference of Afro-Asian powers in April, 1955, not to interfere in the internal affairs of Laos.[9] In December more than 2,000 Pathet Lao troops took part in the strongest offensive for half a year, but they were easily defeated, and except for early February, 1956, the next months were comparatively free of Communist military activity.

Despite the Pathet Lao insurgency problem, the last half of 1955 witnessed considerably greater stability in Laos than was evident in the immediate post-Geneva period. The Geneva conference on Indochina had been followed in Laos by a series of violent cabinet crises which appeared at times to threaten the advantages derived from the peace settlement. Fortunately, the situation was stabilized by Premier Kathay, long identified with the Laotian nationalist movement.

The first indication that Laos' newly acquired political stability might be short lived came with Kathay Sasorith's replacement as premier by Prince Souvanna Phouma. It soon became evident that Souvanna Phouma's government was by no means as vigorously anti-Communist as that of Kathay Sasorith. This was indicated by two major developments: a political settlement with the rebel Communist Pathet Lao movement on generous terms, and the emergence of neutralism as a vital force in the formulation of Laotian foreign policy.

A major reason for the decision by the Pathet Lao to call off their rebellion probably was a realization that their con-

[9] New York *Times*, November 12, 1955.

Indochina

tinued occupation of the northern provinces was driving the government into the camp of the anti-Communist West. The Pathet leadership also undoubtedly realized that the Communist charge that failure to hold unification elections in Vietnam was a breach of the 1954 Geneva settlement could be countered with the accusation that what the Pathets were doing in Laos was equally illegal.

As a result of negotiations between Premier Souvanna Phouma and his half-brother and leader of the Pathet Lao, Prince Souvanna Vong, agreement was reached in early August, 1956, for the cessation of all hostile acts by each side toward the other. The two northern provinces of Phong Saly and Sam Neua, it was agreed, would pass from control of the Pathet Lao to the jurisdiction of the royal government. The military arm of the Communist Pathets, moreover, would be integrated into the royal Laotian army. The communique issued by Princes Souvanna Phouma and Souvanna Vong also noted that the Laotian government would be guided in its various policies and actions by the five principles of coexistence outlined by Communist China's Chou En-lai and Indian Prime Minister Nehru. Details of the agreement, including those relating to the integration of Pathet Lao elements into the royal government, would be worked out by joint military and civilian committees.

In late December, 1956, the government of Premier Souvanna Phouma announced the signing of an agreement for the integration of the Pathet Lao into Laotian national life. According to this agreement, the Pathets would not only be accepted back into national life as individuals and given full rights as citizens, as provided for in the 1954 Geneva settlement, but Pathet representatives also would receive posts in the government (including the cabinet and the army). The Communists, in addition, would be allowed to set up workers', students', and women's organizations throughout Laos. The agreement was not immediately submitted to the national assembly for ratification, but this was expected to follow and to be successful. The Communists clearly were making progress towards their goal of eventual assumption of power in newly independent Laos.

They were making greater progress, it seemed, than in their period of armed opposition to the government.

Simultaneous with the rapprochement between the royal government and the Pathet Lao leadership was the emergence of neutralism as a major factor in the determination of Laotian foreign policy. This will be different from the neutralism of India, Burma, Indonesia, and Ceylon, Premier Souvanna Phouma has stated. "Our country," Laos' prime minister declared in mid 1956, "has no intention of joining any bloc, even the neutralist bloc." "Neutrality," according to Souvanna, "is even more neutral than 'neutralism'." Laos, he said, aspires to be truly the Switzerland of the Far East (not the India of Indochina). In mid-August, 1956, following his negotiations with Prince Souvanna Vong, Laotian Premier Souvanna Phouma visited Peiping, where he undoubtedly pleased his Chinese Communist hosts by declaring that his country would not join any military alliance—that is, the Southeast Asian Treaty Organization—as long as there was no interference with its security. He further promised that his kingdom would bar new foreign military installations from its territory. For its part, Communist China promised to "respect and wholly support" the neutral position of Laos.[10] Laos' premier went further than signing a declaration espousing neutralism; he also accepted the principle of Chinese help to his country in meeting the economic goals it had drawn up for itself, becoming the second non-Communist country to accept such aid from Peiping.

The Laotian leader's action had implications for his country's relations with Communists elsewhere in Southeast Asia—as evidenced by his visit to north Vietnam on his way back from Peiping. Souvanna Phouma signed a declaration of peaceful coexistence with the Viet Minh and said his nation would have economic and diplomatic relations with north Vietnam shortly.

Back in his native Laos, Souvanna Phouma seemed to sing a different song than he had sung in Peiping or north Vietnam. He told a news conference upon his arrival at Vientiane that his government was "not ready to establish diplomatic or economic relations with either" the Chinese Communists or the Viet

---

[10] Washington *Post and Times-Herald*, August 26, 1956.

Minh.[11] He admitted that his country had been offered economic aid by the Communists during his Peiping visit, but he said that he was not yet ready to accept more foreign help. He also announced that he was asking for a revision of United States aid with an eye toward obtaining more economic development assistance and less military help. For all his naivete, Souvanna Phouma obviously knew how to put on the economic "squeeze." Yet Peiping could not have enjoyed everything Souvanna Phouma said upon his return from Communist China. "A Communist government will not work in Laos," he declared, "and I would not hold office under such a government." Moreover, despite the joint Sino-Laotian communique of 1956, Laos still maintained formal military links with the West through French bases at Seno and Xieng-Khouang and a mutual defense treaty with France, a charter member of Seato.

THE ECONOMIC PROBLEM IN INDOCHINA

The political problems raised by the postwar fighting in Vietnam, and the related agitation for greater freedom in neighboring Cambodia and Laos, have obscured economic conditions prevailing in Indochina since 1945. In 1940 Indochina was able to export 1,500,000 tons of rice, but in 1951 it sent only 303,000 tons to the world market. Similar export drops took place in rubber and coal. It was presumed that the Geneva-established peace would be accompanied by an economic revival in both free and Communist Indochina. To a certain extent such hopes have been justified, but the long road to economic recovery and rehabilitation still has been only partly traveled, particularly in the two Vietnams.

A key area of economic competition between the two Vietnamese regimes is land reform. In most of the territory they occupied prior to the Geneva settlement the Communists carried out land-reform programs, including many areas of south Vietnam. In the north, following Geneva, Ho Chi Minh and his associates continued their efforts in behalf of land redistri-

---

[11] See New York *Times*, September 5, 1956.

bution, at the same time embarking on a more unpopular program of agricultural collectivization. In the south in the early months of the Diem regime, land previously distributed by the evacuated Communists was taken back by the dispossessed landlords—which did not increase the popularity of the Saigon government.

The south Vietnamese government of Premier Ngo Dinh Diem had good intentions for land reform, although it experienced considerable difficulty in translating these intentions into action as long as it was preoccupied with military actions against dissident groups like the Binh Xuyen, Hoa Hao, and Cao Dai. Fighting in the provinces interfered extensively with rice plantings in south Vietnam in the spring of 1955, for example, which could not help but have undesirable consequences at harvesttime. Diem tried, however—though possibly not hard enough—to effect important land reform changes in the territory he ruled. The land-reform law signed by the premier early in 1955 provided that rentals on farms should not exceed 15 to 25 percent of the value of the crops grown on them, a considerable improvement over past practices under which rentals frequently soared as high as 70 percent of the crop. This measure has been successfully implemented in only a few areas of the Diem-governed territory, partially as a result of the lack of trained, efficient, and honest personnel to administer the program. In addition, the premier's economic program has met opposition from the landlords, who resent not only the lower rentals, but the imposition of taxes—conveniently overlooking the fact that although the Viet Minh "eliminated" taxes, they substituted far heavier economic exactions and, where they were able, took the land away from its owners.

That Ngo Dinh Diem would push forward with an agrarian reform program was evidenced in October, 1956, by the issuance of a government decree under which absentee landlords were to be dispossessed of their lands (with compensation) and landless peasants were to be given an opportunity to buy such lands for their own plots. The October land-reform decrees produced an instantaneous reaction against Diem on

Indochina

the part of powerful landed interests and presaged probable future trouble for the south Vietnamese leader. Diem seemed determined, however, that he would not retreat in the face of this opposition to his reform efforts.

Undaunted by the opposition of vested interests, Premier Diem announced on September 18, 1955, what he termed his "new long-range economic program," aimed at "perfecting the independence of the country in the economic field" by eliminating colonial monopolies and giving the Vietnamese businessman and farmer alike a dominant role in the country's economic life, increasing credit facilities, "modernizing" agriculture, and creating new light industries to meet the country's internal needs.

Not only did Diem desire a reduction in French economic influence in south Vietnam, but he also wished to limit the role of the Chinese in his country's commercial life. South Vietnam's Chinese minority, like the overseas Chinese in the rest of the countries of Southeast Asia, have played a major role in national economic life. In south Vietnam, where the Chinese comprise only one-tenth of the population, they have controlled an estimated two-thirds of the country's economic activity. In October, 1956, President Diem moved to alter this situation by declaring it illegal for noncitizens to own businesses in eleven important categories, including transport and many retail trades, previously dominated by Chinese nationals. Vietnam-born Chinese were to be regarded as Vietnamese citizens, but Chinese born outside Vietnam were designated foreigners and, therefore, were forbidden to participate in the eleven restricted businesses. The Chinese minority responded with a campaign of economic retaliation. Rice exports, which provide south Vietnam with a major percentage of its foreign exchange, came to a virtual halt (fortunately only temporarily) as a result of Chinese reprisal activity. The long-term consequences for the Diem government of the October, 1956, anti-Chinese decrees probably will be similar to those resulting from like moves in Thailand and the Philippines. In these countries such discriminatory action served only to intensify resentment of the Chinese toward the land of their domicile and increased the potentiality for Chinese Communist exploitation of overseas Chinese communities in Southeast Asia. The south Vietnamese Chinese minority's retaliation campaign clearly revealed the power which the overseas Chinese hold over the Vietnamese economy. Rather than surrendering this power, the Chinese probably will seek ways of circumventing the October, 1956, decrees.

A major step toward economic rehabilitation—and the solution of one of south Vietnam's leading social problems—was taken by Premier Diem in late December, 1955, when he announced plans to settle one hundred thousand of the refugees from the north on rich abandoned rice land in southwestern Vietnam. The Cai San project, as it was called, was designed to reclaim lands formerly under Hoa Hao domination and to give refugees from the north, many of whom lived under almost intolerable conditions, an opportunity to establish their own farms and homes and to provide for their own subsistence and that of their families. In the north the refugees, on the average, had rented holdings of less than two acres. Under the Cai San permanent settlement project it was planned that each family would rent eight to ten acres. During the first year of occupancy the farmer would pay no charge for the land he tilled. In the second year he would begin paying rent—but only one-quarter of the normal amount. The third year of his occupancy, the farmer would pay one-third of his rent, while in the fourth year he would start paying full rent. Although no plan was announced whereby tenants might eventually own the land they tilled, the Diem government did indicate its hope that a way might be worked out whereby the rice tenant farmer could in time possess his own land. Diem and his aides were most enthusiastic over the Cai San project, the government stating in February, 1956, that if this project were successfully carried out, efforts would be made to resettle similarly the remainder of the eight hundred thousand refugees from the north. The task, however, was a big one.

Fortunately, President-Premier Diem realizes the importance of the economic factor in his battle with the Viet Minh.

Indochina

"The shooting for the moment has ended," he stated in June, 1956, "but a fresh danger has emerged"—an economic war between the Communist north and the democratic south. Diem declared that the most humble rice farmer in his country must receive benefits from being a citizen in the new republic. Then he would appreciate the republic, the south Vietnamese leader said, and be willing to support and defend it. Communist China and the Soviet Union were trying to dress up north Vietnam as an economic showplace, according to Diem.

Although occupied with internal security problems during most of its first two and a half years of existence, the Diem government in south Vietnam has been fully aware of the need for economic reform and progress if it is to compete effectively with its northern Communist rival. The main device chosen by Diem to fight this economic battle is a five-year plan similar to that in operation in India (though much less spectacular). This development program, scheduled to be launched in 1957, will attack the problem of economic progress from several approaches—including a considerable increase in the country's power resources and the establishment of small manufacturing industries.

It is none too early for the south Vietnamese government to be turning a major portion of its attention to development projects, for the economic problems facing the Diem regime are sizable (although less formidable than those confronting the Viet Minh in the north). South Vietnam's economic problems stem in large measure from the breakdown of the old French commercial structure. They also derive, however, from the impact of American economic assistance, which has not always been used in the wisest ways. Financial help from the United States, indeed, has tended to help perpetuate the old system of small-scale importers of luxury goods—which still can be purchased, despite the French withdrawal. Although there has been governmental economic assistance from abroad (mainly the United States), there has been a glaring lack of private foreign investment in south Vietnam. This has resulted from uncertainty concerning the ultimate form of the country's economy—and who will comprise its future political leadership. The seriousness of south Vietnam's economic situation is perhaps best illustrated by the fact that, according to the National Bank of Vietnam, in the first four months of 1956 only 18 percent of the country's imports were paid for by exports. There were signs of improvement in the second half of 1956, but the basic economic situation in south Vietnam remains serious. South Vietnam has the ingredients for a healthy future economic development, but hard work and continued foreign assistance will be required.

Both the south Vietnamese and the Communists have in fact received considerable economic help from the two rival camps which support them on the international scene. The United States, a much interested party in the outcome of the internal political struggle in Vietnam, allotted $385,000,000 for use in Vietnam in 1954. The Viet Minh, for its part, received considerable assistance from the Chinese and Russian Communists—culminated by the promises of greater help made to Ho Chi Minh in Moscow and Peiping in 1955—as well as some aid from the satellites. China would like very much to have a Communist country on its exposed southeastern flank and can be counted upon to continue to aid the Viet Minh economically, as it helped Ho Chi Minh's side with both material and technical assistance in the war against the French. Nor has Moscow forgotten Lenin's dictum that the shortest route to Europe was by means of the backward territories upon which Europe allegedly was so dependent.

That the United States and its allies—and the Chinese and the Soviets and the other Communist states—should have been so willing to assist the two rival sides in Vietnam was indicative of the importance both major camps in the cold war placed on once little known Indochina. For the Communists, control of Vietnam would mean not only additional territory added to their bloc, but also protection for China as well as a possible jumping-off point for additional expansion in Southeast Asia, not to mention a further dimunition of Western prestige in the Far East and the world in general. The United States and its allies, conversely, sought ardently to prevent the fall of Vietnam to the Communists in order to keep the inter-

Indochina

national Communist coalition from continuing its growth of the postwar years. All of Southeast Asia would be threatened in Washington's eyes, should the Viet Minh take over the whole of Vietnam. Moreover, the West would have suffered still another setback in a string of Far Eastern foreign-policy defeats, which already allegedly included the fall of China to Communism and the Korean stalemate.

The stakes are high in Vietnam and Indochina in general. The eventual outcome of rival efforts to unify Vietnam will have the most important of consequences for international politics as well as for the Vietnamese themselves. Besides the struggle between the Communists and the non-Communist nationalists of Vietnam, there is the continued interest of the United States, the Soviet Union, China, and other nations in the final solution of the Vietnamese problem. The French interest would seem to be a diminishing one, especially in light of the agreement by Paris in February, 1956, to withdraw its remaining troops from Vietnamese soil.[12]

The peace which returned to Indochina in July of 1954 was an uneasy peace. How long it will continue to reign over Indochina depends not only on the people and politicians of Vietnam, Cambodia, and Laos, but also upon those who sit in seats of power in Moscow, Peiping, and Washington. Peace came to Indochina in the summer of 1954 only with the acquiesence of these powers. One or more of them could have a change of heart.

---

[12] Washington *Post*, February 22, 1956. The peculiar post-Geneva position of France in Indochina was illustrated in October, 1955, by the announcement that the French had signed a three-million-dollar, one-year trade agreement with Ho Chi Minh's north Vietnam government. It would appear from this agreement that France does not intend to abandon economic ties with that part of Vietnam under Communist rule. Although the influence of France in Vietnam is decreasing rapidly, a few Frenchmen seem still not to have given up all hope of a turn in their fortunes in Indochina. Their ranks are thinning, however.

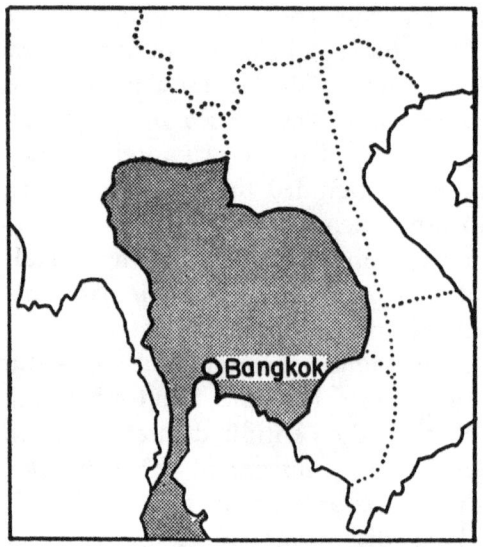

CHAPTER 5

THAILAND
Diplomatic and Political Phenomenon

POLITICS IN Thailand since the bloodless revolution of 1932 has been a rough-and-tumble struggle dominated by colorful personalities who have jockeyed with one another for control of the state. This competition involves serious implications for the whole world, particularly as it increases political instability in Thailand and so reduces the country's capacity to resist Communist pressures.

Central among Thai political personalities of the last quarter of a century has been Phibun Songgram, a field marshal who led the military faction against the Chakri dynasty in 1932, and who now is premier. His arch foe is Pridi Banomyong, a civilian politician, who masterminded the 1932 coup and who now from Communist China attempts to rally dissident Thai elements to revolt. The period since 1947 has witnessed the apparent eclipse of Pridi and the rise of a new rival, ambitious and scheming Police General Phao Sriyanon. Phao, generally regarded as Phibun's heir apparent, boldly increased his strength during these years to the point where he appeared to many to be the chief man in the country—in fact if not in title. In early August, 1955, however, Phibun struck out at Phao's growing strength, stripping him of a key cabinet post and moving to cut off the sources of his lucrative income. As a result, it may well be that the prime threat to the Thai premier at the present time comes once again from his old opponent, Pridi Banomyong.

HISTORICAL BACKGROUND

The Thai, descended from a racial group closely related to the Chinese, came down from south China. By 800 a formidable Thai kingdom had emerged, but rival kingdoms rose and fell during the succeeding centuries. The Thai accepted Chinese suzerainty, though not without repeated assertions of independence. Repeatedly the Thai sought to conquer neighboring peoples, especially the Shans and the Laotians, who are racially closely related to them.

During the latter half of the nineteenth century, when a recrudescence of Western imperialism threatened the independence of Siam,[1] the country was fortunate in having very able kings in Mongkut (1851-1868) and Chulalongkorn (1868-1910). King Mongkut opened his country to Western influence by signing a treaty of friendship and commerce with Britain in 1855. Similar treaties were negotiated with the United States and France in 1856, and with a number of other European countries in the next few years. Mongkut saw the need of modernizing his administration if his country was not to fall a prey to Western imperialism. He brought in Westerners as advisers and teachers, who in many cases actually served as department heads. Most of his advisers were retired British officials from India and Burma, but he was careful to avoid getting too many from any one country. Belgians, Danes, Dutch, Italians, and Americans served in this capacity.

King Chulalongkorn was a progressive and reformer like his father. He abolished slavery, ended the practice of prostration in the royal presence, set up schools for the education of

---

[1] The official name of the country was changed from Siam to Thailand in 1939, back to Siam in 1945, and to Thailand again in 1948.

the children of the nobility, modernized the postal system, and reformed provincial administration and the administration of justice. The king traveled extensively and sent young aristocrats abroad for study.

Siam is the only country in Southeast Asia which escaped becoming a Western colony. This can be explained in part by the desire of both Britain and France for a buffer state between their respective territories in the region. Nevertheless, the story might have been different if the Siamese had not displayed a remarkable cleverness in diplomacy. France put heavy pressure on Siam to renounce control over Laos, Luang Prabang, and the provinces of Battambang and Siemriep, which had once belonged to Cambodia. In 1883 it blockaded Bangkok, after which Siam yielded to most of France's demands. Other concessions were made in 1904 and 1907. As a result of "the long drawn-out series of diplomatic contortions" Siam succeeded in retaining its independence, but at the cost of 90,000 square miles of territory.

Siam emerged from the diplomatic struggle with a territory of nearly 200,000 square miles. A small strip of Burmese and Laotian territory in the north separates Siam from China; in the south its territory extends almost two-thirds down the Malayan Peninsula. Northern Siam is mountainous, and the eastern part of the country is an infertile plateau. The large alluvial plain and rich delta of the Menam River constitutes the heart of the country. The population of Thailand is far from homogeneous; its 20,000,000 inhabitants include some 750,000 Malays in the south and 2,500,000 persons of Chinese blood. Outside of the country's boundaries are two peoples ethnologically closely related to the Thai, the Shans of northern Burma and the Laotians. These three groups constitute material for potential irredentism.

THE PRIDI-PHIBUN RIVALRY

Until 1932 the government of Thailand was an absolute monarchy, with government positions a practical monopoly of members of the numerous Thai noble families. Discontented

Thailand

young intellectuals joined leaders of the armed forces in a bloodless revolution which ushered in the constitutional monarchy. The political history of the country since then has been one of revolution and counterrevolution—some successful, more abortive. During this period Thailand has had five constitutions, but most of this time the government has been a thinly veiled dictatorship.

The political life of Thailand since 1932 has largely centered around two rival personalities: Pridi Banomyong and Luang Phibun Songgram. Both studied abroad under government scholarships in the years immediately following the First World War; Phibun studied military science in France, and Pridi, law in Paris. Pridi was one of the leaders of the 1932 revolution, but it was not long before he was suspected of holding Communist views and was forced into exile. After about six months abroad he returned to Bangkok, declared under oath that he neither was the head of a Thai Communist party nor had Communistic ties. He was officially cleared of the charge of being a Communist and quickly recovered political influence, but he lost in the struggle for political power to Phibun, who had the backing of the army. The latter had acquired a favorable reputation by reestablishing order after an abortive royalist attempt to take over the government in 1933. Phibun became prime minister in December, 1938. Although nominally a constitutional, semiparliamentary monarchy, the government under Phibun was actually a dictatorship. A large number of the appointed members of the assembly and of the ministers were army or police officials, and officers of the armed forces held the chief positions in the civil service. The press was rigidly controlled. Just enough debate in parliament was permitted to create the impression that there was a semblance of democracy. In January, 1939, a plot to overthrow the Phibun regime was uncovered and ruthlessly suppressed.

As the Phibun government became increasingly fascist in character, its policy became more and more pro-Japanese. Under Japanese aegis it succeeded in obtaining the session of a considerable area from Indochina, and with Japanese consent it annexed four Malay states and two Shan states of Burma. Thailand offered only a token resistance to Japanese invasion and thus opened the way for the land attack on Malaya. After a few days it entered into an alliance with Japan, and shortly thereafter declared war on Great Britain and the United States. The United Kingdom answered in kind, but the American government chose to ignore the Thai declaration of war and to treat Thailand as a victim of Japan.

The next phase is one of the strangest in all political and diplomatic annals. A "Free Thai" movement was organized among the few Siamese abroad, which with the cooperation and aid of Great Britain and the United States gave aid to an underground resistance movement which developed under the leadership of Phibun's bitter rival, Pridi. In August, 1944, while Japanese troops were still in the country, Marshal Phibun's regime was overthrown and a new government, secretly sympathetic with the "Free Thai," came to power. Immediately after the collapse of Japan the Thai government issued a "Peace Declaration" in which the declaration of war against Great Britain and the United States was proclaimed null and void because made against the will of the Thai people. Seni Pramoj, minister to the United States and organizer of the "Free Thai" abroad, became prime minister, and a new, more democratic constitution was adopted. Marshal Phibun was arrested as a war criminal, but was released after spending a few months in jail.

Pridi, who was the logical person to head the government after the overthrow of Phibun, held back until after the general election in 1946. On March 24 he became premier, and on June 9, 1946, occurred the death, by bullet wound, of King Mahidol. As a result of rumors, probably set afloat by Pridi's political enemies, the prime minister's name became widely associated with the death of the king. His government was also charged with unbridled corruption, and the pressure became too great for him to withstand; in August, 1946, he resigned the premiership in favor of Admiral Thamrong. On November 8, 1947, leaders of the armed forces overthrew the Thamrong government in the third successful coup d'etat since 1932.

Pridi fled into exile, and Marshal Phibun, who had engineered the plot, took over the reins of government five months later. Thus "the man who declared war on the Allies" was back in the saddle. Pridi's forces twice attempted to overthrow the Phibun regime, but failed. General Luang Kach, one of the chief agents of Phibun in the 1947 coup d'etat, was himself later accused of plotting against the Phibun government and was sent into exile in January, 1950.

How are these events to be interpreted? A cynic might conclude that in the Second World War the Thai again outwitted the Great Powers. With the Phibun government linked up with Japan and the "Free Thai" in association with the Allies, Thailand could not lose much, no matter what the outcome of the war. After the war the United States government obligingly intervened on behalf of Thailand with the British, who quite naturally did not feel kindly disposed toward Thailand, which, because of its collaboration with Japan, had contributed to British woes in Malaya. Malaya was in desperate need of rice, and the British government thought it not unreasonable to demand that Thailand contribute its surplus of that commodity. The British were outmaneuvered; Thailand got off very lightly, in spite of its declaration of war on the Allies. There were rumors among the Thai that the struggle between Pridi and Phibun was mere show, and that they were actually in collusion. According to these rumors, Phibun in the postwar crisis was taking the side of the Western powers, as that seemed to be the best policy at the moment, but with the knowledge that in case this policy failed, Pridi could step forward to make peace with Communist China. This is fantastic, of course, but it does indicate something of the Thai mentality. This policy of diplomatic reinsurance does not seem at all unreasonable to them.

Marshal Phibun has definitely committed his country to the side of the non-Communist nations. A few Thai have frankly stated that Thailand cannot repeat the performance of the last war. "The doctrine of extra-legality will not appear in the Thai dictionary for future use," states a Thai nationalist paper, and it warns the Thai not "to hope for a hopeless chance of remaining neutral." The only sensible policy now is to take sides from the beginning, according to this view.

RETURN OF PHIBUN

The coup of November, 1947, did not result in Phibun's immediately becoming premier. Khuang Aphaiwong, who could be a friend of both sides, was selected by Phibun and his associates to be prime minister for the third time in a little more than three years. On April 6, 1948, however, a supreme state council set up by Phibun named its creator premier once again.

Pridi, meanwhile, was not to be counted out of the Thai political picture. On the night of February 26, 1949, the former law professor tried to return to power in a dramatic coup d'etat, which misfired when a premature radio broadcast warned Phibun and his supporters that a revolution was about to be attempted. Reaching tank and armored-car headquarters in advance of Pridi's tank-corps associates, they saved the day for the government. Reprisals of an ugly sort followed, giving indication of the political climate of Bangkok and the morality of those who ruled Thailand. Not only were a number of arrests made, including Pridi's brother, but within the first four days of March six known supporters of Phibun's opponent were killed.

In June, 1951, still another attempt was made to seize the reins of government from Phibun. Before many of Thailand's dignitaries and the entire diplomatic corps, a small naval vessel, the *Sri Ayuthia*, pulled up beside the American dredge *Manhattan*, which at the moment was being ceremonially transferred from the United States to Thailand, and kidnapped the Thai premier. When the Royal Thai Air Force later bombed and sank the *Sri Ayuthia*, Phibun had to leap for his life and swim to shore.

Was this still another instance of the Phibun-Pridi rivalry? The evidence is conflicting. First reports were that this was a routine Thai coup, differing only from past coups in that this one was very bloody compared to its predecessors. Pridi, it was reported, was the power behind the rebellion, although for safety's sake he did not put in a personal appearance. However, the naval officer who headed the group which kidnapped Phibun vehemently denied Pridi's leadership of the revolt, and some observers termed the "Manhattan Affair" a last desperate attempt on the part of the Thai navy to wrest some power from the army and police.

In terms of the scanty evidence presently available, there is reason to think that the "Manhattan Affair" was the work of an underground Communist body known by its abbreviated title Ku-Sap-Be, the translation of the full name of which means "Liberation Party for the Salvation of the Fatherland: Vietnam-Laos-Cambodia-Thailand-Burma." Founded in 1944 at Sakorn Nathorn in northeastern Thailand by a very able Viet Minh agent, Moscow-trained Nguyen Van Long, the Ku-Sap from the start sought to enlist persons who might not consider direct affiliation with the Communist party itself. It was claimed by many in Bangkok that the "Manhattan Affair" was in fact a Ku-Sap revolt.[2] The would-be new regime's program, as broadcast over the captured Thai radio at the time, coincided with the Ku-Sap program, even in many cases down to exact words.[3] Moreover, the Viet Minh radio just three months earlier had predicted an early "civil war" in Thailand.[4]

PRIDI AND COMMUNIST CHINA

Whether or not Pridi was a partner to the 1951 coup attempt, he is still a factor of significance in Thai politics today, supporting a Thai irredentist movement from Peiping as part of Chinese Communist foreign policy in Southeast Asia. His defection came as a great surprise to most of his friends outside Thailand. Some immediately recalled the charges of Communist leanings made against him in the 1930's, but most regarded

[2] See Denis Warner, "Communist Techniques in the Attempt on Siam," London *Daily Telegraph*, July 10, 1953.
[3] Copies of the Ku-Sap program and the text of the broadcast in question were both available at C.I.D. headquarters in Bangkok in August, 1953, when one of the authors of this book was in that city.
[4] New York *Times*, March 8, 1951.

his earlier economic policy and his present conduct as unrelated events. Although Pridi may be a real Communist today, perhaps convinced that such a course is the only alternative to the dictatorial rule of Phibun, it seems more likely that he is using the Chinese Communists to pave the way for his own return to power in Bangkok.

The appearance of Pridi in mid 1954 as an ally of the Chinese Communists in Asia followed the announcement in late January, 1953, that Peiping had set up a "Thai Autonomous Peoples' Government" in the southern province of Yunnan in China, bordering on Burma and Laos. The apparent objective of the establishment of this "nationality autonomous area" was to appeal to irredentist feeling of the fourteen million Thai in Thailand and the more than two million Thai in the Shan states of neighboring Burma and in adjacent Laos.

If Pridi is not really a Communist, he is nevertheless part of Peiping's policy toward Thailand. In the same sense, Phibun is the democratic camp's ally in Thailand despite his lack of affinity with the basic precepts of democratic government. Thailand at the present time is an oligarchy pure and simple, and there is little real evidence that it is moving in the direction of democracy despite Premier Phibun's assertions following his return from the United States in the summer of 1955 that the time was at hand for the democratization of his country.

The early postwar years did see the emergence of a number of political parties in the country as well as the establishment of a bicameral national legislature with all the members elected. Traditional Thai political apathy, however, continued to plague those who would provoke popular interest in government. Only 22 percent of the electorate went to the polls in the election which followed the November, 1947, coup, but the victor was the Democratic party, a group of liberals who opposed both Phibun and Pridi. Phibun's personal assumption of power again in April, 1948, served to disillusion the Thai people further, with the result that less than half as many persons turned out to vote in 1949 as had gone to the polls in 1947.

In 1951 democracy's prospects in Thailand were further dimmed by the abrogation of the new constitution with limited advances toward popular government. The two-house national assembly was replaced by a unicameral parliament comprising 123 appointed members and 123 elected ones. In the elections of February, 1952, approximately thirty opposition candidates won seats—weak voices to serve democracy.

A subsequent so-called democratization drive of Premier Phibun seemed to gain new impetus in November, 1956, with the announcement that the Thai cabinet had accepted the prime minister's proposal for elimination from the constitution of "second category," or appointed, members of the national assembly. The constitutional revision proposed by Phibun would also establish a bicameral parliament, comprising a senate and a house of representatives, but this was not due to become effective until after the February, 1957, elections. These elections were for the purpose of filling half the seats in the existent one-chamber national legislature, whose total membership had been increased from 246 to 320.

Just how soon after the February, 1957, elections these reforms would take effect was the big question. Phibun was quoted in December, 1956, as stating that elections for national assembly seats then filled by nominated members would probably be held in May, 1957, only three months after the February voting.[5] There were those who wondered, however, why Thailand would go to the bother of electing one-half of its national legislature in February and the other half in May. Phibun's November announcement that the electoral reforms would not become effective until after the February voting was interpreted by many to mean that they would not actually come into being until four years later, 1961, when national elections again would be held. A lot could happen before that time, including Phibun's own departure from the scene as Thai premier.

RIVALS WITHIN PHIBUN'S REGIME

In spite of the fact that Phibun has remained at the head of the Thai government since 1948, he has not been as complete a master of the political situation as during the time of his

[5] *The Economist* (London), December 15, 1956.

earlier premiership. The men who staged the November, 1947, coup d'etat formed a junta to govern the country collectively. Phibun was but one leader of the Coup party, as the junta came to be known, possessing a strong voice in its councils, but not so strong that it could not be overruled.

In the years after 1950 three men in particular in the Coup party markedly increased their strength and so vied with one another, as well as with the premier, to increase their influence over affairs of state (and business) in Thailand. Participants in this struggle for power were ambitious and scheming Police Director General Phao Sriyanon, who also has served as deputy minister of interior and deputy minister of finance; General Sarit Thanarat, commander in chief of the army; and aging Field Marshal Phin Chunhawan, Sarit's predecessor as head of the army, whose positions also have included deputy defense minister, minister of agriculture, and deputy premier. These men so increased their personal strength between 1950 and 1955 that Phibun at one time appeared to survive as premier only because he represented a balance among the various factions attempting to succeed to his power.

Although Field Marshal Phin, father-in-law of General Phao, possessed both considerable power and marked ambitions, especially in the economic field, it was between Generals Phao and Sarit that the real contest existed. As the prestige and power of General Phao grew, Phibun's position clearly was threatened. In the first week of August, 1955, Phibun struck out at the increasing power of his foremost rival. Phao, on a financial mission to the United States, was removed as deputy minister of finance. This coincided with announcement of the details of the police director general's involvement in a sensational opium scandal in which a $1,500,000 reward was concerned.[6] At the same time, Phibun removed several Phao followers from prominent posts in his government, including the venerable Field Marshal Phin, who lost his deputy defense ministership, while keeping his portfolios of minister of agriculture and deputy premier. Other pro-Phao casualties included a deputy communications minister, a deputy premier, and a

[6] See New York *Times*, August 7, 1955.

deputy minister of cooperatives. Admitted to cabinet ranks for the first time were two prominent supporters of General Sarit. Relinquishing his post as minister of culture, Phibun himself assumed the portfolio of minister of interior, under whose jurisdiction fell the national police network previously controlled exclusively by General Phao.

Phibun did not content himself with a cabinet shakeup. On September 2, 1955, he stripped from military and police commanders the authority to mobilize Thailand's armed forces and police, declaring that only he, in his joint capacity as minister of interior and minister of defense, would possess such power in the future. A day previously the premier had taken two other moves of considerable political significance: he had withdrawn from the police the power of press censorship and had announced the dissolution of the legislative study commission, before which bills had previously been examined prior to being presented to the national assembly. General Phao had been secretary general of the commission and, consequently, had exercised considerable influence over legislation.[7] And two days before these actions, Phibun appointed a new chief of the police central investigation bureau, the first indication that the premier intended personnel changes in Phao's agency.

Political tensions in Thailand mounted in the weeks following. By late November, 1955, the political atmosphere in Bangkok was described as being near the "boiling point."[8] Hardly a newspaper appeared which did not headline violent denunciations of high-ranking cabinet officials. Rumors were widely circulated that Phibun was on the verge of effecting a drastic reshuffling—one which would result in the complete removal of General Phao and Field Marshal Phin from the government. Sidewalk orators and the press openly attacked Phao and his police followers for their past oppressive activities. Although the premier seemingly went out of his way to dissociate himself from these attacks on the Phao faction, it is most significant that some of the strongest criticisms of this group appeared in Phibun's own newspapers. The November

[7] See New York *Times*, September 3, 1955.
[8] New York *Times*, November 23, 1955.

political tensions reached their high point when word spread about Bangkok that Police Director General Phao had been arrested at the instigation of Phibun.

The reports of Phao's arrest were not true. On the other hand, they most likely were not as wild a set of rumors as the government subsequently sought to suggest. Tensions among Thailand's leading political figures decreased, however, following a meeting on November 28 attended by Phibun, Phao, Sarit, and Phin. While it is not known what specific discussions and bargaining took place at this secret session, it is obvious that a political rapprochement of some sort was reached among the top Thai politicians. It was only a matter of time, however, until a new crisis would emerge.

Such a crisis appeared sooner than was generally anticipated —indicative, perhaps, of the seriousness of the stresses within the Thai political hierarchy. On December 23, 1955, Field Marshal Phibun announced his intention to resign as premier in early 1956 to make way, as he put it, "for greater democracy."[9] "I have heard," he said, "many criticisms from the people and I think the Government should resign and permit the political parties to decide on a new Government." Seemingly, the purpose of Phibun's announced plans to resign was to get rid of certain cabinet ministers he might not otherwise be able to remove from the government—using as an excuse for their exclusion from a new government "democratic criticism" of their actions. The prime minister blandly admitted that if he resigned, he probably would be asked to form a new government, and that he very likely would do so and would include in his new cabinet men whom he felt the people trusted. The Bangkok *Tribune,* Phibun's own paper, quoting "inner circles," openly attributed the premier's decision to resign to the refusal of certain ministers, recently under public attack, to give up their posts in the government. The chief target of this public criticism, of course, was Phao.

On January 4, 1956, somewhat surprisingly, the Thai premier announced that he no longer intended to resign his office as previously planned. He said that he had talked the

[9] See *Christian Science Monitor,* December 23, 1955.

matter over with members of the Seri Menangkhasila party, which he heads, and that they did not wish him to resign.[10]

Phibun's party, formed after the 1955 legalization of political parties in Thailand, is composed mostly of the military leaders—including Phao, Sarit, and Phin—who helped him return to power in 1948 and who have dominated key public positions since that time—in other words, the 1947 Coup party. The explanation behind Phibun's change of plans about resigning the premiership would seem to lie in a sufficient show of strength within the party to indicate to Phibun that if he proceeded with his announced plans, he would do so virtually without allies. It is possible that the likelihood of bloodshed also was mentioned.

That the Thai political situation continued in a state of flux was evidenced in April, 1956, when Phibun announced a new cabinet shakeup in which Phin Chunhawan lost his deputy premiership while retaining his agriculture portfolio. The balance of contending forces was maintained by the appointment of the ousted deputy communications minister as minister of industry.

The February, 1957, election turned out to be a far more hectic affair than Phibun probably envisaged. The Seri Menangkhasila party won a majority—but not without opposition charges of widespread electoral irregularities. The most torrid of a number of close contests was in Bangkok, where Phibun's party emerged with seven of nine seats. Phibun himself led the field, but second in the race was the more democratically inclined Khuang Aphaiwong, a former prime minister and leader of the Democratic party.

The charges of irregularities in the Bangkok voting resulted in demonstrations by students and the political opposition, followed by the declaration of a state of national emergency on March 2. The government claimed that this action was necessary because there were organized groups "with foreign support" which were attempting to incite unrest in order to overthrow the government. A high government spokesman identified the "foreign support" as Communist, but not "Com-

---

[10] See New York *Times*, January 5, 1956.

munist China, the Soviet Union, or Czechoslovakia"—"It just means Communist support in the form of morale, subversive and financial help."

To make sure the government was ready militarily in the event of a coup attempt, Phibun named Commander in Chief Sarit Thanarat to be commander of all of Thailand's armed forces, including Phao's police. Sarit, addressing demonstrating students on March 2, told them that the election was "completely dirty from all sides." This was an unusual position for a spokesman of the government to take and most likely was a bid by Sarit for popular support for himself.

Although the elections left much to be desired by Western democratic standards, they did represent a step forward along Phibun's alleged "road to democratization" in Thailand. The campaign was a spirited one, there was a surprising degree of free speech, and government corruption and inefficiency were subjected to constant attack. Probably equally significant, at least in the short run, was Sarit's emergence as the leading administration spokesman in an hour of crisis. The first days of March, 1957, indicated that he might have become more than his chief rival's equal.

Although confusion dominated the Thai political scene in the last two years, two facts above all others are clear: the relationship among the three leading figures in Coup party rule of Thailand is in delicate balance, and Phibun is an exceptionally clever politician. Both Phao's police and Sarit's army are self-contained military organizations which still might strike out at one another or at Phibun. Thailand's peace is a peace of accommodation, not of acceptance. As for Phibun, the very fact that he survived in Thailand after nearly a quarter of a century of coup and countercoup is testimony to his political adroitness.

THE ECONOMIC SITUATION IN THAILAND

The present instability in Thailand is by no means entirely political. A major part of it also stems from economic adjustments following decreases in the international price of rice, which provides nearly two-thirds the value of Thai exports, and changes in demand for other Thai primary products as a result of the ending of the Korean war. With more than enough resources to support its present population, Thailand has been traditionally pictured as a pleasant, happy-go-lucky country where everybody has enough to eat, this being offered as a partial explanation for the Thai lack of interest in politics. But Thailand, like other backward countries in this and other parts of the world, is changing. Economic discontent is beginning to appear, especially in the traditionally restive northeastern part of the country. Thailand may have at least one million tons of surplus rice to sell on the world market each year, but with rice prices off, this is not the all-sufficient economic bulwark it was once thought to be. Moreover, the considerable drop in rice production in 1952-1953—6,500,000 tons in that season as compared with 7,310,000 tons in 1951-1952—gave vivid evidence that the country's rice supply was subject to significant variation. As a consequence of this drop in production, the southern provinces actually experienced a seasonal rice shortage—an almost unheard-of event in Thailand.

Several factors have contributed to Thailand's budding economic discontent. Foremost among these has been the drop in the price of rice. Thai rice is of high quality, and through mid 1956 at least, Thailand, unlike Burma, had been able to sell its surplus of the grain.[11] But the price which Thailand was able to obtain for its rice in 1955 was $18.00 a ton below what it had received in 1952. This total drop of $50,000,000 in export value provides a partial explanation for Thailand's present adverse balance of overseas payments, which began in 1953. In 1954 the government tried to reduce its trade deficit by tightening exchange and import controls, but this served primarily to discourage private commerce and to introduce further complications into the country's foreign-trade position.

Another factor contributing to Thailand's newborn economic discontent has been the increasing desire of the Thai peasant to buy a variety of consumer goods which he does not produce for himself. Prices for such goods, however, are today high,

[11] See New York *Times,* May 24, 1956.

partly because many of them have to be imported and partly because a large percentage of the cost of all items for sale in Thailand includes bribery for import licenses.

The fact that Thailand is dependent on imports for so many commodities also is the cause of discontent among more enlightened elements. Money flowed into Thailand during the period 1948-1953 when world demand for the country's products was at an alltime high. Little of this wealth, however, made its way into capital investment for industrial development, hydroelectric plants, and the like. Most of it was squandered on conspicuous spending among the ruling elite, a fact which agitators do not neglect in telling the farmers why there are no modern irrigation projects to permit crop diversification when rice prices are low. The mounting popular discontent with the present government of Premier Phibun, reported in mid 1956, would seem to indicate that the words of such agitators are not falling on infertile ground.[12]

Fundamentally, however, Thai economic discontent is mild, compared to its counterparts elsewhere in Asia. Thailand is not marked by the hunger or extreme poverty so common in many lands of the Far East. Total annual rice consumption, as an indication of the comparative well-being of the Thai people, is the same as for Indonesia, which has four times the population of Thailand. Fish, Thailand's second food staple, also is in plentiful supply. Moreover, Thailand is not afflicted with a land tenure or ownership problem such as exists in the Philippines. The great majority of those engaged in agriculture, which provides approximately one-half of the Thai national income, own their farms, small though these may be in many instances. This absence of a land-tenure problem may yet turn out to be one of Thailand's strongest economic bulwarks.

Although economic discontent is stronger in Thailand today than at any other time in its recent past, and although the country's leaders seem less responsive to such discontent than does, for example, the leadership of Burma and the Philippines, it cannot be said that they are unaware of its existence or that they are not tackling the problem in a number of ways. In

---

[12] See, for example, New York *Times*, May 24, 1956.

July, 1956, for example, General Phao Sriyanon as a spokesman for the government pledged a broad program of rural reforms to the Thai peasantry, including an increase in the income of the average family, which in 1955 was only about fifty dollars a year, and vast improvements in the country's roads so that the farmer might bring his products to market more easily. The response of the Thai government to economic discontent, however, has generally been controlled by expediency rather than by a genuine desire for improvement.

The welfare activities of the Thai government relate particularly to housing and agriculture, but extend also to land reform in those comparatively limited areas where it is required. The present large-scale housing program tackles a major social problem in an enlightened manner, providing, as it does, for government mortgages for the building of new houses or the renovation of old ones and for the rental or purchase from the government of both houses and land. The self-help settlement scheme, if fully implemented, also offers the promise of a brighter future to many Thai peasants. By this scheme the government undertakes the responsibility for setting up whole new communities, surveying the sites for them, constructing roads and irrigation systems, and providing their inhabitants with public utilities, basic machinery, and medical care. Settlers are advanced loans by the government to be used for building homes and acquiring farming implements, feed, and livestock. Under the scheme, settlers are given ten acres of land, which becomes their own at no cost if they repay the government's loan in eight years and if three-fifths of the land is cultivated at that time. Several such settlements already exist, with more promised by the government.

These housing and settlement schemes do not represent the full extent of the Thai leadership's moves to reduce economic discontent in the land. In a somewhat belated attempt to encourage crop diversification, efforts now are being made to increase the output of jute, cotton, and sugar, among other products. In 1954, moreover, plans were announced for an agricultural bank offering farmers credit at low interest rates. In addition, the traditional problem of usury is being dealt with by not renewing pawnbroker's licenses upon expiration. Although much more could be done in the field of irrigation, work is proceeding, nevertheless, on the large-scale irrigation project at Chainat, financed by a loan from the International Bank for Reconstruction and Development. On another social welfare front, free medical treatment—already existent in Bangkok and other towns—is being extended, although not as rapidly as it could be.

The Thai government also is seeking to increase the industrialization of the country as well as to develop its basic resources. The government has made extensive attempts to discover and develop adequate resources of fuel and power, although its efforts to date have not fulfilled the high hopes entertained for such projects. Industrialization is severely hampered by a serious lack of capital; neither foreign nor domestic capital is eager to invest in a land where corrupt business and governmental practices inflate the costs of operation to levels equaled in few other countries in the world. Domestic capital, moreover, tends to be channeled into various areas of short-term investment—loans covering limited periods of time and bearing high interest rates. In spite of this uninviting climate for capital investment, a new cement plant has been constructed, for example, and the port of Bangkok is being rebuilt, the country's inadequate railroad system rehabilitated, and production of electric power increased. In most of the major projects foreign loans have played a leading role.

One bright spot in the Thai economy is the increase in rubber production, which by 1955 had reached 130,000 tons a year and brought Thailand about $75,000,000 in foreign earnings. This accounted for 30 percent of the country's total foreign-exchange receipts as contrasted with 10 percent of such earnings two years earlier. The loss in rice revenues, therefore, has been partly compensated for by the growth in rubber earnings. In addition, Thailand's two other leading exports—tin and teakwood—have remained in demand.

For all the economic changes of the past five years, however, Thailand has remained a primarily agricultural country, highly dependent upon the whims of world demand. Until major changes are made to reduce this dangerous reliance on the demands of distant lands, the country will continue to be in a vulnerable position economically.

THAILAND'S CHINESE MINORITY

If the Thai farmer has become increasingly discontented in recent years, the 2,500,000 Chinese of Thailand have long been dissatisfied with the Phibun regime. Ever since Phibun first became premier in 1938, they have been subject to legal discriminations seeking to reduce the economic stranglehold they are believed to have on the country and to increase Thai participation in business and commerce. With the consolidation of the power of the Chinese Communists in Peiping, fear has increased in government circles concerning the dangers to the state inherent in the presence of such a sizable minority which is both unassimilated and discontented. The present government, however, is doing little to win the Chinese over to its side. The twentyfold increase in 1952 in the alien registration fee, for example, was not designed to increase loyalty among Thailand's Chinese.

The drive to decrease the Chinese (and European) hold on the Thai economy and to induce more Thai to enter commercial and business pursuits is Thailand's own version of the nationalism which has swept Southeast Asia with such furor in recent years. Thailand never having been a colony of a Western power, the developing nationalism of the Thai, as spearheaded by the ultranationalist Phibun, directed itself against the most conspicuous example of foreign domination in the country, alien control of the nation's economy. Nor did the Chinese, who bore the brunt of this attack, really attempt to reduce the furor of this emotionally potent economic nationalism. Increasingly nationalistic themselves, they continued their open allegiance to China, under Chiang Kai-shek as well as Mao Tse-tung, with the result that they further stimulated Thai nationalism. This anti-Chinese discrimination could provide an excuse for intervention by Peiping in the country's affairs.

In late 1956, indications were that the Communists were tightening their grip on Thailand's Chinese, who represent 20 percent of the population of the country and 30 percent of the inhabitants of the capital city of Bangkok. The Communists, as their influence expanded, were gaining control of many organizations which were once pro-Nationalist. Five of Thailand's six Chinese newspapers, for example, look with favor on the Peiping government.

There were several reasons for the growth of Communism among the Chinese of Thailand. Chief among these was a swelling nationalistic pride in a China which was once more laying claim to great-power status. The fact that the leadership of this new China comprised totalitarian Communists made little difference to many Chinese who were more concerned with the fact that the soldiers of Mao's China had held the powerful West at bay in Korea. Many Chinese also were proud of the cheap serviceable goods which began to flow into the Bangkok market from mainland China in 1955. The psychological effect of Chinese-made goods competing with the manufactures of the United States, the United Kingdom, France, and other Western countries should not be underestimated. Large numbers of young Chinese, moreover, frustrated in their efforts to retain their Chinese citizenship while seeking higher education and important positions in Thailand, turned to Communist cells as a means of furthering their ambitions. Here they were indoctrinated in Maoist-Leninist dogma, helped to escape to mainland China for further education, and frequently smuggled back into Thailand to serve themselves as carriers of the Communist propaganda.

Fear also played a major role in the growth of Communism among Thailand's Chinese minority in the years after 1950. The Communists were ruthless in their efforts to play upon the fears of those Chinese who still had members of their family living in mainland China. All weapons were employed in the campaign to intimidate Thailand's Chinese into supporting the Mao regime. In mid 1956 the president of the Chinese Chamber of Commerce sought to resign his office; he said he was overburdened with business activity, but friends

Thailand

said he was mainly influenced by the fact that the two previous presidents had been murdered. Many Chinese join Communist front organizations for safety's sake alone. "It is all right for you Americans to speak against Communist China," one Chinese told a New York *Times* reporter. "If Communist China is recognized, you will be personally safe."[13]

Another cause of anxiety to Thailand's leadership—and, like the Chinese, a source for Communist exploitation—are the estimated fifty thousand Vietnamese refugees who inhabit the Thai side of the Mekong River, which separates Thailand from adjacent Laos. Residents of Thailand since 1946, when they fled from the French who were then reoccupying Indochina after the defeat of the Japanese, they are overwhelmingly Communist in their political orientation. In their homes are to be found pictures of their venerated hero, Ho Chi Minh, leader of Communist north Vietnam. Located in Thailand's traditionally most troublesome area in the northeastern part of the country, these Vietnamese afford excellent opportunity for subversive activity of a variety of sorts. The Communist government of north Vietnam, indeed, has made overtures to the Thai government to permit it to open a consulate in Thailand to handle the affairs of these refugees. The Thai, however, have replied in the negative, fearing Ho and his associates were using the refugee issue to obtain a diplomatic foothold.

Since it would appear that Communism's offensive in the future against Thailand probably will take the form of an intensified effort at infiltration and subversion, rather than overt aggression, the existence of discontented minorities, like the Chinese and Vietnamese, does not augur well for the Phibun government's hopes for future internal tranquillity.

A major source of stability, on the other hand, is the overwhelmingly dominant religion, Buddhism. As in Burma, Laos, Cambodia, and Ceylon, the form of Buddhism adhered to in Thailand is Hinayana or Little School Buddhism. Antagonistic as Communism is to all religions, it would appear that this faith constitutes a major social barrier to Communism's future development in Thailand, particularly in light of the strong

---

[13] Quoted in New York *Times*, May 18, 1956.

hold it has on the hearts and minds of the Thai common people. The Buddhist priests of Thailand, moreover, have been historically apolitical, which would seem to make it unlikely that they will become active workers for Communism, should they ever fall for its glib promises. On the other hand, Buddhist monks in other lands have been far from politically inactive in the past—as, for example, Burma's Buddhist priests, who strongly supported their country's nationalist revolution in the 1930's.

FOREIGN RELATIONS

It is in the realm of foreign relations, rather than domestic affairs, that Thailand has most recently captured the world's headlines. The defection of Pridi Banomyong to the Chinese Communists and the emergence of Phibun as one of the United States' chief allies in the Far East have already been noted. The importance of these events stems in large part from the rise to power of the Communist Mao Tse-tung in China and the considerable attention which his Peiping government is giving to Southeast Asia. The establishment of the Asia-Australasian Liaison Bureau of the World Federation of Trade Unions in late 1949 and the Peace Liaison Committee of the Asian and Pacific Regions in 1952 are examples of the role Communist China is assuming with respect to the other peoples of Asia. The report made on the various Asian "working class liberation movements" at the 1949 Peiping conference of the A.A.L.B. indicates that China is seeking to assume the leadership of Far Eastern Communism, an objective which many say it has already attained. In addition to the contacts China possesses with sympathetic overseas Chinese elements in Thailand today, it also is trying to play on Thai irredentist feelings through its "Thai Autonomous Peoples' Government," set up in early 1953 in the province of Yunnan in south China. The broadcast support from Peiping of Pridi Banomyong for the Chinese Thai state in 1954 was part of Communist China's policy of seeking to control, or at least neutralize, the Thai kingdom through an appeal to irredentist sentiments.

The Chinese moves have alarmed both Phibun Songgram

Thailand

and the United States, which is the main reason for the present alliance between these onetime enemies. This alliance, which was all the easier to arrange because of Thailand's lack of a colonial past with its resulting hatred and suspicion of the West, took formal shape in October, 1950, when Thailand signed a military assistance agreement with the United States. Since that time Phibun has assumed an increasingly larger role in American Far Eastern "cold war" strategy, as witnessed by an American economic aid contribution of $111,900,000 between 1950 and 1956 and "hundreds of millions" of dollars of military help.[14] In September, 1954, Thailand was among the eight nations represented at the Southeast Asian Treaty Organization founding conference at Manila. Much had happened in Southeast Asia between August, 1944, when Phibun stepped down from the premiership, and September, 1954. The fact that a Phibun-premiered government was a participant at Manila was one indication of these changes. Thailand was subsequently the first nation to ratify the Southeast Asian Collective Defense Treaty.

The friendship of the United States has brought many major benefits to the Thai people, aside from the considerations of international politics. Deadly malaria, for instance, has been eliminated as a consequence of American aid. The United States has given Thailand, which depends so vitally on its rice production, a new rice seed which will raise yield threefold. New roads and railroads have been built, and many acres of arid land have been irrigated. A major consequence of American economic and technical assistance to Thailand is the fact that the Thai people today are as friendly toward the United States as are the people of any land in the Far East.

Thai-American cooperation has been evidenced in many ways. Militarily, for example, Thai troops participated in "Operation Firm Link," the first joint maneuvers of the Southeast Asian Treaty Organization powers. Held in February, 1956, the exercise comprised a mock landing in the vicinity of the Thai capital of Bangkok and provided clear evidence of

[14] See report of Bangkok press conference of United States Ambassador Max W. Bishop in New York *Times,* March 4, 1956.

Thai willingness to cooperate with the United States in maintaining a sturdy defense posture against aggression in Asia. On another level of joint endeavor, the government of Phibun Songgram has cooperated with the United States in carrying out an ambitious anti-Communist indoctrination program among the Thai peasantry. Instruction teams associated with this program have gone into almost every corner of the country in order to bolster the spiritual barrier against the spread of Communism, and while some have criticized the program for introducing Communism to many peasants who had not heard of it previously, the record would seem to be one of genuine accomplishment.

The rise of the Chinese Communists to power was only one of two developments to bring Thai and American foreign policies closer together in the postwar years. The other was the increasing success which greeted the efforts of the Viet Minh to achieve power in adjacent Indochina and the infiltration of Thailand by agents of Ho Chi Minh. The Geneva Agreements of 1954, which established the Viet Minh in northern Vietnam and permitted the Communists to maintain an enclave in Laos (the part of Indochina which borders Thailand on the greater part of its eastern boundary) alarmed Phibun and his foreign minister. Viet Minh infiltration into the troublesome northeastern sector of the country has particularly worried the government, but this by no means represents the extent of the Indochinese Communists' efforts to bore away at Thai stability. The Ku-Sap-Be, which appears to have directed the *Manhattan* revolt of June, 1951, was clearly inspired by the Viet Minh, and another body, the Southeast Asia League, existed briefly just before the coup of November, 1947, as a cover for various forms of assistance to Ho's insurgents, including the shipment of military supplies. Few events in the present century, however, have alarmed the Thai government more than the Viet Minh thrusts into relatively defenseless Laos in 1953 and 1954, which dramatized to Phibun and his associates the precarious position in which their country was situated. The reality of this position was brought home at the same time to the United States, which has steadily increased its aid to

Phibun. The collapse of French fighting against Ho in Vietnam, climaxed by the Geneva Agreements, was primarily responsible for the haste with which Washington engineered the Southeast Asian Treaty Organization meeting in September, 1954, attended by Thailand, the United States, and six other nations.

Despite Thailand's record of strong opposition to Communism, reports began to appear in the fall of 1955 of a creeping trend toward neutralism in Thai foreign policy. The Thai reportedly were having second thoughts regarding their hitherto uncompromising stand against Communist China, in large measure as a consequence of the direct negotiations then taking place between Peiping and the United States at Geneva on various matters of dispute between them. The Thai leadership allegedly feared that if Washington made its peace with the Chinese Communists, this might leave Bangkok in an extremely awkward position. As one Western diplomat in Thailand put it, "Thailand is afraid that it is going to be caught way out on a limb alone in Asia."[15]

At about the same time Thai foreign policy was claimed to be veering toward neutralism, the stores in Thailand's capital city of Bangkok were being flooded by a flow of indirectly imported goods from Communist China. The Communist products included such items as bicycles, fountain pens, sewing machines, radios, and alarm clocks—these having reached Thailand through the British crown colony of Hong Kong. Some thought it more than a coincidence that talk of Thai neutralism and large-scale imports from Communist China were occurring almost simultaneously. There was no question, however, regarding Chinese intentions in flooding the Thai market with low-cost, serviceable goods. So cheaply priced were the Communist products that Peiping clearly was losing money on them. China's purpose obviously was political, not economic.

Some observers believed that Thai foreign policy had begun to feel the impact of neutralist sentiment at the Bandung conference of Asian and African nations in Indonesia in the spring of 1955. Reports that a neutral foreign policy was under dis-

---

[15] Quoted in New York *Times*, November 19, 1955.

cussion by the Thai cabinet were alleged to be a logical development of seeds sown at Bandung. The personal overtures made to the Thai foreign minister by Chinese Communist Premier Chou En-lai were said to be enjoying a natural flowering.

Thai Premier Phibun, however, denied emphatically that his country was drifting in the direction of the sort of neutralist foreign policy pursued by the Indians and the Burmese. Speaking at a press conference following American newspaper reports that neutralism was on the rise in Thailand, Phibun not only declared that "we still adhere to *SEATO*," but also noted that "the world situation presents no basis for optimism." "Bulganin is visiting Burma and India and he still adheres to his policy of world domination," the field marshal stated; "so our Army must be ready for any emergency."

The prime minister's words were in harmony with the remarks of General Sarit Thanarat, commander in chief of the Thai army, made three weeks earlier before the national assembly. Discussing the 1956 budget bill, which allocated $41,000,000 to the ministry of defense, General Sarit called for an army and air force "three times the present strength and a Navy four times as strong." Sarit said such a military expansion was necessary, because "Thailand is being subverted more and more by our enemy."

In Sarit's November 11 speech also was to be found a possible indication of why Bangkok had suddenly produced a spate of rumors regarding a rise in neutralist sentiment among Thai officials. "Our Army today could not stop any aggressor," Sarit had told the assembly. "Our Navy could not even keep our gulf clear of mines," he had declared. "I cannot wait for United States aid," he said; "we shall use our own money to make our Army stronger."

The alleged proneutralist turn in the Thai foreign outlook in 1956 and early 1957 could be a mid-twentieth-century instance of the truth of the old Thai saying: "Like the bamboo, we bend with the wind." The Thai did bend with the wind of growing Japanese importance in the Far East in the nineteen-thirties and of increased American influence in the second half of the nineteen-forties and the first half of the fifties. The newest winds are those of Asian neutralism and national sensitivity, and there are those who claim to see signs of the beginning of a "bending with the wind" in Thailand. In September, 1956, for example, there were no less than fifty-five anti-American editorials in Bangkok newspapers (including those owned by Phibun, Phao, and Sarit), compared to only three in the same month of the previous year. In the campaign for the 1957 national assembly elections the charge that United States aid was an expression of "imperialism" was a major platform issue. The governing Seri Menangkhasila party defended its acceptance of American assistance, and the other main campaign participant, former Premier Khuang Aphaiwong's Democratic party, supported United States help but questioned the need for more military than economic aid. The small opposition parties and much of the Thai press, however, were frequently violent in their attacks on United States assistance to Thailand. The criticism leveled at the American aid program by responsible elements, who also were those in power or who had once held power (like Khuang), seemed designed to get more assistance from the United States. There was a growing, very vocal but still very small group of Thai, however, who inclined toward neutralism—and it was this group, which was not part of the ruling elite, which attacked the concept of American aid (rather than the amount). Despite its size and present insignificance, this small anti-American minority will bear watching in the future.

The most likely explanation of Thailand's reported tendency toward neutralism in late 1955 was that the United States was being reminded that Thailand, one of its major Far Eastern allies, was not to be taken for granted. The fantastic expansion in the Thai military services proposed by Sarit was most likely an instance of hyperbole in the service of foreign policy. The Thai leadership felt that the United States was too much concerned with winning over such avowed neutral states as India and Burma, and in the process was neglecting faithful Thailand. The Thai also were genuinely concerned over a possible American-Chinese Communist rapprochement at Geneva.

If in late 1955 the Thai leadership seemed to be seeking to

convince the United States that Thailand might go neutralist if Washington did not pay more attention to it, there were signs a year later that a mild but real revision of Thai foreign policy was taking place. However, Thailand still was a stanch ally of the United States and still a strong foe of Communism, as evidenced, for example, by the July, 1956, police roundup of Chinese newspapermen in Bangkok believed to be Communists. At the same time Thailand seemed to be moving away from its previous inflexible policy of rejecting all Communist overtures. The most conspicuous example of this change in policy was Thailand's lifting of its ban on nonstrategic trade with Communist China and North Korea in the summer of 1956. The announcement of the lifting of the ban, significantly, came only four hours after a Chinese Nationalist good-will mission, headed by Taiwan's foreign minister, had landed at the Bangkok airport. Included in the list of nonstrategic goods which may now be traded with Communist China are rice, timber, industrial tools, agricultural implements, pharmaceuticals, chemicals, cement, fuel oil, lead, and zinc.

The lifting of Thailand's ban on trade in nonstrategic goods with Communist China followed a long and clever campaign for such action by certain Thai opposition assemblymen and the leftist press in Bangkok. These elements, who also called for Thai recognition of Communist China, claimed that China had solved its own economic problems and was now in a position not only to sell cheap goods to Thailand but also to supply technicians to help Thailand in its efforts to industrialize. Some of those who took this line undoubtedly were Communists or Communist sympathizers, but most of the opposition politicians and newspapers backing direct trade with the Chinese Communists showed no signs of being ideologically pro-Communist. Their views did not seem to be shared by Premier Phibun, however.

In March, 1956, Phibun told American Secretary of State John Foster Dulles, visiting Bangkok, that "it is not possible in the world of today to be neutral." General Phao, however, told a press conference in July that the reason the Thai press seemed so sympathetic to Communist China was that the Thai people felt a certain closeness to the Chinese and that, "after all, for the Thai people, mainland China is China."

Former Premier Seni Pramoj put it this way: "Communism is dynamic. Check it in the West and it expands in the East. . . . Adherence to Marxism-Leninism by the Soviet Union means no peace for the world until and unless the whole world is Soviet. The Communists pose a long-range threat to us. The question is not whether, but when."[16] There were indeed signs of new Communist pressures in the states to Thailand's immediate east and west. In July, 1956, Chinese Communist troops had crossed over the Sino-Burmese border; in August, 1956, the Laotian government entered into an agreement with the Communist rebel Pathet Lao movement.

The meaning of the Communist moves have not gone unperceived by the Thai premier. Thailand has relaxed its foreign policy a little bit—possibly to test the outcome of such a relaxation. There are no indications that Phibun and his associates will seek to send strategic goods to China, or that they are less firm in their backing of the Southeast Asian Treaty Organization, or that they will not seek to continue their support of United States policy in Asia and the Far East. If the pressures are increased, Thailand may move in the direction of the sort of neutralism espoused by India, Indonesia, and Burma. There is greater likelihood, however, that such a move on the part of the Communists will serve to reinforce the presently close Thai-American defense cooperation. Collaboration between the two states would seem to be firmer today than at any other time in history, despite the recent relaxation in a hitherto inflexible Thai foreign policy.

Postwar Thailand's international relations clearly owe their complexion to the tensions and urgencies of the cold war between the Sino-Soviet bloc and the United States and its allies. The country's future, moreover, will probably be determined by the outcome of that competition.

[16] Quoted by Arnold C. Brackman in *Christian Science Monitor*, September 19, 1956.

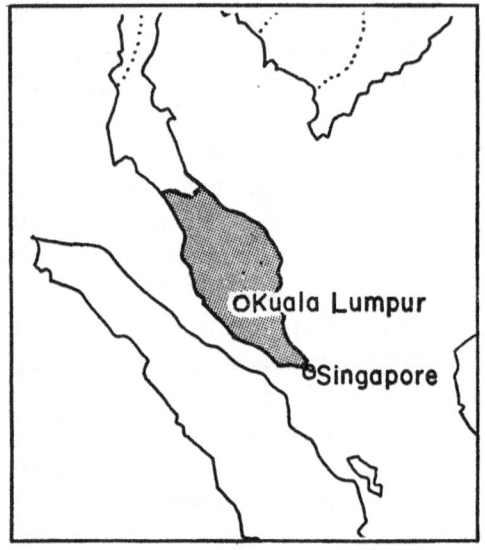

CHAPTER 6

MALAYA
A Problem in Nation Building

THE SITUATION in Malaya is quite different from that in any of the other countries of Southeast Asia. Before the Second World War, Malaya was politically asleep. For most of the area the governmental structure was feudal—sultanates under a complicated system of British protection. The native population had become a minority as a result of immigration chiefly from China and India. As if to make up for lost time, the political tempo since the war has steadily accelerated. The British government has now promised the people of the Malay Peninsula self-government within the Commonwealth in 1957, but the three main population groups—Malayans, Chinese, Indians—are still a long way from having merged into a nation. How to unite these culturally divergent groups into a national community on which a democratic political superstructure can be built, and that in a relatively short time, is the formidable and urgent problem of Malaya.

The Portuguese were the first Europeans to establish themselves in Malaya. They set up a trading post and built a fortress at Malacca, where they remained for over a century. The Dutch conquered Malacca in 1641, but they did not extend their control over the peninsula; in 1824 they traded Malacca for Bencoolen in Sumatra, a post which the British had retained after returning the East Indies to the Netherlands in 1816. Earlier, in 1786, the British had obtained the cession of the island of Penang from the sultan of Kedah, and in 1800 they obtained from the same ruler some territory on the peninsula opposite Penang. In 1819 the British acquired the island of Singapore, just off the tip of the peninsula, from the sultan of Johore. This strategic point was secured by Sir Thomas Stamford Raffles, who had been governor of Java during the British occupation of the Indies (1811-1816) and who at the time he obtained the cession of the island was governor of Bencoolen. Raffles realized the strategic importance of the island for both trade and defense, and was determined to get control over it for his country.

After establishing themselves at these key points, the British did nothing for half a century to extend their control. However, in the last quarter of the nineteenth century, the British government induced a number of Malay sultans to accept its protection, and in 1909 Thailand by treaty transferred to Great Britain "all rights of suzerainty, protection, administration and control" over the sultanates of Kedah, Perlis, Kelantan, and Trengganu. In 1914 the sultan of Johore accepted British protection, and with this agreement all of the Malay states except Patani, which was under Thailand, had been brought under British indirect rule.

British Malaya before the war was composed of three different parts, the Straits Settlements, the Federated Malay States, and the Unfederated Malay States. The Straits Settlements included the island of Singapore, Penang with Province Wellesley, and Malacca, together with Christmas Island and the Cocas-Keeling group in the Indian Ocean. These areas were British territory and were directly governed as a crown colony. The Straits Settlements had an area of only 1,260 square miles, but had a population of 1,114,015 (1931 census). At the head of the administration was a governor who acted under instructions from the secretary of state for the colonies in London. He was assisted by an executive council which was composed of eight official and three unofficial members, the latter nominated by the governor. The executive council had only advisory powers. There was also a legislative council composed of the governor as president and thirteen official and thirteen unofficial members, eleven of whom were nominated by the governor. The remaining two unofficial members were elected by the British members of the chambers of commerce at Singapore and Penang. There was little evidence of a desire in the Straits Settlements for a more democratic constitution.

The Federated Malay States were composed of the sultanates of Perak, Selangor, Negri Sembilan, and Pahang. They had a combined area of 27,540 square miles and a population in 1931 of 1,713,096. The division of so small a country as Malaya into so many separate administrations was an obvious disadvantage. By agreements with their rulers these four states were federated in 1895 under a resident general. It was hoped that all of the states would eventually enter the federation, but when the nonfederated states saw that membership involved considerable loss of freedom, they were not attracted by it. In 1909 a federal council was established, with the governor of the Straits Settlements as president under the title of high commissioner, and with the president general transformed into the chief secretary. The state councils now lost nearly all of their powers. In 1935 the British introduced a policy of decentralization, and the state councils recovered much of their former authority.

The Unfederated Malay States were five in number, namely, Johore, Kedah, Perlis, Kelantan, and Trengganu. They had an area of 22,080 square miles and a population in 1931 of 1,526,604, about half of which was found in the single state of Johore.

All of the Malay states were protectorates of the British crown. The rulers had agreed to accept the advice of a British adviser or resident except in matters connected with Malay custom or the Mohammedan religion. The sultans or rajas were assisted by councils composed of official and unofficial members, with the former in a majority. The rule was in form "indirect," but most of the services were under a united British Malayan civil service responsible to the governor of the Straits Settlements, who served simultaneously as high commissioner for the Malay States.

The British rule in Malaya was successful, especially in view of the situation which had developed. A great influx of foreign capital and of immigrants into a country with a feudal society created a large number of problems, but the administration ran smoothly and was highly efficient. The social services, judged by Asian standards, were very good. Much of the credit for this goes to the Malayan civil service, but it was made possible by the high level of prosperity which Malaya enjoyed.

THE JAPANESE OCCUPATION

Before Pearl Harbor, Malaya was placid; during the war it completely lost that character. This was in large part due to the impact of the Japanese occupation. The defeat of the British and the imposition of a new foreign rule caused shock and brought upheaval. The Japanese treated the three main population groups, the Malays, the Chinese, and the Indians, differently; hence the effects of the occupation varied widely. The experience did not make for national unity but for increased antagonism between the three races. However different the treatment of the various races by the Japanese, all were exposed to anti-Western and pro-Asian propaganda. Many acquired habits of violence.

The Malays continued to carry on the government under the Japanese as they had under the British. They were entrusted with higher positions, if not always more responsible ones, than they had held under the British. They acquired a taste for the top positions and won confidence in themselves. The Japanese also indoctrinated the Malays with patriotic sentiments for Malaya, the Coprosperity Sphere and Japan. Feeling for the last two did not take or was quickly lost, but the first found fertile ground.

The Chinese community suffered severely in the war. The Japanese were bent on destroying active supporters of the Kuomintang, active Communists, and members of the volunteer forces who had not surrendered. Chinese were massacred in the early days of the occupation. The British had trained and armed a nucleus of guerrillas before Singapore fell, and as a result of Japanese brutality their number increased. Organized as the Malayan People's Anti-Japanese Army, they became strong and were very effective in disrupting Japanese supply lines, but they became more and more under the control of Communist leadership. They punished collaborators, levied contributions on whomever they could, and collected them by fair means or foul. They were joined by persons who had no political motives but who resorted to terrorism and extortion as a means of making a living in the prevailing economic chaos.

The effects of the period on the Chinese is succinctly summarized by two Malayan scholars as follows: "No one is likely to underrate the importance of the Occupation period in stimulating guerilla organization among the Chinese. But other effects may have been in the aggregate more important: the inculcation of the habit of paying extortion money; the vast increase in bribery and irregularity of all kinds; the undermining of the pre-war respect for Government and law; and the stimulation to fantastic extremes of the tendency among the South Seas Chinese to be steadfastly neutral on all political issues and concentrate on personal advancement."[1]

The Indians were likewise stirred up by the Japanese occupation, but in a quite different manner. They were used by the Japanese as a base and instrument for a drive to "liberate" India. An "Indian National Army" was recruited, often by duress, from the Indians in Malaya and financed by extortion levied on wealthy Indians with the protection of the Japanese authori-

---

[1] T. H. Silcock and Ungku Abdul Aziz, *Nationalism in Malaya* (Secretarial Paper No. 8, Eleventh Conference, Institute of Pacific Relations, Lucknow, India, October 3-15, 1950) (New York, 1950).

Malaya

ties. No doubt many of the leaders in the movement were sincere Indian patriots, and they may have thought that they were using the Japanese for their own cause. The "Indian National Army" was defeated, and the movement came to nought. However, the Indians became more politically conscious, they learned how to organize, and they acquired a sense of importance.

Much of what happened in postwar Malaya can be better understood if it is remembered that the war ended abruptly and in a quite unexpected manner. The British believed that the liberation of the country would require a campaign fought in Malaya. They planned a series of troop landings on the coast combined with attacks on the Japanese forces by guerrillas operating from the jungles. But Japan capitulated before the campaign got under way, and unfortunately, the British were unable to reoccupy Malaya for several weeks. Into this power vacuum the Communist guerrillas, previously armed and supplied by the Allies, moved rapidly and expanded. They organized labor unions in all the chief centers and in practically every trade. Where necessary, they used intimidation and terrorism. The British army which finally moved in was unprepared for the task of reoccupation. The conduct of some of the troops and of some members of the military administration did little to restore British prestige. Small wonder that the peoples of Malaya at long last began to think about governing themselves.

POSTWAR POLITICAL REORGANIZATION

It will be helpful, before turning to the specific plans for governmental reform, to have a good look at Malayan society. According to the 1947 census, Malaya, including the Straits Settlements, had a population of 5,848,910. Of this number a little more than 38 percent of the total were Malays; about 5.5 percent were Malaysians (chiefly Indonesians); nearly 45 percent were Chinese; about 10.5 percent were Indians and Pakistanis. Europeans and Eurasians accounted for 0.3 percent each. These figures were for the whole of Malaya. The racial complexion of Malaya and Singapore separately was quite different. In Malaya exclusive of Singapore the Malays and Malaysians accounted for nearly 50 percent of the total population, the Chinese for a little more than 38 percent, and the Indians and Pakistanis for a little less than 11 percent. In Singapore the Chinese constituted nearly 78 percent, the Malays and Malaysians slightly more than 11 percent, and the Indians about 7.5 percent of the population. Singapore, with a population of 941,000 in 1947, and estimated at about 1,200,000 in 1957, is predominantly a Chinese city. Penang is also strongly Chinese, with over 55 percent of the population of that urbanized island belonging to that race.

The population of the country was growing rapidly, even though Chinese and Indian immigration during the depression and since the war had almost ceased. The rate of population growth was well over 2 percent—highest among the Chinese and lowest among the Malays. The fertility of all the communities was high, but the death rate among the Malays was much higher than among the Chinese and Indians.[2]

About 60 percent of the Chinese in Malaya and about 50 percent of the Indians were locally born. The number returning to their native country was considerably greater among the Indians than among the Chinese. Since the Second World War, immigration has ceased to be an important factor in population growth. Religiously the population of Malaya was divided as follows: Islamic—2,575,000 or 44 percent; Confucian-Buddhist —2,560,000 or 43 percent; Hindu—510,000 or nearly 9 percent; and Christian—120,000 or about 2 percent. Religious divisions ran along racial lines; the Malays and Malaysians are Moslems almost to a man, the Chinese are Confucianist-Buddhist, and

[2] The total population in 1957 was well over 7,000,000. Malaya is generally regarded as underpopulated, but T. E. Smith in his *Population Growth in Malaya: An Analysis of Recent Trends* (London, 1952) sounds another note. "Although Malaya is a small country it does not yet suffer from the same population pressure as Java, China, India and the Philippines. Nevertheless there must clearly be a fairly low upper limit to the number of years during which Malaya can absorb an annual population increase of this order without feeling acute indigestion. Over Malaya as a whole, the density of the population was estimated at 115 persons per square mile in the 1947 Census Report; and it must be borne in mind that the country includes very considerable areas of steep mountainside which are not likely to be opened up in the foreseeable future." Page 2.

Malaya

the Indians are predominantly Hindu, with a small number of Moslems and Sikhs.

The literacy rate for the whole population of Malaya, including all ages, was 32 percent. It was highest among the Indians (40 percent) and lowest among the Malays (25 percent).

Malaya had, and still has, what is sometimes called a "plural society." The inhabitants of Malaya were not culturally and economically integrated; on the contrary, they were divided into sharply separated racial communities. The native Malays were the rice growers and small-holder producers of rubber. The lower and middle positions in the government were their patrimony. Few were found in wage-earning employment, in the professions, or in commerce. About 70 percent of the Indians and Pakistanis were laborers, chiefly on rubber plantations. A considerable number were in commerce and the professions. The Chinese were engaged in rubber cultivation both as laborers and as small holders, and they provided most of the laborers in the tin mines and a very large percentage of the factory workers. They also owned and operated tin mines, were strong in the professions, and very nearly dominated the commercial life of the country. The Europeans held the top positions in the government, were large producers of tin and rubber, and played a leading role in finance and shipping.

The economy of Malaya is heavily concentrated on the production of rubber and tin for export. Malaya is the world's largest producer of tin and is second only to Indonesia in the output of natural rubber. These two commodities generally total over 80 percent of the value of all domestic exports and account for about a fifth of the national income. Singapore has a large entrepôt trade. The Malayan per capita income is the highest in Asia ($250 in 1953).

The British government planned a thoroughgoing reorganization of the government of Malaya after the war in the direction of unification and democracy. The Malay aristocracy would be deprived of their privileged positions and the constitutional patchwork replaced by two governments; a Union of Malaya, which would include all the territories on the peninsula and the island of Penang, and Singapore. The latter was to be detached from the mainland and made a separate unit of government for two reasons. First, Singapore was a cosmopolitan free port, whose prosperity was in large part due to its entrepôt trade. Its economic interests were not wholly tied up with Malaya. Secondly, exclusion of Singapore from the union would give a majority to the Malays, the racial community least politically conscious and least advanced economically, and thus make the proposed changes more acceptable to it.

The British plans were based upon the assumption that it would require a campaign of heavy fighting to drive the Japanese out of Malaya and that in this campaign British forces landing on the shores would be assisted greatly by Chinese guerrillas operating in the Japanese rear, with the Malay rulers, civil servants, and police giving passive if not active military aid to the enemy. The British prewar policy of "protecting" the Malays was regarded by the Chinese as unjustifiable favoritism. With the record of Malay collaboration with the enemy and active resistance by the Chinese, the old British policy could not be restored. However, the British did not return to Malaya in the manner expected. The Japanese surrendered without the necessity of a campaign in Malaya; as a result the plan had either to be abandoned or carried out under unanticipated conditions. The British government decided on the latter course.

In pursuance of the decision to proceed with the plans, Sir Harold McMichael was sent to Malaya with essentially similar treaties for the rulers to sign. The sultans apparently felt that they had no alternative, for they all agreed to sign away most of the independence of their states and practically all of their own prerogatives. Strangely, the non-Malay communities, which stood to gain greatly by the proposed Malayan Union, did little or nothing in support of the proposal, but the response to it of the Malays, and especially of the Malay intellectuals, was immediate and strongly adverse. A United Malay National Organization (U.M.N.O., as it became popularly known) was formed under the leadership of Dato Onn Bin Jaafar as a peninsular movement to oppose the union proposals. Other organizations sprang up with the same purpose. Though the Malayan Union constitution was inaugurated in April, 1946, and nominally remained in force for two years, some of its more important provisions were never given effect, and negotiations with the sultans and the U.M.N.O. for a revision of the constitution were begun almost immediately. Out of these negotiations emerged the new federation constitution which went into effect on February 1, 1948.

With the replacement of the union by the federation the Malay community had scored a victory over the non-Malay communities. The Malays were bitterly opposed to a democratic, unified government, for such a system would give the Chinese and Indians great influence in the government, if not control over it. The intellectual Malays had no love for the old feudal system, but they were unwilling to see it swept away if political reform should open the door to political power by the nonnative groups. They were caught in a dilemma. There was only a limited place for them in the old system, but they feared that a more democratic system would improve their position little, if any. Citizenship and the right to vote were the crux of the problem. In the union proposals the provisions for citizenship were quite liberal; under the federation constitution they were more restricted. By excluding Singapore from the federation, the Malay electorate was given an additional advantage on the peninsula.

The Malay nationalists were caught in a difficult position between the foreign rulers and the nonnative Chinese and Indian masses. They were torn between their desires and their fears. They desired self-government, but they feared that they could not obtain this without making political concessions to the Chinese and Indians which would give the latter great political power. The Chinese and Indians already had great economic power; the Malays hesitated to give them political power in addition, for that would give them almost complete domination of the country. As the Malays saw it, Malaya was their country and all others were intruders. They were bitter about the British policy which had encouraged the immigration of alien races to develop the tin and rubber industries. The Malays felt that they had become stepchildren with little share in the prosperity of the country, that British policy had made it possible for the Chinese to take over the country economically.

The Chinese community was reproached for having only an economic interest in Malaya but otherwise being wholly apathetic to things Malayan. The Chinese answer to this charge was that by their hard work, thrift, and enterprise they had made modern Malaya—without enjoying any economic or other privileges as did the Malays. The latter had preference in government positions, and the best rice lands were reserved for them. As the Chinese saw it, the great weakness of the Malay was his narrow communal attitude and his obsession with the idea that the Chinese and Indians were determined to keep him down economically. They rejected the charge that there was any conscious or concerted attempt to exclude the Malay from commerce. The Chinese contended further that little inducement was offered them to become loyal Malayans, since they were practically denied citizenship in the states, and though all Chinese born in the Straits Settlements were British subjects, this citizenship meant little because it conferred no political rights. Their loyalty, the Chinese declared, could be won by giving them a better status.

The Malays were obviously in a weak position to resist reforms. They had collaborated with the Japanese. Moreover, more than half of the population under the old governmental system was excluded from participation in government. The need for unification and democratization was obvious, especially in the atmosphere of the postwar world. The Malays were nevertheless able to defeat the union. They were in a powerful position because the traditional, existing feudal system favored them, and any attempt to impose a radically new constitutional system against their opposition would lead to chaos. They were also aided in their opposition to the union by a number of influential British who were former Malayan civil servants, including Sir Frank Swettenham, a former governor of the Straits Settlements. The British government very probably had also come to see the advantage of federation over union, in that it favored the conservative Malays over the Chinese, among whom there was a strong radical element. The Malays hoped to put off democratization of the government until their economic and social position had improved.

In June, 1948, the Communist insurrection began. Thus to the problem of communalism there was added militant Communism. There had been sporadic violence and lawlessness before this, but now it became more general, continuous, and systematic. The purpose of the movement was to set up a Communist republic of Malaya. To cope with the situation, the government declared a state of emergency.

The Malayan Communist party is an offshoot of the Chinese Communist party. It gained some strength and prestige in the mid twenties, during the period when Dr. Sun Yat Sen, in order to gain his ends, had resorted to collaboration with Soviet Russia. The organized terrorism which has disturbed Malaya for nearly a decade had its base in the Malayan People's Anti-Japanese Army. This group, recruited mainly from young Chinese, operated in the jungle behind a screen of agents in every village. Toward the end of the war they were supplied with arms by the British. The Communists burrowed deeply into this movement. After the war the British encouraged the development of labor unions; the Communists promptly infiltrated them. In 1948 the Communists turned to organized violence to achieve their ends. Chinese Kuomintang leaders were killed in their homes, European planters were murdered, and police stations were attacked. The terrorism thus begun was prolonged over months and years. In April, 1950, an attempt was made on the life of Sir Franklin Gimson, the governor of Singapore, and in October, 1951, Sir Henry Gurney, British high commissioner to the Federation of Malaya, was assassinated.

Though the number of guerrillas was estimated at only 3,000 to 6,000, the campaign to suppress them has been costly. Some 35,000 British soldiers and some air force units, together with a large number of extra police and special constables, were mobilized to fight the Communist guerrillas. The cost of the campaign in money was about $100,000,000 a year.

A number of factors explain why the war against the Communists has been difficult and costly. Much of Malaya is still jungle, which is ideal for guerrilla warfare. The large rubber plantations offer much the same advantage. The British commanders said that fighting the guerrillas was like using a sledgehammer to crack a nut or like hunting for a needle in a haystack. In addition the guerrillas could make use of some 500,000 Chinese who had squatted on the fringes of the jungle. During the depression in the 1930's Chinese laborers in tin mines and on the rubber plantations turned to the lands on the edge of the jungle for a livelihood. Under the Japanese occupation their numbers were greatly increased by thousands of Chinese who fled from the towns. The squatters were in the clutches of the bandits. Since they lived in areas where the police could not protect them, they were forced to furnish food, supplies, money, and information. The guerrillas also obtained recruits from the squatters. Thus no real progress could be made against the bandits unless something were done about the squatters. The solution was a resettlement program. The squatters were given small plots of land in accessible communities where they could enjoy the advantages of education and social services.

The resettlement of so many people was necessarily an arduous and expensive task. It also made for more bad feeling on the part of the Malays toward the Chinese. Ninety percent of the guerrillas were Chinese, but the Chinese community did little to help suppress them. Few Chinese joined the police force of the federation. And now the government was spending huge sums on the community which was economically least needy.

TOWARD SELF-GOVERNMENT

Malaya's problems are indeed formidable. While still fighting to suppress a Communist insurrection, the multiracial society is proceeding with a rapid democratization of its government. This may seem a dangerous undertaking, yet an argument frequently made is that the battle against the Communists cannot be won without the active aid of the whole Chinese community, and the allegiance and support of the Chinese cannot be won unless they are given citizenship and the right to participate on equal terms with the Malays in a democratic government. Sometimes it is made to appear very simple: that the Communist disturbances will subside almost immediately after political reforms have been instituted.

The Federation of Malaya, which was set up in 1948, comprises eleven units: the nine Malay States and the Settlements of Penang and Malacca. At the head of the government is the high commissioner appointed by the British crown. He is assisted by a deputy high commissioner and a federal executive council. The federation agreement also provided for a legislative council composed of 75 members, of whom 50 were unofficial, 9 were the presidents of the state councils, 2 from the settlement councils, and the remainder were ex officio and official members. While the majority of the members were unofficial, they were nominated by the high commissioner to represent the various racial and interest groups of the country. The federation agreement also established federal citizenship "designed to draw together with a common loyalty all those who can be said to regard Malaya as their true home."

The federation agreement provided that "as soon as circumstances and local conditions [would] permit," legislation would be introduced for elections to the federal legislature and to the state and settlement legislative councils. In pursuance of this purpose, municipal elections were held in 1951 in Penang, Malacca, and Kuala Lumpur, and in 1952 the legislative council passed a law providing for the election of village councils throughout the federation.

A step in the direction of responsible government was taken in 1951, when Sir Henry Gurney, the British high commissioner, broadened the central secretariat to include three Malays, a Chinese, and a Ceylonese. Dato Onn Bin Jaafar, the chairman of the United Malay National Organization and a leading advocate of early self-rule for Malaya, was made head of the department of home affairs. The new appointees directed their departments, but they were responsible to the high commissioner.

Another step forward on the road to democratization was a citizenship law which became effective in September, 1952. By this law some 1,100,000 Chinese, which was between 50 and 60 percent of the federation's Chinese population, acquired citizenship. Of the Indian population, 180,000—about 30 percent—acquired citizenship. The Indians and the Chinese were not altogether happy about the provisions of the law. The law did not automatically grant citizenship to all persons born in Malaya, as the non-Malays demanded, but only to second generation non-Malays.

After these progressive steps the British government seemed to hesitate. Oliver Lyttelton, colonial secretary, in the house of commons in July, 1952, warned against moving toward self-government in Malaya too rapidly, stating that there was not yet enough fusion and unity to make self-government successful. He expressed the belief that the establishment of an effective system of self-government would take a decade or two. He declared that an immediate grant of full self-government would soon be followed by bitter racial strife, conflict, and confusion. Early in 1954 the colonial secretary rejected a request from the leaders of the Alliance formed by the U.M.N.O. and the M.C.A. (the Malayan Chinese Association) for direct talks in London on federal elections and constitutional issues. In September, 1954, five members of the British parliament visited Malaya and made a statement that Malaya should not set a target date for self-government.

The political leaders of Malaya reacted strongly to these declarations. The strongest Malay party, the U.M.N.O., and the large Chinese organization, the M.C.A., had already formed an alliance in order to present a common front. They were now joined by the Malay Indian Association (M.I.A.). Sir Cheng-lock Tan, president of the powerful M.C.A., in December, 1953, issued a strong statement in protest to the trend of the British pronouncements. He demanded self-government for Malaya within "a reasonable time." He declared that if the transfer of power was delayed too long, the people might be provoked into impatience and hostility, and the contention that national unity must precede self-government and that communal antipathies made such unity impossible would be interpreted as a policy of "divide and rule." The idea that the Chinese monopolized the wealth of Malaya, he declared, was a myth; they actually controlled less than 20 percent of the rubber industry and 25 percent of the tin mines. Big business was almost entirely in European hands, asserted Sir Cheng-lock.

Regardless of the official British views on the feasible rate of progress toward self-government, events from 1952 moved rapidly and irresistibly toward that end. In the Kuala Lumpur municipal elections of that year the U.M.N.O. and the M.C.A. formed a local alliance and won nine of the twelve seats. The alliance was so successful that it was extended to the municipal election campaigns throughout the country. In March, 1953, the U.M.N.O. and the M.C.A. announced an agreement for the extension of the alliance to the general elections for the federal legislative council. In August of that year the Alliance held a national congress which adopted a resolution making an independent state within the British Commonwealth and full responsible democratic government its goal and demanding that elections to the federal legislature be held in 1954. Tengku Abdul Rahman, president of the U.M.N.O., and Sir Cheng-lock Tan, president of M.C.A., had accepted the challenge of Colonial Secretary Lyttelton and were seeking to prove that the Malays and the Chinese could cooperate for constructive purposes. In this connection it should be noted that this movement was in no small measure due to the work of Malcolm MacDonald, who since 1946 had served the British government as commissioner general for Southeast Asia. He instigated the formation of the Communities Liaison Committee, which by its studies, recommendations, and work did much to bring the leaders of the various races together.

In 1954 another step forward was taken. The legislative council was enlarged to 98 members, of whom 52 were to be elected. Moreover, after the elections to the legislative council the members of the executive council would be appointed in consultation with the leaders of the group or groups commanding a majority of the elected members, thereby creating a sort of limited responsible government. In the elections held in July, 1955, the Alliance, of which the Malay Indian Association had also become a member, won 51 of the 52 elective seats. As a result of this triumph, the leader of the U.M.N.O. and of the Alliance, Tengku Abdul Rahman, was named chief minister by the high commissioner.

Chief Minister Rahman and his Alliance now pressed hard for a timetable for independence within the Commonwealth. A Federation of Malay Constitutional Conference met in London in January, 1956, attended by representatives of the Malay rulers, the Alliance, and the United Kingdom. It was announced on February 6 that an agreement had been reached. "Every effort" would be made by the parties to enable Malaya to achieve independence within the British Commonwealth "if possible" by August, 1957. In the meanwhile, Britain was to speed the turnover of full internal self-government as rapidly as possible, reserving control of foreign relations and defense until full independence was achieved. A treaty of defense and mutual assistance would regulate the special relations between the United Kingdom and the Federation of Malaya. Under the terms of this treaty the United Kingdom would be given the right to maintain in the federation the forces necessary to fulfill its Commonwealth and international obligations. In January, 1957, London announced that such an agreement had been signed. Under its terms the federation is to receive £20,000,000 ($56,000,000) in financial assistance.

A draft constitution for independent Malaya was published in February, 1957. The constitution aims to provide a common nationality for the future, but during a transition period the Malays will continue to enjoy certain special privileges with respect to Malay reservations and quotas for admission to public services, eligibility for scholarships, and the issuance of permits and licenses. The draft constitution further provides that Malay shall be the national language, but with English also the official language for a decade. The supreme head of the federation will be the senior among the rulers of the nine constituent states. The parliament will consist of a house of representatives of one hundred members, entirely elected, and a senate of twenty-two elected and eleven nominated members. Malaya would become a dominion within the Commonwealth.

SINGAPORE

It was felt that to incorporate this large island-city, whose population was 80 percent Chinese, in the federation was politically unwise. As a result of this separation, Singapore's problems and development must be traced independently of the federation.

The legislative council was reconstituted in 1951 with a membership of 25. Of the 16 unofficial members, 4 were nominated by the governor, 3 were named by the Chamber of Commerce, and 9 were elected by constituencies. Only a fraction—48,000—of the persons qualified to vote had registered, and of these only 52 percent actually voted. In 1953 automatic registration was introduced, whereby the number was increased to 300,000. In 1954 a commission was appointed, with Sir George Rendel as chairman, to advise on the amendment of the constitution. The commission recommended changing the name of the legislative council to legislative assembly and increasing the number of elective members to 25. These recommendations were adopted by the government, and elections under the new arrangement were held in April, 1955. The results surprised everyone. Five main parties ran candidates. Three of these (the Progressives, the Democrats, and the Alliance) were rightwing, and two (the Labor Front and Peoples' Action Party) were leftwing. The Labor Front won 10 seats; the Progressives, 4; the Peoples' Action Party, 3; the Alliance, 3; the Democrats, 2; and independents, 3. The left wing won its victory on promises of repealing the emergency regulations, the immediate achievement of independence, and the creation of a socialist society.

The governor called upon David Marshall, the unofficial leader of the Labor Front, to form a government. He made a coalition, not with the Peoples' Action Party, but with the Alliance. With the support of two Labor Front members appointed by the governor and the three ex officio members, Marshall had behind him only 18 of the 32 members of the legislative assembly. Marshall had a short and stormy career as chief minister. The extreme left made war upon him and his government. The life of the city was crippled by a series of strikes aided and abetted by the Chinese middle-school students. Student strikes and violence are a strange phenomenon of Singapore society. The students rioted against national military service in May, 1954, and they struck on the eve of the 1955 elections against the government's refusal to register their newly organized Students' Union. In May they aided the bus strikers and furiously attacked the police.

Marshall, the first chief minister, hoped to achieve self-government for Singapore, and the union of Singapore with Malaya. Tengku Abdul Rahman, the chief minister of the federation, rejected the advances for union. He apparently had no desire to endanger the present favorable political developments on the peninsula by bringing into the federation this urban center with its large Chinese population and its strongly leftist, if not Communist, tendencies. Marshall also failed in obtaining self-government for Singapore. He headed a delegation to London for a conference like that which had brought success to Rahman and his federation delegation only a few months earlier, but Singapore was a different story, due primarily to its position as an important military base. The British government offered extensive concessions, but not enough to satisfy Marshall, who said he wanted the whole loaf or none. Britain offered to replace the present constitution with one in which the legislative assembly would be enlarged by 25 seats and which would provide full responsible government. Marshall was willing to concede to Britain the right to maintain the military base and to retain control over external affairs, but no powers over internal security unless and until the Singapore government should completely fail to maintain order. The British argued that external defense and internal security were inseparably intertwined, that internal disorder would affect the security of the military base, and that therefore Britain must have emergency powers with respect to the maintenance of law and order. On this issue the negotiations broke down. Marshall's emotional temperament and the lack of unity in his delegation were contributing factors. In conformity with the declaration he made before leaving for London that he would resign if he failed in his mission, Marshall quit as chief minister in June, 1956. He was succeeded by Lim Yew Hock, a seasoned labor leader. Lim is less spectacular than Marshall but a more effective administrator. He seems to be determined to put Singapore's house in order and then press for self-government.

MALAYAN PROBLEMS

The chief problem which confronts Malaya is that of transforming its multiracial, "plural" society into a Malayan nation. Malaya's political leaders contend that democracy and self-government will aid the process of amalgamation—indeed, that it is a necessary condition. Marshall and Rahman have also argued that for Malaya it is either nationalism and independence, or Communism. While there is much validity in the first contention, it is also true that popular elections can be very divisive. Closely connected with this general problem of nation building are others, such as citizenship and the right of suffrage, education, and the future relation of Singapore to Malaya.

The Chinese and Indians fear that they will not be accorded equal rights, equal justice, and equal opportunities with the Malays in an independent Malaya. At the moment Malays have a great political advantage in the federation, and they are loath to surrender this until their economic condition has much improved. Some 1,600,000 people in 1955 had the right to vote in the federation. Of these, 350,000 were non-Malays. Because of their participation in the Alliance, the non-Malays were accorded more generous treatment in the distribution of seats in the legislative council (17 of the 52 elective seats) than their voting strength would warrant, but still much less than their percentage of the total population. As the Malays see it, the Chinese have the tremendous advantage of having most of the productive property of the country, by far the largest number of the more educated people, and nearly all of the important economic contacts. To grant the Chinese political power while they are still economically and socially backward would be to commit communal suicide. In effect, this means that the Malays are demanding that the Chinese aid the Malays in entering the world of trade and finance, and that the government expenditures on education and social services primarily for Malays be greatly increased.[3] The Chinese, of course, can have little interest in independence for Malaya if the qualifications for citizenship are going to be such as to restrict suffrage to a small number of their community. They want the right of citizenship extended to all persons born in Malaya and making it their home.

The Malays feel that their predicament was created by the encouragement by the British rulers of the non-Malay immigration. How to solve this problem is the Malay's chief concern. The Malays have thought of ways in which the position of the non-Malays, and especially the Chinese, can be reduced. Legislation of recent years has already made it difficult for Chinese who were born in Malaya or have long been resident there to reenter the country. To exclude the Chinese from citizenship is no longer possible. The prohibition of further Chinese immigration and the encouragement of Indonesian immigration might help redress the balance somewhat. The incorporation of Sarawak, Brunei, and British North Borneo[4] into the federation would decrease the proportion of Chinese in the total population, though it would not increase the Malay element very much. The expansion of the federation in this

---

[3] For example, the Selangor branch of the U.M.N.O. in 1956 submitted a memorandum to Tengku Abdul Rahman opposing citizenship by birth for the non-Malays, Chinese as a national language, the recruiting of physicians from Hong Kong, and the conduct of lotteries by the Malay Chinese Association (the proceeds of which were being used for social services in the Chinese community). They also demanded that half of the positions in any new industry be reserved for the Malays.

[4] The three British-controlled states in North Borneo. Sarawak, with an area of 50,000 square miles and a population of nearly 600,000, was governed for nearly a century by the Brooke family. Sir Charles Vyner Brooke, the last of the "white rajas," ceded the territory to Britain as a crown colony in 1946. Brunei, with an area of less than 2,500 square miles and a population of about 60,000, is a sultanate under British protection. It is rich in oil. North Borneo, a crown colony, has an area of nearly 30,000 square miles and a population approaching 400,000.

manner is an idea which Rahman has endorsed and which the British government has instructed its commissioner general for Southeast Asia to promote. A solution to the Malay's problem might be found in the union of Malaya with Indonesia. The success of Indonesian nationalism naturally made a marked impact on the Malays, since the vast majority of Indonesians are of the same race and religion, and many Indonesians have settled in Malaya. The Malay Nationalist party broke away from the U.M.N.O. in 1946 on the issue of the use of the Indonesian flag, but it was unable to gain much of a following. There are also about 700,000 Malays in the southern part of Thailand who are by no means happy in their minority status, a situation which might in the future lead to an irredentist movement. The solution of becoming a part of Indonesia is not very attractive, as Malaya would be lost in a much larger unit. In the last analysis, there remains only one real solution, and that is the development of a Malayan outlook on the part of all the races and their amalgamation into a nation. Though this solution is in many ways unpalatable to the Malays, they are coming to recognize it as the only feasible one.

Probably the most powerful instrument at hand to forge a Malayan nation is a national or public educational system with facilities for giving all of the children at least a common-school education. Such a program runs into a number of difficulties, aside from the formidable problem of finding the funds to finance it. These difficulties were recently summarized as follows:

"Malaya's problems of education are unusually intricate because of the diversity of schools and the large backlog of children, adolescents and adults without the advantages of even elementary education or literacy. The Federation's schools, classified according to the language of instruction, are Malay, Chinese and Indian (known as vernacular schools), and English. All types have primary schools, but only the English and Chinese offer secondary courses. They have diverse management and financing—there are schools maintained by government, non-profit schools to which government gives financial aid, and private schools wholly dependent on their own resources. English schools are the only ones attended by children of all races.

"There is little cross-over from one type of primary school to another. The only formal bridge is between Malay and English schools—special classes in the latter give intensive training in English to enable selected Malay pupils to join the last primary classes. Almost no pupils go directly from the vernacular primary schools to the government or aided English secondary schools. The Chinese primary schools lead to the Chinese secondary schools. There are large variations in the qualifications of teachers and the facilities for training them, and consequently in the level and quality of teaching."[5]

For a long time the only education really available to the Chinese was what the Chinese community itself provided. After 1920 the Chinese schools were brought under government supervision and inspection, and a modest system of subsidies was introduced. While some Chinese students attended the subsidized English schools, four times as many (1951) attended Chinese schools. Somewhat the same division existed among the Indian and Malay children. This produced cultural divisions within the communities. Moreover, the poorly paid Chinese teachers in the Chinese schools, most of them China-born, were strongly leftist. An authority on the Chinese of Malaya states that these teachers, "Communists almost to a man, passed on their doctrine to their pupils in spite of all the precautions taken."[6] This explains the revolutionary activity, especially in Singapore, of Chinese school students.

The Chinese dissatisfaction with the inadequate opportunities offered their children and the desire to preserve Chinese culture led to the establishment of a Chinese university in Singapore in 1954, with Lin Yu-tang as its first chancellor.[7]

---

[5] *The Economic Development of Malaya. Report of a Mission organized by the International Bank for Reconstruction and Development* (Singapore, 1955), 102.

[6] Victor Purcell, *Malaya: Communist or Free?* (Stanford, Calif., 1954), 153. Purcell is a former member of the civil service of Malaya and assistant director of education in charge of Chinese schools.

[7] Lin Yu-tang ran into trouble and resigned before "Nanyang University," as it was called, opened its doors in 1956. He declared the troubles leading to his resignation were of Communist instigation.

Graduates of the Chinese schools lacked sufficient knowledge of English to be admitted to the University of Malaya.

The discussion of the educational problem has tended to turn Malaya into a "cockpit of aggressive cultures." Malay and English are the official languages of the country; hence it was planned to use Malay as the medium of instruction in the national primary grades and English in the secondary schools and in the higher institutions. This implied the elimination of Chinese schools, which is sharply resented by the Chinese, who fear the extinction of their culture in Malaya. To most Chinese "Malayanization is anathema, in view of the absence of a culture, or even a society, which can as yet be called Malayan."[8] The Chinese demands will require trilingualism for the Chinese children—a rather heavy burden. In Singapore there are demands that all education in the primary schools be bilingual, and in the secondary schools, trilingual. There is logic behind this demand, since the Chinese constitute about 80 percent of the population, English is the language of commerce, and Malay (including Indonesian) is the language of the nearly 90,000,000 people which live in the region of which Singapore is the commercial center.

The relation of Singapore to the federation is an unsolved problem and will undoubtedly continue to be so for some time. At the time of the formation of the federation it was thought unwise politically to include Singapore, because of its preponderantly Chinese population, but to exclude it is economically unsound. It is true that Singapore thrives on its large entrepôt trade, which makes it one of the greatest ports in the world, but it could be given the status of a free port in the federation. Singapore is, and will continue to be, the leading commercial, financial, and cultural center of Malaya, whether it is in the federation or not. A joint coordination committee, established in 1953 under Malcolm MacDonald, at the time commissioner general, reported that there are fifty-one

---

[8] *Chinese Schools and the Education of Chinese Malayans. Report of a Mission Invited by the Federation Government to Study the Problem of Education of Chinese in Malaya* (Kuala Lumpur, 1951). Quoted by Purcell, 156-57.

subjects with respect to which consultation and coordination are highly desirable. Tengku Rahman, chief minister of the federation, has shown little enthusiasm for admitting Singapore to the federation, for obvious reasons. He declared in January, 1957, that there would be no merger of Singapore with the federation. He pointed out that in independent Malaya, Malay will be the official language, Islamism the religion, and a Malay the paramount ruler—conditions unacceptable to the predominantly Chinese population of Singapore.

The suppression of Communist terrorism continues to be the first problem of Malaya. Tengku Rahman offered the Communist guerrillas a general amnesty, but on condition that the Communist party be dissolved. He met with the Communist leader, Chin Peng, in December, 1955, but the talks collapsed. Some people have naively assumed that as soon as Malaya becomes independent, "Communism will be destroyed by a twist of the hand." How serious the problem of Communist influence is was evident again in October, 1956, when the Singapore government began a campaign against Communist influence and agitation in its schools. It ordered the dissolution of the powerful Chinese Middle Schools Students Union as a "Communist Front Organization," and also ordered the dismissal of two teachers and the expulsion of 140 students. A student revolt ensued, and student riots spread into various parts of the city. Thirteen persons lost their lives and over a hundred were injured before the riots were brought under control. Police were rushed into Singapore from the federation to help quell the riots.

The struggle against Communism will not have been won with the suppression of the bandits. Infiltration and subversion may be more difficult to meet than terrorism. And there is always the possibility that Peiping may at any moment take a more active and direct interest in the Communist movement in Malaya than it has yet done.

While Malaya is a very productive dollar earner and its per capita income is considerably higher than that of its neighbors, there is, nevertheless, concern over its economic future. Malaya has "too many eggs in the same basket." The economy of the country is highly dependent on rubber and tin, but chiefly the former. The producers of these commodities complain that their products are taxed too heavily. Export taxes on rubber provide much of the public revenue. A drop of one cent in the average price of rubber means a loss of two million Malay dollars in export duties and about twelve million Malay dollars in gross national income. Competition with synthetic rubber tends to drive the price of natural rubber down. For all of these reasons the estates have lagged behind in replanting trees. The government is seeking to encourage both the estates and the small holders to replant at a faster rate and to replace low-yielding with high-yielding trees. Malaya must import much of its staple food, the country producing less than half of its total rice requirements. "Grow more food" programs and campaigns have so far not been successful. The soil of Malaya is not well suited to large-scale mechanical production, and it is not especially fertile.

Malaya, like its neighbors, very much needs industrial expansion. The mission of the International Bank for Reconstruction and Development concluded in its report that "By and large, we are favorably impressed with Malaya's economic potentialities and prospects for expansion. There remains, nevertheless, a serious question whether rates of economic progress and additions to employment opportunities can move ahead of or even keep up with the pace at which the population and the labor force are growing."[9]

[9] *The Economic Development of Malaya*, 26-27.

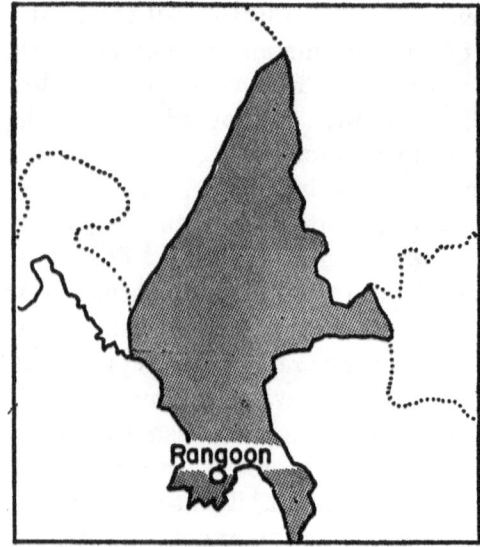

CHAPTER 7

BURMA
Land of Contradictions

THE LEADERSHIP of the Burmese government is, at one and the same time, passionately socialist and devoutly Buddhist. Socialism has a greater foothold in Burma at the present time than it has ever before had in any Far Eastern country. At the same time Buddhism is receiving more official support in Burma today than it has received in any land in modern times. This philosophical contradiction is nowhere better illustrated than in the fact that one man, U Win—presently Burmese ambassador to the United States—served until late 1955 as both minister of national planning and minister of religious affairs and culture.

It is difficult to conceive of two philosophies more basically opposed than Buddhism, devoted to escape from the world, and socialism, seeking to make the world as enjoyable as possible for the great mass of men. Yet Burma in recent years has been host to the Asian Socialist Conference, in January, 1953, and to the Sixth Great Buddhist Council, or Sangayana, which met in two-year session from May, 1954, through May, 1956. The first of these meetings chose Rangoon as the site for its permanent secretariat. For the second, the government of Burma constructed a mammoth assembly cave on grounds of more than one hundred acres; four hostels, each to accommodate one thousand monks; a refectory capable of feeding fifteen hundred monks at a time; and an international Buddhist library at a cost of $4,620,000—not including labor.

The present drive to gain maximum popular participation in the establishment of a welfare state *(pyidawtha)* in Burma has engendered immense support among the masses. Likewise, Buddhism is undergoing a revival among the Burmese people, following a temporary eclipse in the immediate postwar period. Besides seeking to encourage the faith for its own sake, the Burmese government obviously hopes by the revival of Buddhism to build up resistance to communism in Burma. But if its efforts are really successful in checking the spread of communistic ideas, they may also cause the Burmese to lose interest in building socialism. The very fact that both Buddhism and socialism are espoused by many of the same people in Burma today is an obvious indication that intellectual coexistence is possible between the two philosophies, but in the long run one or the other will emerge triumphant—or a new composite philosophy of some sort will be formed.

Burma is a relatively large country with an area of nearly 262,000 square miles. Geographically it is isolated. Overland communication with India is difficult because of formidable mountains and jungle-covered ridges, high mountains and vast stretches of hilly country keep Burma and China pretty well separated from each other, and mountains form a natural boundary with its eastern neighbor, Thailand. But Burma is easily accessible by sea, and as a result this Mongoloid people has been strongly influenced by the culture of nearby India. The heart of the country is the central Irrawaddy-Chindwin river valley and its delta, in which is located Rangoon, the capital and largest city.

In 1941 Burma had a population of 16,800,000. Of this number about two-thirds were Burman. Important ethnological groups are the Karens and the Shans. The former constitute nearly a tenth and the latter about an eighth of the total population, which in 1957 was estimated at about 20,000,000. Before the Second World War there were over a million Indians in Burma, but their numbers since the war has been much less. The Chinese population in Burma does not exceed half a million.

DEVELOPMENT OF NATIONALISM

The history of Burma as a distinct political entity begins with the great ruler Anawrahta, who founded the early Burmese kingdom of Pagan in 1044. Anawrahta is important to the development of the Burmese national tradition in yet another way. It was he who established Hinayana Buddhism as the official religion of Burma.

The kingdom of Pagan perished in 1287 before the Tartar armies of China's infamous Kubla Khan. The next four and a half centuries were marked by the absence of even the semblance of unity in Burma, except for the reign of Byinnaung, 1550-1581. This era of disruption came to an end in 1754, when Alaungpaya rose to defeat the last of the Mon kingdoms in northern Burma and established the last Burmese dynasty. Alaungpaya's Burma, like that of Anawrahta, was not a state in the modern sense. It was a feudal arrangement, but sufficiently unified to serve as the nucleus for the development of the present Burmese national state.

The British conquest of Burma spanned sixty-two years. As the result of the attempted Burmese invasion of British India in 1824-1826, the British East India Company, acting for the throne, took possession of the Arakan and Tenasserim coastal strips of Burma. In 1852 the governor general of India was provoked into sending another expedition against Burma, the immediate cause of his action being the treatment of British subjects and shipping in Rangoon. The British as a consequence acquired the remainder of coastal or lower Burma. On January 1, 1886, following Burma's defeat in the third Anglo-Burmese War, Britain announced the annexation of the rest of Burma. Incorporated into the British Indian Empire, Burma was administered as a province of India until 1937, when it became a separate colony.

It is difficult to indicate the precise origins of nationalism in any land, and Burma is no exception. Although nationalism as a political force in Burma did not emerge until after the First World War, the seeds of its development were sown well before that time. British abolition of the traditional feudal institutions following the rebellion of 1886-1889, for example, created a vacuum from which some new allegiance inevitably had to spring. The introduction of commercial rice cultivation, which upset traditional village economic self-sufficiency, necessitated a new sort of social integration. Increasing foreign domination of the country's economic life, including the growing stranglehold possessed on the nation's economy by immigrants from India, was an important element in stirring the Burmese to revolution. Culturally, too, the British made inroads on traditional Burmese habits. In particular, they withdrew official governmental support of the Buddhist religion.

A number of external events also influenced the emergence of nationalism in Burma. Japan's victory over Russia in 1905 gave vivid evidence that the white man was not invincible. The activities of the Congress party in India revealed that gains could be made against colonial domination by effective organization. The lofty phrases of American President Woodrow Wilson regarding national self-determination, made both during and after the First World War, also inspired many a Burmese patriot.

As in other parts of Southeast Asia, cultural nationalism preceded political nationalism. In Burma it assumed the organizational form of the Young Men's Buddhist Organization, modeled in many ways after the Y.M.C.A. The step that bridged the gap between cultural and political nationalism in Burma was taken in 1921, when the General Council of Buddhist Associations sought to direct nationalist sentiments into political channels, and openly declared home rule as its goal. Although nationalism grew in Burma throughout the twenties and thirties—Burma's first race riots in early 1930, directed against the Indians, marked a highlight of its growth—it was not until 1935 that it assumed its present form. In this year there was organized at the University of Rangoon, traditionally a hotbed of political radicalism, a group of Marxist-minded students who called themselves the Thakins. Included among the Thakins were Aung San, later called the "father of the Burmese nationalist revolution" by his people; U Nu, independent Burma's first premier; and Than Tun, subsequently the leader of the orthodox wing of Burmese Communism and architect of the postwar Communist revolt against the government. The Thakins called for immediate and complete freedom for Burma, and advocated a radical economic program. In the urban areas they organized strikes, some of them very effective, and in the country they championed the cause of agricultural reform.

Burma's first premier following separation from India, Dr. Ba Maw—still a contestant, though a weak one, in the Burmese political arena—led those Burmese who collaborated with the Japanese during the occupation of the country in the Second World War. Rangoon fell to the Japanese on March 8, 1943, with the aid of the "Burma Independence Army," led by General Aung San. Dr. Ba Maw remained as prime minister in the puppet government, Aung San was minister of defense, and Than Tun served as minister of communications. Serving as foreign minister for a year in the Ba Maw government was U Nu, then known as Thakin Nu.

Nationalists like Aung San and U Nu had joined hands with the Japanese to oust the British from Burma because they were impatient for their country to achieve its independence from colonial rule. When Premier U Saw on a special mission to London in 1941 failed to obtain an unqualified British promise of postwar dominion status for Burma, no other action seemed possible. But Burma's young nationalists were to be sorely disappointed; it was soon evident that "Asia for the Asiatics" meant Asia for Japan. In response to this wholly unanticipated situation General Aung San converted his "Burma Independence Army" into the "Anti-Fascist People's Freedom League" and prepared to strike a blow at the Japanese occupation of Burma when the occasion arose. This came with the British return to Burma, when Aung San led his A.F.P.F.L. forces in support of the liberation army.

Relatively inconspicuous in the prewar years, U Nu joined hands with Aung San to undermine the puppet regime and aid the Allies in ousting Japan from Burma in the late years of the Pacific war. When Aung San and six of his cabinet associates were murdered in July, 1947, U Nu succeeded to the leadership of the new Burma.

The first task facing U Nu was the completion in August, 1947, of the formal arrangements which would make Burma independent once again. In October the Nu-Attlee agreement was signed by the British and the Burmese, and on January 4, 1948, the sovereign Union of Burma, approximately the size of France, came into being, the third country in modern history to free itself completely from the British Empire.

There is evidence that both U Nu and Aung San would have preferred that Burma remain a member of the Commonwealth, as did India, Pakistan, and Ceylon. But by 1947 this was no longer possible. The postwar plans for Burma devised by the Churchill government in England forced the nationalists to take such an extreme position in their demands for independence that retreat was impossible. The British in their White Paper of May, 1945, offered only restoration of Burma's prewar status by 1948 to a people who had received a taste, limited though it may have been, of independence under the Japanese.

DEVELOPMENT OF SOCIALISM

That the present rulers of Burma are thoroughly committed to socialism is beyond question. As youthful a ruling group as is to be found anywhere in the world today, the men who comprise the Burmese government are mostly graduates of Rangoon University in the 1930's who constituted the revolutionary Thakin group. Not only did they focus their sights on the ending of British imperial political control, but they also planned for the day when the new free Burma would expropriate the alien capitalists and supplant their control of the nation's economy with direction by a native government.

When the young nationalists came to power in independent Burma in January, 1948, they proclaimed the socialist ideas for which they had propagandized since their student days. The constitution of the new Union of Burma, a curious mixture of Western liberal and Marxist ideas, proclaimed the right of the state to limit private property or to expropriate it in accordance with the law. The state, moreover, was the owner of all land, and in free Burma there were to be "no large land holdings whatsoever." One-third of Burma's privately owned timber concessions were immediately nationalized, as was the British-owned Irrawaddy Flotilla Company, which controlled almost all of the inland water transport in prewar Burma. Prior to the actual attainment of independence a State Agricultural Marketing Board was created, which was to control the rice export trade, and an early step of the new Burmese government was to open the State Bank of Burma. Before the first year of independence was half over, the government announced a "Two Year Plan" for the economic development of Burma, which, among other things, provided for nationalization of the power industry as well as of all water and land transport facilities and for establishment of certain state-owned basic industries as well as several consumer-goods industries. The plan also called for a land redistribution program.

The goals of the "Two Year Plan" were too high. In the four years which followed the announcement of the plan, only a spinning and weaving factory was established. Burma had neither the capital nor the technical talent to set up overnight the sort of socialist economy envisioned by its young and inexperienced leaders. Moreover, the various revolts by assorted brands of Communists and ethnic minorities which plagued the country during its first years of freedom did not provide the sort of environment in which Burma's socialists were given maximum opportunity to implement their schemes. As much as 40 percent of government revenues were diverted to military operations against rebels, who at one time controlled more than half of the country.

The failure of the "Two Year Plan" of 1948 did not discourage Burma's leaders. It did, however, lend a much needed sobering influence to their economic thinking and policy making. Plans for an early and complete nationalization of the country's economy have been abandoned, and Burma today is not only encouraging internal private enterprise but also help from abroad. In August, 1949, even before the expiration of the "Two Year Plan," it was announced that "until such time as the State can undertake sufficient production," a number of industries previously earmarked for state ownership might be developed by private capital "either on its own or in partnership with the State." Industries of importance to the security of Burma, like atomic energy and defense, were excluded from the change in policy, but private enterprise might now participate in such major Burmese industries as oil and mineral extraction, railway transport, electric power, coal mining, and several others.

A second change in Burmese economic policy came in 1952-1953, when the Industrial Development Corporation was established to direct future government-sponsored industrial development of the country. Allocated more than two million dollars by Rangoon for 1953-1954, the corporation soon commenced construction of a brick and tile factory, and announced plans for a steel rolling mill with a capacity of 20,000 tons a year. Other projects included the establishment of salt, jute, and paper and pulp factories, as well as a cement plant in which the government would have as its partner the private Burma Cement Company.

The general policy of the government is to contract with a Western corporation to construct a factory and operate it for a few years, and, after having trained personnel to run it efficiently, to turn it over to the government. A Scottish drug company, for example, is constructing a pharmaceutical plant on such a contract. These Western capitalist companies are thus aiding Burma in establishing socialism. One of the odd, contradictory things to be seen in Rangoon is a New York capitalist corporation helping Burma plan a socialist society.

If the Burmese government has slowed down the pace of its nationalization of industry, it is attempting to increase the tempo of its land nationalization program. Passed by the Burmese parliament in October, 1948, the Land Nationalization act has as its goal the abolition of landlordism and the redistribution of the land to the cultivators. Implementation of the program was begun in January, 1949, in selected "experimental" areas, but it could not be continued because of the rebel hostilities. Later resumed in a single township near Rangoon, it was not until 1953 that land redistribution in Burma really began in earnest, and even then at a much slower pace than was anticipated. Close to seven million acres of land had been redistributed by mid 1956, representing about one-twelfth of the total scheduled for redistribution. Present plans for a "new order" among Burmese peasants call for completion of the current phase of Burma's land distribution program by 1962, with high hopes of achievement.

Another agricultural goal of the government was the restoration of production to the prewar level by 1956-1957. A five-year plan for agricultural and rural development was drawn up for this purpose in 1952, and an Agricultural and Water Resources Development Corporation was created to supervise the plan. An ultimate rice production increase of one and three-quarter million tons was aimed at, and to achieve this, the government sought to rehabilitate two and a half million acres of paddy land thrown out of cultivation through war and civil insurrection, to bring an additional five hundred thousand acres of new paddy land under irrigation, and to improve cultivation methods by the use of fertilizers and improved seed strains. By 1960 Burma's socialist leadership hopes that the 1938-1939 over-all gross output of the land will be exceeded by about 30 percent.[1]

Whatever the achievements, Burma at the end of a decade of struggle still faces very great difficulties. The country's population has increased by 21 percent since the Second World War, but the gross national product is still only 81 percent of what it was before that war. The mines at Namtu, normally one of the world's richest producers of silver, lead, and zinc, have reached only 20 percent of their prewar output. The

[1] Frank N. and Helen G. Trager, *Burma: Land of Golden Pagodas* (New York, 1954), 31.

Yenangyaung oil fields, Burma's largest, are still not back in production after being blown up by the retreating British at the time of the Japanese invasion in 1942, and the Chauk fields produce about one-third of what they did before the Second World War. Burma's postwar rice export high is two million tons a year. The export price of rice, which earns about 80 percent of Burma's foreign exchange, fell from $168 per ton in 1953 to about $100 a ton in 1955. Foreign-exchange reserves toppled from approximately $211,000,000 to about $92,000,000.

BUDDHIST REVIVAL

While socialism gained an increasing hold on the Burmese mind, Buddhism also received growing support from the government as well as among the people. In October, 1950, for example, three important religious bills were passed unanimously by the Burmese parliament. One of these was the Dhamma Chariya act, which established a pair of government-sponsored ecclesiastical courts to restore order once more among Burma's more than fifty thousand Sanghas (monks), some of whom were believed unfit to wear the yellow robes of Buddhism. The second act was the Vinissaya act, setting up the Pali University to coordinate monastery teaching of the language in which the great books of Buddhism are written. Most important of the three bills was the Buddha Sasana act, which provided for the establishment of a government-operated Buddha Sasana Organization to coordinate Buddhist activities in the country. In addition, the Buddha Sasana Organization was charged with the task of translating the Pali Tripitaka into Burmese as well as of sending missionaries abroad to propagate the faith of Gautama Buddha.[2] The most conspicuous example of official Burmese support of Buddhism in recent times, however, was the Sixth Great Buddha Council, which met in a two-year session at Rangoon in 1954-1956. The council, which brought together Buddhists from Thailand, Ceylon, Laos, Cambodia, and Burma, enjoyed the full support of the

---

[2] For a detailed account of these three acts, see John F. Cady, "Religion and Politics in Modern Burma," *Far Eastern Quarterly*, XII (1953), 158-61.

Burmese government, which met all of its expenses. Surely no further evidence need be summoned that the leadership of Burma is uniquely devoted to the Buddhist faith, despite its simultaneous passionate attachment to socialism.

Burma's socialist-Buddhist contradiction is nowhere better symbolized than in the person of U Nu. A revolutionary who subsequently devoted himself to the effective establishment of socialism in his country as its first prime minister, U Nu is also an ardent Buddhist who, more than any other single person, is responsible for the present state support of Buddhism in Burma. Indicative of his religious nature is his frequently stated intention of eventually retiring from his worldly chores to devote himself to spiritual work or contemplation. He has often stated that he would like to retire to a monastery.

It was U Nu who in 1950 went before the Burmese parliament in support of the Buddha Sasana act to plead, most dramatically, for funds for Buddhist missionary work at home and abroad. It was he, too, who initiated the drive to build Rangoon's Kabe-Aye, or World Peace Pagoda, which holds the share of the relics of Sariputta and Maha Moggallana, chief disciples of Buddha, which Burma received from India. U Nu it was, also, who, once when a representative of his was going to an international conference and asked for instructions, pulled a little religious book out of his pocket and told his countryman to read two verses every morning before breakfast. His support of a translation of the Buddhist scriptures into Burmese—they previously had been available only in Pali—caused one writer to observe that Nu was "becoming to Buddhist scriptures what King James was to the King James version of the Bible."[3]

PROBLEMS AND ACCOMPLISHMENTS

One of the first problems U Nu had to face after independence had been achieved was the need for economic and social rehabilitation. Before the Second World War more than twelve

---

[3] Robert Sherrod, "Man on a Rickety Fence," *Saturday Evening Post*, CCXXVII (April 23, 1955), 111-12.

million acres had been under rice cultivation in Burma. In the 1945-1946 season only six and a half million acres were devoted to the growing of rice, although during the next two years rice farming land increased by almost two million acres. Rice production in the year following the war's end was only 2,770,000 tons, which was hardly sufficient to feed Burma's own population, let alone have an export surplus; in the years leading up to the Pacific war, British Burma had exported three million tons of rice annually, making it the world's principal exporter of the grain. By the 1947-1948 season agricultural production had risen to 77 percent of the prewar average and the country exported 1,251,000 tons of rice, but this still left the leaders of newly independent Burma with a sizable economic recovery problem.

The status of Burma's oil and timber industries was similarly dismal, and the country's transportation facilities were in chaotic condition. In 1938-1939 Burma had sent abroad 651,000 tons of petroleum; in 1947-1948 it exported no oil at all. Its exports of timber in 1947-1948 were in a somewhat better position; they were nearly half of what they had been in 1938-1939.

In spite of a variety of domestic insurrections, the Burmese recovery under the Nu government was considerable. The crop output had increased to 81 percent of the prewar level by 1952-1953, and the yield per acre had reached 96 percent. In the same season total acreage sown had increased to 85 percent of what it had been in the prewar years. Between 1950 and 1952 the country's mineral production also improved, nearly doubling in this two-year period as internal security progressively returned to the country, although in 1952 it was still only 12 percent of what it had been in 1939. Teak output was up, too—amounting in 1952, however, to only 25 percent of the prewar production. The gross national product (the value of all goods and services) had been $927,000,000 in 1938-1939; in 1954 it had risen only to $741,000,000.

The most important accomplishment of the government in terms of economic recovery was its resumption of rice exports, the bulwark of the Burmese economy. In 1953 Burma's exports of rice totaled about 50 percent of the prewar level, with a value, at postwar inflated prices, of four times the 1939 figure. This factor more than anything else permitted the financial survival of Burma in the trying first years of its newly resumed independent existence. In 1954, however, for the first time since it attained its independence, Burma was forced to sell its rice at a price much below that which it sought, and even then it did not sell all its surplus.

The price for Burmese rice dropped even lower in 1955, and Burma suddenly found itself faced with a serious balance-of-payments problem. The government was thoroughly alarmed by this situation. Because of its heavy economic reliance on the receipts from a single export crop, Burma would be unable to fulfill its elaborate socialist plans if the demand for rice continued to drop. Moreover, were the pyidawtha, or welfare state, program to be abandoned at this time, it might well mean political suicide for the Burmese leadership and a triumph for their internal Communist opponents. It was in apparent recognition of such realities that U Nu in the summer of 1955 asked for—and received—a $42,000,000 loan from neighboring India, the second time within a year that India had come to Burma's aid because of its rice price difficulties. In late 1954, when Burma had found itself overloaded with rice, India had purchased nine hundred thousand tons of the surplus on what Nu called "our suggested terms."

Foreign economic assistance, however, does not solve Burma's basic economic problem, which is to continue to sell its surplus rice at a high price until it is able to diversify its underdeveloped economy to such an extent that it is no longer dependent on the export receipts from a single agricultural product. This the leaders of Burma realize, and they were exceptionally industrious in 1954 and 1955 in seeking out markets for their surplus rice while at the same time continuing to work for the economic advancement of their comparatively backward country. The moves they took to bolster their sagging rice exports, however, may prove more harmful than helpful in the long run. For in addition to attempting to increase the sales of Burmese rice to such countries as Japan and India, they also looked for customers among the Communist lands. Probably nothing was more significant for Burma in 1955 than the emergence of Communist China, the Soviet Union, and the satellites as major customers for Burmese rice.

Burma had tried elsewhere to dispose of its surplus rice. The United States would not take Burma's rice off its hands, however, because it had a rice surplus of its own—and a powerful farm lobby. The Soviet Union and Communist China were willing, and so were Poland, Hungary, East Germany, Czechoslovakia, and Rumania. The terms of the several Communist rice barter pacts with the Burmese were essentially the same. For stipulated quantities of Burmese rice the Communist countries promised both goods and services—mostly heavy capital equipment, although some consumer goods also were pledged. The "services" consisted mainly of Communist technicians to be sent to Burma to teach the Burmese how to use the equipment supplied under the pacts.

The Communists' intentions in concluding such agreements appear to have been purely political. With the exception of Communist China, none of the countries involved in the barter pacts could be said to be in need of Burmese rice. The U.S.S.R. and its allies, however, would like to draw Burma as close to the Communist bloc as possible, economically as well as politically. Even if the Burmese do not renew the several rice barter agreements with the Communist countries, the capital goods which they will receive under the present pacts will require replacement parts and associated equipment—all of which will have to come from Soviet bloc nations. A major result of Burma's economic agreements with the several Communist countries would seem to be the prospect of a marked reorientation of Burmese trade toward the lands of the Soviet bloc.

On the eve of the visit of Soviet leaders Nikolai A. Bulganin and Nikita S. Khrushchev to Burma in late 1955, U Nu announced that the U.S.S.R. was prepared to extend the duration of its rice barter pact with Burma, originally a three-year agreement, to five years. The enthusiasm with which the Burmese premier greeted such a prospect was an indication of his strong concern over his country's surplus rice; it was also, unfortunately, an indication of his lack of perception of Soviet designs.

The impact the barter pacts with the Soviet bloc countries would have upon the Burmese economy was evident within a year. Prior to the conclusion of these trade agreements, the Communist countries had accounted for only 3 percent of Burma's imports. By mid 1956 this figure had risen to 25 percent and was increasing each month. From the U.S.S.R., Czechoslovakia, Hungary, and other Communist countries heavy capital equipment was flowing into Burma ostensibly to help that newly independent land in its efforts to modernize its backward economy. The Soviet bloc barter deals were not all milk and honey, however, as Burma's leadership is coming increasingly to realize. The main eye opener to date has been cement—cement which Burma has received in return for its rice and which has caused the government more headaches than it is willing to admit. In mid-May, 1956, cement literally was to be found everywhere along the Rangoon waterfront. As a New York *Times* correspondent described it: "It [the cement] is piled high in the warehouses, the docks are choked with it, and more ships are waiting to unload it when berthing room becomes available."[4] Some ships, loaded with consumer goods badly needed by the Burmese, were kept waiting for weeks in the harbor. Other ships with important cargoes were informed of the tieup while still at sea and skipped the port of Rangoon.

Cement was not the only commodity which Burma received in exchange for its rice and with which it was dissatisfied. There also were complaints about Czechoslovak whisky and beer, Communist Chinese toothpaste, Soviet vehicles, and other items. Burmese consumers bought Soviet bloc goods only when they had no other choice. Czech canned milk, they complained—for example—was watered and was much inferior to British and American canned milk.

There was another side to Burma's discontent with the several rice barter pacts with the Sino-Soviet bloc countries. This related to the subsequent appearance on the scene of cash

[4] New York *Times*, May 9, 1956.

customers whose orders for rice Burma could not meet due to its recently assumed commitments. An Indonesian order for one hundred thousand tons of rice followed almost on the heels of the conclusion of the barter agreements, and this was followed by an order from Pakistan, in the grip of famine, for sixty thousand tons. These orders Burma was just barely able to fill. Then came Malaya with an order of ten thousand tons, and Burma had to say no. Pakistan next came back with a request for more rice, but the Burmese had no more rice to sell to their Pakistani neighbors. So Pakistan went to Communist China, where it bought the same rice the Chinese had received from Burma, or rice which Peiping felt able to sell to Pakistan as a consequence of the additional grain it had got from the Burmese. From Burma's point of view, the important thing was that China was receiving cash for rice for which the Burmese had to accept barter goods.

Burma's leadership apparently was very much aware in late 1956 that for every ton of rice that had to be shipped to the Communist bloc under one of the barter pacts, there was one less ton available for sale for cash with which it could buy what Burma wanted, not just cement, Czechoslovak canned milk, and Communist Chinese toothpaste. One Burmese official flatly stated that the day of making barter deals with Communist countries was over. There were even indications that the Burmese were trying to get the Communists to call off the deals. The Communists, however, held a trump card. Burma had signed contracts setting up the several rice barter deals, and the Burmese were an honorable people. The dangers of long-term economic commitments with the Soviets and their allies were only too clear.

Meanwhile, not only did Communist capital equipment flow into Burma, but also Soviet, Bulgarian, Czech, and Polish economic advisers to help the Burmese use the heavy goods acquired from the Soviet bloc as well as to build a new technological institute, a huge sports center, a hospital, a hotel, and an exhibition hall. In the spring of 1956 hardly a plane landed at Rangoon's Mingaladon airport which did not carry more Soviet technicians. This was economic infiltration, Soviet style, in all its glory and with all its sinister intentions. There was genuine reason for Burmese alarm. There also was cause for American concern.

The United States revealed its concern in mid 1956 by agreeing—finally—to buy ten thousand tons of Burmese rice in order that Burma might have one million dollars with which to pay American technicians who might otherwise have had to leave Burma, leaving a completely open field to the Soviets. This was only a small amount of rice, however, compared with the maximum of 1,600,000 tons of the grain Moscow had contracted to take under barter arrangements over the four-year period 1956-1960. A loan of $25,000,000 (and another $17,500,000 in Burmese currency), reported imminent in early 1957, underscored United States concern.

The extent of Burmese rice commitments to the Soviet Union and its allies was considerable. In the original July, 1955, barter pact between Burma and the U.S.S.R. the Soviets had agreed to take only 150,000 to 200,000 tons of rice annually —this in exchange for Soviet machinery, goods, and technical and other services. In April, 1956, however, in formalization of U Nu's announcement of late 1955, the Soviet Union and Burma agreed to extend their trade pact, originally planned for only three years, to five years. The Soviets also agreed to increase the amount of rice they would take annually to four hundred thousand tons. The new trade agreement was signed on the occasion of the visit to Burma of Soviet First Deputy Premier Anastas I. Mikoyan.

Communist China, meanwhile, had signed its own rice barter pact with the Burmese. In late December, 1955, Peiping agreed to take 150,000 tons of Burmese rice annually in return for Chinese exports of the same value. Before the several Communist countries were through bidding for its rice, Burma had committed itself to move a sizable share of its rice crop annually to Communist countries. The amount was half of Burma's total rice exports in the 1953-1954 season.

So dissatisfied was Burma's leadership with the barter agreements with the Soviet bloc as a result of their first year of operation (1956) that it was decided to reduce considerably rice shipments to the Communists in 1957. Burma planned to sign contracts to export only 55,000 to 105,000 tons of rice to Communist countries in 1957, although under the several barter pacts it might ship up to 740,000 tons annually and although the 1957 rice surplus was expected to be greater than that of 1956. In addition, the Burmese would send approximately 165,000 tons of rice to Communist countries in 1957 to satisfy contracts signed in 1956 but not filled in that year. Burma's future trade relations with the Soviet Union, Communist China, and the satellites was expected to depend, in large measure, on how satisfied the Burmese were with the goods supplied in fulfillment of these obligations.

Although the several rice barter agreements were concluded during the premiership of U Nu, it is clear that Nu's leading lieutenants, U Ba Swe and U Kyaw Nyein, agreed in principle that conclusion of such pacts was a necessary move. There is evidence, however, that one of the several factors causing these men to disagree with Nu, which they did frequently, was the degree to which Nu committed his country to supply the Soviet Union and other Communist countries with Burmese rice. This may have been one reason why Nu was eased out of the Burmese premiership in early June, 1956, just as dissatisfaction with the barter deals began to be strongly evident.

POSTWAR CIVIL DISTURBANCES

Imposing though aspects of Burma's recovery have been, the record probably could have been more impressive had it not been for the series of domestic revolts which afflicted the nation beginning in 1948. These revolts combined three major elements of instability only too obvious in the political personality of postwar Burma. First to raise the standard of rebellion were the Communists, whose thinly disguised objective was control of the state for themselves. Also revolting against the central government were various groups of Burma's ethnic minorities, the most important of which were the Karens, who never did favor the break with Britain for fear that reprisals would follow against them by the ruling Burmese majority. Finally, there were the brigands, armed gangs who found it difficult to return to a quiet settled life after the fury and excitement of the wartime years.

When the Japanese or British were still about and constituted the common foe, Communists and non-Communists worked side by side in the nationalist revolution. When the common enemy bowed out of the picture, however, this unity quickly dissolved. In 1944, however, when the Japanese still occupied the country, Burma's varied revolutionaries banded together in an omnibus coalition called the Anti-Fascist People's Freedom League, which Aung San organized together with the Communist Than Tun. When the war ended, the A.F.P.F.L. emerged as the only political body of any significance in Burma, comprising socialists, Communists, the army, peasant unions, student groups, and others. The unity this coalition represented was not to last long, partly as a result of personality conflicts among the various elements of its leadership and partly because of the altogether different objectives of the socialists and the Communists. That the Communists sought more than just independence was never more evident than when they turned against U Nu in late 1947 for accepting the terms of the Nu-Attlee agreement, which hardly could have been much more generous but which they attacked as favoring British military and economic interests. Control of the machinery of state for themselves was the Communist objective, this goal becoming only too clear in 1948, when, apparently on orders from outside Burma, the Communists rose in revolt against the government.

If the A.F.P.F.L. was beginning to disintegrate, losing much of its former unity, the Communists also were to display a singular lack of common purpose. Led by two revolutionaries of rather strong personalities, the Communists themselves were divided into two competing groups, the White Flag Communists, or Stalinists, and the Red Flags, or Trotskyites. The able organizer Than Tun, who formed the A.F.P.F.L. with

Burma

Aung San in 1944, was at the head of the orthodox Stalinist Communists, and at one time he possessed very close contacts with Peiping. The extremely uncompromising and volatile Thakin Soe led the Red Flags. Ostensibly the two Communist groups were divided by their adherence to the rival Stalinist and Trotskyite interpretations of Marxism, but the real difference appears to have been in the realm of personality differences between their two leaders. As for the supporters of the two groups, a good many of them have been out-and-out dacoits, and others were shiftless adventurer types, attracted by the strong personality of either Than Tun or Thakin Soe. More than one observer has described Burma's postwar Communist troubles as a bad case of "follow the leader" brigandry.

There were times in 1949 when the Communists or other rebel groups controlled more of Burma than the government, whose area of effective jurisdiction often did not extend much beyond Rangoon itself. By the fall of 1950, however, the tide had begun to turn, and since then the strength and effectiveness of the various insurgents, including the Communists, have declined enormously. This has been matched on the government's side by an increase in the size and fighting ability of the Burmese army. That the White Flags, the stronger of the two Communist groups, were beginning to see the handwriting on the wall was most evident when they made the proposal to U Nu that they form a coalition government with the A.F.P.F.L. Nu promptly turned down the Communist offer. After trying an alliance with Thakin Soe's Red Flags, the Karen rebels, and the insurgent leftwing of the People's Volunteer Organization (onetime armed auxiliary of the A.F.P.F.L., a part of which revolted in 1949), Than Tun's forces began to shift from guns to propaganda in their offensive against the government. The failure to achieve success in this change of tactics, and the major military defeat the government forces inflicted on them in November, 1953, reduced the potency of the White Flags considerably. By March, 1956, when the military campaign against the insurgents was halted temporarily with the approach of the annual rainy season, both Communist groups were badly shattered. However, the Communists continue to possess considerable support among various elements in the countryside as well as among the youth of Burma.

The Burmese army in its campaigns against the Communists had been able to split the foe into small units, but these small bands of insurgents, generally comprising from thirty to fifty men, have been able to continue to terrorize large areas of rural Burma. The government, though it once offered the insurgents a full amnesty if they would lay down their arms, has refused to negotiate with them—at least on a formal basis. There have been reports from time to time of private meetings between Communist leaders and cabinet members, but these have not been successful in ending the rebellion. The government's amnesty offer, which failed to bring in many Communists, was withdrawn in late April, 1956.

Burma's army has about 60,000 soldiers, and there is also a 13,000-man military police. The Communist technique against these forces had been to strike quickly, in limited numbers, against villages unsympathetic with the Communists' cause and then to withdraw before the government forces arrived upon the scene. The government forces' numerical strength, training, and better weapons would undoubtedly wipe out the rebels if pitched battles were fought more frequently.

Although considerably reduced in numbers over what they once were, Burma's Communist insurgents still comprise a serious security problem—although they are far less of a threat to the state than they once were. In mid 1956 it was still impossible to drive safely more than twelve miles from the capital city of Rangoon at night. Rail service between the major cities of Rangoon and Mandalay was disrupted at least once a week as a result of Communist work in blowing up bridges and tampering with the railroad tracks. The road from Rangoon to the important city of Moulmein is not even safe to travel during the day. Ambushes still occur throughout the country, and villagers in many areas are so terrorized by the insurgents that they do not tell the authorities of their movements. The threat to the state is diminished, but the threat to internal security remains.

There were those in Rangoon in early 1957 who believed Burma's Communists had decided to step up their stalled guerrilla operations and wage an all-out nuisance campaign against the government. In late January, 1957, Communist rebels swept down on the city of Pegu, forty-five miles north of Rangoon, inflicting considerable property damage and killing at least twelve persons. The Communists had turned down an earlier amnesty offer and asked the government to end the eight-year-old civil war on their terms—which Rangoon authorities refused to do. The Communists, as a consequence, attempted to expand their campaign of violence as a means of exerting pressure on the government to accept their terms. The Communists were weak enough, however, that Burma's non-Communist leadership did not fear a military defeat at their hands. What Burma's rulers did fear was that the populace, increasingly critical of the government's failure to end the guerrilla warfare, might increase its support of the Burma Workers' and Peasants' party or other psuedo- or near-Communist elements. This fear the Communist rebels sought to exploit as Burma's smoldering civil insurrection entered its ninth year.

The Communists were not the only groups to revolt against the government in the postwar years. The Karens, one of Burma's larger minority groups and one which has feared repression from the central government from the very inauguration of independence, took up arms against the state in 1949 and have been allied with several of the other insurrectionists at various times since then. Partly because of the effectiveness of government action against them and partly because more moderate Karens have assured them they will not be the subject of future discrimination, Karen rebels have been surrendering in increasing numbers since early 1954, with the result that nearly nine-tenths of Karen territory is now under government rule. Forceful action also has caused the surrender of many of the leftwing Peoples Volunteer Organization rebels as well as members of other smaller insurrectionist movements. Peace is gradually being restored to Burma, so recently afflicted with so much domestic disorder.

DEMOCRACY IN BURMA

With the return of law and order in Burma, democracy's chances of success may be increased. Its present status, however, poses another of Burma's many contradictions.

On paper, Burma is a parliamentary democracy. It has a two-house national legislature, comprising the 250-member chamber of deputies, forming the lower assembly, and the 125-seat chamber of nationalities, the upper house. The chamber of nationalities, modeled after its Russian namesake, is required by the constitution to allot a specified number of seats to representatives of the Shans, Kachins, Karens, and Chins, all of whom represent major minority groups in Burma. The other house is a popular assembly with representation based on population. The prime minister is responsible to the chamber of deputies, following the British parliamentary example.

The largest party in the chamber of deputies today is the still powerful Anti-Fascist People's Freedom League, which in the last general elections in April, 1956, won 169 out of 250 seats. No longer the omnibus coalition it was in the early postwar years, the A.F.P.F.L. is presently composed in the main of members of the Burmese Socialist party, who prefer to run under its label in order to capitalize on its still enormous prestige as the organ of the revolution. Associated with U Nu in the A.F.P.F.L.'s leadership during his first eight years' premiership were two of Asia's more competent political figures —U Ba Swe, who was Nu's minister of mines and defense as well as chairman of the 40,000-member Trade Union Congress of Burma, and U Kyaw Nyein, his minister of industry and secretary general of the A.F.P.F.L. Both were ardent socialists —Kyaw Nyein so much so that the London *Economist* once described him as a "more ruthless Stafford Cripps."

U Nu, U Ba Swe, and U Kyaw Nyein were generally pictured as a smooth-functioning triumvirate, collectively ruling Burma, with Nu the philosopher-statesman heading the government, Ba Swe in charge of party organization, and Kyaw Nyein serving as chief socialist theoretician. But there were major differences which usually found Ba Swe and Kyaw Nyein lining up against Nu. Ba Swe and Kyaw Nyein, more doctrinaire socialists than Nu, sought to return to the more radical economic measures of the early independence years. In the realm of foreign affairs they felt that in its operation Burmese neutralism tended to advance the goals of the Sino-Soviet bloc at the expense of the democratic camp. Ba Swe and Kyaw Nyein also were continually incensed by the highhanded way in which Nu disregarded cabinet views on foreign matters and frequently took actions which he knew the other leading members of his government opposed.

The day of reckoning came for U Nu in June, 1956, following the Anti-Fascist People's Freedom League's electoral victory of the preceding April. Nu, a good vote getter, particularly among the minority groups, who were less trusting of other A.F.P.F.L. leaders, was ousted as premier little more than a month after the election returns were in. His successor was his capable defense minister, U Ba Swe. Various reasons were given for Nu's departure from the post of premier. Some reportedly informed sources said Nu felt his policy of neutralism in world affairs was a complete failure, yet his successor pledged himself to continue this very same policy, which he described as genuinely wise and in the best interest of the Burmese nation. The official explanation given for Nu's resignation was that he wished to devote his full energies to a reorganization and general house cleaning of his political party, the A.F.P.F.L. Nu reportedly felt that certain party weaknesses had been brought out in the April elections and that he should now devote his political talent to remedying these defects. It was indicated, however, that Nu would be available for consultative duties with the Ba Swe government.

U Ba Swe was a singularly qualified individual and a man

highly representative of the new and independent Burma. Only forty-one years old at the time he ascended to the premiership, he nevertheless had behind him a lengthy career in politics. As minister of defense in the Nu government, he had been responsible for the prosecution of the campaign against Burma's several insurgent movements, including the two Communist insurrections. He also was head of the influential Trade Union Congress of Burma and was vice president of the Anti-Fascist People's Freedom League. In addition, Ba Swe (known throughout Burma as "Big Tiger") had played an active role in the Asian Socialist movement, which made its organizational headquarters in Rangoon. Like U Nu, U Ba Swe was a Buddhist and a socialist. He, too, saw no basic contradiction in these two rival philosophies and seemed equally devoted to both of them. Unlike Nu, however, Ba Swe was less a product of the British period, although he was well acquainted with the history, aims, and accomplishments of the British Socialist movement, and he was significantly influenced by the example of British political institutions.

U Nu's claim that he was stepping down from the premiership only temporarily proved to be correct. Only a little more than six months after Nu had been replaced as Burma's prime minister, a terse government announcement stated that he would resume that office. According to the announcement, Ba Swe would become one of three deputy premiers. On March 1, 1957, U Nu resumed the office following repeated announcements that he had already done so or was about to do so.

The circumstances of Nu's return were no less mysterious than those surrounding his earlier departure from office. Perhaps Nu really had resigned to reorganize the Anti-Fascist People's Freedom League, some observers thought. Others believed that the differences dividing Nu, Ba Swe, and Kyaw Nyein had been resolved. Both of these interpretations left many questions unanswered, however. The most important consideration in Nu's return to power was the fact that he was an extremely skilled practitioner in the art of Burmese politics. Nu used his months out of power to mend political fences—and build some new ones. The differences among

Burma's key triumvirate of Nu, Ba Swe, and Kyaw Nyein remained, however. Nu's hold on political power, despite his comeback, is more precarious than generally believed.

It is well to remember that the power of the A.F.P.F.L. government today rests as much on its armed strength as on the will of the people. Even though it enjoys much popular support, it would not exist long if it did not possess an army to keep down that segment of its citizenry, mainly the Communists, who would topple it by force if they could.

Although the Anti-Fascist People's Freedom League is far from professing totalitarian political beliefs, it is clear that Burma today is in many ways a one-party state. This situation derives from the fact that the major opposition to the government, Communism, is scornful of parliamentary methods, preferring shortcuts and direct action to slower constitutional methods. It is not, of course, primarily the A.F.P.F.L.'s fault that it has no real opposition, although its formidable organization, its control over patronage and welfare benefits, and its close association with the idea of pyidawtha undoubtedly help perpetuate this condition. Yet the condition is not encouraging the growth of democratic government in Burma.

A grave problem which Burma's leadership must face as it seeks the effective establishment of a democratic state is the fact that Burma is by no means a homogeneous nation. Indicative of the seriousness of Burma's ethnic problem was the action taken by representatives of the important Shan minority at a January, 1957, regional conference. These Shan leaders passed a series of resolutions, the chief of which declared that the 56,000-square-mile Shan state (located on Burma's eastern border) should prepare for secession from the Union of Burma and establishment of a "separate existence" in 1958. Though permitted by Burma's constitution, this is not a move which Rangoon authorities are likely to permit. It will take all their ingenuity to prevent it, however, and, even then, they probably will not be able to put an end to Shan secession aspirations.

Because of Burma's inexperience in democratic ways, it may well be that democracy will find the most fertile soil for its roots at the village level, where a system of local government based on elections of local councils is being introduced today. It may prove the key to future effective popular rule.

FOREIGN POLICY

Still another contradiction is to be found in Burma's foreign policy. The Burmese leaders openly fear the return of Western imperialism, but less often do they express concern over the much more virile imperialism of Communist China. This attitude is reflected in a most ambivalent foreign policy toward the United States and the Chinese Communists.

Following their defeat by the Communists, remnants of the Nationalist forces in southwestern China fled into Burma, from where they occasionally made raids across the border. Such activities were taking place with official American approval, Burmese leaders claimed, or at least could be halted by the United States, to whom Chiang Kai-shek owed the existence of his regime on Taiwan. As a reprisal for this alleged American responsibility, Rangoon announced it wished an end of American aid to the country. This came about in June, 1953.

China has received quite different treatment. Burmese Communists, including Than Tun, have crossed the border to confer with Chinese Communist authorities, and Communist cadres from Burma at one time poured in a continuing stream to China for training, yet the Burmese government made no public protest. Communist China, presumably, was not responsible for what happened in Communist China.

Although U Nu stressed the fact of his country's neutrality in the cold war on virtually every possible occasion, he frequently conducted himself in such a way as to suggest considerable naivete about the workings of international politics. In the summer of 1955 Nu made a trip to the United States. His visit to the Soviet Union in the fall of the same year was to have evened the balance; his neutrality demanded that since he had visited Washington, he must also pay a call on Moscow. Yet what he said in Moscow and in Washington indicated a strong partiality to the Soviet outlook. Although Nu spoke most kindly of his American hosts, he did not attempt to identify himself with the main aims of American foreign policy. In Moscow, however, he and Soviet Premier Nikolai A. Bulganin issued a communique in which, among other things, they denounced the "policy of creating blocs" and agreed to base their relations on the five principles formulated by Indian Premier Jawaharlal Nehru and Communist China's Chou En-lai: nonaggression, noninterference in internal affairs, peaceful coexistence, cooperation based on equality and mutual economic benefit, and respect for each other's territorial integrity and sovereignty. The Burmese premier also asked the U.S.S.R. for major help in Burma's efforts toward industrial advancement and requested the Soviets to buy greater quantities of Burmese rice, promising reciprocal Burmese purchase of Soviet goods.

At U Nu's invitation, Soviet Premier Bulganin and Communist Party Secretary Nikita S. Khrushchev visited Burma in December, 1955. Although the popular reception of Bulganin and Khrushchev in Burma was not as overpowering as that accorded them in India's major cities, there is much to indicate that they made a significant impression on the Burmese people. Excepting Khrushchev's ferocious tirades against the West, especially Great Britain, with whom Burma maintains cordial relations—and to which Nu made no objection—the Russian leaders did their utmost to appear as warm, friendly, and sincere men. As a consequence, it probably will be difficult in the future to convince the Burmese that the Soviet leadership is sinister.

The Russians also apparently continued to charm U Nu. As they had done in Moscow two months previously, Premiers Nu and Bulganin issued a joint communique in Rangoon which seemed to indicate Burmese acquiesence in all the major publicly declared aims of Soviet foreign policy. In particular, the Burmese prime minister identified himself with three specific avowed aims of Soviet Far Eastern policy: the transfer of Taiwan (Formosa) to Chinese Communist control; resolution of the Indochinese problem "in accordance with the decisions of the Geneva Conference of 1954," the letter and spirit of which have been violated in numerous ways by the Communists; and the reunification of Korea, the Communist northern half of which continues to refuse foreign inspection of its so-called "democracy."

Taking their cue from the success of the American foreign-aid program throughout the world and replying to U Nu's request in Moscow for Soviet economic help, the Russian leaders took advantage of their Burma visit to offer the Burmese technological aid in seemingly generous portions. Specifically, the Soviets signed an economic agreement with the Nu government whereby the Russians promised to assist Burma in such important economic tasks as agricultural development, new irrigation projects, and the establishment of a variety of industrial plants. The Burmese agreed to pay for this help with rice; if not enough rice should be available to meet the scheduled payments, the Soviet Union agreed to permit deferment. In addition, the Russians offered to build and equip at Soviet expense a new technological institute in Rangoon. U Nu, who had frequently refused gifts from the West because they would seem to compromise Burmese neutrality, apparently had no qualms about accepting Soviet donations.

The general reaction in Burma to the Soviet visit was favorable. Many important Burmese felt that the Bulganin-Khrushchev visit and the economic aid resulting from it was proof that Burma's policy of nonalignment in world affairs was paying off. Moreover, it was pointed out that the new Burmese economic ties with the Soviet Union would help to solve the problem of Burma's rice surplus. As one Burmese businessman put it, "If we can make a deal, why shouldn't we? If the Russians are willing to give us what we need for something we can't get rid of, then let's take it."[5]

U Nu's joining with the Soviet leaders in such declarations as those made in Moscow and Rangoon probably were not dictated by a pro-Communist outlook, regardless of the lack of wisdom evident in some of his actions. Yet Rangoon has not always spoken with one voice. The pronouncements of Kyaw Nyein, one of Burma's leading political figures and a powerful member of the present government, indicate a

[5] Quoted in New York *Times*, December 2, 1955.

considerably clearer comprehension of the realities of mid-twentieth-century world politics. Chairman of the Anti-Colonial Bureau of the Asian Socialist Organization as well as Burma's leading socialist theoretician, he has been a frequent outspoken critic of the "new imperialism" of the Soviet Union. Ba Swe also is more critical of the U.S.S.R. than Nu.

If Burma's approach to its relations with the United States and China partook of the contradictory under Nu, he yet was much concerned over American-Sino relations. Nu sought diligently, for example, to bring Washington and Peiping closer together. Concluding a good-will visit to Communist China in December, 1954, the Burmese premier asked Peiping's leaders to seek an "understanding" with the United States in order to reduce tensions in the Far East. On an earlier occasion he told Secretary of State John Foster Dulles in Rangoon that "we want to be friendly toward both sides." Nu, whose government was the first non-Soviet-bloc country to recognize Communist China, seemingly sincerely believed that the United States and Peiping could resolve their differences. But if these countries were not willing to work to reduce tensions between themselves, then he and his nation certainly were not going to align themselves with either side. In this policy U Nu had the support of both U Ba Swe and U Kyaw Nyein, who agreed with Nu that peace was possible only if coexistence replaced the cold war and its accompanying arms race. Ba Swe's and Kyaw Nyein's differences with Nu stemmed, not from disagreements over policy objectives, but rather from some of the ways in which Nu frequently seemed to manipulate this neutralism to the advantage of the nations of the Communist camp.

That Nu's departure as premier was not the signal for a reorientation of Burmese foreign policy was stated by his successor, Ba Swe, upon his assumption of office. Much of this talk was designed to placate the ousted Nu, but even so, it was generally believed that Ba Swe would continue to pursue a neutralist foreign policy, although his means of implementing such a policy might differ from those of U Nu.

Despite its concern for a revival of Western imperialism in

Southeast Asia, Burma under Nu was, nevertheless, a supporter of Western values in the field of foreign relations. In June, 1950, Burma gave its backing, for example, to the Security Council resolutions calling for United Nations action against North Korea, although it claimed it was "not in a position to render any effective assistance." A close ally of Nehru's India and a key member of the Colombo Powers, Burma under both Nu and Ba Swe has displayed a passionate belief in the right of all nations to run their own affairs. This applied to Chinese and Russians as well as Americans and Englishmen—and, of course, to Burma itself. In this respect Burma offered no contradictions whatsoever.

U Ba Swe's assumption of the premiership, which included primary responsibility for the direction of foreign relations, was followed by the first open crisis between Burma and Communist China. In July, 1956, *The Nation,* an influential Rangoon newspaper, broke the story that Chinese Communist troops had infiltrated into Burma and had engaged in shooting incidents with Burmese army units. Burma's foreign office, seemingly somewhat reluctantly, announced on July 31 that much of what *The Nation* had said was true: Chinese Communist troops had set up outposts on Burmese territory. According to Ba Swe, Chinese forces had slowly moved into the border area of northern Burma over a period of two years. The premier did not consider the situation as serious and expressed the belief that removal of the Chinese troops could be settled by negotiations between the two countries.

Three separate "invasions," or incursions, seem to have taken place. One of these reportedly consisted of some three thousand troops which in mid-October, 1956, were claimed by the Rangoon newspaper *The Nation* to be only nine days' march from the north Burma center of Putao (Fort Hertz). A second incursion took place in the wild and only partly settled border area of Kachin state in northern Burma. In early October, 1956, Burma's premier stated that Burmese forces had recently probed this region and that "no Chinese troops were found anywhere." It was generally conceded by Burmese authorities, although reluctantly, that there had been Chinese Communist troops in this area but that they had withdrawn. The other region into which Chinese Communist forces had moved was the former "Wa states" area, part of present-day Shan state (one of the members of the federal Union of Burma). Rangoon newspapers claimed that there were more than fifteen hundred Chinese troops in the northern part of the Wa states, but Ba Swe estimated the number at "around five hundred only."

Burma protested the incursions into its territory to Peiping, but there were conflicting reports as to the Communists' response to Rangoon's action. Negotiations were begun, however, and Ba Swe announced in early October that Communist China had agreed to withdraw its troops from the areas in dispute—which the Rangoon newspaper *The Nation* later stated had not been done. China itself in August had admitted through Peiping radio that Chinese troops had occupied outposts in "disputed" Chinese-Burmese frontier areas, stating that these troops would not be withdrawn until a settlement had been reached. *The Nation,* which seemed to be forcing the Burmese government to release more information on the subject than it appeared inclined to do, claimed that the Chinese had suggested to Burma that if the Burmese would withdraw their troops stationed along the northern frontiers in territory claimed by Peiping, China would remove its forces from the Wa states in Burma. *The Nation* noted that Chinese Communist maps included part of Burma's northern Kachin state as Chinese territory. What the Peiping leadership seemed to be saying, with apparently little shame, was that if Burma would recognize Chinese Communist claims to part of Kachin state, the Communists would withdraw their troops from the Wa states as a territorial *quid pro quo.* There were other reports out of Burma and Communist China that Peiping had indicated it would make no major concessions on the issue until former Premier U Nu visited China in late October, a visit he had been planning for some time. Communist Chinese Premier and Foreign Minister Chou En-lai also was scheduled to visit

Rangoon in December, 1956, and it was indicated that this might serve as the occasion for a final resolution of the border problem.

Burma's frontier with China was defined in a 1941 treaty between the United Kingdom and the Chiang Kai-shek government. Upon achieving its independence, Burma believed it took over the territory previously governed by Britain. The border had never been properly demarcated in many areas, however, giving the problem an element of vagueness which the Communist Chinese obviously were seeking to exploit.

It soon became apparent that Burma's leaders were willing to settle border differences with the Chinese Communists on terms less than favorable, if necessary. In November, U Nu, returning from his visit with Chinese Premier Chou En-lai in Peiping, disclosed that his country would relinquish its perpetual lease of one hundred square miles of Chinese territory (known as the Namwan Assigned Tract) on Burma's northern frontier. Burma also would cede three villages in northern Kachin state to Peiping, Nu said. The Chinese, in return, would recognize Burma's claim to the rest of the territory inherited from the British.

In spite of the willingness of the Burmese leadership to compromise, the December, 1956, visit of Chou En-lai to Burma did not result in a final settlement. The Burmese and Chinese premiers discussed the matter at length, but the statement they issued stated that the border dispute was near solution, but still unsettled. It was generally believed, however, that a final agreement on the subject would soon be reached.

But why did the Peiping leadership choose this time to raise the issue? There are several possible explanations. One is that China did not wish to raise the matter publicly at this time; it was *The Nation,* after all, which broke the story. Burmese authorities obviously knew of the situation, but they gave no public notice of the problem until *The Nation's* story, which probably derived from leaks by officials who were discontented with the government's tightlipped policy on the controversy. Such a move would have had the advantage of revealing the border situation without involving the Burmese government. A second explanation is that Communist China may have sought actually to lay effective claim to certain territory before such territory had been under Burmese jurisdiction for sufficient time for it to derive legal validity from that factor alone. After all, Chinese maps, under Chiang Kai-shek as well as Mao Tse-tung, have shown a good part of Kachin state as Chinese territory. It also is possible that the Chinese move was designed to keep pressure on the Burmese government as a means of reminding the Burmese of the possibility of trouble with China if their foreign policy moved in a direction inimicable to Peiping.

The Burmese reaction to the situation, once it had been brought out into the open, was less clouded than the factors motivating the Chinese. U Nu, still his party's leader as head of the Anti-Fascist People's Freedom League, stated in July, 1956, that Burmese relations with the United States had shown "a tangible improvement." In the same speech Nu also noted that there were "stooges, spies and fifth columnists" aplenty in Burma who were working for "big powers" and "threatening Burma's independence." His remarks seemed aimed at pro-Communist groups and individuals, elements of Burma's Chinese minority, and persons associated with the Soviet and Communist Chinese embassies. A further indication that Burma might in fact be drawing closer to the United States was given in March, 1957, with the report that the Burmese government would accept a $25,000,000 loan and a $17,500,000 loan in Burmese currency from the United States government, both repayable over a forty-year period. The possibility is strong that the United States and Burma will draw closer together in the years ahead.

CHAPTER 8

THE INTERNATIONAL RELATIONS
OF SOUTHEAST ASIA

THE EVENTS of the last fifteen years have had immense consequences for Southeast Asia in the realm of international relations. After a frustrating era of colonialism, when their relations with other nations and among themselves were directed from London, Paris, The Hague, and Washington, the countries of this part of the world gained in the years after the Second World War, among other aspects of national independence, the right to conduct their own foreign affairs. For the Philippines, ruled first by Spaniards and then Americans, the ending of the colonial period marked the first time in nearly four hundred years that it had been able to direct its relations with other peoples. The era of external control of their foreign relations had not been nearly so long for the Burmese, Indochinese, and Malays, but in their eyes it had been long enough. The Indonesians, who had given birth to the empires of Srivijaya and Majapahit in the age before the Western penetration of Southeast Asia, also had had no control over their country's international relations since the effective establishment of Dutch rule in the islands. Thailand had never lost nominal direction of its foreign relations, never having been a Western colony, but its contacts with the rest of the world, particularly with its Southeast Asian neighbors, had been limited nevertheless. When the foreign office at Bangkok had cause to concern itself with neighboring Burma or Indochina, for example, it had been to far-off London or Paris that it directed itself, not Rangoon or Saigon.

One of the consequences of the period of Western colonialism is that the political leaders of these lands are today lacking in experience in the art of foreign-policy determination and implementation. If these leaders have seemed unnecessarily wavering in some aspects of their foreign policies in the years since independence was gained, and unduly rigid in others, it is partially because of this inexperience. This factor also explains the naivete which has marked much of the foreign-policy outlooks of these states in their first years of freedom.

This conspicuous inexperience in foreign affairs is not the only legacy for Southeast Asia's international relations of the Western colonial period. Of equal importance is the sense of isolation which the long years of alien rule impressed upon these lands. During the Western colonial era the orientation of the average educated Burmese was to London, as that of his Indonesian counterpart was to The Hague. This orientation was by no means purely political; it was economic and cultural as well. Although there was great interest in other Asian peoples among intellectuals in these countries, there was little knowledge of them and even less contact. The legacy of this period of isolation cannot help but influence the political personality of Southeast Asia today. Nations, like individuals, do not readily escape from their past. The countries of Southeast Asia are no exception. Their foreign policies today display a strong imprint of the centuries of enforced isolation. The fact that few Southeast Asian cabinet members know their opposite numbers in the other countries of this part of the world is but a single example of the impact of this tradition of isolation. This situation is being remedied, but slowly.

If the reality of present-day relations among the states of Southeast Asia is to be comprehended, the isolating impact of the division of the area into several separate Western colonies must be fully realized. Even before the beginning of the Western intrusion, intraregional relations were considerably limited by the geography of the area—a geography of mountainous islands and peninsulas, mitigated partially by calm seas. This mountainous terrain explains in good measure the historic division of the region into a multiplicity of small states. If relations among the peoples of Southeast Asia were restricted before the arrival of the West, they were limited even more by the arbitrary boundaries erected by the European imperial powers to separate their colonies. So effective was this isolation that no real contact can be said to have existed among the several nationalist movements in Southeast Asia, even on the eve of the Pacific war. Because each of the nationalist movements was brought into being in opposition to colonial rule, there was a regionwide spiritual link among the various nationalist leaders, but this assumed no organizational form.

The Second World War greatly stimulated regional feeling in this part of the world. The creation of the Allies' Southeast Asia Command under Admiral Lord Louis Mountbatten in 1943 popularized the concept of Southeast Asia as a distinct region. The Japanese occupation also stimulated regional consciousness, for this was the first time the area had ever known a single ruler. Moreover, Japan played a prominent part in the encouragement of regionalism by introducing various of the Southeast Asian nationalist leaders to one another. The Assembly of the Greater East Asiastic Nations, held in Tokyo in November, 1943, for example, was attended by President José P. Laurel of the Philippines, Prime Minister Ba Maw of Burma, and Prince Wan Waithayakon of Thailand, present in place of Premier Phibun Songgram, said to be ill in Bangkok. This was the first meeting of these three prominent Asian leaders.

SOUTHEAST ASIAN REGIONALISM

In the years which followed the end of the Pacific war, several proposals for closer political collaboration among the peoples of Southeast Asia were put forward by indigenous leaders. No governmental international organization of the peoples of this part of the world took place, however, although an unofficial body called the Southeast Asia League was set up in Bangkok in September, 1947. Organized by the Viet Minh agent Tran Van Giau, who came to Thailand in 1945 to build support for Ho Chi Minh's Viet Minh movement in Vietnam, the Southeast Asia League was a front organization to cover up a variety of activities, including gunrunning, in aid of the Indochinese Communists. It included such well-known Southeast Asian Communists as Tran Van Luan, later to head the Viet Minh news service in Rangoon; Le Hi, then editor of the Viet Minh propaganda publication in Bangkok; and Prince Souvanna Vong, a prominent leader in the Communist movement in the Indochinese state of Laos. Several prominent Thai, including former Premier Pridi Banomyong, then Prime Minister Thamrong Nawasawat, and Tiang Sirikhand, Thailand's controversial onetime deputy minister of interior, were associated in one way or another with the league, but they appear not to have been in on the Community conspiracy.[1]

If the Communist-sponsored Southeast Asia League was the only postwar regional proposal to assume even tentative organizational form, it was by no means the only one to be advanced. That none of the others ever came into being is not so surprising when it is recalled that these countries have enjoyed the right to conduct their own foreign policy for only a few years. Yet there have been those Southeast Asian politicians who wanted closer political collaboration and who worked sincerely in its behalf. Such a leader was General Aung San, moving spirit of Burma's wartime guerrilla army and deputy head of the postwar interim government in Burma as well as president of the Anti-Fascist People's Freedom League, the nationalist coalition which won independence for Burma. As early as October, 1945, at a moment apparently when he had lost hope that British gratitude for his belated military assistance against Japan would result in the grant of freedom to Burma, Aung San called for an Asian "Potsdam Conference" to "plan a united campaign to achieve freedom within the shortest possible time."[2] In January, 1947, further elaborating

[1] For a fuller account of the Southeast Asia League, see Richard Butwell, "Communist Liaison in Southeast Asia," *United Asia*, VI (1954), 146-51.
[2] New Delhi *Hindustan Times*, November 10, 1945.

this idea in a broadcast from New Delhi, he forecast the formation of an Asian Commonwealth, which would constitute a united Asian front "against imperialistic rule." Expanding what he meant by an Asian Commonwealth, Aung San declared, "While India should be one entity and China another, Southeast Asia as a whole should form an entity—then, finally, we should come together in a bigger union with the participation of other parts of Asia as well."[8] Again in April the Burmese leader called for greater regional cooperation, publicly urging the formation of a Southeast Asian economic union consisting of Burma, Indonesia, Thailand, Indochina, and Malaya.[4] Burma's leadership in the attempt to establish a Southeast Asia league or union ended, however, with the tragic assassination of General Aung San in the summer of 1947. The support of subsequent Burmese national leaders, U Nu and U Ba Swe, for their country's participation in the Colombo Powers grouping and their desire to improve relations with neighboring Thailand indicate a sincere wish on their part for friendship with other South and Southeast Asian countries, but this policy does not represent a continuation of Aung San's efforts to establish governmental organizational links among Burma and the lands to its east and southeast.

In the early postwar years Burma was not the only Southeast Asian state in which projects for closer regional political collaboration were proposed. On July 1, 1947, the then Thai premier, Thamrong Nawasawat, announced that Thailand and France would jointly sponsor the formation of a Pan Southeast Asian Union, which would include Thailand, Cambodia, Vietnam, and Laos, to begin with, and which later would be expanded to embrace Burma, Indonesia, Borneo, and India. The union would concern itself primarily, according to Thamrong, with regional plans for the joint development of irrigation, fisheries, communications, and other such resources of the area. Public opinion in Bangkok, usually most apathetic, was opposed to the union from the start, the opposition parties leading the attack with charges that the Thamrong administra-

[8] Edinburgh *Scotsman*, November 28, 1947.
[4] Singapore *Straits Times*, April 19, 1947.

tion was subservient to the French. The union never was formed, being killed in its embryonic stage by this almost instant reaction against it.

The proposed union, however, did inspire the Communist Tran Van Giau and his colleagues to set up their Southeast Asia League, which was formed in September, 1947, and suppressed two months later after the return of supporters of Field Marshal Phibun Songgram to power in Thailand. Phibun's suppression of the league, together with his general aloofness from postwar movements to back the cause of nationalism in other Southeast Asian lands, has led some observers to state that the Thai premier—a known nationalist of strong convictions—has no wish to associate more closely with Thailand's neighbors. Such statements are far too strongly put. Like the leaders of Thailand's several Southeast Asian neighbors, Phibun supports regional collaboration, if such cooperation can be arranged in the form he wishes. His state visit to Burma in late 1955, his first such trip to a Southeast Asian country since assuming power in the 1930's, gave indication of his willingness to meet Burmese Premier U Nu at least halfway in the latter's efforts to improve relations between the two countries. Thailand's desire for closer relations with the Indochinese states, particularly Laos, also reveals Phibun's concern for friendly association with neighboring countries. The visit of Laotian Prime Minister Kathay Sasorith to Thailand in 1955 was only one indication of the conscious efforts being made by the governments of both Thailand and Laos to strengthen the ties between them.

On more than one occasion between 1947 and 1950 Thai Premier Phibun Songgram expressed his anxious desire for a Southeast Asian defense pact. In October, 1949, he took the initiative in inviting Burma, the Philippines, and India to Bangkok for talks on political and economic matters in Southeast Asia. The conference was never held, however, because of lack of enthusiastic response from the invited states. Thailand itself participated in the Philippines-convened Baguio Conference of the following year, although it subsequently announced that it was not ready to join any Southeast Asian bloc. This came after the Thai government had concluded a military assistance agreement with the United States in October, 1950, which apparently gave it the security it was seeking. Phibun thereafter gave up whatever limited ideas for regional collaboration he possessed until the Anglo-American declaration of April, 1954, calling for a Southeast Asian collective defense organization. The Thai premier quickly associated his country with that project, and Thailand was represented at the September conference at Manila which set up the Southeast Asian Treaty Organization.[5]

Support for closer regional collaboration in Southeast Asia also was forthcoming in the postwar years from Ho Chi Minh, leader of the Communist-captured nationalist movement in Vietnam. In 1945, in the wake of the Japanese defeat, the Viet Minh leader sent a message to President Sukarno in Djakarta, asking the Indonesian nationalist to join with him in a common declaration of purpose in their mutual struggle against colonialism as well as to participate in the formation of a preparatory commission to organize appropriate machinery for future cooperation among the Southeast Asian countries.[6] Since nothing came of the proposal, it would appear likely that it was turned down by the Indonesians. It would seem highly plausible that Sukarno, already under attack from some Dutch quarters as being a Communist and hoping for support from the United States, would have been most cautious and circumspect in replying to Ho Chi Minh's overtures.

Unlike those of Burma, the attempts of the Philippines to establish a regional organization in Southeast Asia did not end in the early postwar period. The island republic, in contrast to the former British colony, continued to propose a variety of plans for closer Southeast Asian relations long after it was apparent that nobody was really interested in the idea. The leader of the Philippines' efforts to draw the nations of this part of the world nearer to each other was General Carlos P. Romulo, who before the war advocated a Pan-Malay Union.

[5] The Southeast Asian Treaty Organization is examined in the next chapter.
[6] Harold Isaacs, in Phillips Talbot (ed.), *South Asia in the World Today* (Chicago, 1950), 165-66. See also Milton Sacks in the same work, pp. 206-207.

Following the New Delhi Conference of 1949, called by India to support Indonesia's bid for independence, he began working for an anti-Communist South and Southeast Asian bloc, which he hoped would include India, Pakistan, Ceylon, Australia, and New Zealand as well as the countries of Southeast Asia proper, with future American support also anticipated. Most of these countries did not want to align themselves with either side in the cold war, and so nothing much came of the Baguio Conference called by the Philippines in the summer of 1950. The Philippines received an opportunity to revive its plans for a Southeast Asian regional organization in April, 1954, when American Secretary of State John Foster Dulles and Sir Anthony Eden, British foreign secretary, jointly called for a collective defense body in the area. Negotiations eventually resulted in the Philippines serving as host to the conference which drafted the treaty for the organization.

The most unreceptive of all the Southeast Asian lands to any form of regional political collaboration has been Indonesia. In April, 1951, when the suggestion was advanced that the Southeast Asian countries should be included in a Pacific pact, Foreign Minister Mohammed Rum declared that his government had no intention of associating itself with any alignment inconsistent with Indonesia's foreign policy of "active neutrality." Sunarjo, foreign minister in the Ali Sastroamidjojo cabinet which ruled the country from mid 1953 through mid 1955, expressed himself in a similar vein on several occasions, indicating a desire for greater Asian-African cooperation rather than closer relations limited to the states of Southeast Asia. On one occasion in recent years, however, Indonesia has been seen to deviate slightly from what has otherwise been a most consistent foreign-policy line. This was early in 1951 when it sounded out the other Southeast Asian countries on holding a conference to discuss the conflict between Bao Dai, France, and the Ho Chi Minh revolutionaries, a conference which, probably because it failed to get the response Indonesia hoped for, was never held.[7]

Another fence-sitting country with respect to regional col-

[7] Paris *Le Monde*, February 3, 1951.

laboration has been the Indochinese state of Cambodia. On September 27, 1953, Penn Nouth, then Cambodian prime minister, declared that the Southeast Asian lands, including his own, should sign a common defense pact in view of their common danger of foreign invasion. Yet two weeks earlier this same leader had told the Communist-led Viet Minh by radio that if it would get out of their kingdom, the Cambodians would not fight the Communists in neighboring Vietnam. An examination of Cambodian policy statements since 1950 will reveal that this wavering has been one of the most constant factors in the country's extremely flexible foreign policy. Because Cambodia, like Laos, was excluded from participation in the Manila Southeast Asian Treaty Organization Conference in September, 1954, by the terms of the Geneva agreement signed the previous July, it was not required to commit itself with respect to the Western-sponsored Seato. There are strong indications, however, that if it had been forced to make such a decision, Cambodia would have declared in favor of remaining outside the new regional defense grouping—despite its friendship with the United States and its strong reliance on American aid. Prince Norodom Sihanouk, formerly Cambodia's king, stated following his smashing electoral triumph in the fall of 1955 that Cambodia would follow a policy of neutrality. The trend toward neutrality in Cambodian foreign policy would seem to have strengthened since that time.

PRIMACY OF NATIONALISM

The most important thing to note about the several indigenous proposals for closer regional political collaboration, from General Aung San's suggestions to those of the Vietnamese Communist leader Ho Chi Minh, is that they were, for the most part, made during the early postwar years. Although nobody ever seemed to want to second anybody else's plan, almost everybody had his own proposal. The unity of feeling created by the common experience of colonial rule was, no doubt, the basis of these several plans. With the attainment of independence, however, this unity began to wane. Nationalism commenced to display its divisive tendencies. This, probably more than any other single factor, explains the continuously lessening appeal which political regionalism seems to have had for the leaders and peoples of Southeast Asia.

There can be little doubt that this newly triumphant nationalism is the most singularly influential political factor in the region at the present time. Where the old loyalties were primarily to the village or the family, the present ones follow political boundaries to an increasing extent. And the primary objective of the nationalism which has so aroused them is political, economic, and social freedom—independence in all ways possible from the peoples of other lands.

In the years before the Second World War one of the consequences of this nationalism had been to bring its advocates in the several Southeast Asian lands closer together, spiritually if not in actual experience. Its hour of triumph, however, has revealed its inherent divisive tendencies. Closer political collaboration has not made progress in Southeast Asia in the years since the Pacific war, because adherence to such regional cooperation would lessen the freedom of action of the new national states—which freedom of action they wish to maintain above all other things. Rather than drawing closer together in the postwar years, these states are becoming increasingly differentiated, not only in their attitudes toward each other, but also in their approaches to larger world problems, such as the cold war, Chinese Communist expansionism, and other matters. The upheaval of the postwar years to fulfill the urge of nationalism brought with it civil war and economic dislocation, but in spite of this, the leaders of the Southeast Asian states believe their fight for national independence was justified. They do not wish now to give up any of their newly acquired sovereignty to a regional supranational political entity.

PAN-ASIAN SENTIMENTS

If divisive nationalism has served as a barrier to closer regional collaboration in postwar Southeast Asia, the same also might be said of quite an opposite tendency, that of thinking in Asia-wide terms. The idea of an all-Asian grouping, which has attracted some of Southeast Asia's leaders in recent years, is by no means a new one. It can be traced back to such ventures as the Russian-convened Congress of the Nations of the Orient at Baku in September, 1920, the Nagasaki Pan-Asiatic Conference of 1926, and the 1934 Pan-Asiatic Labor Conference in Ceylon, among other events, its past sponsors including such distinguished Asian figures as Jawaharlal Nehru.

A large number of plans for closer political relations among the several Asian states were put forward in the postwar years. The unofficial Asian Relations Conference in New Delhi in March-April, 1947, in fact, was hailed in many quarters as the beginning of the establishment of some kind of Asian union. All of the Southeast Asian countries were represented among the thirty-one states sending delegates to the conference, but the unity of the many prominent Asians attending the New Delhi meetings appears to have been limited to an almost unanimous anti-European sentiment, moral support for the liberation struggles in those Asian lands not yet independent, and a widespread belief in the possibility of Asian neutrality in any future world war. The representatives of the Southeast Asian countries seemed very much afraid that integration into any Asia-wide bloc would be at the cost of their newly acquired political independence. A nongovernmental body called the Asian Relations Organization was set up by the conference, however, its work to be carried on by national units in the several countries of Asia. More than six years later the A.R.O. had succeeded in establishing national councils in only Burma and Malaya of the Southeast Asian countries. An East Asian Conference in Djakarta, to include Burma, Malaya, Thailand, Vietnam, and Indonesia, was to have been called in 1948 preliminary to the next planned Asian Relations Conference in China in 1949, but neither the Indonesian nor the Chinese meeting ever took place.

If the Asian Relations Conference of 1947 did not itself result in the formation of a continuing Asia-wide organization of any importance, it did establish contacts which were to produce an all-Asian grouping of considerably more strength than the A.R.O. In New Delhi in March-April, 1947, such Asian Socialists as Indonesia's Sutan Sjahrir, Burma's U Ba Swe and U Tun Win, and India's Jayaprakash Narayan met for the first time. They decided on this occasion that the formation of a South Asian Socialist organization of some kind was imperative, but circumstances were to prevent the establishment of such a body in the years which immediately followed the New Delhi Conference. In March, 1952, representatives of the Socialist parties of the three countries met in Rangoon, together with observers from the right and left wings of the then split Japanese Social Democrats, and plans were laid for the Rangoon Conference of 1953, expanded from a South Asian to an all-Asian conference "because the problems to be solved are Asia-wide." Full delegations from Malaya, Pakistan, Israel, and Egypt, as well as from Burma, Indonesia, India, and Japan, attended the Rangoon Socialist Conference in January, 1953, with observers present from other Asian lands, although there was no representation at all from such countries as China, Vietnam, Thailand, the Philippines, Cambodia, or Laos. An Asia-wide organization was set up, to be called the Organization of Asian Socialist Parties and comprising a conference (to be held every other year), a bureau (to meet twice annually), and a permanent secretariat (to be located in Rangoon). One of the major drawbacks of this organization at the present time is that only two of its national parties (the Burmese and the Israeli) are in power in their countries.

Neither the Asian Relations Conference nor the Asian Socialist Organization set up by the Rangoon Conference of 1953 represented collaboration of the governments of Asia. On only one occasion prior to 1955 did these governments gather together on an Asia-wide basis, and this was in January, 1949, at the Indian-convened Indonesian Conference, following the second Dutch "police action" of December, 1948, against the nationalist revolutionaries in the former Netherlands colony. This conference was called by Prime Minister Nehru of India, at the suggestion of the premier of Burma, U Nu, to deal specifically with the Indonesian situation, and was attended by nineteen states, including Australia and New

Zealand. At its final session it passed a resolution calling upon the United Nations Security Council, among other things, to arrange for the complete transfer of power by the Dutch over Indonesia by January 1, 1950, to the United States of Indonesia. It is generally agreed that the action taken at New Delhi in January, 1949, was an influential factor in the ending of the Dutch-Indonesian war in the same year.

The several suggestions for an Asian federation or union have been paralleled in the postwar years by a number of proposals for a Pacific pact which would include the United States and other Western powers as well as the East Asian countries. Such suggestions have come, for the most part, from the late President Elpidio Quirino of the Philippines, Chiang Kai-shek of the Nationalist Chinese regime on Taiwan (Formosa), and President Syngman Rhee of South Korea, thus partially explaining their lack of appeal to Southeast Asians, who regard Chiang and Rhee as unrepresentative of modern Asia. It was in line with such proposals that the Philippines called the Baguio Conference of 1950, which, though comprising only South and Southeast Asian states to begin with, was to have been expanded later, according to Philippine expectations. The Baguio meeting was a singularly ineffective gathering, its basic purpose from the Filipino point of view having been completely changed in order to attract such neutralist countries as Indonesia and India. Originally intended to be a conference to set up an anti-Communist alliance, it turned out to be a general discussion of economic and social questions, with Communism a taboo topic. Typical of most of Southeast Asia's reaction to the Philippine overtures was Premier Nu's declaration that Burma was not prepared to join any such union unless it were "sponsored by the right people at the right time" —neither of which conditions, by implication, was met by the Quirino plan.

SOUTH ASIAN BLOC

Still another kind of political association in this part of the world to be proposed in the postwar years was a bloc among the states of South Asia, which is generally defined to include

India, Pakistan, and Ceylon as well as Southeast Asia. In January, 1949, S. W. R. D. Bandaranaike, leader of the Ceylonese delegation to the Indonesian Conference in New Delhi and presently premier of Ceylon, proposed closer economic and political cooperation among India, Pakistan, Burma, Indonesia, and Ceylon. Nothing came of the proposal at the time, and it was not until April, 1954, that leaders of these five South Asian states met together, or so it was declared ahead of time, specifically for talks about relations among themselves. This was the result of an invitation extended by the then premier of Ceylon, Sir John Kotelawala, to meet in Colombo for such talks. Sir John called upon the countries of South Asia to unite in a "joint endeavor" to become an effective force in the preservation of world peace, expressing the hope that the premiers of the five lands would frequently come together for consultations along the lines of the meetings of the Commonwealth prime ministers. So preoccupied were the five premiers with matters related to the Geneva Conference on Indochina then in session, and so divided in their views about some of them, that they ignored the main reason for the meeting being called in the first place, with the result that no standing machinery emerged from the conference. However, the Colombo Powers, as the five states have come to be called, did gain recognition as a significant bloc in world politics.

Meeting for the second time in Bogor, Indonesia, in late December, 1954, the premiers of the five Colombo Powers authorized the Indonesians to invite various Asian and African nations to a "peace conference" in April, 1955. Indonesian Prime Minister Ali Sastroamidjojo had proposed such an Afro-Asian conference at the first meeting of the Colombo Powers, but no definite date for the gathering was set at that time. Indonesian leaders immediately announced they hoped the April talks would "bring lasting peace to Asia by reconciling the conflicting viewpoints of East and West," which seemed quite a chore for a conference at which only the East would be represented. At their December meeting the Colombo Powers also decided to invite Communist China to the parley, which some doubting elements outside Asia thought might serve to drive a further wedge between East and West rather than reconcile the two. On the other hand, there were those, more limited in number and vocal strength, who hoped this action might help start regularizing outcast Communist China's relations with the rest of the world and so bring closer together East and West, as the Indonesians had suggested.

One thing was certain, however. The fact that the five South Asian countries decided to hold an all-Asian conference indicated that the idea of a community of interests among the lands of Asia was by no means dead. The 1947 Asian Relations Conference in India received much publicity as marking the beginning of closer Asian political relations, which, it is generally admitted, failed to materialize. Due partially to the Communist rise to power in Peiping, the projected second meeting of the conference in China in 1949 was not held, nor was a session convened at an alternative location. Likewise, the 1949 Conference on Indonesia failed to produce any permanent machinery for closer collaboration, while the Organization of Asian Socialist Parties has been limited by the fact that there are no Socialist parties of any consequence in many lands of the Far East, including Vietnam, the Philippines, Thailand, Pakistan, and Korea, not to mention mainland China and Taiwan (Formosa). Despite past failures, however, the idea of an Asian community persisted in the minds of such leaders as Jawaharlal Nehru, Ali Sastroamidjojo, U Nu, and others—although some of these, like Dr. Ali, who undoubtedly thought Indonesia's leading role in holding the parley might raise the faltering prestige of his much-criticized government, clearly were not motivated by such thoughts alone.

With respect to the composition of the Bandung Conference, it is worthy of note that not all the lands of Asia and Africa were invited. The Nationalist Chinese government of Chiang Kai-shek was conspicuously snubbed, which, though probably not justified, made more sense than the exclusion of some other countries, such as Israel, Nigeria, and the Union of South Africa. Syria, Jordan, and Lebanon were part of Asia in the eyes of the Colombo Powers—as was Turkey!—but not Israel, which had been part of Asia for the 1947 Asian Relations

Conference as well as for the Organization of Asian Socialist Parties. Indonesia's affinity with the Moslem lands of the Middle East was responsible for the exclusion of Israel, indicating that the ties between the Southeast Asian archipelago republic and the Moslem Middle East are of consequence to the region's international relations. Also not invited were the rival regimes of north and south Korea, although north and south Vietnam were extended invitations.

Significantly, the April, 1955, conference—which was held in the beautiful Indonesian city of Bandung—included African as well as Asian nations. This was but a continuation of the trend observable in the so-called Arab-Asian bloc's concern, inside and outside the United Nations, for the colonial countries of Africa and in the Asian Socialist Organization's establishment of an Anti-Colonial Bureau primarily to assist the several African nationalist movements in their efforts toward independence. It is altogether possible that the world is heading toward a bipolarity somewhat different from its present two-bloc anatomy: a bipolarity of Asia and Africa versus Europe and the Americas. Indonesia was reported on the eve of the first meeting of the Colombo Powers as desiring the creation of a permanent Asian organization, on the lines of the United Nations, to obviate Western interference in purely Asian matters.

THE BANDUNG CONFERENCE

Although the fact that the Bandung Conference was held indicated that the idea of an Asian community of interests was not dead, the actions of the conference gave vivid proof that such a community still had a long way to go before it became a vital reality. If the Bandung Conference pointed out one thing above anything else, it was that there was not yet a true Afro-Asian bloc—indeed, not even an Asian bloc!

The delegates from twenty-nine nations, only sixteen of which were then United Nations members, agreed on many matters during the course of the conference. They agreed, for example, to condemn colonialism, which did not come as much of a surprise, considering the fact that anticolonialism was the strongest bond among them. They backed Nehru's proposal that the testing of nuclear weapons be suspended. As was to be expected, they very strongly championed the cause of peace. And they backed Indonesian claims to Dutch-held West New Guinea, supported Yemen's pretenses to the British protectorate of Aden, and generally championed the cause of the Arab peoples of the Middle East, whether fighting for independence against the French in Morocco or Tunisia or seeking redress of the grievances of the Palestine refugees.

If they concerned themselves vitally with Aden, however, they ignored the problem of Korea completely. And although they talked about the difficulties in Vietnam, they did not do or say anything which brought solution of these difficulties any closer. In short, their discussions were conspicuous for the fact that they concerned themselves with matters over which they had little direct control, as in the case of nuclear weapons, or which represented grievances against nations not in attendance at the conference—for example, the Dutch in West New Guinea, the French in North Africa, the British in Aden, and the Israelis and the problem of the Arab refugees. A pattern only too obvious at the April, 1954, meeting of the Colombo Powers was being repeated—the less the assembled nations could do about a given problem, the louder they talked about it. When it came to problems over which Asians could exercise some influence and for which they bore some responsibility—Kashmir, Vietnam, and Korea, for instance—the delegates spoke in more subdued terms.

It was not, however, the fact that the Asian community failed to shoulder its responsibilities which was the most significant thing about the Bandung Conference—it was, rather, that it was obvious that there was no real Asian community to begin with except on a superficial sentimental level. Asia at Bandung spoke with three voices, not including several brands of whispers. Loudest of these three voices at the outset of the conference was that of the pro-Western nations: the Philippines, Thailand, Pakistan, Iran, Iraq, and Turkey. They condemned Communism as the new imperialism and strongly defended their alliances with the West. In their attack upon

Communism they were joined, somewhat surprisingly, by Ceylon's Sir John Kotelawala, who called the first meeting of the Colombo Powers. Sir John, democrat but neutralist, charged that Communist policy aimed at converting the free nations of Asia and Europe "into satellites of the Soviet Union and Communist China."

Ranged against the vocal pro-Western elements were the more soft-spoken Communist representatives. Chief Communist spokesman at the conference was China's sly and personable Chou En-lai. The Communists' sweet talk at Bandung failed to dim the perception of the pro-Western nations as to the real intentions of the Sino-Soviet bloc: the division and weakening of the ranks of all who would oppose them—in Asia and Africa, as well as Europe and America. Unfortunately, however, the Communists' true colors were not perceived by all who attended the Bandung meeting—including, apparently, such a key Asian figure as U Nu.

Finally, there were the neutralists, comprising most of the countries participating in the conference. Jawaharlal Nehru was the leading spokesman for this group, although he was not particularly conspicuous for guiding the conference's development along the lines he wished. The neutralists, including U Nu and Ali Sastroamidjojo as well as Nehru, had hoped that cold-war alignments could be forgotten amid the triumphant unity of pan-Asian sentiments. They could not have been more wrong. The impact of the cold war pervaded almost all aspects of the Bandung meeting. There were the pro-Western elements, and the Communists, and the neutralists—and they succeeded in reaching no more agreement among themselves than these forces have accomplished in the world at large. The communique which the Bandung delegates presented at the conference's closing session was a facade of common views. There was no genuine meeting of the minds at Bandung—despite the bond of anticolonialism—because deep divisions continued to afflict the so-called Asian community, divisions which reflected to a very great extent the tensions of the worldwide cold war.

The Bandung nations did agree to meet again in the future.

The details of the meeting were left up to the Colombo Powers, although there was much talk that the second session would be held in Cairo. It may well be, of course, that Bandung was the first step to closer Afro-Asian relations; a new bipolarity, as already noted, may be in the process of development. At the same time it should not be forgotten that the great hopes of an earlier all-Asian gathering, the 1947 Asian Relations Conference, failed of fulfillment. The same nice words were said in New Delhi in 1947 as were heard in Bandung in 1955—but nothing came of New Delhi. Indeed, there is good reason to believe that even the ranks of the sponsoring Colombo Powers were somewhat ruptured by the Bandung experience. Sir John Kotelawala's strong attack upon international Communism visibly annoyed neutralist Jawaharlal Nehru, for example. Even the unity of the Colombo Powers is by no means an assured thing.

Although political cooperation has yet to assume organizational form in Asia—which it may never do—economic cooperation among the lands of South Asia and the more highly industrialized of the British Commonwealth nations, together with the United States, already exists under the Colombo Plan, which originated at a meeting of the Commonwealth foreign ministers in the capital of Ceylon in January, 1950. The objective of the Colombo Plan is "to raise the standard of living by accelerating the pace and widening the scope of economic development in the countries of South and Southeast Asia by a cooperative approach to their problems, with special emphasis on the production of food." The members of the Colombo Plan today include Burma, Indonesia, Malaya, Vietnam, Laos, Cambodia, India, Pakistan, and Ceylon as well as the United Kingdom, Australia, New Zealand, Canada, and the United States.

BACKGROUND OF PAN-ASIAN SENTIMENTS

In the years since the Second World War the lands of Southeast Asia, quite clearly, have shown considerably more interest in all-Asian and South Asian regionalism than they have in pro-

International Relations 265

posals for closer relations among themselves. No true Asian political bloc can be said to have emerged during these years, however. General Aung San never got beyond the overture stage of his proposed regional grouping before his untimely death, the Thai and Philippine conference attempts of 1949 and 1950 were unqualified failures, and Indonesian indifference to closer regional relations could hardly be less encouraging. On the other hand, all the Southeast Asian lands did attend the Asian Relations Conference of 1947, all except excluded Vietnam were on hand for the Indonesian Conference in 1949, and all turned out for the 1955 Bandung meeting. The Philippines has shown great interest in a Pacific pact, although other lands, like Burma, have had doubts about both the timing and membership of such an alignment. Burma and Indonesia possess high regard for the Colombo Powers grouping, and the Socialists of these two lands are ardent in their support of the young Asian Socialist Organization. Colombo Plan membership also has proved inviting to the Southeast Asian countries.

Why have the Southeast Asian nations displayed so much more enthusiasm for South Asian and Asia-wide alignments than for closer ties among themselves? A partial explanation is to be found in the related factors of the large respect they have for their bigger Asian neighbors, particularly India under Nehru's leadership, and the little respect they hold for one another. A good part of the mechanics of the several Southeast Asian nationalist movements was modeled after the example of the Congress party in India. It is natural that these countries should continue to look to India for leadership after independence was attained, and they have been encouraged by Nehru's bid, sometimes revealed more strongly than at other times, to lead the way in foreign policy for the several lands of this part of the world.

Allied with this has been the low regard most of the Southeast Asian political leaders have had for their comparatively powerless neighbors within the region. To Indonesian foreign-policy makers the Thai are a fickle people who bend with the wind, as illustrated by their alliances under Phibun's leadership, first with Japan and now with Japan's recent enemy, the United States; the Thai scratch their heads in bewilderment at an Indonesian leadership under Ali Sastroamidjojo which is in tacit alliance at home with Communists, who seek the ultimate destruction of Indonesian independence; the Burmese think of the Philippines as a country of hardly any consequence in the world of power politics; and the Filipinos regard the Burmese as sitting on top of a powder keg, with a variety of potentially explosive dissident groups.

The belief that all, or almost all, of history's wars have started in Europe, or have been started by Europeans, also has influenced the approach of Southeast Asia's leaders to the subject of pan-Asianism. A number of these lands are neutralist in their foreign-policy outlook—that is, they refuse to be drawn into either camp in the worldwide cold war. The feeling of a number of leaders is that they should all draw together and form a single Asian neutralist bloc. There is a feeling that all Asians are peace loving, or at least moderately so, and this has served to draw Burma and Indonesia, particularly, toward a larger all-Asian alignment, especially since two of their Southeast Asian neighbors, the Philippines and Thailand, are possessed of nonneutral points of view, making alliance with them rather difficult in the circumstances.

Finally, the sense of Asian solidarity derives considerable impetus from the fact that all of the lands of Asia were at least partially subjected to the yoke of Western political, economic, or cultural imperialism. Each of the present nationalist governments owes a major part of its backing to its anti-Western outlook. This is one of the reasons why the Southeast Asian lands of Indonesia and Burma have been as tolerant as they have of the conduct of Communist China. There is a feeling of kinship with Peiping, because these countries and China all represent facets of a successful continentwide revolution against Western domination. In a sense all are members of the same family, and in a family of this sort, as in families of individuals, the faults of the members are often glossed over, but the disliked next-door neighbor can hardly ever do anything worthy of commendation. China, Indonesia, Burma, and India are to be compared with members of a family, and the role of the suspicion-provoking neighbor is played by the recently imperial West.

GLOBAL OUTLOOK OF THE NEW NATIONS

It should not be thought, however, that the international relations of Southeast Asia are limited to relations with other Asian countries. Nothing could be more distant from the truth. Besides thinking in Asia-wide terms, the foreign-policy architects of Southeast Asia also have a distinctly global outlook, limited though it may be in many respects as a result of the long era of enforced isolation.

The allegiance which these lands give to the United Nations as a focal point of their foreign policies is one example of this outlook. Indonesia and Thailand may disagree drastically on various aspects of their foreign policies, but both these foreign policies have cooperation with the rest of the world's nations within the United Nations as one of their major objectives. Burma, too, has strongly backed the United Nations, as witnessed by its moral support of the police action in Korea, and the Philippines has similarly oriented its foreign policy with an eye toward closer cooperation at New York. Membership in the United Nations gives these young countries a position on the world stage out of all proportion to their economic and military power, thereby bolstering the national ego. At one and the same time it satisfies nationalist emotions and gives the foreign policies of these countries a distinctly global outlook. There is, therefore, no conflict between their internationalism and their nationalism—the former in many ways feeds the latter.

The general acquiesence of most of the Southeast Asian countries in the decisions of the so-called Arab-Asian bloc, functioning outside as well as within the United Nations, is still another example of the global outlook of these lands. The sponsorship of Indonesia and Burma, together with the other

Colombo Powers, of the April, 1955, Bandung Conference, as well as the participation of other states of the region in it, is an instance of the importance these countries place on good relations among the peoples of the Asian lands. Several Southeast Asian nations also are members of the United Nations Economic Commission for Asia and the Far East, and countries like Burma and the Philippines have reaped considerable benefits from this association. Moreover, each of the lands of this part of the world has associated itself with many of the specialized international agencies, such as the World Health Organization, the Food and Agriculture Organization, and the International Labor Organization.

Indonesia, in addition, has interested itself very much in the other Moslem countries, as have certain Malay elements in Malaya. Malaya, furthermore, through its imperial ruler, the United Kingdom, is a member of the A.N.Z.A.M. strategic unit, together with Australia and New Zealand. Military, mutual defense, and economic agreements still tie the Philippines very much to the United States, and Indochina has yet to escape completely from the vestiges of French colonial rule. The Viet Minh in Vietnam clearly is a member of the Sino-Soviet bloc, thus determining the approach of its foreign policy to the rest of the world.

SOUTHEAST ASIA AND THE COLD WAR

It should be apparent from the foregoing analysis that the foreign policies of the several Southeast Asian states are alike in their approach to closer regional political collaboration in that they do not, for the most part, favor a regional link among themselves. These several foreign policies also resemble one another with respect to relations with other Asian lands. Each is premised on some vague kind of kinship with the peoples of the rest of Asia—and, Vietnam excluded, each looks to India to some degree for foreign-policy leadership, although there is considerably less unanimity concerning the proper attitude toward Communist China. Indonesia, Burma, the Philippines, Thailand, and Indochina all seek, or have sought at some time in the postwar years, closer relationships with bigger, more powerful Asian states. The foreign policies of these several states have displayed their greatest differences—not in the realm of Asian relations—but in their approaches to the worldwide Russo-American cold war.

The governments of the Philippines and Thailand have aligned themselves with the United States in its effort to contain Communism within its present confines. These two countries were among the charter signatories of the American-sponsored Southeast Asian Treaty Organization, organized at the September, 1954, Manila Conference. Malaya, through its colonial ruler, the United Kingdom, also is covered by this defense alliance, although there was a considerable amount of initial opposition to the pact in Malaya. When Malaya does attain its independence and becomes a member of the British Commonwealth, which it is scheduled to do on August 31, 1957, it will enter a mutual defense pact with the United Kingdom. Under such a treaty the United Kingdom would have the right to station the Commonwealth strategic reserve in the Far East in Malaya and would provide British troops to help Malayan forces fight the Communists in the peninsula's continuing insurrection. A bloc led by Senator Claro M. Recto in the Philippines also has opposed the treaty, as does the pro-Peiping Thai politician Pridi Banomyong, the former premier now attempting, from the soil of Communist China, to rally dissident elements in Thailand.

At the other end of the spectrum from the Philippines and Thailand is the Viet Minh, ruler of north Vietnam by the Geneva agreement, which, as a member of the international Communist coalition, violently attacks the United States, alleged successor to the European colonial powers, as Southeast Asia's foremost enemy.

Between these two extremes are to be found Indonesia and Burma. The Indonesians, suspicious of almost all of the outside world, are trying to walk a tightrope with few parallels in recent history; theirs is a policy of "active independence" in the cold war, this being defined by the Indonesian foreign office as a "positive approach of noninvolvement." As a consequence of this policy of neutrality, Djakarta has been cautious concerning American economic assistance because it might commit Indonesia to the side of the United States in its opposition to the Communists. Because China is a copartner in the great Asian revolution against Western dominance, however, the Indonesians have frequently watered down their so-called neutrality when Peiping has been involved. The Indonesian government of Ali Sastroamidjojo, for example, did not question the listing of China's Mao Tse-tung as an honorary chairman of the country's Communist party, although in the words of dynamic speechmaking President Sukarno, at least, the United States is a "liberal imperialist" nation seeking to interfere in other countries' affairs.

Burma likewise espouses neutrality, but this would appear to be a bit more neutral "neutrality" than Indonesia's, despite the somewhat pro-Soviet joint statements issued by then Burmese Premier U Nu and Soviet Premier Bulganin in Moscow and Rangoon in 1955. Burma seems to fear Communist China more than it sympathizes with it. A David-sized state in comparison with giant China, with which it shares a disputed border, Burma—which has been afflicted with a variety of uprisings at home—would like to avoid involvement in the cold war at almost all costs. There are some indications, however, that it realizes that involvement eventually may be necessary. Ideologically, the Burmese would seem to incline toward the West; economically, however, Burma's several rice barter pacts with the Communist countries have drawn it dangerously close to dependence on the Sino-Soviet bloc.

In all the countries of Southeast Asia there is considerable suspicion of both the Soviet Union and the United States. A good part of this suspicion stems, not unnaturally, from the efforts of both powers to build up blocs in support of themselves throughout the world. The element of right may be on the side of the United States in its cold-war struggle with the Soviet Union, but the American policy of seeking out alliances with like-minded powers has not always been differentiated by Southeast Asia's leaders from the more sinister policies of the Russians. The American search for allies has often been

International Relations

misunderstood, whether a country is receptive to it, as the Philippines is, or whether it turns a cold shoulder to it, as Burma does. One thing is certain about Southeast Asians: they have no desire to be pawns in Soviet-American political maneuvering. Even a state like Thailand, in alliance with the United States, asks a big enough price for its support to disqualify a description of it as a simple pawn—as the U.S.S.R. describes it.

Of the two states, the Soviet Union is clearly the less trusted and the more feared, even though this fear is not always openly declared. Many Southeast Asians admire its economic accomplishments, but resent its efforts to interfere in their internal affairs through the medium of the Moscow-coached local Communist party.

China's position differs considerably from that of the U.S.S.R. It is recognized as a partner in the Soviet imperialist camp at the same time as it is admired as a coarchitect of the Asian revolution. This dichotomy confuses some Southeast Asian political leaders and partially explains their wavering in the shadow of a potential Chinese Communist thrust south.

The close relations of Indonesia and Burma with India are a consequence of three factors primarily: traditional Indian leadership of Asia's fight to rid itself of colonialism, geography, and the fact that Indian foreign policy seems so sensible in the eyes of the leaders of present-day Burma and Indonesia. For Burma and Indonesia to be neutral all by themselves would require considerable strength and conviction. It is much easier for these countries to be neutral in the company of a large India. Burmese and Indonesian relations with India are based both on a genuine affinity of foreign-policy outlook and a gratitude that there is an India to lead the way along an admittedly precarious path.

Japan's relations with Southeast Asia are colored both by the experiences of the war years and Tokyo's ties with the United States. Burma, Thailand, and Cambodia appear much more willing to normalize relations with former conqueror Japan than do the Filipinos or the Indonesians. The fact that the Philippines, a close ally of the United States, and neutralist

Indonesia have been reluctant to regularize completely their relations with Japan, while neutral Burma and pro-American Thailand have done so, would seem to indicate that cold-war considerations are secondary to the memories of the Second World War.

Relations with the former imperial powers also differ among Southeast Asian countries. American-Filipino relations are genuinely cordial, while Indonesian resentment against the Dutch is very strong, particularly in light of the still unsettled West New Guinea controversy. The Burmese and the British remain on good terms, although they are not as close as Washington and Manila. The French, ousted from Indochina, are generally despised by their former colonial subjects.

GREAT POWER INTEREST IN THE REGION

Traditionally, China has held a position of suzerainty over much of the area, the Chinese regarding Southeast Asia as a proper outlet for their expansive tendencies. It is significant that no strong power has ever arisen in the region when there also was a strong China. The old Southeast Asian empires of Funan, Kambuja, Srivijaya, and Majapahit all achieved the zenith of their achievements when their strong northern neighbor's strength was at a low ebb. Moreover, on at least two occasions in the past the establishment of a new regime in China has meant trouble for the states along China's southern border. Such was the case when the Mongols came to power— so also was it in the early years of Ming rule. Mao Tse-tung's passionate espousal of the "rights and interests" of the Chinese living abroad, Communist China's policy toward minorities along its southern border (as evidenced by its "Thai Autonomous People's Government"), and Chinese leadership of Far Eastern Communism in general clearly indicate the possibility that still another new Chinese regime may begin its reign with an exhibit of expansionist tendencies. A participant in the Viet Minh's colonial-civil war with the French and anti-Communist elements in Vietnam, the Chinese Communists also have actively interfered in the area through their contacts with the overseas Chinese resident in the region.

Chinese Communist policy toward Southeast Asia has seemed to comprise three elements: economic, military, and political. One of the most significant developments in the Far East in 1956 was the emergence of the Chinese Communists as active participants in the sharpening trade-and-aid contest between the United States and the Soviet bloc in South and Southeast Asia. In May, 1956, Prince Norodom Sihanouk of Cambodia announced that his country would receive economic assistance from Peiping totaling $22,400,000. There also were reports that China was pressuring Laos to accept economic help from its big northern neighbor, and the Communist regime in north Vietnam had been receiving significant financial, material, and technical help from the Peiping government since its emergence in 1954. In addition to extending such aid, the Communist Chinese also have sought to expand their trade ties with the countries of Southeast Asia. Indicative of the success which has met Peiping's efforts was the announcement in the fall of 1956 that Communist China had made its first purchase of rubber from the British crown colony of Singapore since 1950—a purchase which amounted to more than two million American dollars.

The Chinese Communist military threat to Southeast Asia has been an ever-present one. In 1956 United States military officials in the Philippines estimated that Communist China then had about a 2,500,000-man army south of the Yangtse River, where it could readily be used against the Southeast Asian countries. Some military units were used against a Southeast Asian state, Burma, although both the Burmese and Chinese governments strongly denied that their border difficulties (which received considerable publicity in the summer of 1956) involved either an explicit or implicit military threat. But China's military strength and Burma's physical weakness unquestionably were major factors in both countries' thinking on the subject of the border question.

Peiping did not confine itself to economic and military

weapons. Politically, the Communist Chinese leadership seemed not to let up in its efforts to persuade, enchant, deceive, and intimidate both the rulers and the ruled of Southeast Asia. The triumphant return of Chou En-lai from the Geneva Conference on Indochina in the summer of 1954 was the occasion for the unveiling of the now famous "five principles" of peaceful coexistence. Chou, in both his 1955 appearance at the Bandung Conference and his 1956 visit to several of the lands of South and Southeast Asia, sought to win friends and dispel doubts as to Peiping's designs for domination. Throughout 1955 and 1956 red carpet after red carpet was laid down in Peiping for the seemingly endless processions of political, economic, and cultural delegations which journeyed from Southeast Asia to enjoy the ego-flattering receptions for which Mao Tse-tung, Chou En-lai, and comrades were justly famous. Only too many of these visitors seemed not to realize that there might some day be an hour of payment for the hospitality of the brief present hour. Few seemed aware of Peiping's intentions to assert the territorial and political claims of the traditional Chinese state.

The visit of Communist China's Chou En-lai to Southeast Asia in late 1956 provided additional evidence of Peiping's continuing concern for the state of its relations with the countries of this region. Chou visited Cambodia and Burma, in addition to Communist north Vietnam and the South Asian lands of India, Pakistan, Afghanistan, and Ceylon. Indicative of the importance China attached to relations with Southeast Asia was the fact that Chou, busy premier and foreign minister of the world's largest national population, spent nearly a week in tiny Cambodia. In Cambodia, Chou strove to portray the Chinese and the Cambodians as equals. Chou seemed to be seeking to show the rest of Asia how well giant China could get along with its neighbors, big or small, neutralist, or even pro-West. This was an impression Chou also tried to create in Pakistan (a charter member of the anti-Communist Southeast Asian Treaty Organization) as well as in other countries he visited. In Cambodia, too, Chou asked that country's Chinese minority of 250,000 to observe rigorously the laws of the kingdom and "to abstain from carrying on political activities."

Chou met with criticism and challenges at several points on his late 1956 tour of Southeast Asia. Student placards in Burma's capital, Rangoon, proclaimed to the Chinese leader: "We greet you—with tears." In Cambodia, Prince Norodom Sihanouk, the leading political figure in that former French colony, told Chou that "noninterference" in the affairs of other nations was "the key to world peace." There was, quite clearly, a shift in sentiment in Southeast Asia in 1956 concerning Communist China. How strong a shift this was or how permanent it would be was not clear. The reasons for this shift were twofold: Soviet suppression of the Hungarian revolt in the fall of 1956, which Chou endorsed; and the Sino-Burmese border controversy, which some Asians at least felt revealed the Peiping regime in its true light as an imperialist power. Other Asians, however—like the Ceylonese—drew closer to Peiping as a result of Chou's tour. Chou and Ceylon's premier signed on February 5, 1957, a pact of "peaceful cooperation and resistance against aggression and expansion of the imperialist and colonial forces."

Southeast Asia's other large neighbor, India, also shows expansionist tendencies at the present time, as the large colonies of Indians in East Africa as well as Southeast Asia attest. "I am not thinking in terms of India as the leader of Southeast Asia or dominating the region," Prime Minister Nehru has said. But he also has declared that "in the modern world it is inevitable for India to be the center of the affairs of Asia, and in that term I include Australia and New Zealand and even Eastern Africa." India clearly is a much interested power in what takes place in Southeast Asia—as evidenced, for example, by its cease-fire proposals for Indochina in the spring of 1954 and its subsequent chairmanship of the three-power team to watch against violations of the 1954 Geneva agreement in Vietnam. It was India, after all, which convened the unofficial Asian Relations Conference of 1947 and the official Indonesian Conference in 1949. New Delhi, moreover, has long been recognized as a leader of the so-called Arab-Asian bloc.

The United States and the Soviet Union, the two leading

powers in the great global cold war, also are vitally interested in this part of the world. In addition to the links it retains with the Philippines, America has developed close relations with Thailand in the post-Second World War years. Its economic and military aid programs, operative to different degrees in various lands of the area, are a clear indication of American interest in Southeast Asia—as was the backing given France by the United States in the former's fight against Communism in Vietnam. That American concern for Vietnam has not lessened since the signing of the Geneva agreements in July, 1954, is evidenced by continuing United States political and financial backing of the anti-Communist south Vietnamese regime of Ngo Dinh Diem. Moreover, it is Washington which is today the most prominent advocate of a collective security system in Southeast Asia and the western Pacific. The United States, content to leave the fate of Southeast Asia to other parties in the early postwar years, is today keenly awake to the strategic and economic worth of this part of the world, as its post-1950 policy toward the area has indicated.[8]

Russia, too, is very much concerned with happenings in Southeast Asia, although it has taken no known direct role in subversive activity in the area since the Calcutta conference of Southeast Asian Communists in February, 1948, which touched off a wave of revolts throughout the region. The Soviet Union has continued to be the capital of conspiratorial international Communism, however, and a material and moral supporter of Communist China. The Soviets' interest in the region has been no less because their political partner has acted in their behalf.

If the Soviet Union has come to lean less conspicuously on subversive activities as a means of increasing its influence in Southeast Asia, this is because it now believes other methods may better achieve its aims. Its current tactic may best be termed a "friendship offensive" in its political phase and "peaceful competitive coexistence" in its economic aspect. The exchange of visits between then Burmese Premier U Nu and

---

[8] American foreign policy in Southeast Asia is treated in detail in the next chapter.

Soviet leaders Nikolai A. Bulganin and Nikita S. Khrushchev in 1955 was an example of Moscow's new diplomatic offensive. Bulganin and Khrushchev also visited India and Afghanistan in 1955 as part of the same attempt to win friends for the Soviet Union in important Asian lands. The successful efforts of the Soviet Union and its allies to increase economic ties with various of the South and Southeast Asian countries, especially through the medium of barter agreements, is another instance of the "new look" in Soviet Asian policy. Burma by mid 1956 was sending more than a quarter of its exports to Sino-Soviet bloc countries, and Indonesia in September, 1956, revealed the details of a sizable economic and technical aid agreement with the U.S.S.R. Under this agreement the Soviets promised to grant $100,000,000 worth of credit to Indonesia in the form of capital goods, machinery, and heavy industrial equipment. Moscow also offered to cooperate with Indonesia on the peaceful uses of atomic energy, with the Soviets promising to train Indonesian technicians in nuclear research. As result of the Soviet-Indonesian loan agreement, which followed by only one month a trade pact between the two countries, the Indonesians probably will have to purchase spare parts and replacements from the U.S.S.R. for many years to come.

The 1955 visit of Soviet leaders Bulganin and Khrushchev to South and Southeast Asia took place against the background of a change in Soviet policy in the world at large. By its tactics at the Geneva Foreign Ministers' Conference in October, 1955, the U.S.S.R. gave indication that it had been brought to the point of acceptance of the status quo in Europe, at least temporarily. In 1948, following the strengthening of the Western position in Europe, the Soviet Union had turned its attention to Asia, where it helped kick off the several Southeast Asian Communist revolts which broke out in that year while also assisting in the rise of Communism to power in China. In 1955, as in 1948, the Soviets turned their eyes eastward as a consequence of a European stalemate and the prospect of more valuable advances in Asia.

The political-military vacuum which had resulted in South and Southeast Asia from the withdrawal of the Western colonial powers was an obvious temptation to the imperialistically inclined Soviet Union. Southeast Asia also was an area where there was a stronger likelihood of success than in Japan or the European nations, which could hardly be called political vacuums in 1955 and which were, moreover, strongly committed to the side of the United States in the great cold war. By the inauguration of its friendship offensive in South and Southeast Asia in 1955 the Soviet Union sought to take advantage of the decline of Western power and influence in this part of the world. It also sought to utilize the large body of neutralist nationalist sentiment which flowered in many vital areas along the onetime strong British defense arc from Suez to Singapore. The Bulganin-Khrushchev visit to Burma, India, and Afghanistan was the curtain raiser of this offensive. A later act in the same important drama was the wooing of the key Middle Eastern nations of Egypt, Syria, and Saudi Arabia. The Southeast Asians were at one end of the old British defense arc, the Arabs at the other. Soviet policy was essentially the same toward both areas—as it was toward India, Pakistan, Afghanistan, and Ceylon, lying between the widely separated fronts of Southeast Asia and the Middle East.

The Soviet Union was only partly leading from a position of strength. If the Western position in South and Southeast Asia in 1955 was but a shadow of what it had been in the 1930's, it was in many respects better in 1955 than it had been in 1948. Likewise, in the Middle East the West stood in a far stronger position in 1955 as a consequence of the establishment of the Baghdad Pact—designed to protect the so-called "northern tier" against Soviet aggression and including as members Iraq, Iran, Turkey, Pakistan, and the United Kingdom—than it had three years earlier when the Iranian oil nationalization problem was occupying world attention and the Egyptians were agitating for the removal of British troops from the Suez Canal zone. Although the deficiencies of the Southeast Asian Treaty Organization loom largest in Western eyes perhaps, to the Soviets the mere establishment of such an organization, however limited in its infant stage, was a significant setback. Moscow's change in tactics in 1955 to a wholesale wooing of the neutral nations of South and Southeast Asia (as well as of the Middle East) may be regarded as partly an effort to consolidate Asian neutralist opinion to offset the gains of the West—potential as well as actual—embodied in the establishment of the Southeast Asian Treaty Organization and the Baghdad Pact. The aim of the Soviets was a neutral bloc of nations, stretching from Suez to Singapore and including Egypt, Saudi Arabia, India, Afghanistan, Burma, and Indonesia (among other states). The Soviets sought to establish an arc of neutralist countries where once stood, in proud confidence, the British Empire South Asian defense arc. Although Moscow had not attained its goal in late 1956, partially as a consequence of its repressive action against freedom-seeking Hungary in the fall of that year, the Soviets are not known to give up easily and may be expected to continue their efforts to neutralize key Asian areas—to the psychological and strategic disadvantage of the West. There were indications in late 1956 that the U.S.S.R. was closer to a victory in the Middle East than it was in Southeast Asia. Leaders of the Asian Socialist Conference, which met in India in early November, stated strongly their objections to collaboration with the Communists through the medium of so-called "united front" governments. That the Soviets were meeting with at least limited success in Southeast Asia, however, was indicated by Indonesia's strong condemnation of the Anglo-French military action against Egypt, following Israel's attack on that Middle East nation, and the Indonesian foreign office's tardy disapproval of the Soviet invasion of Hungary.

The South and Southeast Asian policy of the U.S.S.R. does not conflict with the long-term Communist goal of the establishment of the Soviet order throughout the world. It is, indeed, merely a means toward the attainment of that end. The Soviet Union is well aware that it is not possible to bring such nations as India, Burma, and Indonesia into the Communist camp at the present time. It is willing, therefore, to shift its efforts to the accomplishment of a more possible objective, the neutral-ization of the ring of nations which stretches from Suez to Singapore. Its ultimate aim of Communist conquest has not changed, however. Its short-term policy has merely been brought into line with political realities.

Some observers in late 1956 felt that the U.S.S.R. was abandoning the "friendship offensive" policy of Bulganin and Khrushchev to return to hard-line Stalinist policies. Cited as evidence were the repressive Soviet moves in Hungary and the repeated threats of Soviet military intervention in the Middle East. Such a change may be in the process of taking place, but it is more likely that the developments in Soviet foreign policy in late 1956 represented fewer changes than suggested by some observers. Certainly the Soviet's espousal of the Arab cause against the Anglo-French and Israeli military actions was most consistent with Moscow's policy of seeking Arab friendship. The anti-Soviet and anti-Communist rebellion in Hungary, moreover, served to underscore the slim prospects for new gains in Europe for the Soviet Union. The Hungarian affair, if fully appreciated by the Soviet leadership, pointed a finger at other areas of the world as the regions in which the U.S.S.R. should seek to register further advances. Soviet policy in the Middle East, therefore, was most intimately tied to developments in eastern Europe. Southeast Asia also would seem to qualify for new Soviet attention in the months and years ahead. An increase, rather than a reduction, in Soviet activity regarding Southeast Asia should be expected. World opinion having been so opposed to the Soviet moves in Hungary, it would also seem that the Soviets will seek, as quickly and cleverly as possible, to replace the image of Russian tanks in Budapest with new pictures of the so-called "happiness twins"—Bulganin and Khrushchev—doling out smiles to the peoples of the backward Middle East, Africa, and Southeast Asia.

Although postwar attention has focused on the relations of India, China, the Soviet Union, and the United States with Southeast Asia, the strong probability of future closer relations between Japan and the countries of this region should not be overlooked. Japan remains Asia's most advanced industrial power, and the economic problems which partly prompted Japanese expansionism in the 1930's and 1940's have worsened, rather than lessened, in recent years. In the thirties Japan made a tremendous impact on the economies of the Southeast Asian lands with its cheap manufactured goods; its seizure of the region in 1940-1942 was partly to acquire the vast raw material resources of the area. There is nothing to indicate that Japan is less interested in Southeast Asia today than it was in the thirties and forties.

Japan's role in Southeast Asia has grown steadily in the last few years. The Burmese, for example, have shown themselves most pleased with machinery received under the reparations agreement with Japan and with the technical experts who have come to Burma to assist in the use of this machinery. Burma, in need of help with its several development plans, has shown increasing interest in obtaining Japanese cooperation in the fulfillment of these projects. The Japanese, for their part, are interested in renewing their influence in Burma as well as Indonesia, Thailand, Indochina, and the Philippines —for political as well as economic reasons.

Britain's interest in the region is declining, creating new problems. With the withdrawal of the British from Malaya scheduled for August, 1957, there is increasingly strong feeling for greater self-government in adjacent Singapore, too. A thoroughgoing redefinition of that colony's status (including steps toward independence) is likely before 1960. The big question in Singapore's future concerns its predominantly Chinese population, who incline increasingly toward support of the Peiping government of the Communist Mao Tse-tung. If the British leave Singapore, the Chinese Communists are likely to succeed them (in actual fact if not in name). Neither the British nor the United States desire such a development, but it is not yet clear what they plan to do to prevent it.

Since anticolonialism has swept almost all of the rest of Asia, it also may be expected to visit the three British possessions on the island of Borneo: Sarawak, Brunei, and North Borneo. Philippine Moslem inhabitants of the southern island of Mindanao took advantage of the visit of North Borneo's governor to Manila in January, 1957, to renew their agitation for the session of the British crown colony of North Borneo to the Philippines. If the British do give up their present holdings in northern Borneo, which seems unlikely in the immediate future, such Filipino claims to all or part of this area undoubtedly will meet with opposition from Indonesia, which rules the greater part of the large island of Borneo. This could lead to new intraregional bad feeling.

Other nations also have played significant roles in the international relations of Southeast Asia. Australia was a champion of Indonesian independence in the second half of the 1940's, and in the 1950's it sent troops to Malaya to help the British repress the Communist rebellion in that territory. Egypt, even before the Suez crisis strengthened the great bond of anticolonialism between the Middle East and Southeast Asia, had embarked upon a policy of strengthening its relations with the nations of the Far East. Not only did Egypt recognize Communist China, but it also was reported on the eve of the Suez crisis to be about to expand its diplomatic missions in Burma and Indonesia and to press for diplomatic ties with Cambodia, Laos, and Vietnam. Both Yugoslavia and Israel have been exceptionally active in seeking out Burma's friendship in the years since that ancient Buddhist country regained its independence from the British.

A political "low pressure" area historically, as noted in the opening chapter of this survey, Southeast Asia today would seem to have a major task before it if it is to avoid falling once more under foreign control. A power vacuum as a consequence of the withdrawal of the Western colonial powers, the region seems unable to invoke at the present time the sort of unity which might prevent outside interference. It ignores closer regional collaboration, preferring to seek the protection of bigger powers—which well may prove to be the key to its survival as an area of independent states, but which also could be the beginning of a new era of external domination.

The problems facing Southeast Asia in the realm of inter-

International Relations

national relations today are obviously immense. It is regrettable that many of the leaders of these lands are not better prepared to meet them. This is one of the most unfortunate legacies of the colonial period—one which may prove decisively fateful to the Western cause in its conflict with the Communist conspiracy.

CHAPTER 9

AMERICAN POLICY IN SOUTHEAST ASIA

THE UNITED STATES has had responsibilities in Southeast Asia since 1899, when it acquired sovereignty over the Philippine Islands, but American interest in the region as a whole remained slight until the eve of Pearl Harbor. The amount of American capital invested in the region was small. Senator Albert Beveridge, in 1899, predicted that Americans would swarm to the Philippines and American capital would flow to the newly acquired dependency in an ever-swelling stream, but this did not happen. The total amount of American investments in the region in 1941 was estimated to be $325,000,000, or only about 2 percent of the total of American foreign investments at the time. It is probably less than that today. The value of American trade with the region was more significant, due in large part to the 100 percent preferential tariff policy instituted by the United States in the Philippines in favor of its own trade, as a result of which about three-fourths of the external trade of the islands was artificially channeled to the United States.

As a great industrial and military power, the United States has an interest in the region because it is an important source of strategic materials. Southeast Asia produces two-thirds of the world's tin and over 75 percent of its natural rubber. While its output of oil is not large in terms of total world production, it is nevertheless of great strategic importance because so little oil is produced in South or Eastern Asia. In 1954 Free Asia (which for these particular commodities meant chiefly Southeast Asia) supplied the United States with 99 percent of its imports of copra, 91 percent of its natural rubber, 67 percent of its Manila hemp, 61 percent of its spices, and 58 percent of its tin. The loss of these supplies of strategic materials to the West would be serious but probably not irreparable. But free access to them by Communist countries would greatly strengthen the Red orbit. Before the war, the region also produced 65 percent of the world's copra, 40 percent of its palm oil, 85 percent of its pepper, 90 percent of its quinine, and 70 percent of its kapok. Burma, Indochina, and Thailand are also capable of producing tremendous quantities of rice. Control of this surplus of the basic food of most Asians would greatly strengthen Communist economic and political power.

The strategic importance of the region is great, if for no other reason than the extent of its area and the size of its population. The region covers some 1,650,000 square miles of land spread over a large section of the globe, with a population of about 175,000,000. Half continental and half peninsular and insular, it lies astride the great trade routes of the eastern world. The strategic importance of the region, and of Indochina in particular, became painfully apparent in the Second World War. Once in Indochina, Japan was in a position to overrun Southeast Asia almost at will, and to threaten Australia and India. Today Communism has a foothold in Indochina, backed by China, a great continental power, whose territory adjoins it. This is a situation far more alarming than that of 1941. It is true that China's striking power is in some respects more limited than that of Japan. For example, it lacks naval power and is not yet as highly industrialized. But it possesses certain advantages, such as its geographic position contiguous to Southeast Asia, and in the nearly 10,000,000 Chinese living in the region, China has something Japan did not have. Among these millions of Chinese there is abundant material for the infiltration and subversion which Communists use so effectively.

Undoubtedly the region is of great importance in world politics; President Eisenhower in a press conference in March, 1954, declared it to be of "transcendent importance." The free world cannot afford to have any more territory and people go over to the Communist world if the balance of power is to remain in its favor. The economic gain to the Communist bloc, and the corresponding loss to the free world, would be serious, if not disastrous, if this region should move into the Communist orbit. The psychological advantage to the Communist world would be great, for nothing succeeds like success. Communist control of Southeast Asia would strategically endanger our "defense perimeter," the offshore island chain which stretches from Japan to the Philippines.

OBSTACLES TO AMERICAN DIPLOMACY

Unfortunately Southeast Asia is a region in which American diplomacy faces numerous and difficult obstacles, especially in combating Communism. The entire region, with the exception of Thailand, was until recently subject to Western colonial rule. In the long struggle for independence there naturally developed a strong anti-Western feeling. The Philippines, Burma, Indonesia, and very recently, the peoples of Indochina, have acquired their independence, but the colonial issue is not yet dead. Malaya and Borneo remain under British rule, and Indonesia is bitterly contesting Dutch control over West New Guinea. Because American sentiment has been traditionally anticolonial, the Southeast Asians expected outright support from the United States in their struggle for independence. Many Southeast Asian nationalists feel that American support of their cause was feeble and vacillating.

There is among the peoples of the region a cultural reaction to Western penetration. This is quite evident from the revival of Buddhism in Burma and Thailand and the irreconcilable Darul Islam movement in Indonesia, which seeks by violence to establish a theocratic Islamic state. The collision of Western with Eastern culture has had an extremely disturbing effect on the minds and feelings of many of the Southeast Asians, and has caused hostility not only towards Westerners but also tension between groups within countries. In addition to this there is the clash of the ideologies of communism and democracy. All of this makes for hostility toward the Western world and for disunity within the nations.

Another important factor in the situation is the presence of large alien population groups: between eight and ten million Chinese, a million or more Indians, a few hundred thousand Europeans, and a scattering of Arabs. These groups constitute a disturbing social factor because they control a large part of the economic life of the region, they are not easily assimilated, and they are, for the most part, nationals of large and powerful neighboring countries. Nearly every country in the region has passed legislation discriminating against these alien elements with the object of helping their indigenous nationals improve their economic position.

Still another factor which must be noted is the low level of living in the region. Its total population is about 15 percent greater than that of the United States; its combined national income is only 3 percent of that of the American people. There are areas, such as Java, central Luzon, and the Red River Delta, where the population pressure is intense. The last named area has a "nutritional density" of 475 persons per square mile of cultivated rice land. Wherever the population pressure is severe, there almost invariably is a center of grave social and political unrest.

It is wholly understandable that people living under these conditions would ascribe their poverty to foreign exploitation. The presence of prosperous foreign enterprises and numerous affluent aliens in the midst of their poverty-stricken society seemed to point to but one explanation. To people in their condition, Marxism seemed to explain nearly everything. Moreover, the nationalist leaders found the Marxist theories useful in arousing resentment against foreign rule. In contrast with the nationalist revolutions in the West, which were middle-class movements, those in Southeast Asia (with the exception of the Philippines) are headed by intellectual proletarians. The result is a strong socialistic inclination in all of these countries, the phenomenon of weak governments attempting vast socialistic programs. In view of the political and administrative inexperience of these peoples, it is surprising that the results have not been more disastrous. Though their leaders have unlearned and learned a great deal about economics, the suspicion of foreign capital is still strong. The political leaders of Southeast Asia regard the economics of their country as "colonial," and they are determined to make them national in as short a time as possible. This accounts in large part for their socialistic fervor. Important sectors of their economies are foreign owned. Moreover, the economic life of these countries is heavily dependent on the export of a few commodities. In 1954-1955 rice constituted 76 percent in value of the total exports of Burma, and in the other countries of the region the percentages of chief exports were as follows: Indonesia—rubber, 38, petroleum, 25, tin, 7, and copra, 6; Philippines—copra, 31, and sugar, 26; Thailand—rice, 33, and tin, 21; Malaya—rubber, 60, and tin, 23.

Americans are often surprised and shocked that Asians are not repelled by the cruelties of Communism as we are. There are some explanations for the Asian attitude. Asians are not instinctively repelled by the cruelties of Communism because they live in the midst of malignant poverty, with its attendant suffering. Many of them have experienced nothing but suffering and have lived with it all their days. They are inured to it. Moreover, their religious systems have not tended to make them as sensitive to suffering as have the teachings of Christianity. Furthermore, Communist theory, however fallacious it may be, offers much that is attractive to Southeast Asians, and they are prepared to overlook some of the cruelties in practice. Communism offers a simple explanation of the causes of the plight of the colonial peoples through Lenin's theory of imperialism, the idea that poverty is not inevitable, the concept of a planned economy, and political techniques suitable for backward peoples.[1] Moreover, Communist belief

[1] Max Mark, "Nationalism versus Communism in Southeast Asia," *Southwestern Social Science Quarterly*, XXXIII (1952), 135-47.

in the inevitability of a proletarian victory seems to have a strong attraction for the Asian mind, which is intensely preoccupied with the idea of fate.

The peoples of Southeast Asia were led by their nationalist leaders to believe that with independence their living conditions would immediately improve. This has not happened. In general, the trend has been in the other direction; in some countries there has been serious deterioration. In Indonesia, in which is found half of the population of the region, the level of living is considerably below what it was in 1938. In spite of this deterioration, school attendance, and especially college enrollments, have boomed, pouring large numbers of intellectuals into a market which can absorb very few of them. It is not surprising, therefore, to find young intellectuals turning in frustration to dictatorship and totalitarianism as the only solution to their difficult problem.

In conclusion, it must be pointed out that there is little unity in Southeast Asia, either regionally or within the countries individually. Nearly every country has significant minorities, both religious and ethnic. In Malaya, where the native Moslem has become a minority in his native country, the divisions are sharp. It will take history a long time to merge the three leading communities of Malaya into a nation. Developments in Indonesia indicate rather clearly that the Dutch had not yet succeeded in molding the peoples of the myriads of islands into a real unity, for when the Dutch withdrew, the seeming unity of Indonesians fell apart. It is much the same regionally. The population of one state is predominantly Christian; that of another, Moslem; that of several, Buddhist; and Malaya has no majority for any one faith. Because they were ruled for long periods by different powers, these countries were drawn in different directions culturally. The absence of political and cultural unification enabled the Western powers to establish their control originally, and today the region is again a power vacuum. The colonial administrations have been replaced by weak, independent states, the economy of most of the region has deteriorated, the work of well-trained, experienced colonial officials and able foreign entrepreneurs has been taken over by untrained, inexperienced natives. Social and civil unrest, insurrection and armed strife, and political ineptitude have rendered the region exceedingly vulnerable to direct and indirect Communist aggression. Even if there were no threat of external aggression, the situation would be acute, for in several of these countries the forces of disintegration are strong. With their societies open to Communist infiltration and subversion, the situation is very serious. The region is utterly lacking in economic and military power with which to defend itself, and what is worse from the Western point of view, it seems to lack the will to defend itself. Large sections of the population are not aware of the existence of the threat to their security.

AMERICAN POLICY IN SOUTHEAST ASIA

With respect to American policy in Southeast Asia, a distinction must be made between our policy with respect to the Philippines and our policy with respect to the rest of the region. Our Philippine policy was one of cultural and commercial assimilation and a rapid preparation for self-government and independence.[2] That these policies involved contradictions is apparent, and they have left some unsolved problems. The United States is pledged to defend the islands, and for this purpose it has been granted a number of military bases. Since the Philippine Islands are a part of Southeast Asia, the United States pledge to defend them gives it a strong interest in the defense of the region.

Before Pearl Harbor the United States manifested little official interest in Southeast Asia apart from the Philippines. American imports of rubber and tin and a few other commodities of the region were considerable, which led our government to oppose schemes to restrict rubber and tin production. The United States also had a diplomatic controversy over access of American capital to the right of the exploitation of the oil resources of the Netherlands Indies. When in 1940 the Japa-

---

[2] American-Philippine relations are discussed in Chapter 3.

nese occupied Indochina and put severe pressure on the Dutch to make extensive commercial concessions, the United States became aroused and gave the countries with responsibilities in the region some diplomatic support in resisting Japanese demands.

Little has yet been made public about American diplomacy with respect to the region in the Second World War. It is well known that President Roosevelt held strongly anticolonial views and that he was especially critical of French policy in Indochina. He apparently was strongly inclined to oppose the return of the dependency to French rule except as a trust territory under the proposed trusteeship system. Of the Dutch he was not so critical, probably for the reason that blood creeps where it cannot walk.

The Netherlands Indies, exclusive of Sumatra, was included under General Douglas MacArthur's Southwest Pacific Area command. Dutch New Guinea became a base for the next leap northward, but beyond that, Morotai in the northern Moluccas and Tarakan and Balikpapan, the oil ports on the east coast of Borneo, were the only parts of the Netherlands Indies recaptured by the forces of this command. General MacArthur had proposed, immediately after the Borneo campaign, to move on to Java "and restore the Dutch Government under Van Mook, which would have rapidly brought law and order there as it had done in New Guinea." This plan for a further thrust into Java was, according to General MacArthur, "for some reason never understood, peremptorily called off and forbidden from Washington, in spite of my insistence of its complete success with little loss." MacArthur further declared that the cancellation of this movement "was one of the grave mistakes of the war and ultimately resulted in the chaotic conditions which followed in that part of Indonesia. It completely violated the basic principle of American foreign policy to support the orderly development of dependent areas toward self-government."[3]

---

[3] Charles A. Willoughby and John Chamberlain, *MacArthur: 1941-1951* (New York, 1954), 275.

Though the reasons for this action by Washington have not been revealed, some seem quite obvious. It may be adequately, if not wholly, explained by the need of all available forces for an early move on Japan proper. Shortly before the capitulation of Japan, the Netherlands Indies was shifted from General MacArthur's area to that of Admiral Mountbatten. Washington probably felt that it had a large enough area of responsibility in the Philippines, China, and Japan. Also, in the background there may have been a reluctance, and even fear, of becoming involved in restoring the former colonial governments in these territories. It is interesting to speculate on what might have happened had this change of plans not been made. One can hardly avoid the conclusion that the United States narrowly escaped being drawn into a situation which would have been embarrassing at home and abroad. As it was, our government did not escape all embarrassment in Indonesia or in Indochina, or even in the Philippines. It was caught in an awkward position. It could ill afford to alienate the Dutch and the French, whose cooperation in Europe it needed badly, yet it wished to win the good will of the nationalist movements in Southeast Asia and to use its influence to end colonialism wherever it had outlived its usefulness. In Indochina the situation was desperate; the war there seemingly could not be won either with or without the French. The outcome was not happy. The United States gave too little aid to win the good will or gratitude of the nationalist leaders, but enough to offend the colonial powers.

From 1948 on, the United States government became increasingly concerned about Communist activity in Southeast Asia. In 1950 (February 27) Secretary of State Dean Acheson declared in a public address that the countries of that region "find themselves in the path of a main thrust of Soviet subversion and expansion," but he was nevertheless unfavorably disposed toward the idea of an Asian defense pact. In May, 1949, he turned down a suggestion that such an alliance be formed. In July, 1950, President Everett Case of Colgate University and Raymond Fosdick of the Rockefeller Foundation were appointed to assist Ambassador Philip C. Jessup on Far Eastern policy. Jessup himself later visited the countries of Eastern and Southeast Asia, and on February 13, 1950, presided over a conference in Bangkok of all chiefs of United States missions in the region.

Much thought was given in 1950 by the state department to United States policy with respect to Southeast Asia. The Case-Fosdick recommendations have not been made public, but Fosdick unofficially gave his views in an article in the New York *Times*.[4] He depreciated military power as a solution, and emphasized economic and social aid and diplomatic support for the peoples of Asia in their aspiration "for freedom and justice and more abundant living." The United States should make the just and humane purposes of this revolution "its own and become the friend and counselor of revolutionary Asia."

Acheson made one of his most important policy addresses as secretary of state on January 12, 1950. His views were in many respects similar to those of Fosdick. He warned against the obsession with military considerations in seeking solutions to Asian problems. American policy toward the region must recognize the revulsion of Asian peoples "against the acceptance of misery and poverty as the normal condition of life," and "revulsion against foreign domination." He declared that the basic interests of Americans and Asians are the same, that the United States stood ready to help the peoples of Asia to improve their social and economic conditions, but that American assistance can be effective only when it is the "missing component in a situation which might otherwise be solved." The United States could not furnish all the components that might be required. "It cannot furnish determination, it cannot furnish the will, and it cannot furnish the loyalty of a people to its government." This remark probably reflected the bitter experience of the United States in China. He also implied that, except for the Philippines, Southeast Asia was not regarded as an area vital to the security of the United States

[4] February 12, 1950.

which this country would fight to defend, except in conformity with its obligations as a member of the United Nations.

Ambassador Jessup on his visit to Asia indicated an increasing concern about the situation in Southeast Asia and especially Indochina. He declared in Singapore on February 6, 1950, that armed aggression against Indochina would be regarded as a grave matter. In January, Communist China and Soviet Russia announced their recognition of Ho Chi Minh's regime; on February 7 the United States announced the recognition of Vietnam, Cambodia, and Laos. A few days later the Export-Import Bank granted Indonesia a $100,000,000 loan. At Bangkok on February 12, on the eve of the conference of American diplomats to discuss the situation in the region, Ambassador Jessup indicated that the United States government was sympathetic with the idea of an Asian military alliance. According to the official communique, the conference considered the problem of how the United States could best implement its announced policy "to support the independence and nationalist aspirations of all Asian peoples."

It is clearly evident that a new and more active American policy was rapidly taking form in these days. On February 16, Secretary Acheson made his fighting speech on "total diplomacy," in which he declared that the only way to deal with Russia was "to create situations of strength." The United States must be prepared to meet wherever possible all thrusts of the Soviet Union "and at the same time to create those economic, political, social and psychological conditions that strengthen and create confidence in the democratic way of life." A week later, Washington announced that a special economic mission would soon be sent to Southeast Asia under the leadership of R. Allen Griffin. In July a military survey mission under John Melby was sent to Southeast Asia. Military and economic aid began to flow to Southeast Asia in increasingly large quantities. For the fiscal year 1954 the total United States aid to Indochina alone was over $800,000,000, nearly all of it for arms and military supplies. Substantial amounts also went to Thailand and the Philippines. On August 30, 1951, the United States and the Philippines signed a mutual defense treaty, and on September 1 the United States, New Zealand, and Australia signed the A.N.Z.U.S. pact.

THE GENEVA CONFERENCE

The crisis which developed in Indochina in the spring of 1954 was a painful experience for the American people and the Eisenhower administration in particular. In the 1952 campaign the Republicans had flayed the Roosevelt and Truman administrations for the loss of China to the Communists and for getting the United States into a war in Korea which American forces, under the conditions imposed upon them, could not win and which threatened to go on forever. Moreover, the Eisenhower administration had cut military expenditures, contracted the armed forces, and reduced American troops abroad. Having taken credit for ending the war in Korea, it could hardly justify entering another and similar one in Indochina. But the loss of Indochina to the Communists would also be embarrassing in view of the capital which the Republicans had made of the American diplomatic disaster in China. Moreover, the United States had become deeply involved in the war in Indochina. In the last months the United States was bearing about 80 percent of the cost of the military operations in that unhappy country.

Secretary Dulles was determined not to lose any more territory to the Communists, but the policies of Secretaries Humphrey and Wilson tended in an opposite direction. The secretary of state himself had promised that the United States would not again become bogged down in local wars. Caught in the vortex of conflicting policies and forces, Dulles in desperation proclaimed his "instant, massive retaliation" threat.[5] This outburst was understandable under the circumstances, but its effects were bad. It frightened and alienated our friends, and provided our enemies with propaganda. When the military situation steadily worsened and the French at long last decided to get out of the war in Indochina at once, the administration

[5] See James Reston's interview with General Walter Bedell Smith in the New York *Times*, October 10, 1954.

apparently seriously considered the idea of sending American troops into the conflict. The Vice President on April 6, in an off-the-record, off-the-cuff speech, declared that if the French withdrew from the fight, the United States would have to dispatch forces to Indochina. As the leader of the free world, the United States could not afford a further retreat in Asia. Dulles' replies to the press, when questioned about the issue, were a bit equivocal. The President kept his balance. He repeatedly pointed out the seriousness of the situation, but he made direct participation by American troops in the war conditional upon Allied support and the approval of congress. The decisive factor, however, seems to have been the opposition, on military grounds, of General Ridgeway, army chief of staff. The attitude of the senate was not very constructive. Most senators were opposed to direct military intervention, but also to making any concessions which would help reach a compromise settlement.

The secretary of state now engaged in a piece of sudden and unilateral diplomacy. Without ascertaining in advance whether he had the support of congress, the French, or the British, he went to Europe and publicly appealed for a "united action" policy to stop Communist aggression in Indochina. The result was a public rebuff. Because of political sentiment at home and Commonwealth ties, as well as a determination to attempt a peaceful settlement with the Communist countries, the British government refused "to give any undertakings" for military action "in advance of the results of Geneva." The European foreign offices feared that Dulles wanted to scuttle the Geneva Conference, but it is quite clear that he wished only to strengthen the anti-Communist position in order to get a more favorable settlement. With this rebuff, the secretary of state returned to Washington, and the Geneva Conference ground to a conclusion without active American participation.

Though the United States was not actively present at Geneva, American military strength and American sentiment had much to do with the final settlement. The Communists did not dare to press their demands too far, lest they drive France into the arms of the United States and arouse America to large-scale intervention. The Geneva agreements meant in effect the practical withdrawal of France from Indochina, the withdrawal of the Communist Viet Minh forces from Cambodia and Laos, the temporary division of Vietnam at about the seventeenth parallel, and a plebiscite in two years to determine the future status of the whole.

In Indochina, American diplomacy suffered a setback. China won a puppet state with important mineral resources, a strategic location, and 13,000,000 people. The plebiscite scheduled for July, 1956, has not been held, chiefly because of the refusal of the Diem government to cooperate in holding it. It does not look as if the elections will be held soon, if ever. Vietnam thus joins Germany and Korea as divided countries—victims of the titanic struggle between Communism and the free world for the strategic areas of the globe.

The President, who in his press conference had stated it might be necessary to work out a modus vivendi with Russia, was philosophic about the Geneva truce, and the secretary of state was both philosophic and somewhat chastened. In his press conferences the President talked about American partnership with other nations rather than of American leadership. In a press statement of July 23 Dulles declared that the "important thing from now on is not to mourn the past but to seize the opportunity to prevent the loss in Northern Vietnam from leading to the extension of communism throughout Southeast Asia and the Pacific Southwest." He stated that there were two lessons which the free nations should learn from the past; namely, "that resistance to communism needs popular support, and this in turn means that the people should feel that they are defending their own national institutions," and "that arrangements for collective defense need to be made in advance of aggression, not after it is under way."

THE MANILA CONFERENCE—SEATO

The United States now proceeded without delay to call the conference which it hoped would draft a security plan for Southeast Asia to prevent further Communist expansion in that region. A conference was called and held within a matter of weeks. On September 8, eight countries signed a Southeast Asian Collective Defense Treaty. There had been rumors of proposals to form a Southeast Asian defense organization from 1947 to 1953. In those years the British, French, Dutch, and Australian governments were interested in creating such an organization, but the United States was lukewarm to the idea. In May, 1951, a military conference was held at Singapore, at which the United States was represented by observers. It was agreed to exchange information. In January, 1952, the chiefs of staff and other high-ranking military officers of the United States, the United Kingdom, and France, together with representatives of Australia, New Zealand, and Canada, met in Washington for a series of talks described by the American defense department as a continuation of the Singapore discussions. It was reported that the military leaders discussed the pooling of their air, land, and sea forces in case of a Chinese Communist attack on territories held by Western or pro-Western nations. Further talks were held at the Pentagon in March, but no organizational arrangement was set up. Some months later, Prime Minister Churchill proposed to the incoming Eisenhower administration the formation of a Southeast Asian defense pact, similar to Nato, but Washington was not ready for it.

In seeking to create "a dependable barrier to further Communist expansion" in Southeast Asia, Dulles took on himself a formidable task. He had to find a formula for the defense of the region which would win the acquiescence, if not the enthusiasm, of France, Britain, Australia, New Zealand, Cambodia, Laos, Vietnam, Pakistan, India, and other neutralist countries of Southeast Asia as well as the various factions of the United States congress. The difficulties encountered at Manila reveal many of the problems which American diplomacy confronts in Southeast Asia.

It is clear that if Seato is to be effective psychologically and militarily it must have the support of a large number of Asian states. Suspicion of the West is strong, and the slogans of "Asia for the Asians" and "the peace of Asia should be

American Policy

maintained by Asians" have a compelling appeal. Unfortunately, the attempt to enlist Asian states in the movement and to give it an Asian character was not successful. The idea of the defense treaty originated in the West, was advocated chiefly by the United States, and received the support of only three Asian states, namely, Pakistan and Thailand, which were already receiving military assistance from the United States, and the Philippines, which is regarded by Asians as an American satellite and on whose territory the conference was held. The three Indochinese states might have joined at the time if the terms of the Geneva truce agreement had not precluded it, but Cambodia and Laos have since turned neutralist in their foreign policy. As it is, there is little about Seato which is truly Asian. Whatever power the pact can have will necessarily come from the Western members.

The treaty could not be given a broader Asian base for a number of reasons. The American policy of not extending recognition to Communist China and of continuing to recognize the Chiang regime as the government of China, while the British government, for one, adopted the opposite policy, made it impossible to include either Nationalist or Red China. Moreover, the inclusion of Formosa would dispel any hope of ever getting India, Burma, or Indonesia to join. To avoid these difficulties, Hong Kong and Formosa were excluded from the operation of the treaty. Japan could not be included as a member either, for all the countries of Southeast Asia profoundly distrust her, and Burma, Indonesia, and the Philippines were still wrangling with her over reparations. Thus to include some states or regimes would have wrecked the chances of getting a treaty at all, and the inclusion of others would have barred all hope of getting the later adherence of any other countries in the region. The result was a small and weak Asian base for the pact.

Then there was the problem which no secretary of state can ever forget when he is negotiating a treaty, namely, that of getting an international agreement which will be acceptable to two-thirds of the membership of the United States senate. To insure approval by the senate and to avoid becoming involved in any war between India and Pakistan, Dulles wished to have the treaty state specifically that it was directed against Communist aggression. The inclusion of such a statement would have alienated neutralist India and several of the Southeast Asian states beyond any hope of future adherence to the pact. Britain opposed it. As a compromise, it was agreed that the United States could attach a memo to the treaty expressing its own views.[6] It was probably also out of similar considerations that the obligations of the defense treaty were made not automatic, as in Nato, but merely consultative, though vulnerable states like Thailand and the Philippines strongly pleaded for the former.

Under the terms of the treaty, the signatories undertake, "separately and jointly, by means of continuous and effective self-help and mutual aid" to "maintain and develop their individual and collective capacity to resist armed attack and to prevent and counter subversive activities directed from without against their territorial integrity and political stability" (Art. II). They further "undertake to strengthen their free institutions and to cooperate with one another in the further development of economic measures, including technical assistance, designed both to promote economic progress and social well-being and to further the individual and collective efforts of governments towards these ends" (Art. III).

From a military point of view, Article IV constitutes the heart of treaty. In case of aggression by means of armed attack in Southeast Asia against any of the parties, the signatories agree to meet "the common danger in accordance with its constitutional processes." By separate protocol the states and territories of Cambodia, Laos, and free Vietnam are designated as falling within the scope of the treaty, though these are not parties to it. However, no action will be taken on the territory of any of these states except "at the invitation or with the consent of the government concerned." The delegates to the

---

[6] The statement of "Understanding" of the United States attached to the treaty is to the effect that in case of an armed attack which is not a Communist attack "in the treaty area against any of the Parties or against any State or territory which the Parties by unanimous agreement may hereinafter designate," the United States is under no obligation to act under the terms of the treaty. The reservation applies only to Article IV, paragraph 1.

American Policy 301

Manila Conference were well aware that the chief threat to the region might not be direct attack but infiltration and subversion. They therefore further agreed that if the territorial integrity or political independence of the parties in the treaty area or the three states of Indochina "is threatened in any way other than by armed attack or is affected or threatened by any fact or situation which might endanger the peace of the area, the Parties shall immediately consult in order to agree on the measures which should be taken for the common defense." Since the treaty is so definitely consultative in character, a council so organized as to be able to meet at any time is provided for in Article V.

States not original signatories may be invited to adhere. Article VII provides that "any other State in a position to further the objectives of this Treaty and to contribute to the security of the area may, by unanimous agreement of the Parties, be invited to accede to this Treaty."

These are the chief provisions of the Southeast Asia Collective Defense Treaty. It is hardly necessary to add that, like all other defense treaties to which the United States is a party, it is carefully drafted so as not to conflict with the obligations of the parties under the Charter of the United Nations, or the responsibility of the United Nations for the maintenance of international peace and security.

At the suggestion of President Magsaysay of the Philippines, the conference also drafted a declaration called the Pacific Charter, which proclaims the principle of "equal rights and self determination of peoples." It is not clear what good this anticolonial declaration will do. It is not likely to make the treaty more acceptable to neutralist countries. Seato members emphasize that part of the declaration which states that they "will earnestly strive by every peaceful means to promote self-government and to secure the independence of all countries," while the Asian doubters draw attention to the qualifying clause "whose people desire it and are able to undertake its responsibilities." If it made Asians aware of the dangers of Communist imperialism, it would have some value, but most Asians think only in terms of Western imperialism. As former

Premier Mohammed Ali of Pakistan once said, "they are worried by a disease they are getting rid of and ignoring the one with which they are threatened." Where colonialism still exists, as in Malaya and North Borneo, the declaration may do harm by putting pressure on the British to grant self-government faster than these plural societies can be prepared to receive it, and thus lead to more disorder, which can only help the Communists. Nor will the declaration do anything to solve the complicated problem of West New Guinea.

ASIAN RESPONSE TO THE TREATY

The Indian response was unfavorable from the beginning. Long before the Manila Conference met, V. K. Krishna Menon, Indian delegate to the United Nations, denounced the proposed collective security action as "an incipient and embryonic infringement of our peace area approach." Mrs. Pandit, Nehru's sister and herself a leading Indian diplomat, dismissed Seato with the quip that it was "a Southeast Asian Alliance minus Southeast Asia." Prime Minister Nehru described the treaty as an interesting and odd document which seeks to give protection to countries which do not want it. "Asian problems," he declared, "Asian security and Asian peace are not only discussed but treaties are drawn up in regard to them chiefly by non-Asian powers." He felt that the treaty would have the effect of halting "the process of calming down" begun by the Indochina settlement and of increasing tension and unrest in the world. He also criticized the economic aid provisions of the treaty and contrasted them with the Colombo Plan, which is without military implications. He wished to know whether economic measures of the treaty would supplant, rival, or duplicate the efforts now being made under the Colombo agreements. Even before the Manila Conference was called and Seato was drafted, Nehru was given the opportunity of putting his "peace area" idea into something like specific form. Chou En-lai, prime minister of Communist China, on his return home from the Geneva Conference visited New Delhi for conversations with the Indian leader. In a joint Chou-Nehru statement issued on June 28, 1954, the two prime ministers on behalf of themselves and their governments affirmed faith in the five principles of mutual respect, nonaggression, noninterference, equality, and peaceful coexistence. From New Delhi, Chou went to Rangoon, where he won prime minister Nu for this policy. The Burmese and Chinese premiers made their affirmation of faith in a joint statement similar to the one made by Nehru and Chou in New Delhi a few days earlier. Nehru wished to conciliate Communist China, whereas he seemed convinced that the American policy was one of provocation. A few months later, after a visit to China, Nehru declared in parliament that Chou and he had agreed on the principle that "everything possible should be done to remove fear and apprehension from men's minds so as to produce an atmosphere which is more helpful in the consideration and solution of problems."[7]

It is difficult to believe that the Indian prime minister accepts all of Communist China's assurances at face value. Aware of the military weakness of India and Southeast Asia and opposed to Western intervention in any form in the region, he may feel that the best policy for India is to get commitments from Peiping against aggression and intervention in Asia and to serve as mediator between China and her neighbors.

A view quite the opposite of that of Nehru and Menon was expressed by the *Straits Times,* an English-language newspaper published in Singapore. It declared the day following the signing of the treaty at Manila that "The situation in Southeast Asia is transformed by the simple fact that there is a treaty at all. Security at once is immeasurably strengthened. . . . The Treaty's economic clauses, and the Pacific Charter which has been written into the preamble, affirm Seato's noble purpose. It is no longer the old imperialism which threatens the rights and liberties of Asian peoples. Colonialism everywhere is departing decently. Seato stands between Southeast Asia and the imperialism of a new and vicious creed."

Prime Minister Ali of Indonesia, the largest country in the treaty area, reacted strongly to the Manila defense treaty.

[7] New York *Times,* November 23, 1954.

Almost immediately he went to India to confer with Nehru about creating an All-Asian alternative to Seato's military-economic commitments to ensure peace for the region. Later he visited Premier Nu in Burma to confer with him on the same subject. As a result of Ali's initiative, a Colombo Powers conference met in Java to make plans for an Afro-Asian conference. As an immediate measure to counter the Manila treaty, Ali proposed a mutual nonaggression treaty with Communist China.

BANDUNG CONFERENCE

If Prime Ministers Nehru and Ali Sastroamidjojo expected an unqualified triumph for their ideas of foreign policy at Bandung, they were disappointed. A neutralist bloc was not created; indeed, neutralism won few unalloyed victories at the conference. Anti-Communists showed remarkable strength at Bandung. Led by such able parliamentarians as Romulo of the Philippines and Sir John Kotelawala of Ceylon, the anti-Communist countries defeated any plan Communist China and some neutralist countries may have had of making the white man's colonialism or imperialism seem the principal menace confronting Asia and Africa. In the final communique of the conference not just Western imperialism but "colonialism in all of its manifestations" was condemned. The conference avoided endorsement of the "five principles" of Chou and Nehru; instead, it adopted ten principles, among which was included "Respect for the right of each nation to defend itself singly or collectively in conformity with the Charter of the United Nations." The use of the term "coexistence" was rejected, and instead the phrase of the preamble of the Charter of the United Nations, "live together in peace with one another as good neighbors," was adopted.

The conference may not have met the high expectations of the neutralists, but it was, nevertheless, a historic meeting. It was a great diplomatic gathering from which the West, so long dominant in world affairs, was excluded. There was the feeling that at long last the destiny of Asia was being determined in Asia, that Asia was free. The debates were of a high order and the proceedings were carried on with decorum. Asians and Africans felt their stature increased.

While the conference did not turn out as badly as Americans feared it might, it did take a position on a number of matters which have not made American foreign policy easier. The Asian-African countries wield a considerable influence in the General Assembly of the United Nations because of their numbers. The conflict between the anticolonial, underdeveloped countries and the technologically advanced Western states in the United Nations has been sharper as a result of the Bandung Conference, and the United States not infrequently finds itself in an embarrassing position on certain issues. For example, the conference declared its support of the Arabs against Israel, of Indonesia against the Netherlands on the West New Guinea issue, and of Yemen against the British in Aden and the protectorates in the southern parts of Yemen. The Asian-African bloc made its influence strongly felt in the Suez Canal conflict in the United Nations in 1956-1957.

The prime minister of Communist China won few victories on the floor of the conference, but he nevertheless achieved some diplomatic gains for his country. The traditional Chinese principle of indelible nationality was a cause of serious friction between China and the countries of Southeast Asia, for in accordance with it, China claimed the allegiance of all persons of Chinese descent born abroad, no matter how many generations removed from China. Indonesia, and the Netherlands before it, had long sought to get China to give up the claim of Chinese nationality for persons of Chinese descent born in Indonesia and continuing to live there. A dual nationality on the part of so large a part of its population was a matter of serious concern to the Indonesian government. At Bandung, Chou entered into an agreement with Indonesian Premier Ali under the terms of which the Communist Chinese government accepted broad limitations on this principle. There was general rejoicing at first among Indonesians over this diplomatic victory, but upon closer analysis and after second thought their enthusiasm cooled. It was discovered that under the agreement many persons who under Indonesian law were Indonesian nationals again became Chinese nationals. The agreement created some uncertainty and confusion. However, Indonesians who are not completely blind to the methods of Communism know that many ways remain open by which Communist China can intervene in the internal affairs of Indonesia, such as in family relations between Chinese in Indonesia and Chinese in China, and in using Indonesian-Chinese whose loyalty is to Peiping.

Chou created a sensation on the last day of the conference when he issued a statement that the Chinese people were friendly to the American people and did not want a war with the United States. He declared that the Chinese government was willing to enter into negotiations with the United States government to discuss the question of relaxing tensions in the Taiwan (Formosa) area. Probably because of the attacks on Communism on the floor of the conference, Chou felt that he had to take a conciliatory attitude. He had already given the conference delegates the impression of mildness, friendliness, and great reasonableness. With this offer Chou confirmed that impression and won supporters for the position of his government. When the United States government received the Chou offer with considerable reserve, there was rather general disappointment among the delegates to the conference. Chou also had given support to the stiff anti-Israel resolution which was adopted by the conference, thereby winning the favor of the Arab states.

REORIENTATION OF AMERICAN POLICY

United States policy in Southeast Asia underwent something of a change in 1956. A number of factors may account for the shift. The United States government was undoubtedly influenced by the "new look" in Russian foreign policy which followed the Geneva "Summit" Conference of July, 1955.[8] The Soviet shift involved more than a change of manner from

[8] See the statement by Secretary Dulles to the senate foreign relations committee in support of the administration's foreign-aid program. New York *Times*, May 1, 1956.

growling to purring; it was accompanied by an announcement of willingness to provide technical assistance and agricultural and industrial equipment to underdeveloped countries. When Bulganin and Khrushchev visited India in the closing months of 1955, they paid Burma the high compliment of including it in their itinerary. This was followed by an agreement to provide technical assistance and equipment in exchange for Burma's surplus rice, which was not readily finding a market. Russia also offered, as a gift, to build and equip an industrial institute. In September, Djakarta announced an agreement between the Soviet and Indonesian governments whereby the former is to extend the latter a credit of $100,000,000 at an interest rate of 2½ percent and with repayment in 12 years. The specific projects were still to be determined, but equipment and training in atomic-energy research was prominently mentioned.

The beginning of a change in United States policy is evident in a proposal made in October, 1955, by John B. Hollister, director of the International Cooperation Administration, to the meeting of the consultative committee of the Colombo Plan countries at Singapore. Hollister proposed the establishment of a center for nuclear research and training, with the promise that the United States would contribute substantially toward its construction and operation. Some months later a mission of atomic specialists was sent to confer with officials and scientists in the free Asian countries about the proposed project. By its bomb tests in the South Pacific the United States had alienated Asian public opinion; it now hoped to change this unfavorable sentiment by offering to help Asian countries use the atom for constructive purposes.[9] In March, 1956, Secretary Dulles attended a Seato conference in Karachi and visited several Asian countries. Indonesia seems to have been selected for special treatment on this trip. The anticolonial theme, so dear to President Sukarno and most Indo-

---

[9] The American offer was renewed and made more specific at the meeting of the consultative committee of the Colombo Plan countries at Wellington, New Zealand, in December, 1956. The United States government declared it was prepared to contribute about $20,000,000 to the establishment of a center at Manila.

nesians, was played up very effectively (though stretched a bit). Shortly after his departure Dulles cabled President Sukarno, "You are grappling with the same problems that our own nation faced nearly two hundred years ago and which are still a vivid part of our tradition. I believe that only those who have gone through the process of transformation from being a colony can understand the problems that are involved. You and we have had a common experience which we can share with a special sense of fellowship." On behalf of President Eisenhower the secretary invited President Sukarno to visit the United States. The latter accepted with alacrity. He visited the United States in May and was given an enthusiastic reception.[10]

At about the same time the United States government seemed to be groping for a new attitude toward neutralism. President Eisenhower at a press conference on June 6 made a statement in which he declared that military alliances were not always an advantage to the United States and involved a risk for the country entering them. That same evening Vice President Nixon in a speech followed the President's train of thought, explaining that uncommitted nations wanted time for economic development and "are not going to be frightened into alliances with the West by military power, nor can their allegiance be purchased by dollars." Reactions by America's allies to the President's statement apparently were immediate and strong, for the White House on the next day issued an explanatory statement. The President did not believe that association for

[10] The invitation to President Sukarno was a good diplomatic move, though not without its drawbacks, coming at the time it did. The Thais and Filipinos were surprised and hurt at the rousing reception given a "neutralist" head of state and began to make unfavorable comparisons. The Dutch were unhappy because to them it seemed to put the American stamp of approval on the recent unilateral denunciation of the economic and financial agreements signed at The Hague Round Table Conference with the encouragement of the American representative there. It also made more difficult a movement of Indonesian leaders to restrict President Sukarno's role. Because parliament had not been elected, it had had little moral authority, and Sukarno was able to assume a position of political leadership without responsibility to cabinet or parliament. Now that elections had been held and parliament had a mandate from the people, the time had arrived to put an end to the anomaly, but the president's warm reception in the United States increased his already great prestige and made it more difficult than ever to control him.

mutual security with the United States will involve any country in added danger, but, on the contrary, will provide added security on the basis of mutuality and scrupulous respect for the independence of each. In disparaging military alliances, the President apparently meant only to disparage alliances with Communist countries, "great powers which have shown an aggressive disposition." A few days later, Secretary Dulles declared neutrality to be immoral. Vice President Nixon visited the Philippines and some of the countries of South and Southeast Asia in July. In speeches and statements at Manila and Karachi he was back on the old theme of the immorality of neutralism and warned against trade agreements with the Soviet bloc.

It is evident that a change of attitude, at least, had taken place in Washington, however badly the government spokesman explained this change. The right of neutrality was recognized, and aid was promised to countries even if they did not align themselves with the West; and instead of stressing the military aspects of defense, the government began to emphasize the need for economic and social progress in the underdeveloped countries. With respect to East-West trade policy a relaxation had also set in. When the United States government in the United Nations opposed the actions of Israel, France, and Great Britain with respect to Egypt in the closing months of 1956, the United States became almost popular in the countries of South and Southeast Asia. However, that popularity began to decline when the United States government began to press for a basic, permanent solution to the problems of the Near East.

SOME GENERAL OBSERVATIONS

The drive against Western foreign rule has been practically won throughout most of Southeast Asia; the reestablishment of Western domination is unthinkable and impossible. But the peoples of the region have not yet succeeded in establishing strong and efficient, to say nothing of democratic, government. Their societies are far from healthy. There is disillusionment, discontent, dissension, corruption, governmental weakness, and inefficiency. These conditions facilitate the penetration of the government by the Communists, who themselves work hard to help create weakness and disorder. They then take over as the bearers of order. This happened in China and in northern Vietnam, and the big question is whether this Communist success is going to be repeated in other countries of the region. The discussion of the question of how much the West and the colonial powers have contributed to producing the present situation is no longer profitable. It is necessary to deal with the situation as it is.

It is clear that the advance of Communism in Southeast Asia cannot be checked by a military alliance alone, but the military problem had become so acute by 1954 that it had to be given priority over the economic. Unless the line is held militarily, the West cannot assist the governments of these countries in working at the solution of the economic and social problems. However, the chief danger is not direct attack, but infiltration and subversion, with Moscow and Peiping using local residents and nationals (Chinese and indigenous persons) to spearhead the troublemaking. The conference of the Seato members which was held at Bangkok in February, 1955, gave this difficult problem careful consideration. The council, in the communique issued at the conclusion of the meeting, declared that it recognized the gravity of the situation, that the threat "demands special efforts in all aspects of the national life," that there was "agreement on the need for cooperation among the member governments to assist one another in combating the subversive activities of international communism," and further that the council had decided "to arrange for continuing consultation and mutual assistance and to make it possible for each member government to draw upon the experience of the others in dealing with this danger." This is good so far as it goes, but it does not seem to go very far in meeting an immediate and dire threat. Of course, the Seato powers rely upon the individual and collective efforts of the governments in promoting "economic progress and social wellbeing" to destroy the attraction of Communism for Southeast

Asians, but it will take some time for these measures to become noticeably effective.

Thailand and the Philippines, as well as Australia and New Zealand, wanted armed forces placed in the area of immediate danger, but the United States would not go along with this. It did not wish to tie down its troops at various points in the treaty area; it chose rather to "rely largely upon mobile Allied power which can strike an aggressor wherever the occasion may demand," in the belief that this capacity will deter aggression. The policy of not stationing troops or maintaining bases in the region is less likely to alienate neutralist countries. For Seato to be made acceptable to noncommitted Asia, the United States and its allies must convince these peoples that their intentions are strictly defensive.

This may still leave the Seato powers, and especially the United States as the country with the largest forces in the area, the problem of determining whether to incur the risk of precipitating a global war, with the possibility of atomic warfare, by an attack on China in case of overt aggression by Communist China or aggression by another state, say north Vietnam, backed by China. Certainly the world, and not only Asians, would be shocked at the bombing of China in retaliation for infiltration and subversion in one of the countries of Southeast Asia.[11] It is not inconceivable that due to these considerations the great military striking power of the United States might be rendered immobile and thus not deter infiltration and subversion, or even aggression. If China and Russia reach the conclusion that the danger of massive retaliation is not great, they will be tempted to risk local thrusts. It would seem that the only alternative to a war with Communist China, probably supported by Russia, is to become involved again in a local war with conventional weapons like that of Korea and Indochina. These are not pleasant alternatives.

Southeast Asia is not going to be saved from Communism

[11] General Maxwell D. Taylor, army chief of staff, expressed the view before the senate armed services subcommittee that "small wars" are more possible now that mutual deterrence "of atomic weapons has lessened the likelihood of general war." Other military specialists hold that nuclear weapons will be used in any war, and that the Communists know this and therefore will not start a war of any size. See New York *Times*, July 27, 1956.

unless its peoples and governments have the desire and the will to be saved from it. This will at the moment does not seem to be strong. But desire and will are not sufficient; there must be the capability to defend itself from Communism, both internally and externally. The region must be made capable of defending itself. Can this be done?

The problem was sharply stated by Syed Amjad Ali in an address while he was Pakistani ambassador to the United States: "The illiteracy and poverty of the hundreds of millions of Asia stares at the better living conditions of the Free World. . . . [The mass of Asians are] not only illiterate but uncertain about the value of democracy. Asia, the oldest inhabited continent, is today overcrowded. . . . Unlike Europe, this spectacular increase in manpower has not been accompanied by a corresponding increase in production nor are there any avenues of migration to new colonies. Hence the population, which is already desperately poor, is getting poorer. The problem of democracy is to give these people something to struggle for, to give their life a dignity out of which will come a desire to preserve individual freedom."[12]

The level of living in Southeast Asia is extremely low. The contrast with the United States is startling. The figures compiled for 1949 by the statistical office of the United Nations show that the per capita annual income in the United States was $1,453; in the same year the figure was $36 for Burma, $36 for Thailand, $44 for the Philippines, and $25 for Indonesia.[13] These figures are only approximations, it is true, but they nevertheless reveal extreme differences in the levels of living. All of the available social statistics, such as the percentage of illiteracy, birth and death rates, and food consumption, emphasize this startling contrast. And the disparity in living levels is increasing, not decreasing.

This is what gives Communism its strong attraction for many Asians. In nearly every Western country the levels of living

[12] New York *Times*, February 20, 1955.
[13] *National and Per Capita Incomes of Seventy Countries in 1949, Expressed in American Dollars* (New York, 1950).

American Policy   313

are higher, and generally considerably higher, than in Russia; but in Asia, with the exception of Japan, the levels of living are much lower than in the home of Communism. What impresses many South Asians about Communism in China is that already marked economic advances have been registered, and that confusion has given way to discipline and order. A terrible price has been paid for this, especially by certain sections of the population, but to people living under conditions of malignant poverty, the price may not seem very high.

The problem was succinctly stated by the Indonesian ambassador to the United States, Mukarto Notowidigdo, in an address before the American-Indonesian Chamber of Commerce in New York on January 14, 1954. "The future development of the political as well as the economic stability of the world obviously," declared the ambassador, "cannot rest on a solid basis when so significant a part of the world as Southeast Asia remains unstable, uneasy, and a source of increasing social discontent. The significance of the danger inherent in the failure of economic developments in Southeast Asia to keep pace with those in other parts of the world has not been fully appreciated by the West. The emphasis of the Western Powers has been on achieving a military balance of power. They have neglected the even more basic problem of the balance of power with respect to Southeast Asia. The danger stems from a number of factors. First is a psychological one—the achievement of substantial progress in Communist countries cannot fail to exercise powerful attraction on underdeveloped countries whose rate of progress has not been so rapid. In the second place, a nation which has no sound economic base is vulnerable both politically and militarily because it cannot retain the loyalty of its population when it does not satisfy their basic needs and their aspirations for the future. The consequence of this economic unbalance is to create pressures which may tend to attract underdeveloped countries to a system which, in a similar stage of development, has apparently succeeded in some degree in meeting the problems which they have not begun to solve."

To promote economic progress and social well-being, great reliance is being placed on technical assistance and economic aid. It has been said that the peoples of Southeast Asia have no ills which a full stomach cannot cure. Assuming the basic truth of this statement, though the problem is by no means as simple as that, much has to change before the peoples of Asia can enjoy an adequate diet, good health, and a few of the amenities enjoyed by the masses in the West. Profound changes must take place in the inherited social and religious attitudes, the political climate, and the social structure. The environment has to change before economic development can flourish. There must be more than just discontent with their social conditions if a people are to achieve substantial material progress. A mere desire for economic progress is not enough, there must also be the determination to achieve it. It is true that the introduction of superior techniques of production help to change the environment, but this is a slow process. The process is also accompanied by dangers. Education, better hygiene, and medical facilities are basic necessities if the society is to be more effective in production. But since they can be extended more easily than the economy can be developed, their extension is accompanied, at least in its early stages, by two effects which make the general problem more difficult, namely, a rapid rise in the population and a rapid rise in the level of expectations. Americans have too easily assumed that with technical assistance and economic aid the peoples of underdeveloped areas would soon be able to enjoy better living conditions, but we have already learned not to expect results immediately.

Though the pressure of population in Southeast Asia is not as great as in China and India, it is, nevertheless, severe enough to present grave obstacles to economic progress. On Java, in central Luzon, and the Red River delta of north Vietnam the pressure of many people weighs heavily on the productive capacity of the land. Modern developments in medicine and disease control have brought about a marked decrease in the death rate in these countries, but a drop in the birth rate

American Policy 315

waits upon a change in the social environment.[14] The result is an explosive population situation. Population is increasing in the countries of Southeast Asia at a rate of 1½ to 2 percent annually. To keep the production of food abreast of the population increase is no small task. Even though Indonesia and the Philippines are 80 percent agrarian, these two countries have been rather large importers of rice and are only now succeeding in attaining self-sufficiency in this staple of consumption. To improve the level of living, production must increase more rapidly than the population. To date, food production has barely kept up with the rapidly expanding population, but the purchasing power of Asians is so low that there has developed a glutted market. While many Asians are starving, rice is deteriorating in warehouses.

The contrast between Southeast Asia and the United States in this respect is indeed startling. The number of people in the United States engaged in the production of food has steadily fallen, until now it is less than 15 percent of the population; yet the food supply, in spite of governmental restrictions on the acreage of some crops, outruns the demand, and huge surpluses pile up. The truth of the matter is that the United States can produce rice more cheaply than the Asian peasants, and the 1,000,000 tons of surplus in this country help to depress the price of this important export commodity of Burma, Thailand, and South Korea, and thus create economic difficulties in these countries. Wheat and barley provide the same amount of nutrient as rice at half the price, but they cannot compete with the latter on the Asian market because Asians much prefer their customary diet. Should Asians develop a taste for the cheaper imported cereals, Asian agriculture would face enormous difficulties.

Southeast Asia does not have the capital to finance its economic development; its per capita income is so low that little

---

[14] The death rate in Ceylon declined from 31.2 in 1921 to 12.6 in 1950, but the birth rate continued as high as ever, at between 34 and 41 per thousand of the population. Though Ceylon is not in Southeast Asia, conditions there are very similar to those which prevail in some of the countries of Southeast Asia.

saving or capital accumulation is possible. The capital will have to come from the outside, which would seem to offer a golden opportunity to Americans and the United States government to join in fruitful cooperation with these countries. These countries desire technical and economic assistance, but they are afraid of it. They fear a return of "colonialism." By "colonialism" these peoples do not mean merely political subordination of their country to another; they mean by it dependence upon Western countries in any form, whether political, economic, or cultural. As a result of the many years of agitation against what their political leaders called exploitation by foreign capitalists, they have come to regard all capitalism as a hidden form of colonialism. They regard their economy as colonial because it is highly dependent upon a few export commodities to a few highly industrialized countries. They regard their low living levels as a phase of colonialism.

Because of these sentiments, governments of Southeast Asian countries are loath to induce private foreign capital to invest in their countries. And government aid, to be acceptable, must be without strings attached. It will be recalled that an Indonesian government fell in 1952 because it had signed an agreement for economic aid from the United States in the amount of only $8,000,000. The agreement contained a mild clause linking Indonesia with the free world, but it was considered a departure from the policy of neutralism, and the cabinet was overthrown. Burma in 1953 renounced American economic aid for somewhat the same reasons. When the Burmese government first accepted American aid, critics accused it of selling the country to capitalist America, and for a paltry sum. During the early years of the Indonesian Republic the United States contributed loans and grants to the extent of $200,000,000; during the last five years the amount has been only $30,000,000. At present, Indonesia is again receiving assistance from the United States, but only in the form of technical cooperation in the amount of $8,000,000. The Philippines and Thailand, members of Seato, and Cambodia, Laos, and south Vietnam receive large amounts of military as well as smaller sums for

American Policy

technical cooperation assistance.[15] In the election campaign in Cambodia in 1955, former King Norodom Sihanouk was charged by his opponents with having sold the little kingdom to the United States in a secret treaty granting the latter military bases in Cambodia. In the election in September, 1955, the former king won a resounding victory, but since then he has taken a neutralist line.

Under the provisions of the Mutual Security act of 1955 the President was granted a special fund of $200,000,000 to be used primarily for projects contributing to economic development of the Asian region as a whole. This fund is available for obligation until June 30, 1958.

SUMMARY AND PROSPECTS

There is grave danger that the 175,000,000 people of Southeast Asia may be lost to the free world. This loss would come near to tilting the balance of power in favor of the Communist bloc. The United States, as the leader of the free world, must do all that it can to prevent this from happening, not simply out of national pride or out of a desire to win a victory over a rival or enemy, but because of what this would mean for the Southeast Asians and for the world.

American policy in Southeast Asia has been based upon the deterrence of aggression by the threat of massive retaliation, collective security, technical assistance, economic aid, and military support. Unless the potential enemy should commit a clear, single, outrageous act of aggression, the United States

---

[15] Under the Mutual Security act of 1955 the countries of Southeast Asia were to receive during the fiscal year 1955 assistance as follows:

	Military Assistance		Technical	Total
	Direct forces support	Defense support	Cooperation	
Indonesia			$8,000,000	$ 8,000,000
Philippines	$ 2,300,000	$ 19,700,000	6,500,000	28,500,000
Thailand	8,200,000	31,800,000	5,500,000	45,500,000
Indochina	38,200,000	379,300,000	7,500,000	425,000,000

For the fiscal year 1957, appropriations for technical cooperation in the countries of the region were as follows: Indonesia, $8,000,000; Philippines, $5,900,000; Thailand, $4,600,000; Cambodia, $2,500,000; Laos, $1,500,000; and Vietnam, $5,000,000.

could not resort to massive retaliation because of the unfavorable reaction it would produce in Asia and the whole world. Resort to massive retaliation would also involve the risk of a global nuclear war. Moreover, by putting so many of its eggs in the nuclear basket, the United States has weakened its capacity for engaging in a limited war, if it should now find that engaging in this kind of war is the only alternative to enemy aggression or global atomic war. Seato is weak. It is for the region but not of it. It lacks strength because there are few Asian states in it, the few Asian states who are in it are weak, and there is little agreement among its Western members. The strongest cornerstone of Seato, namely, the American-Philippines military relationship, is weakening because of the friction which has developed between the two countries over jurisdiction in the American bases in the islands.

From the point of view of American objectives in the region, the situation has not improved since 1954. Elections in Burma and Indonesia gave the Communist parties increased strength in the national parliaments. Cambodia and Laos adopted a markedly neutralist policy in the same year. Malaya has been promised early independence, and leftist elements in Singapore have been causing more trouble with increasing insecurity. Under the conditions prevailing, no great value can be attached to the British air and naval bases on the key island of Singapore. Moreover, Russia and China have begun an active cultivation of the countries of the region. Burma has made several barter deals with Communist countries; Russia has extended Indonesia a $100,000,000 credit; and China has entered a trade and economic aid agreement with Cambodia. Khrushchev and Bulganin have visited Burma; Chou En-lai continued the assiduous cultivation of the countries of the region by a visit to Cambodia and Burma in November and December, 1956; leading statesmen of Southeast Asia have visited Russia and China; and Mao Tse-tung has promised to visit Indonesia. Economic conditions in the countries of the region have improved little, if at all.

The United States must place its chief reliance on technical assistance and economic aid. Because of south Vietnam's key position, its formidable problems, and the danger of imminent collapse, the United States has had to put enormous sums of money into that small country. It is amazing what obstacles have been overcome, but its position, nevertheless, remains precarious. There is danger that the peoples in the region, and Americans too, will become discouraged with the slow progress in economic development, especially in the early stages. Great gains cannot be expected at once, or even very soon. Once the groundwork has been laid and attitudes have undergone change, an entrepreneurial spirit will develop, innovations will become easier, and the people will desire a higher standard of living and will be prepared to make sacrifices for it. Economic development will then be self-generated, with American capital accelerating the process with marginal assistance.

The thermonuclear stalemate in world politics has brought about a shift in thinking from armaments to ideology, from the material to the spiritual. This ought to be to the advantage of the United States if it knows how to present this side of its character in an effective manner. There are other good reasons why the United States should be careful not to limit its help to technology and capital. There is no guarantee that if these peoples win the struggle against poverty, they will be democratic and peace loving. Advancement in technology is not inevitably accompanied by peaceful attitudes. Better economic conditions and scientific and technological progress do not necessarily make "nice" people, as the recent examples of Germany, Russia, and Japan prove. Technology produces social changes, and this aspect of the problem should receive far greater emphasis in technical assistance programs than it now does. Americans must give aid in such fields as education, journalism, labor movements, democratic political organization, women's movements, and civic activities, in order to make certain, so far as it is possible, that the economic changes will produce a democratic society. This will require great skill and human understanding on the part of the Americans sent to give this assistance, for Asians are even more suspicious of cultural than economic imperialism.

Mention must be made at this point of certain American policies which Indonesians, Malayans, and other Southeast Asians find difficult to understand. The economic life of Indonesia and Malaya is to no small extent dependent upon a few major exports, principally tin and rubber, which account for about two-thirds of her foreign exchange. The price of these commodities fluctuates greatly. The price of tin was 78 cents a pound in June, 1950; 183 cents in February, 1951; 85 cents in December, 1954; 95 cents in October, 1955; and 106 cents in December, 1956. The price of rubber varied even more: 17.5 cents a pound in December, 1949; 31 cents in June, 1950; 78 cents in December, 1950; 20 cents in December, 1953; 45 cents in September, 1955; and 37 cents in December, 1956. Indonesians and Malayans point to the encouragement of synthetic rubber production and the heavily subsidized tin smelter in Texas to process Bolivian ore imports as evidences of an official policy on the part of the United States government to beat down the price of rubber and tin. These peoples are inclined to associate their economic difficulties with deliberate American policy. Apropos of this problem, the Ceylonese delegate in 1956 at the conference on the General Agreement on Tariff and Trade at Geneva declared that if the Western countries cannot provide better than erratic markets for rubber and other primary commodities, the underdeveloped countries would have to turn to the Communist bloc. The Communist countries would very likely welcome this opportunity, as foreign trade is becoming their chief instrument of policy in underdeveloped countries.

Indonesians find it difficult to reconcile what they believe to be official American policy in this matter with the offer of technical assistance and economic aid. Because wages on the rubber plantations are low and the bulk of their rubber and tin go to the United States, Indonesians see in this situation another case of "colonialism." When they contrast their low wages with the high American incomes, they are easily convinced that they are being exploited. This is a bad situation and ought to be remedied. The Indonesian government would like to see the prices of its export commodities stabilized at what it regards as a fair level by means of an international commodity price agreement. The United States is reluctant to enter into any such agreement, and it may not be the best answer to the problem, but our government should show a willingness to join in seeking a solution to a real problem. Likewise, by selling our surplus agricultural commodities in the region, we alienate important elements in these countries and create apprehension. The American people are going to have to consider the necessity of bringing their domestic and foreign policies in line with each other. As it is now, certain aspects of our domestic policy tend to neutralize our foreign policy. The ban on the shipment of strategic goods to Communist countries has also caused resentment. This policy has had results adverse to Western interests. It has not only been a cause of friction in this vital region (and elsewhere), but it has probably also forced the Communists to develop their own production of the embargoed items. Fortunately, the United States is relaxing its stand on this matter.

That American technical assistance and economic aid is making an impression in South Asia is apparent from the fact that the Soviet Union is now offering technical assistance to countries of the region. The natural American impulse will be to try to head this off. It would be unwise to urge these governments to reject the proferred aid. Maybe Americans should welcome it, as they should welcome increased trade between South Asian countries and the Soviet Union. Communist countries—and this is especially true with respect to the Soviet Union—are not regarded by the peoples of Southeast Asia as exploitive or imperialistic, because they take no goods out of the region nor put any capital in, and no Russians are to be seen. In this they have a tremendous advantage psychologically. It is not likely that the Communist countries would permit much trade, but as it is, the United States opposition plays into the hands of the Communist propagandists. Trade might very well cause friction to develop between the Communist and Southeast Asian countries. Burma's experiences with barter agreements with Communist countries indicate that increased contacts may lead to friction.

There remains the difficult problem of creating in Southeast Asia a regional community with a common will and purpose. There must develop the conviction that their survival as independent countries can be assured only by common action against all encroachments on their territorial integrity and political independence. In this connection the question rises of whether to carry on our programs directly, on the basis of bilateral agreements, or channel all of our technical assistance and economic aid through the Colombo Plan and the United Nations. The neutralist countries would be less suspicious of United States motives, and more convinced that Americans are genuinely interested in their welfare, if the latter were to become our policy. Our present policy has a tendency to divide the nations of the area into two opposing groups; action through the United Nations or the Colombo Plan might be more effective in developing a regional community spirit.

American policy in Southeast Asia is made more difficult because of United States policy toward Japan and China. The peoples of this region still fear Japan; they are not convinced that the Japanese have been really converted and are now peaceful. They fear an economically strong Japan; they distrust the American policy of mobilizing and integrating Japanese resources with those of the free world. When the Japanese peace treaty was negotiated, Australia, New Zealand, and the Philippines urged and obtained security pacts with the United States designed to insure them against a recurrence of Japanese aggression as well as Communist military expansion. Indonesia and the Philippines signed the Japanese peace treaty, but did not ratify it because its terms precluded reparation payments except in services. Burma, as well as these two countries, demanded reparations so large that Japan could not possibly pay them without a long economic servitude. Burma and the Philippines have finally settled for a greatly reduced amount, and Indonesia may also gradually scale down its demands to a point where Japan may agree upon a settlement. But distrust of American policy in building up Japan as a bulwark against Communism remains.

It would be very unfortunate if this situation should continue much longer, for the solution of Japan's problem is in no small measure dependent upon greatly increased commercial relations with Southeast Asia. Japan cannot live without extensive foreign trade, and commercial relations with the mainland of China will be only on Communist terms. As an Asian nation which has made remarkable progress in technology and economic development, Japan can offer the countries of Southeast Asia a great deal. In an address to the National Press Club in Washington on August 30, 1955, Mamoru Shigemitsu, the foreign minister of Japan, made a significant suggestion. After a brief statement on the thorny reparations question, he asked if it were not possible for the United States government to devise "an over-all plan of economic development of Southeast Asia which will, in the course of its implementation, also help dispose of the reparations issue. . . . We only desire to coordinate, to our mutual advantage, our policy with yours. In short, it is our desire to foster our economic strength, profiting from the American aid plan for Southeast Asia so that we may become better qualified to work together with the United States in stabilizing this critical theatre in the global struggle now raging between the free and fettered nations."

The diversity of policy among the Seato powers as well as among the countries of the region with respect to China is a divisive factor. American effort to prohibit trade in strategic materials with China has caused strained relations with Ceylon, a country more inclined to be pro-West than neutralist, and caused a great deal of resentment in Indonesia. The refusal of the United States to recognize the Chinese Communist regime and the continued support of the Nationalists on Formosa is widely condemned among South and Southeast Asians. The Ceylonese ambassador to the United States declared at a conference held under the auspices of Johns Hopkins University (August 8 to 11, 1955) that the continued control of the veto in the Security Council of the United Nations by the Chiang Kai-shek government was "an affront to Asian democracy." He further declared Formosa to be a militarily occupied island. Until a unified policy with respect to China is arrived at, extensive cooperation between the United States, Thailand, and the Philippines on the one hand, and Burma and Indonesia on the other, will not be possible. Burma, if it did not hold the United States responsible for the continued presence of Chinese Nationalist troops on her soil, did assume that the American government could exercise enough control over Chiang Kai-shek to force him to remove these troops. The Nationalist forces in north Burma were not only causing domestic difficulties, but they threatened to involve Burma in serious trouble with Communist China. It was probably the latter consideration which led Burma to renounce further American aid.

The American diplomatic problem in Southeast Asia is indeed formidable. The United States must find a policy which is acceptable to a number of states without and within the region whose policies in Eastern Asia differ from ours, especially with respect to China, but also with respect to Japan. It is almost impossible to do anything positive in the region without alienating as many countries as are won. By arming Pakistan, we alienate India; by continuing to protect Chiang, we irritate and embarrass Burma; by making Japan its chief Asian ally, the United States made several countries of Southeast Asia resentful and apprehensive. The United States must seek to equate Asian anticolonialism with its own anti-Communism. This is no easy matter, for it may require a change in American policy with respect to China and Formosa. Most Asians regard American policy as a continuation of Western imperialism—a form of colonialism. Asians fear war. The United States will do well to talk less about force as a deterrent to aggression. The United States government is wisely emphasizing working through the United Nations, though this is accompanied by difficulties. Because of the structure of the General Assembly, with each member state having one vote, the United Nations gives states which are weak socially, economically, and militarily a tremendous political power. Southeast Asia has a population somewhat larger than the United States, but in 1956 it had six votes in the General Assembly, and may in the not too distant future acquire two more, while the United States has only one vote. Frequently these states take an unreasonable position on certain matters. Nevertheless, more can be achieved through the United Nations than outside of it. In fact, attempts to bypass the United Nations would hopelessly weaken our position in the underdeveloped, anticolonial world.

Asians dread war, and especially the prospect of nuclear warfare, even more than Westerners. American spokesmen talked too much about force as a deterrent to aggression, while Communist leaders were talking peaceful coexistence. Chou En-lai is going to great lengths to assure Southeast Asians of Chinese peaceful intentions. The American nuclear bomb tests in the Pacific have stirred up the Asian fear of war, and unfortunately, associated atomic war with the United States. All of this strengthens Asian sentiments of neutralism. Even President Eisenhower has said repeatedly that there is no longer an alternative to war. Asians feel the same way, but unlike the President, they feel that military alliances provoke war. It will be difficult to wean most Asians from this point of view. Americans should remember that neutralism once held a strong appeal for them, and that not so many years ago.

In conclusion, it should be pointed out that recent events are by no means all to the disadvantage of the United States. Developments in the satellite states in eastern Europe, especially Russia's cruel repression of the anti-Communist revolt in Hungary, must have at least raised doubts in the mind of Asians as to the peaceful nature of Communism. Likewise, recent developments in Tibet, with Chinese Communist plans to settle 5,000,000 Communists there, and the controversy between Communist China and Burma over border territory cannot help but arouse suspicion. The Communist-power bloc is no longer monolithic; it is beginning to show serious cracks. The breakup of the two-power bloc system into a number of relatively independent power blocs is not to the disadvantage of the United States, but may in fact make its problems less difficult.

The diplomatic problem of the United States in Southeast Asia is indeed difficult, but it is not hopeless.

RECENT DEVELOPMENTS

THE POLITICAL INSTABILITY in most of the countries of Southeast Asia—especially the deterioration of economic conditions in Indonesia and the civil war in that unhappy land—is favoring the Communist cause by enabling the Communists to play on political rivalries, to intensify disruption, and to spread disillusionment with democratic or non-Communist systems. Indonesian President Sukarno's determination to allow the Communists a role in the government obviously also works in their favor. The arrival in Indonesia of ten ships from the U.S.S.R. in early 1958 to replace Dutch vessels which formerly provided the transportation for this large insular country, and the continuing possibility of military equipment from Communist countries for putting down rebellions in the outer islands, are grave developments for the West.

Indonesia's announcement in December, 1957, claiming territorial jurisdiction over all of the waters between its thousands of islands was undoubtedly intended to exclude communication without its consent through the numerous sealanes traversing this vast area.[1] The Indonesian claim, if successfully maintained, would greatly reduce the effectiveness of the Southeast Asian Treaty Organization.

Security problems of Southeast Asia and their relation to the world situation were critically reexamined by the Seato council of ministers at its fourth annual meeting, which was held in Manila March 11-13, 1958. Pote Sarasin, Thai diplomat and statesman who in 1957 became the organization's first secretary general, declared in his report to the council that the Asian members of Seato during the year had had to face continued efforts of Communists to infiltrate their trade unions and their governments. In its final communique the council declared that Seato had become "a bulwark which has enabled the countries protected thereby to proceed in peace with their programs of national development." It was of the opinion that collective-security measures had resulted in the diversion of the emphasis of Communist activities from the military to the nonmilitary field. Subversion was recognized as "the most substantial current menace."

The council emphasized economic and cultural activities. Economic problems and progress in the area were reviewed. During 1957 more than $700,000,000 for economic purposes was provided for the Asian members of Seato, principally by the United States. It was agreed to continue and to expand Seato's program of cultural activities, which includes round-tables, scholarships and fellowships and the appointment of professors at universities of the Asian members, and traveling lecturers.

The United States and the Philippines announced that they intended to establish a defense college in the latter country, which would be open to members and nonmembers of Seato.

The council's communique did not mention Indonesia; it was agreed that Seato's policy with respect to that country should be one of strict noninterference. That developments in Indonesia were seriously discussed cannot be doubted, for the situation there is of the utmost gravity for the free world. A Communist or pro-Communist regime in Indonesia would isolate Australia, render Singapore's naval base useless, provide the Communist bloc with a rich source of tin, rubber, and other strategic commodities, and open the region wide to Chinese Communist influence. The West is confronted with a series of

[1] The Indonesian government declared that "the delineation of the territorial sea, with a width of 12 nautical miles, shall be measured from straight lines connecting the outermost islands of the Republic of Indonesia." New York Times, international edition, January 18, 1958.

dilemmas in regard to the situation in Indonesia. Inaction may in the end lead to a Communist triumph, but action even of the mildest sort would further alienate Asian neutralists, while positive action might bring on Communist intervention and produce another Korea or Indochina. Djakarta has for some time sought arms from the United States, but the latter has been understandably reluctant to furnish the Sukarno regime with arms with which to build up strength to crush the opponents of its policies. The Indonesians subsequently have sought to acquire military supplies (about $200,000,000 worth) elsewhere, and Foreign Minister Subandrio has indicated the existence of Communist offers on excellent terms. It is also reported that Communist China has offered a $20,000,000 loan on a long-term basis for industrial purposes.

Rather than give the Communist bloc an excuse or even an opportunity for intervention, the West may well prefer to give the Indonesian government indirect aid in putting down the revolt. In this case, smoldering opposition and guerrilla warfare may in the end drag the Sukarno regime down. But in this event there is no guarantee that it would be replaced by a government better disposed toward the West.

The Indonesian government apparently regards American policy as interventionist. President Sukarno in his numerous speeches has insinuated that the United States was behind the rebel movement. John M. Allison, the American ambassador to Indonesia, was in January, 1958, transferred to another diplomatic post after he had been in Djakarta less than a year, presumably for the reason that he disagreed with his government's policy with respect to Indonesia. On February 11 Secretary Dulles stated that he would like to see in Indonesia "a government which is constitutional and which reflects the real interest and desires of the people."[2] The Indonesian foreign minister immediately responded to the secretary of state's comments that he did not think that it was "to the advantage of the United States to get involved with domestic issues in any Asian country, since this may also provoke other big powers to act in the same

[2] New York *Times*, int. ed., February 12, 1958.

manner."[3] Progovernment and leftist papers accused the United States of interfering in Indonesian issues and backing the rebels.

INDONESIA

Increasing dissidence in the outer islands, here and there breaking out into open defiance, forced out the Ali Sastroamidjojo cabinet in March, 1957. President Sukarno promptly declared a state of war and siege, and in April he appointed a cabinet with Djuanda as prime minister. The cabinet, which contains a number of extreme leftists, is more presidential than parliamentary. In fact, since the resignation of the Ali ministry, parliament has functioned ineffectively, with barely a quorum in attendance. The president was authorized by parliament to establish the national council which he had advocated as his plan for a "guided democracy," and in accordance with his previously expressed views, he included Communists in its membership.

Colonel Maludin Simbolon, commander of the territorial army in North Sumatra, who in December, 1956, declared the autonomy of his area, found himself outwitted. The central government reestablished its control in the area by a counter-coup under Colonel Djamin Gintings. Lieutenant Colonel Vantje Sumual in North Celebes fared better. He, too, declared his area autonomous, but the central government was unable to unseat him easily.

Throughout 1957, efforts were made by the moderates to effect a compromise between Djakarta and the dissident areas in the outer islands and to bring about a reconciliation between Sukarno and Hatta. The latter, who is a native Sumatran, is regarded by the peoples of the outer islands as representing their point of view and as a guardian of their interests. The high point of these efforts was a national conference in Djakarta in September, 1957, attended by leaders of the central government and of the disgruntled and rebellious outer islands. Hopes centered around a possible reconciliation between the president and his former vice president. The estranged leaders signed a

---

[3] New York *Times*, int. ed., February 14, 1958.

Recent Developments

joint statement in which they pledged to work with the Indonesian people in striving to realize the ideals of the proclamation of independence in 1945. While this vague statement of "agreement" really did nothing to solve the crisis, it did slow down the widening of the breach between Djakarta and the outlying regions. The conference also made an attempt to solve another of Indonesia's persistent problems, namely, the disunity in the army. A seven-man commission was named, with Sukarno and Hatta as members, to arrive at a solution. The military participants in the conference, which included many "rebel" colonels, took an oath pledging to obey unconditionally the decisions made by the commission.

President Sukarno and Hatta were unable to implement their basic joint statement of September. They met twice, one time with the president calling on Hatta. A third meeting of the two leaders was postponed. Before this meeting was to have taken place, the central government made its decision to use force against the "countergovernment" which had been set up in Sumatra. With this decision, reconciliation between the two leaders probably vanished for good. Sukarno was apparently desirous of having Hatta back in the government, or at least he was willing to take him back to appease the peoples of the outer islands, but he was unwilling to accept the former vice president's conditions. According to reports, Hatta insisted upon the exclusion of Communists from the government, the dissolution of the national council, and the formation of a presidential cabinet with the approval of parliament. It was also rumored that he demanded amnesty for the leaders of the countergovernment.

In the closing months of 1957 Indonesia made its fourth attempt to secure from the General Assembly of the United Nations a resolution requesting the Netherlands to renew negotiations with it for the transfer of West New Guinea to Indonesian administration. A month before the vote on the resolution was taken, Foreign Minister Subandrio declared that Indonesia would take West New Guinea by force if its current appeal to the United Nations were unsuccessful. In late October, about the time this statement was made, the first wave of the anti-

Dutch campaign began. Youths began painting Dutch-owned automobiles and buildings in Djakarta with the slogan, "We are now ready to take West New Guinea by force." President Sukarno in a speech in Lombok declared it was not necessary to attack West New Guinea; Indonesia could obtain control of the disputed territory by attacking Dutch interests in Indonesia and boycotting Netherlanders. The place to carry on the struggle for West New Guinea was not the United Nations or Washington, but Indonesia.[4] Not long before the vote was taken in the assembly, the Indonesian foreign minister warned the Netherlands and the West that the Dutch attitude was "very dangerous" and might lead to unforeseen and even explosive events in the international field. "If we are forced to abandon our present preoccupation with peaceful, constructive activities, and, instead, concentrate on building up our physical strength, the prevailing fundamentals of our foreign relations may change in character, too."[5]

With the failure of the passage of the resolution on November 29, the anti-Dutch campaign was stepped up.[6] Dutch-owned KLM planes were forbidden to land in Djakarta, Indonesian personnel of Dutch enterprises went on a 24-hour strike, and later practically all of the Dutch enterprises were taken over by the native personnel or by the government. The production or distribution of newspapers, journals, or other publications in Dutch, including those imported, was prohibited, as well as the display of films with Dutch subtitles. The Netherlands-owned KPM fleet which engaged in interisland shipping was first taken over by the government, but just before the company was to collect insurance from Lloyds for its loss, the ships were returned but forbidden to engage in Indonesian traffic. The Indonesian government first attempted (but without success) to charter ships from Japan to meet the urgent need for interisland transportation. Later, ten ships were obtained from the Soviet Union.

[4] *Nieuwe Rotterdamse Courant*, November 11, 1957.
[5] New York *Times*, int. ed., November 21, 1957.
[6] The resolution had strong support but failed to obtain the necessary two-thirds vote. The vote was 41 for, 29 against, with 11 abstentions. The United States abstained from voting.

Netherlanders left Indonesia in droves. Of the 250,000 Dutch nationals in the islands in 1949, about 175,000 had either repatriated or left the country by January 1, 1956. It was estimated that there were still about 50,000 Netherlanders in Indonesia in October, 1957, when the bitter anti-Dutch campaign began. About half of these were repatriated within the next few months.

Dutch consular offices in Indonesia were ordered closed on December 5, as well as the cultural, military, and information sections of the Netherlands mission in Djakarta. Further credit transfers to the Netherlands were prohibited.

The Indonesian actions were a severe blow to the Dutch, whose investments in the former dependency are estimated at one and a quarter billion dollars. The repatriation of so many people to the crowded lowlands created difficult physical problems, as well as some psychological ones, for many of these people are Eurasians who had never been in the Netherlands before.

A few months before the vote on the West New Guinea resolution in the General Assembly of the United Nations, the Australian and Netherlands governments issued a joint statement of a common policy with respect to New Guinea. The two administering countries agreed to cooperate in the administration of the "geographically and ethnographically related" territories of the large island, and stated that they were determined "to promote an uninterrupted development until such time as the inhabitants . . . will be in a position to determine their own future" in accordance with the "interests and inalienable rights" of the inhabitants under the United Nations Charter.[7] The statement was in effect a denial of Indonesia's claim that West New Guinea is really Indonesian. Ali Sastroadmidjojo, the head of the Indonesian delegation to the United Nations, branded the statement an attempt to influence the peaceful solution of Indonesia's claim.

Increasing dissatisfaction with the trend of affairs and deepening concern over the direction of President Sukarno's leadership finally led to the formation of an opposition government.

[7] New York *Times*, int. ed., November 7, 1957.

In the closing months of 1957 more and more of the dissidents gathered at Padang in the western part of Sumatra. The group included a considerable number of military leaders, but also outstanding political leaders. It included the president of the Bank of Indonesia and two former prime ministers, Natsir and Harahap. As president of the Bank of Indonesia, Sjafruddin Prawiranegara had fought for a sound economic and financial policy, had warned about the dwindling gold reserves, and had pleaded for greater consideration for foreign capital. The dissatisfied leaders deliberated for weeks and finally organized a council.

An attempt was made on November 30 to take the life of President Sukarno. He escaped uninjured, but the hand grenade thrown at him killed eight people and wounded a number of others. Apparently the attack unnerved the president, for about a month later he went on a six-week Asian-African "rest" tour.

The revolutionary council on February 10, 1958, issued an ultimatum to President Sukarno and Prime Minister Djuanda, with five days in which to comply with its terms. The council demanded that Mohammad Hatta and Sultan Hamengku Buwono of Djokjakarta be named to form a new cabinet to be composed of "men of integrity and free of atheistic influence," this cabinet to function until the next general elections in 1960. The council demanded that Sukarno return to his constitutional position as president. The ultimatum, which was called a Charter in Defense of Freedom and Justice, was preceded by a long preamble in which the grievances and political views of the group were set forth. The Djuanda cabinet was charged with actions hostile to the legitimate desires of the outer regions and with disastrous economic and financial policies culminating in the abrupt liquidation of Dutch economic activities. Sukarno was accused of having gone abroad not to recuperate his health but to try to purchase arms from the Soviet bloc, "apparently to crush the popular movements." The Sukarno-Djuanda regime was charged with seeking "to strengthen the Communist position in the government while intensifying atheistic influence in the community, and to disrupt friendly relations with the Western world in order to bring Indonesia closer into the Soviet bloc."[8]

The Djuanda cabinet rejected the ultimatum and ordered the dishonorable discharge of four colonels associated with the council. President Sukarno returned from his "rest" trip on February 16, and that evening the government ordered the arrest on treason charges of the prime minister of the counter-government, Sjafruddin, and five of its ministers.

The control of the rich oil fields of Sumatra, exploited by American and British-Dutch companies, became of the utmost importance to both government and rebels. The oil companies provided the central government with 60 percent of its total foreign-exchange income. One of the first acts of the rebel government after the expiration of the ultimatum was to order the oil companies to cease all shipments of oil to Java and all payments of other revenues to the central government. By controlling the production and shipment of the central Sumatra oil, the rebels would be able to exert tremendous economic pressure on the central government, but they made little military or administrative effort to enforce their demands. The government went into action against the rebels in the middle of March. Its navy blockaded the rebel ports, and the air force landed parachute troops at Pakanbaru, the oil center, with little difficulty. The rebels offered little resistance. Their strategy may be to make tactical retreats and bleed the government white with guerrilla warfare. The war has been called "a very civil, civil war," with remarkably few losses on either side.

At the beginning of April the outlook for the rebels appeared dark. They had apparently expected to be joined by Colonel Barlian, the military commander of the vital region of South Sumatra, and by the Achinese in the north of Sumatra and by other known pockets of discontent throughout the islands. Nor did they receive political aid from Mohammad Hatta or the sultan of Djokjakarta. The countergovernment movement fell between two stools: it tried to be both a regional and a national movement, but failed to be either sufficiently to rally real support to its cause. In spite of these facts, there is little cause for

[8] New York *Times*, int. ed., February 11, 1958.

optimism on the part of the central government. Sjafruddin was probably not far from the truth when he declared that his regime was much stronger politically than the Djakarta government under President Sukarno, though far inferior militarily. He also feared Soviet intervention after the Korean model. "We do not want to be killed by Russians," he declared. "We started the revolutionary government to prevent Indonesia from being colonized by Russia through Sukarno. Sukarno was dead set to rule Indonesia like a dictator under Russia and ignore the Constitution. He was always trying to get authority without taking responsibility."[9]

Even if the central government succeeds in crushing the present rebellion, the chief issues of anti-Communism, regional autonomy, Sukarno and his "guided democracy," economic deterioration, and incompetence and corruption will remain unsolved.

THE PHILIPPINES

The dynamic and honest President Magsaysay died in a plane crash on March 17, 1957. He was succeeded by Carlos P. Garcia, the vice president.

A hot presidential political campaign ended in the election in November of Garcia, who was the candidate of the Nationalist party. His leading opponent was José Yulo, the Liberal party candidate. The surprising feature of the campaign was the remarkable showing made by Manuel Manahan, a young independent candidate who declared his complete dedication to the policies of the late President Magsaysay. Claro M. Recto, who was also a candidate, ran far behind. Garcia's success in the election did not extend to his running mate, José P. Laurel, Jr. The latter was defeated for the vice-presidency by Diosdado Macapagal, the candidate of the Liberal party. Recto and Laurel were frequently critical of the United States and of the pro-American policies of Magsaysay. The election campaign was hard fought; large sums were spent.

The economic situation in the Philippines remains unfavorable. The trade imbalance is serious; imports steadily and in-

[9] New York *Times*, int. ed., March 22, 1958.

creasingly ran ahead of exports throughout 1957. The foreign-exchange situation is alarming. In December, 1956, the international reserves of the central bank stood at $288,000,000; in December, 1957, they had declined to a record low of $145,000,000. The government budget remains out of balance. About 2,000,000 persons are unemployed. A favorable factor in the situation is the increasing physical volume of production. To help meet the situation, President Garcia at the end of 1957 proclaimed a program of austerity. In March, 1958, he announced his intention to visit the United States to seek aid in the form of a $300,000,000 loan to be used for developmental projects.

VIETNAM

The competing Communist and non-Communist states of north and south Vietnam registered economic gains in 1957 and the early part of 1958, but both still had sizable tasks before them.

North Vietnamese Premier Phan Van Dong announced on April 17, 1958, that the socialized economic sector was now "the leading force." Nguyen Van Tran, deputy chief of the state planning board, declared two days later that particular attention would be paid to the collectivization of agriculture during the next three years. Cooperative agricultural methods, involving mutual-aid teams, previously had represented the government's main efforts on behalf of collectivization.[10] Considering the reaction produced by the Communists' land-reform program, the policy to push collectivization could provoke resistance. The land-reform program, on the other hand, was ultimately carried out in spite of opposition.

Industrialization in north Vietnam has shown progress, with help from the other Communist-bloc countries, but so far emphasis has been on light industry. According to north Vietnam's premier, production in the heavy-industry sector in April, 1958, was only 76 percent of what it had been before the war. The premier also asserted that chronic famine conditions in north Vietnam had been fundamentally ended, while the Soviet

---

[10] See Theodore Shabad, "Economic Developments in North Vietnam," *Pacific Affairs*, XXXI (March, 1958), 46-47.

Union has claimed that Ho Chi Minh's government had a sufficient surplus in 1957 to ship some rice to Indonesia and India.[11] The claim of rice self-sufficiency would appear to be debatable in view of the past record of this part of Vietnam with respect to food production—exports notwithstanding.

Both Vietnams were alike in many ways in 1957 and early 1958 economically. Each continued vitally dependent upon its friends abroad to lend it assistance. In one extremely important respect, however, they differed—in their approach to economic development. North Vietnam apparently devoted a much larger proportion of its budget to development purposes (which, if continued, could prove the difference in the important economic competition between the two states). American aid, moreover, has produced dissatisfaction in south Vietnam as a result of the limited emphasis given by the United States to industrialization there.

South Vietnamese rice exports in 1957 failed to make the recovery desired by the government. Rubber continued to experience the uncertainties of a fluctuating market. The problem of unemployment persisted, and there were predictions of a worsening situation in 1958. Envy and discontent mounted among south Vietnamese farmers over the large share of the budget allocated to the resettlement of refugees from the north. There were bright spots in the economy, however, such as the dedication of a large cotton-spinning factory in Saigon in early February, 1958 (described by Vice President Nguyen Ngoc Tho as the first in a series of projects that would become operational in that year).

North Vietnam in early March, 1958, offered to discuss trade and a reduction of troops in the two parts of the country, but President Ngo Dinh Diem declined, terming the move propaganda. The Soviet Union and Communist China supported the north Vietnamese, both charging the United States with responsibility for the rejection.

The United States also was the subject of attack in south Vietnam in the fall of 1957 in the form of apparently Communist-instigated bombing raids against Americans. Although

---

[11] Shabad, 48.

Communist terrorism and sabotage has been largely eliminated in south Vietnam, President Ngo Dinh Diem stated in March, 1958, that there had recently been a renewal of such subversion and that "all necessary measures" were being taken. "All necessary measures," if they followed the pattern of the past, could represent highhanded authoritarianism on the government's part.

CAMBODIA

Parliamentary elections were held in Cambodia on March 24, 1958, for the second time since the 1954 Geneva accords which ended the Indochinese war. The outcome of the 1958 vote was no different from that of the 1955 elections: the Popular Socialist Community party of Prince Norodom Sihanouk (formerly king and four times premier of his country) won all the seats contested. Only one other party even participated in the election, the People's party (Communist), and four of its five candidates failed to gain even a single vote. Sim Var, who had been premier previously and who is opposed to the Communists within his country, became prime minister in April.

There were no indications in early May, 1958, that Prince Norodom Sihanouk, who has a record of popping in and out of the premiership like a jack-in-the-box, had any immediate intention of resuming office. Sihanouk had stepped down from the premiership in 1957 for the fourth time. He remained, however, the country's most important political figure, genuinely popular with the Cambodian masses and the real power behind both throne and premiership. Such one-man, one-party rule would not seem to be in Cambodia's best interest in the long run—despite the fact that in 1957 the prince made some of the strongest statements against Communism he has ever uttered.

Cambodian economic growth continued in 1957; trade increased over the previous year, with imports and exports more in balance as a result of a substantial rise in the export of rice. Foreign-aid programs were a major factor in this growth, with the United States the largest single source of such assistance and the Soviet Union, Communist China, and Japan also contributing in a significant fashion. This aid more than exceeded the annual budget of $50,000,000, making Cambodia in this respect the best aided country in Southeast Asia. United States assistance in fiscal year 1957 amounted to some $39,000,000, a major American project being the construction of a road to connect the capital Pnompenh with the new ocean port France is building at Kompong Som on the Gulf of Siam. Kompong Som is Cambodia's first deep-sea port, and when the road to it is completed (probably sometime in 1959), Cambodia's dependence on communications by river through Vietnam will be greatly lessened.

LAOS

Communist control of the northern Laotian provinces of Phong Saly and Sam Neua came to an official end on November 18, 1957, when the leader of the formerly insurgent Pathet Lao symbolically handed over the two territories to a representative of the king. The national assembly on November 2 had formally approved a pact between the government and the Pathets ending the more than three years of sporadic fighting which had followed in the wake of the 1954 Geneva Conference.

The agreement provided that the Communist Pathet Lao were to be represented in the cabinet and that about 20 percent of the Pathet troops were to be integrated into the army. The remainder of the rebels were to be placed on a reserve status and returned to their homes.

Two Communists subsequently were added to the government: one (Prince Souvanna Vong, leader of the Pathets and half-brother of Premier Souvanna Phouma) as minister of planning, reconstruction, and urbanism, and the other as minister of religion and fine arts. Fifteen hundred Pathet soldiers were integrated into the army as agreed, although pro-West Chief of Staff Colonel Ouan Rathikoun stated that it would take two years to reindoctrinate all of them.

The agreement with the Pathet Lao also provided that the Pathets be permitted freedom of political activity on the same basis as any other group. The Communists quickly organized themselves into a National Patriotic Front (Neo Lao Hak Xat) and contested elections held May 4, 1958, to enlarge the national assembly from 39 to 59 members. Twenty-one seats actually were at stake (the extra one representing a vacancy caused by death), and the Front put up thirteen candidates and backed eight others from sympathetic factions.

The returns occasioned quite a stir in the West, as the Communists placed nine of their thirteen candidates in office, including Prince Souvanna Vong. Four members of the neutralist Santiphab faction, which had an electoral alliance with the Patriotic Front, also won. The results occasioned the possibility of a leftist bloc of as many as twenty-one legislators in the assembly, including deputies previously elected. Nonleftists still possessed a majority, but their lack of cooperation in the past left little room for optimism. The cause of the electoral defeat of the rightwing parties would appear to be the widening gap between them and the masses, especially in the rural areas, and their failure to form electoral alliances (as the leftists did). Elections for an entirely new assembly will be held in late 1959 or early 1960, and a comparably strong showing by the Patriotic Front and other leftist factions could result in a majority for them.

Prince Souvanna Vong and his supporters called for a reduction in the size of the Laotian armed forces and less American military aid during the campaign. Candidates of the Patriotic Front also were reported as indicating to the voters that they would resume their revolt if not elected.[12] The Communists also made charges of corruption by government officials involving United States aid—charges which were not without substance. American aid to Laos has averaged $40,000,000 a year since 1954, and there has been large-scale graft partly as a result of an unrealistic exchange rate, corruption in the issuance of import licenses, and unskilled administration. The aid program came to a virtual standstill in early 1958 because of a reexamination of the exchange rate as well as various procedural matters. Construction of new roads, agricultural improvements, and the supply of commodities to curb inflation represented accomplishments of the United States aid program in 1957 despite this corruption. The impact of American assistance

[12] New York *Times*, May 4, 1958.

may be expected to be more impressive in the future if the necessary reforms are accomplished—and if the Communists do not come to power. United States aid and its effectiveness could be a major factor in the determination of the important 1959 or 1960 elections.

THAILAND

The political rivalry among Phibun Songgram, Sarit Thanarat, and Phao Sriyanon came to a head in the form of a bloodless coup d'etat staged by Sarit September 15, 1957. Phibun fled to Japan, and Phao to Switzerland. Following elections for a new national assembly on December 15, Sarit (reportedly very ill) named Lieutenant General Thanom Kithachon as premier and in January, 1958, departed for the United States for one year's stay for treatment of cirrhosis of the liver. By the spring of 1958, as a result of the developments of the past six months, all of the big three of Thai politics a year earlier were out of the country: Phibun and Phao in exile, and Sarit in the hospital in the United States. The consequent power vacuum, with a figurehead premier, may prove tempting to one or more of Sarit's ambitious army supporters (among others). Thailand continues a highly unstable political entity.

Sarit's coup apparently had its roots in two considerations: a fear within army ranks that Phibun was maneuvering to better Phao's position at the expense of Sarit, and a desire among Sarit's followers for a larger share of the spoils. Sarit was aided in his action by growing popular dissatisfaction with Phibun and, even more so, Phao—in large part because of charged irregularities in the February, 1957, elections. Although utilizing this discontent, Sarit and his supporters did not make their move as a result of pressures deriving from it. For all practical purposes, the September, 1957, change of governments was merely a switch in the seating arrangements.

The December voting was billed as Sarit's answer to the charges that the February elections were corrupt. The mildly socialist Unionist party, led by Sukit Nimanhemin, won more of the 160 contested seats than any other party: 45. Former premier Khuang Aphaiwong's conservative Democrats won 39, and the comparatively well organized extreme leftist parties only 15 (a drop of 6 seats compared with their February total); independents won 61 seats. Sukit's Unionists, rather than being permitted to form a government, were absorbed into Sarit's own newly formed National Socialist party.

After the September coup, Sarit had asked Pote Sarasin, secretary general of the Southeast Asian Treaty Organization and former Thai ambassador to the United States, to be premier of a caretaker government. Pote accepted, but when asked to serve as premier after the December voting, he declined, stating that the elections would have no meaning "if I, not elected, took office."[13] Named by Sarit to the premiership as second choice, as a result, was a 46-year-old career army officer, Thanom Kithachon, commander of the key First Army. Thanom claimed that he was "too green," but he accepted the post anyway. A loyal supporter of Sarit and strongly pro-West, Thanom is politically inexperienced and may not be able to meet any serious challenge to the authority of the ailing and absent Sarit.

Such a challenge probably would not come from the Thai leftists—who have virtually no influence in either the army or the police, and apparently little among the voters as well. The antileftist trend of the December, 1957, balloting was repeated in provincial byelections March 30, 1958, when the opposition Democrats (14), Sarit's National Socialists (9), and independents (3) won all of the 26 seats contested. The elections were held under a law providing that provinces reaching 50 percent literacy elect all of their national assembly representatives instead of having half appointed. Sarit's party, following the March voting, maintained a comfortable majority (97 elected and 105 appointed) in the 291-seat assembly.

The Thai economy continued stable throughout 1957, rice exports reportedly setting a postwar record (one and a half million tons). Expectations, however, were that the 1958 surplus would be down, perhaps by as much as one-third. The International Bank for Reconstruction and Development gave a major boost to the Thai economy in September, 1957, with the announcement of a $66,000,000 loan to help finance the

---

[13] *The Economist* (London), January 18, 1958.

giant Yanhee hydroelectric project on the Ping River 260 miles northwest of Bangkok.

MALAYA AND SINGAPORE

The Federation of Malaya became independent on August 31, 1957. It is now a member of the British Commonwealth and remains linked to the United Kingdom by a defense treaty. Shortly after receiving its independence, it was admitted to membership in the United Nations. Tengku Abdul Rahman, who previously had been chief minister, became the country's first prime minister, while Sir Abdul Rahman, ruler of one of the Malay states, was elected constitutional monarch for a five-year period. Tengku Rahman's cabinet of eleven members included three Chinese and an Indian.

The Malayan Communist party on September 1 offered to end its war against Malaya in return for legal recognition. This was two days before the federation government made a new and "final" offer of amnesty to the Communist guerrillas. Few Communists took advantage of the offer; desultory guerrilla warfare continues.

With respect to foreign policy, Prime Minister Rahman declared that Malaya is not yet prepared to join Seato. He criticized the countries of Southeast Asia for concerning themselves "with problems outside of their own sphere," for being inclined "to dance to the tune of the bigger nations." He suggested that the Southeast Asian leaders "should make more efforts to study the situation around them and try to build up understanding and unity among the nations which are so closely identified in interest and outlook. Otherwise these small nations will look elsewhere for support and protection and the full meaning of independence will be lost."[14]

In Singapore, due to receive internal self-government in 1959, Chief Minister Lim Yew Hock continued his offensive against Communists and extreme leftist elements in trade unions, farmers' groups, and student organizations. A number of Chinese private schools were closed, and supervision of the re-

[14] New York *Times*, int. ed., February 9, 1958.

mainder was tightened. The Chinese principal of a large Chinese high school was deported. The legislative assembly in October, 1957, approved a bill creating a status of Singapore citizenship whereby the electorate was nearly doubled.

Chief Minister Lim told a group of American editors and radio-station owners in February, 1958, that a merger of Singapore with Malaya was inevitable, but the following day Prime Minister Rahman of the federation told the same group that there could be no merger until the people in Singapore became more Malayan-minded.

Sarawak, Brunei, and North Borneo may soon form an association. Sir Anthony Abell, governor of Sarawak and high commissioner for Brunei, on February 7, 1958, formally proposed an association with a central authority to deal initially with defense, external relations, internal security, and communications.

BURMA

The internal-security situation in Burma improved in 1957 and the first half of 1958, as Communist, Karen, and other insurgents surrendered in increased numbers. Domestic security still posed a major problem for Premier U Nu and his government, however, although there was growing optimism as a result of the mounting surrenders.

Nu himself in June, 1957, had proclaimed the priority of restored law and order over further socialization of the national economy. His program called for a retrenchment of welfare-state measures and more joint ventures with private Burmese and foreign businesses (with the government as a "sleeping partner," as Nu put it). Declaring that it was presently impossible to bar foreigners from participation in the development of the Burmese economy, Nu added that when it is possible to do so, "I will be the first to exclude them."

Despite this brake on socialism and the improved internal-security situation, Burma's economy in early 1958 still was a long way from solving the multitude of problems facing it. Burma exported two million tons of rice in 1957, a postwar record, but failure of the rice crop in certain areas indicated a probable drop of nearly 50 percent in the surplus for export in 1958. Foreign-exchange reserves, meanwhile, fell in 1957, despite loans from the United States, India, the International Bank for Reconstruction and Development, the Soviet Union, Japan, and West Germany.

Burma's improved domestic-security situation should provide the government with an opportunity for genuine progress in the field of economic development and diversification. The surrender of the various brands of insurgents, however—particularly the Communists—does not mean that the evolution of a viable Burmese state will proceed without obstacle. Deputy Premier and Defense Minister U Ba Swe told 500 surrendering Communists in Arakan in February, 1958, that the government would bear them no ill will and would do everything possible to rehabilitate them, but whether democratic rehabilitation is likely is open to serious question. If the Communists are willing to "behave," U Nu's government is prepared to treat them as a regular political party.[15] There is no reason to believe, however, that the Communists will be any less Communist in Rangoon and the villages than in the bush. They may even threaten to resume their rebellion against the government if they are not successful politically, as the "rehabilitated" Communist Pathet Lao were reported doing in the campaign for the May 4, 1958, elections in neighboring Laos.

The Communists' prospects for overt political gains could be enhanced by divisions within the ranks of the government party, the Anti-Fascist People's Freedom League. Premier Nu assumed the additional portfolio of minister of home affairs in late April, 1958, allegedly replacing the prior holder of that office as a result of factionalism within the A.F.P.F.L. Nu also reportedly ordered the arrests of some members of the party on criminal charges. Certain Burmese newspapers in May, 1958, charged that the United States had given Deputy Premier Kyaw Nyein $600,000 to use in an effort to oust Nu as premier. Kyaw Nyein claimed the charges were part of a campaign against him by supporters of Nu.

[15] See Robert H. Estabrook, "Burma's Role," in Washington *Post and Times-Herald,* November 30, 1957.

The Communists could take advantage of such rivalries to advance their cause at the expense of the A.F.P.F.L., seemingly wearying after ten years of independence.

No settlement had been reached, as of May, 1958, of Burma's border controversy with neighboring Communist China. China's Chou En-lai had stated in July, 1957, that agreement in principle had been achieved, but nine months later the dispute still was unsolved.

THE CONTINUING COMMUNIST CHALLENGE

The Soviet Union and Communist China continued their efforts in 1957 and the first half of 1958 to capitalize on the political and economic problems and inadequacies of the countries of Southeast Asia, particularly Indonesia. The Indonesians had sought military equipment from the United States, but when the American government refused, arms-purchasing missions were sent to countries of the Communist bloc. President Sukarno announced in early April, 1958, that negotiations with Yugoslavia, Poland, and Czechoslovakia had resulted in Indonesia's purchase of an undisclosed number of Soviet-built MIG jet fighter aircraft and Ilyushin bombers as well as small arms and other war goods. Indonesian pilots, it was reported later the same month, would undergo training in these aircraft in Egypt—itself a recipient of Soviet military and other types of assistance.

The Communists also supplied Indonesia with ten ships in the spring of 1958 to help replace Dutch vessels which formerly engaged in the republic's interisland trade. There also were charges, not substantiated, of considerable Communist involvement in Indonesia's civil difficulties. Philippine Defense Secretary Jesus Vargas, for example, charged that Soviet technical advisers in Djakarta were really military experts helping the Sukarno government in its struggle against the Sumatran and other rebels.

The United States had been asked to supply arms by those in revolt against Djakarta as well as by the Djakarta government, refusing both requests. Communist China, nonetheless, accused the United States in May, 1958, of supplying the Indonesian rebels with "a continuous stream of arms," and the Soviet Union charged that Secretary of State John Foster Dulles was "instigating the overthrow of the legitimate government of Indonesia."

President Eisenhower, however, had told a press conference in April that "our policy is one of careful neutrality." Dulles previously had proclaimed that the official policy of the United States was to provide arms only for internal police protection within or for a fight against aggression from without.

The first phase of the Indonesian civil war ended in the late spring of 1958 with successful military action by the government against the rebels on Sumatra (with the dissidents subsequently intensifying their activity in the eastern part of the island country). The danger of an internationalization of the conflict had fortunately been avoided—at least for the time being. The possibility continued, however, that foreign intervention might still mark the civil struggle in the months and perhaps years ahead.

The Soviet diplomatic offensive was not limited to the Indonesian question or to attacks upon the United States and its allies, although these certainly were focal points of Communist propaganda. On the eve of the March, 1958, meeting of the Southeast Asian Treaty Organization in the Philippines the Soviets coupled a strong denunciation of the alliance with a vague proposal for establishment of an atomfree zone and a system of collective security in Asia and the Far East. The Soviet Union also urged members of the alliance to refuse American missiles and weapons, threatening powerful retaliatory blows if such bases were ever used against the U.S.S.R. or its allies.

The December, 1957, Afro-Asian conference in Egypt was also part of the Soviet diplomatic campaign among the newly independent peoples of Asia (and Africa). The meeting was billed as another Bandung conference, but its delegates were for the most part unofficial, they were overwhelmingly Communist sympathizers, and the Soviet Union itself (not present at Bandung) was the major voice at the gathering. Communist

Recent Developments 349

China and the other Asian Communist states also were represented, and there were "observers" from five eastern European satellites. The Soviet delegation was reported as offering the assembled peoples economic and technical aid "to the best of our capabilities," but there was no confirmation of such a proposal in Soviet reports of the Cairo conference.

As of early 1958, the Communist bloc's assistance efforts in Southeast Asia were still relatively modest (excepting, of course, in north Vietnam, which was in large part supported by such help).[16] Indonesia had been accorded credit amounting to $110,000,000 and Cambodia a grant of $22,000,000, with Burma a partner to a series of rice-barter deals with various Communist countries as well as a recipient of several "gift" projects for which it will make the U.S.S.R. a return "gift" of rice over an extended period. The Philippines, Thailand, south Vietnam, Malaya, and Laos received no Communist assistance whatsoever. Bloc supply of aircraft and arms to Indonesia, however, indicated the Communists' willingness and ability to move to meet the needs, real or self-styled, of Southeast Asian governments. There were those, indeed, who feared that Indonesia might become another Egypt or Syria in terms of Soviet military and other aid. Such a Communist approach to Indonesia could have an enormous impact on all Southeast Asia.

[16] Information based on a United States Department of State study released January 3, 1958, and carried January 4 in the New York *Times*.

BIBLIOGRAPHICAL NOTE

IN WRITING this book the authors have drawn on their many years of study of the region, based on government documents and publications, books, journals and newspapers from the countries of Southeast Asia, and personal contacts and visits.

Before the Second World War very little was written on the region in English, but in the last two decades many excellent studies have appeared.

GENERAL

Professor Brian Harrison of the University of Hong Kong is the author of the first general history of the region, *Southeast Asia: A Short History* (Macmillan, London; St. Martin's Press, New York, 1954. 268 pp.). It was soon followed by a much longer study by Professor D. G. E. Hall, *History of Southeast Asia* (Macmillan, London; St. Martin's Press, New York, 1955. 808 pp.). Professor Hall was for many years at the University of Rangoon and is now at the University of London. It is to be hoped that we shall soon have a history of the region written by a Southeast Asian scholar.

The geography of the region is described by Professor E. G. H. Dobby of the University of Malaya, *Southeast Asia* (Wiley, New York, 1951. 415 pp.). For an illuminating examination of the social forces of the region, see the small book on this subject by Cora DuBois, *Social Forces in Southeast Asia* (University of Minnesota Press, Minneapolis, 1949. 78 pp.).

The problems of developing democratic governments in the countries of the region is ably discussed by Rupert Emerson in *Representative Government in Southeast Asia,* with supplementary chapters by W. H. Elsbree and Virginia Thompson (Harvard University Press, Cambridge, Mass., 1955. 200 pp.). The important

Chinese communities in the region are comprehensively treated by Victor Purcell in *The Chinese in Southeast Asia* (Oxford, London and New York, 1951. 801 pp.). The author was for many years a member of the Malay Civil Service and in charge of the Chinese bureau. *Southwards from China* (Hodder, London, 1952. 200 pp.) by Woodrow Wyatt is a survey by an English journalist.

The New World of Southeast Asia by Lennox A. Mills and associates (University of Minnesota Press, Minneapolis, 1949. 450 pp.) gives a survey of the political developments in the countries by a number of specialists. For an Australian view of the same subject, see W. Macmahon Ball, *Nationalism and Communism in East Asia* (Melbourne University Press, Melbourne, 2d ed., 1956. 222 pp.).

BURMA

For background and the prewar developments, see D. G. E. Hall, *Burma* (Longmans, London and New York, 1950. 184 pp.), and John Christian, *Modern Burma: A Survey of Political and Economic Development* (University of California Press, Berkeley, 1942. 381 pp.). The former is an English, the latter an American scholar. *Colonial Policy and Practice* by J. S. Furnivall (New York University Press, New York, 1956. 568 pp.), first published by Cambridge University Press, 1948, analyzes and appraises British policy in Burma and compares it with the policy of the Dutch in the East Indies. This is an unusual book, one of the best on colonial policy. Mr. Furnivall was a member of the British Civil Service in Burma and is now adviser to the government of Burma.

For a Burmese view and statement of events and developments, see the following by Premier U Nu: *Burma Under the Japanese* (Macmillan, London, 1954. 44 pp.); *The People Win Through* (Society for the Extension of Democratic Ideals, Rangoon, 1952. 63 pp.); *From Peace to Stability* (Ministry of Information, Rangoon, 1951); and *Towards Peace and Stability* (Ministry of Information, Rangoon, 1951).

See Frank N. Trager, *Toward a Welfare State in Burma: Economic Reconstruction and Development, 1948-1954* (Institute of Pacific Relations, New York, 1954. 60 pp. mimeographed), for an account of the basic policy of Burma's government.

INDOCHINA

For the background of French colonialism in the region, see the excellent study by John F. Cady, *The Roots of French Imperialism in Eastern Asia* (Cornell University Press, Ithaca, N. Y., 1954.

322 pp.). *The Struggle for Indochina* by Ellen J. Hammer (Stanford University Press, Stanford, Calif., 1954. 342 pp.) is the most comprehensive account of developments in Indochina since the war. For an excellent account of the regime in the north, see *The Viet Minh Regime* by Bernard B. Fall (Institute of Pacific Relations, New York, rev. ed., 1956. 200 pp. mimeographed). A useful volume on Indochina is *Conflict in Indo-China and International Repercussions: A Documentary History, 1945-1955* (Cornell University Press, Ithaca, N. Y., 1956. 265 pp.), edited by Allan B. Cole.

INDONESIA

Nusantara: A History of the East Indian Archipelago by Bernard H. M. Vlekke (Harvard University Press, Cambridge, Mass., 1943. 439 pp.) is a splendid work by a leading Dutch historian. Mention has already been made of the unusual volume by Furnivall on British colonial policy in Burma and Dutch policy in the East Indies. *The Dutch East Indies* by Amry Vandenbosch (University of California Press, Berkeley, 3d ed., 1942. 446 pp.) brings the political developments of Indonesia up to the Second World War.

For a detailed account of the revolution, see George McT. Kahin's *Nationalism and Revolution in Indonesia* (Cornell University Press, Ithaca, N. Y., 1952. 490 pp.). *The Birth of Indonesia* by David Wehl (Allen, London, 1948. 216 pp.) is a shorter but a very good account of the revolution by an English journalist. For an extreme Dutch view of the revolution, see *Indonesia* by P. S. Gerbrandy (Hutchinson, London, 1950. 224 pp.). Gerbrandy was the wartime prime minister of the Netherlands government in exile. For a sociological study of postwar Indonesia, see *Indonesia in the Modern World* by Justus M. Van der Kroef (Masa Baru, Bandung; Heinman, New York, pt. I, 1954. 308 pp.; pt. II, 1956. 386 pp.).

MALAYA

Malaysia: A Study in Direct and Indirect Rule by Rupert Emerson (Macmillan, New York, 1937. 536 pp.) is a comparative study of British rule in Malaya and Dutch administration in the East Indies. For brief but good histories of British rule in Malaya, see *Malaya: Outline of a Colony* by Victor Purcell (Nelson, London, 1946. 151 pp.) and *Malaya and Its History* by R. O. Winstedt (Longmans, New York, 1951. 158 pp.). *British Rule in Eastern Asia* by Lennox A. Mills (University of Minnesota Press, Minneapolis, 1942. 581 pp.) contains an analysis of British administration by a political scientist.

For a critical treatment of British policy in Malaya during the "emergency" see *Malaya: Communist or Free* (Stanford University Press, Stanford, Calif., 1954. 288 pp.) by Victor Purcell. *Malayan Problems, from a Chinese Point of View* (Tannsco, Singapore, 1947. 182 pp.) by Sir Cheng-lock Tan represents the point of view of most Chinese in Malaya. The author is the foremost leader of the Chinese community.

THE PHILIPPINES

The best and most comprehensive study of the political developments of the Philippine Islands is Joseph Ralston Hayden's *The Philippines: A Study in National Development* (Macmillan, New York, 1942. 984 pp.). Professor Hayden was a political scientist, secretary of the Woods-Forbes commission, and the last vice governor general under American rule. An interesting book on American administration of the islands is *The Philippine Islands* by W. Cameron Forbes, governor general of the dependency, 1909-1913 (Harvard University Press, Cambridge, Mass., 1928, 1945. 412 pp.).

For background, read *Land and People in the Philippines* by Joseph E. Spencer (University of California Press, Berkeley, 1952. 282 pp.). Carlos P. Romulo, the distinguished Filipino journalist and diplomat, has written several books on events in his country since the Second World War: *Crusade in Asia: Philippine Victory* (Day, New York, 1955. 309 pp.) and *I Saw the Fall of the Philippines* (Doubleday, New York, 1942. 323 pp.).

For a critical view of American policy in the Philippines in the immediate postwar years, see *The Philippine Story* by David Bernstein (Farrar, Straus, New York, 1947. 276 pp.). For a similar view by a Filipino, see *Betrayal in the Philippines* by Hernando Abaya (Wyn, New York, 1946. 272 pp.).

THAILAND

For Thailand before the Second World War the following will be found useful: Sir Josiah Crosby, *The Cross-roads* (Hollis and Carter, London, 1945. 174 pp.); Kenneth P. Landon, *Siam in Transition* (University of Chicago Press, Chicago, 1939. 328 pp.); Virginia Thompson, *Thailand, the New Siam* (Macmillan, New York, 1941. 865 pp.).

For postwar developments, see *Bangkok Editor* by Alexander MacDonald (Macmillan, New York, 1949. 229 pp.). MacDonald, an American, published an English newspaper in Bangkok for about a decade after the end of the war. See also *Brief Authority*

(Harper, New York, 1956. 290 pp.) by Edwin F. Stanton, who served as American ambassador in Thailand for a period in the early 1950's. *Some Aspects of Siamese Politics* by John Coast (Institute of Pacific Relations, New York, 1953. 58 pp. mimeographed) gives the views of an Englishman warmly sympathetic with Asian revolutionary movements.

INTERNATIONAL RELATIONS

Little has yet been published in this field. The following titles are suggested: Philips Talbot (ed.), *South Asia in the World Today* (University of Chicago Press, Chicago, 1950. 248 pp.); Philip W. Thayer, *Southeast Asia in the Coming World* (Johns Hopkins Press, Baltimore, 1953. 306 pp.); W. H. Elsbree, *Japan's Role in Southeast Asian Nationalist Movements, 1940-1945* (Harvard University Press, Cambridge, Mass., 1953. 182 pp.); Werner Levi, *Free India in Asia* (University of Minnesota Press, Minneapolis, 1952. 161 pp.); Franz Michael and George E. Taylor, *The Far East in the Modern World* (Holt, New York, 1956. 724 pp.); Harold M. Vinacke, *Far Eastern Politics in the Postwar Period* (Appleton-Century-Crofts, New York, 1956. 497 pp.).

UNITED STATES POLICY IN SOUTHEAST ASIA

See Miriam S. Farley, *United States Relations with Southeast Asia, 1950-1955* (American Institute of Pacific Relations, New York, 1955. 81 pp. mimeographed) and John Kerry King, *Southeast Asia in Perspective* (Macmillan, New York, 1956. 309 pp.).

INDEX

Abdulgani, Ruslan, 46, 68
Acheson, Dean, 292-94
Achinese, 50
A.F.P.F.L. (Burma), 216, 217, 230, 231, 234, 235, 236, 237, 245, 249
Agricultural Tenancy Act (Philippines), 91
Aguinaldo, General Emilio, 72, 83
Ali. *See* Sastroamidjojo, Ali
Alliance (Malaya), 201, 202, 203, 205
Ambonese, 36, 49, 63
A.N.Z.U.S., 295
Asian-African Conference. *See* Bandung Conference
Asian Relations Conference (Delhi, 1949), 256, 260, 261, 264, 265
Asian Socialist Conference (1953), 212-13, 241
Asian Socialist Organization, 257, 260, 261, 265
Aung San, 216, 217, 230, 249-50, 254, 265
Australia, 2, 3, 7, 64, 94, 253, 264, 268, 275, 282, 285, 298, 311, 322

Ba Maw, 216, 248
Ba Swe, U, 229, 234-43 *passim*, 250, 257
Baguio Conference, 94, 251, 253, 258
Bandung Conference (1955), 42, 67, 94-95, 181-82, 261-64, 265, 268, 274, 304-306
Bao Dai, 111, 116, 117, 120-21, 122, 127, 128, 253
Barter Agreements (Burma), 225-29, 270, 321
Bell mission, 85-87
Binh Xuyen, 111, 121, 123, 124, 126, 150
Boeke, Dr. J. H., 54
Borneo, British North, 2, 14, 206, 281-82

Buddhism, 15-19, 122, 124, 177-78, 192, 286, 289. *See also* Burma, Hoa Hao
Bulganin, Nikolai A., 130, 182, 225, 239, 270, 277, 278, 280, 307, 318
Burma: Buddhism, 212-13, 215, 221-22, 236; Socialism, 212-13, 217-20, 221, 236, 237; geography, 213-14; British conquest of, 214-15; nationalism, 215-17; communism, 216, 218, 229-33, 236, 237, 238; land nationalization, 219-20; economic difficulties, 222-29; political development, 229-45. *Also* 2, 5, 7, 8, 9, 15, 18, 20, 22, 157, 159, 164, 170, 171, 172, 177, 178, 182, 248-325 *passim*
Buwono, Sultan, 40, 41

Cambodia: strategic importance, 136; nationalism, 137-38; communism, 138-39; foreign aid and neutralism, 141-42. *Also* 2, 7, 15, 18, 22, 96, 158, 177, 221, 253-318 *passim*
Cao Dai, 111, 121, 123-24, 126, 150
Center of Asian Studies (Philippines), 95
Chiang Kai-shek, 175, 258, 260
China, Communist: and Indonesia, 43, 68; and Philippines, 97-98, 104; and Indochina, 131, 133, 134, 136, 141, 148-49, 153, 154-55; and Thailand, 161-65 *passim*, 176, 178, 181-84 *passim;* and Malaya, 197; and Burma, 225, 226, 227, 229, 231, 238, 241, 242-45. *Also* 4, 7, 12, 259-60, 266-75 *passim,* 281, 294, 297, 298, 299, 302-306 *passim,* 311, 312, 313, 318-25 *passim*
Chinese: in Indonesia, 50, 56, 305-306; in Philippines, 98-99; in Vietnam, 151-52; in Thailand, 175-77; in Malaya, 190-209 *passim*

Chou En-lai, 131, 136, 147, 182, 239, 243, 244, 263, 274, 275, 302-303, 304, 305, 306, 318, 325
Colombo Plan, 67, 250, 259, 260, 261, 262, 264, 265, 268, 302, 307, 322
Communists, 1, 2, 9, 42, 43, 44, 47, 48, 50, 56, 58, 59, 60, 68, 84, 87, 88, 89, 90, 91, 98, 99, 101, 111, 112, 118-31 passim, 138, 139, 144, 145, 146, 147, 155, 159, 163, 164, 169, 170, 176, 178, 180, 181, 184, 185, 190, 191, 197, 198, 199, 205, 208, 210, 216, 218, 229-33, 236, 237, 238, 262, 263, 269, 285, 286, 287, 288, 292, 295, 296, 297, 298, 300, 301, 302, 310, 311, 312, 313, 318, 321

Darul Islam, 49-50, 58, 59, 286
Delhi Conference (Indonesia, 1949), 253, 257-58, 260, 265
Diem, Ngo Dinh, 110-12, 121-32, 150, 151, 152, 153, 276, 297
Dulles, John Foster, 184, 241, 253, 295, 296, 297, 298, 300, 307, 308, 309

East India Company, 27
East Indonesia, 48
Egypt, 68, 257, 278, 279, 282
Elysee Agreements, 117

France, 1, 9, 246, 247, 262. See also Indochina

Garcia, Carlos P., 101
Geneva Agreements (Indochina), 122-30 passim, 144, 149, 155, 180, 181, 295-99 passim
Great Britain: rule in Malaya, 186-207 passim; rule in Burma, 214-17, 244. Also 3, 7, 131, 160, 161, 176, 268, 269, 281, 282, 298, 299, 302
"Guided" Democracy, 46-47

Halim, Dr., 56-57
Hamid, Sultan II, 34, 36, 63
Harahap, Burhanuddin, 43-44, 60, 68
Hare-Hawes-Cutting Bill, 76
Hatta, Mohammad, 32, 34, 44, 48-49, 67
Hayden, Ralston, 82, 87-88
Ho Chi Minh, 3, 110-54 passim, 177, 180, 249, 252, 253, 254
Hoa Hao, 111, 122, 124, 126, 150, 152
Hukbalahap movement, 86-89

India, 2, 4, 7, 19, 148, 157, 217, 224, 242, 251, 253, 257, 258, 259, 264, 265, 267, 268, 271, 274, 275, 277, 278, 279, 280, 285, 298, 299, 300, 302, 303, 307, 314, 324
Indians in Malaya, 190-96, 200, 205, 208

Indochina: French rule in, 111-12, 137; rise of nationalism, 112-13; Viet Minh movement, 113-21; post-Geneva era, 121-36, 149-54. Also 8, 9, 20, 22, 250, 256, 281, 284, 286, 294, 295-97, 311. See also Cambodia, Laos, Vietnam
Indonesia: under Dutch rule, 27-30; nationalist movement, 30-33; Japanese occupation, 31-32, 49, 55; postwar negotiations with Dutch, 32-33; federal government, 33-37; unitary government, 34-37; political and economic developments, 37-68. Also 2, 9, 14, 15, 18, 20, 22, 94, 148, 172, 181, 207, 227, 250-324 passim. See also Irian
Irian, 37, 38, 44, 63, 64, 65, 262, 272, 302, 305

Jafaar, Dato Onn Bin, 194, 199
Japan: occupation of Indonesia, 29, 31-32, 49, 55; occupation of Philippines, 83-84, 88; occupation of Indochina, 113, 143-44; in Thailand, 159-60, 161; conquest of Malaya, 189-91, 194, 196; conquest of Burma, 216-17. Also 1, 4, 7, 8, 9, 99-102, 248, 266, 271, 272, 280, 281, 285, 286, 290, 291, 292, 299, 322, 323, 324
Jessup, Philip C., 293-94

Karens, 214, 229, 233-34
Kathay Sasorith, 145, 146, 251
Khmer Issaraks, 138
Khrushchev, Nikita S., 130, 225, 239, 277, 278, 280, 307, 318
Khuang Aphaiwong, 162, 183
Kotelawala, Sir John, 259, 263, 264, 304
Ku-Sap-Be, 163, 180
Kuomintang, 98, 99, 175, 197, 260
Kyaw Nyein, U. See Nyein, U Kyaw

Land reform: Indonesia, 39; Philippines, 86-89, 90-92; North Vietnam, 135-36; South Vietnam, 149-51, 152; Thailand, 172-73; Burma, 218, 219-20
Laos: strategic importance, 136; nationalism, 143-44; communism, 144-47; foreign aid and neutralism, 148-49. Also 2, 18, 158, 164, 177, 180, 185, 221, 251, 257, 264, 282, 294, 297, 298, 299, 316, 317, 318
Laurel, José P., 83, 88, 90, 91, 104, 108, 248
Lim Yew Hock, 205

MacArthur, General Douglas, 82, 84, 291-92
MacDonald, Malcolm, 201, 209

Index

Malaya: historical background, 186-89; Japanese occupation, 189-91; plural society, 193, 196; British colonial policy, 189, 195-96; self-government, 198-202; economic, political, and social problems, 196-211. *Also* 2, 5, 8, 9, 14, 18, 20, 22, 158, 159, 160, 227, 250, 256, 257, 264, 268, 269, 281, 286, 288, 289, 302, 318, 320
Malayan People's Anti-Japanese Army, 190, 197
Masjumi party (Indonesia), 37, 38, 39, 43, 44, 45, 46, 48, 58, 59, 68

Nationalism, 8-9, 30-33, 72-79, 112-13, 137-38, 143-44, 195-200, 215-17
Nationalist party (Philippines), 73, 85, 89, 90, 103, 108
Natsir, Mohammad, 37, 43, 59
Nehru, Jawaharlal, 147, 239, 257, 260, 262, 263, 264, 265, 302, 303, 304
Netherlands, 20, 26-33, 40, 41, 57, 62, 63, 65, 66
Netherlands-Indonesian Union, 33, 35, 36, 39, 63
Neutralism: in Indonesia, 66-68; in Cambodia, 96, 139, 140, 143; in Laos, 148; in Thailand, 181-85; in Burma, 235, 238, 241, 242. *Also* 263, 264, 266, 270, 271, 278, 279, 304, 308, 309, 311, 316, 323, 325
Nu, U (Thakin Nu), 216, 217, 222-63 *passim*, 270, 276, 304
Nyein, U Kyaw, 229, 234, 235, 236, 237, 240, 241

Osmena, Sergio, 73, 83, 84
Osmena, Sergio, Jr., 84, 85, 88

Pacific Charter, 301, 303
Pantja Sila, 59
Pathet Lao, 136, 138, 144-48, 185
Penang, 187, 188, 192, 194, 199
Phan Van Dong, 129, 132
Phao Sriyanon, 156, 157, 166-73 *passim*, 183, 184
Phibun Songgram, 156-185 *passim*, 248, 251, 265
Philippines: under Spain, 71-72; American policy, 69-70, 79-82; nationalism and self-government, 72-79; Japanese occupation, 83-84, 88; independence and political developments, 86-107; foreign policy, 92-107. *Also* 2, 8, 9, 10, 14, 15, 18, 19, 20, 22, 28, 151, 248, 251, 256-324 *passim*
Phin Chunhawan, 166, 167, 168, 169
Pridi Banomyong, 156-64 *passim*, 178, 249, 269

Quezon, Manuel, 73, 76, 78, 80, 82, 83, 84, 92

Quirino, Elpidio, 85, 86, 89, 90, 91, 93, 94, 108, 258

Rahman, Tengku Abdul, 201, 202, 204, 205, 207, 210
Rangoon Socialist Conference (1953), 257
Recto, Claro M., 90, 91, 104, 108, 269
Regional bloc, proposals for, 248-68, 322-24
Republic of Indonesia (Nationalist), 33-34, 50
Resettlement program, 198
Romulo, General Carlos P., 90, 92, 95, 252, 304
Round Table Conference (The Hague), 32-33, 49, 63, 66
Roxas, Manuel, 84-85, 88, 103, 108
Rum, Mohammed, 253
Rum-Van Royen agreement, 33

Sarit Thanarat, 166, 167, 168, 169, 170, 182, 183
Sasorith. *See* Kathay Sasorith
Sastroamidjojo, Ali, 41, 42, 43, 46, 48, 59, 60, 67, 68, 259, 260, 263, 266, 270, 303-304, 305
Seato, 67, 96, 97, 141, 148, 179, 181, 182, 185, 252, 253, 254, 269, 274, 278-79, 297-304, 307, 310, 311, 316, 318, 323
Seni Pramoj, 160, 185
Sidik, 38
Sihanouk, Prince Norodom, 96, 97, 137, 138, 139, 254, 273, 275
Singapore, 273, 278, 281, 294, 298, 307, 318. *See also* Malaya
Sisavong Vong, King, 143
Sjahrir, Sutan, 37, 45, 257
Socialism, Burmese, 212, 213, 217-21, 236, 237
Southeast Asia: importance in world politics, 1-3; invasion, 5-7; dependent economies, 10, 21-25; cultures of, 13-17, 287; "cold war" and, 11, 12, 94, 154-55, 185, 297; living standards, 21, 287-89, 312-17; regionalism, 248-55, 322-24; Pan-Asianism, 255-58; South Asianism, 258-64; future U. S. policy and, 318-25
Southeast Asia League, 248, 249, 250
Souvanna Phouma, 146, 147, 148, 149
Souvanna Vong, 147, 148, 249
Soviet Union, 7, 11, 68, 118, 131, 133, 134, 141, 153, 154-55, 225-29, 238-40, 241, 270, 271, 276-80 *passim*, 294, 297, 306, 307, 311, 313, 318, 320, 321, 325. *See also* Bulganin, Khrushchev
Straits Settlements. *See* Malaya
Sukarno, 3, 32, 34, 40-50 *passim*, 56, 59, 60, 63, 68, 96, 252, 270, 307, 308
Sukiman, 38

Sumantri, Iwa Kusuma, 42
Sunarjo, 253
Swettenham, Sir Frank, 196

Tan, Sir Cheng-lock, 200
Taruc, Luis, 88, 89
Thailand: background, 157-58; Japanese occupation, 159-60; political developments, 160-70; economic situation, 170-75; Chinese community, 175-77; foreign relations, 178-85. *Also* 2, 8, 15, 18, 19, 22, 94, 119, 136, 213, 221, 248, 250-324 *passim*
Than Tun, 216, 230, 238
Theocracy, 58, 286
Transmigration, Indonesian plans, 53-56
Tydings-McDuffie Act, 76-77

United Nations, 32, 64-65, 92, 93, 95, 98, 242, 245, 258, 261, 267, 268, 294, 301, 304, 305, 322, 324, 325

United States, 7, 20, 39, 68, 111, 112, 141, 142, 153, 154, 155, 160, 161, 179-85 *passim*, 215, 228, 238, 241, 268, 269, 270, 271, 276, 278, 280, 284-325. *See* Philippines

Van Hinh, Gen. Nguyen, 121, 122, 123
Vargas, Jorgé B., 83
Viet Minh, 113-55 *passim*, 163, 180, 249, 254, 268, 269, 272, 297
Vietnam, 2, 7, 14, 15, 18, 19, 177, 249, 254, 260, 262, 264, 268, 272, 273, 274, 276, 282, 294, 311, 316, 317. *See also* Indochina
Vo Nguyen Giap, Gen., 119, 132
Volksraad, 29

Westerling, Captain Raymond, 34, 63
West New Guinea. *See* Irian
Wilopo, 39, 41, 56
Wongsonegoro, 41, 42